The Law of Fraud

Volume I

The Law of Fraud and the Procedure

Pertaining to the Redress Thereof

By

MELVILLE M. BIGELOW

VOLUME I

BeardBooks

Washington, D.C.

PREFACE.

WHAT shall be said of a treatise on the Law of Fraud which makes no mention of Chandelor v. Lopus? With those who pass by the preface, the author lays himself open to the charge of being ignorant of the *fontes juris*; though it is possible that they who turn the leaves of the text under a pressure of anxiety for the endangered rights of clients may suspect that the omission was intentional, and not regret it.

The truth is, Chandelor v. Lopus — and this case is taken as an illustration of a class — has had its day. So long as authorities were few, and the law remained in an unsettled state, that case served a purpose, — not the best purpose possible, but a useful purpose. It was one of the few decisions upon an important point; and it was cited and discussed because it *was* one of the few authorities, and because the law was not well settled. But the case was imperfectly reported, and for that reason was never perfectly understood; and the courts at last found it useless to struggle longer with it. Within the past twenty-five years, the law has become well settled upon the subject of this famous case; and the decisions are generally reported in an intelligible form. Chandelor v. Lopus has a secure place in the modern history of the English law; but, for the purposes of an accurate statement of the existing law, the question of the point decided by it may well be left to the judges and writers of the past, or relegated to the antiquarian.

Tempting as was the history of so venerable a branch of law, the limits which the author assigned for his work precluded all unnecessary departures from his design of presenting an orderly view of the existing Law of Fraud. Indeed, it was soon found that to attempt to treat the subject properly, in all its features, within the limits of a single volume of convenient size, would be vain ; and the result was that the criminal law of fraud was left altogether untouched, and the statutory law concerning fraud on creditors and purchasers presented simply in the language of the Legislatures, without note or comment.

Whatever may have been the author's original desire, the eliminations suggested are not now regretted. The criminal and statutory branches of the subject have been often and ably treated by others. Besides, criminal law would hardly be looked for in a book treating of the civil jurisprudence of fraud; and, as to the statutory law concerning fraud on creditors and purchasers, each State of the Union, with a few exceptions, has a code of its own, interpreted by independent tribunals, and enforced by distinct and diverse penalties and modes of procedure.

With deference to the views of others who have attempted to present a harmonious view of the statutes of the different States, the author is satisfied that such efforts are both unsatisfactory and dangerous. The decisions of the Courts of New York concerning the interpretation of an ambiguous statute of that State — that is, concerning the *intention* of the Legislature of that State in the passage of the act — cannot be safe authority in another State, even upon a question of the meaning of a

statute framed in the very same words. The Legislature
of New York meant one thing by the language used,
and the Legislature of another State may have meant
something else. And so the courts of each State may
have declared, and rightly. To say, therefore, that the
decisions are in conflict is incorrect, and to attempt to
deduce "the true rule of law" as applicable to both
States is vicious.

The case differs widely from decisions concerning the
common law. The common law is generally based, or
supposed to be based, on reason, and there may be a
true conflict of authority between the decisions of courts
of different States concerning its principles; and as
this implies that one, or both, or all of the divergent
decisions may be wrong, it is proper and important to
endeavor to find the true principle.

The acts of the Legislature, on the other hand, are
dogmatic declarations of law for the particular State;
and, when their meaning is called in question, the courts
of that State must give a final interpretation of it.
The exposition of the common law (when not involving
the meaning of a written instrument) is an exposition
of principles: the interpretation of statutory law is the
interpretation of intention. The decision in the latter
case may be wrong, as well as in the former; but the
fact that different constructions are put upon similar
language by courts of different States is no evidence of
erroneous interpretation.

The author's main purpose, therefore, of presenting
the whole body of the law relating to fraud in its civil
aspects, has been carried out. The common-law doctrines of the subject have been examined with the
greatest care, and stated in the clearest language at the
author's command. The statutory law, so far as it re-

lates to fraud on creditors or purchasers, follows, with appropriate citations of judicial authority (taken from the statute books) as to the construction placed upon the language used. It was deemed unimportant to state the rulings of the courts upon the precise meaning of the statutes. Nor was it thought best to present other statutes than those referred to ; since the rest were generally found to be mere legislative statements of what had been presented as common-law doctrine in the preceding portion of the book, or were special rules of procedure.

In considering the common-law doctrines of fraud, both the substantive law and the principles of procedure have been stated. Following established divisions, the substantive law has been divided into actual and presumptive or constructive fraud ; the former consisting of three chapters, and the latter of two. The chapters relating to actual fraud treat, first, of deceit as the type of all fraud, and, secondly, of frauds not necessarily turning upon the doctrines of deceit; and this second class has been divided into special instances of frauds *in pais* and frauds upon the administration of the law. The doctrines of presumptive or constructive fraud are presented in two chapters, the first of which treats of confidential relations, and the second of notice. The consideration of the adjective part of the law carries the subject of procedure through all of its stages from jurisdiction to damages.

The law, however, cannot be laid out with square and compass, upon mathematical lines, and it will occasionally be found that the topics of one head are presented in their natural place, and again in other places where the connection of subjects required further mention of them.

The labor performed in the conscientious preparation of a law book is not a thing to be contemplated with unmixed pleasure; but there is one part of it which brings a satisfaction great enough to cover, for the moment, all discouragements and vexations, and that is in writing the last line and reading the last page of proof. The one is now done: the other will shortly follow.

Boston, November 14, 1877.

———

NOTE.

The following corrections should be made : —

Change "hence," the last word of line 4, p. 99, to "and."

Change "agent," the last word of line 6, p. 110, to "principal."

To note 4, p. 114, add "*Contra*, Burden *v.* Sheridan, 36 Iowa, 125," — a case sustaining the author's view.

Change "by," in line 2, p. 430, to "from."

Change "And," the first word of the last sentence but one on p. 448, to "But."

CONTENTS.

PART I.

SUBSTANTIVE LAW OF FRAUD.

I. ACTUAL FRAUD.

CHAPTER I.

CHAPTER II.

CHAPTER III.

CHAPTER IV.

II. PRESUMPTIVE OR CONSTRUCTIVE FRAUD.

CHAPTER V.

CHAPTER VI.

PART II.

ADJECTIVE LAW OF FRAUD.

PROCEDURE AND INCIDENTS THEREOF.

CHAPTER VII.

CHAPTER VIII.

CHAPTER IX.

CHAPTER X.

STATUTES.

FRAUD ON CREDITORS AND PURCHASERS.

CONTENTS. XV

CASES CITED.

b

d

1 CASES CITED.

INTRODUCTION.

INTRODUCTION.

THE substantive law of fraud is divided into two branches, actual and constructive or presumptive fraud. Actual fraud is fraud in fact, involving turpitude: constructive or presumptive fraud is fraud in law. In the former, therefore, the essential elements of fraud in the sense of *dolus malus* must be present; while it is consistent with the existence of the latter that such elements should be wanting.

In the case of a charge of actual fraud, it devolves upon the complaining party to prove the elements referred to; and these will vary with the nature of the wrong alleged to have been committed. These elements, however, need not be proved, in all cases, by express evidence directed to the precise purpose of establishing them. The proof of one fact will often establish another. Proof, for example, that A sold to B a horse through misrepresentations of the animal's soundness, known by him (A) to be false, will establish an intention on the part of the seller to deceive the purchaser. This is not, therefore, a case of presumptive fraud, except in so far as it comes within the general rule that a man is presumed to know and intend the consequences of his own acts; under which rule all the legal effects of a man's conduct are presumptive. This, it is sufficient to say, is not the kind of presumption which is meant by the term " presumptive " or " constructive " fraud. Fraud in the above example is as truly proved as it is by express evidence of an intent to deceive in cases in which the action of the plaintiff, and the defendant's knowledge of the falsity of his statements, do not prove the bad intent; as in actions for false representations concerning the solvency of a third person.[1]

It follows that the term " presumptive" or " constructive " fraud has no reference to inferences of fact, drawn from the proof of other facts, when those inferences establish, *prima facie*, the existence of actual fraud (*dolus malus*). Such fraud is fraud in fact, and is to be found by the jury in cases at law, and by the chancellor, acting as a *quasi* juror, in cases in equity. Constructive or presumptive fraud is an inference of law, not to the effect that an actual fraud has, in the absence of explanation, been clearly proved, but either that, judging men as very fallible beings, and likely to yield to strong temptation, it is *probable* that fraud was committed ; or that the existence of certain things in the relation or conduct of parties begets a probability of actual knowledge of fraud, or what will lead to fraud, on the part of the person complained of. In the latter case, the presumption may be conclusive, and thus preclude the party from showing that the inference of fraud is false ; as in certain cases of constructive notice.[2] But the fraud thus fixed is still presumptive only, and in reality may not have existed.

There are many subjects in which the doctrines of both actual and constructive fraud may arise. In all cases of constructive fraud, there may also be actual fraud ; and in most if not in all cases of actual fraud, the doctrines of constructive fraud may arise. The two branches must, therefore, frequently be considered side by side ; and sometimes, on the other hand, a single subject must be divided and examined in

[1] See *post*, pp. 82, 83.   [2] See *post*, p. 288 *et seq.*

widely separate positions under each of the heads of fraud. For example, dealings with illiterate, weak-minded, or drunken persons are looked upon by the courts with great suspicion, and fraud is very easily — indeed, generally — presumed ; and this fact requires the presentation of that subject under the head of constructive fraud. But actual fraud may also be committed upon such persons ; and hence the subject must also be presented under the head of actual fraud. The subject of trusts must be divided, and part of it presented under the one and part under the other head. Transactions, for example, between express trustees and their *cestuis que trust*, such as gifts or sales in the interest of the former, are presumed to have been effected by undue influence ; and this branch of the subject belongs, therefore, to constructive fraud. But when money is put by A into the hands of B, for the purchase by the latter on behalf of the former of a piece of land, and B makes the purchase, but (contrary to the agreement) takes the title in his own name, he has been guilty of gross dishonesty of conduct toward A, for which the law treats him as a trustee. Such a case is a case of actual fraud, and must be treated under that head : and so of other cases.

So much has been deemed important as an introduction to the consideration of the substantive law of fraud, and as an explanation of the basis of the division and subdivision of the subject. It is not necessary to make any preliminary observations concerning procedure, the subject of Part II.

PART I.

SUBSTANTIVE LAW OF FRAUD.

———

   I. ACTUAL FRAUD.

  II. PRESUMPTIVE OR CONSTRUCTIVE FRAUD.

PART I.

SUBSTANTIVE LAW OF FRAUD.

I. ACTUAL FRAUD.

CHAPTER I.

DECEIT.

§ 1. INTRODUCTORY.

DECEIT is the type of fraud, and demands therefore the first
and the chief place in a work on the Law of Fraud. All
fraud, in the proper sense of that term, is accompanied by,
and indeed worked out through, deception. But the deception by which actionable or redressible fraud is effected makes
an extensive and somewhat artificial branch of law, and demands, for the purposes of the present work at least, a minute
and detailed examination; and to such we now proceed.

It is a general rule of law that, in order to obtain redress
or relief from the injurious consequences of deceit, it is
necessary for the complaining party to prove that his adversary has made a false representation of material facts;
that he made it with knowledge of its falsity; that the
complaining party was ignorant of its falsity, and believed
it to be true; that it was made with intent that it should
be acted upon; and that it was acted upon by the complaining party to his damage. But, like all general rules,
this proposition needs both illustration and explanation.
Aside from the situations in which it is strictly true, and
these are not many, it must in several particulars be qualified

by rules of law quite as important as the main proposition
itself. We propose now to examine the proposition in its
several parts, in the order above indicated, and to present
such illustrations and explanations of it as may serve to
enforce the precise meaning and limits of the doctrine.

§ 2. Of the Nature of the Representation, includ- ing Concealment.

First, then, we have to consider the nature of the representation itself, and to ascertain what sort of representation
is necessary (assuming the other elements present) in order
to entitle the complaining party to redress or relief against
the alleged wrong-doer.

The representation need not be in words.[1] There is no
distinction between frauds which are effected by acts alone
and frauds which are effected by words.[2] For example, if
one procure the indorsement of a party to a note or bill, in
order to effect a sale of it, the act is equivalent to an affirmation that such party is competent to indorse; and, if he
be not, the person procuring his signature is liable to the
purchaser of the paper.[3]

Upon the same principle, in order to obtain a decree
of nullity of marriage from a woman on the ground of
fraudulent representations on her part that she was chaste,
when in fact she was with child by another man at
the time of the marriage, it is not necessary to prove
any express representations by the woman.[4] It is sufficient
to prove that the acts and conduct of the party were such

[1] Lobdell v. Baker, 1 Met. 193; Mizner v. Kussell, 29 Mich. 229; Lee
v. Jones, 17 Com. B. N. s. 482; s. c. 14 Com. B. N. s. 386.

[2] Marsh v. Wilson, Busb. 143.

[3] Lobdell v. Baker, 1 Met. 193.

[4] Donovan v. Donovan, 9 Allen, 140. See Reynolds v. Reynolds, 5
Allen, 605.

that a reasonably cautious and prudent person might be misled or deceived as to the existence of a particular fact which formed the basis or contributed an essential ingredient to the contract, and that such acts and conduct were designed and adapted to create a false impression and belief in the mind of the other party.[1]

Again, where actual language is used, no one can evade the force of the impression which he knows another has received from his words and conduct, and which he meant him to receive, by resorting to the literal meaning of his language alone. Every one is responsible for the belief he intentionally creates, whether by words or otherwise, and will be precluded from profiting, for example, by any unconscionable use of an obligation which has been thus wrongfully obtained.[2]

To constitute a fraudulent misrepresentation, it is not necessary that statements should be made in terms expressly affirming the existence of some untrue fact. If the alleged misrepresentation be made by one party in such terms as would naturally lead the other party to suppose the existence of such state of facts, and if it be so made designedly and fraudulently, it is as much a fraudulent misrepresentation as if the statement of untrue facts were made in express terms.[3]

Language, further, is to be interpreted in the sense in which it would generally be understood by persons familiar with its particular use, unless some different intention be manifested. Thus, a vendor representing land offered for sale by him along the Mississippi River as high bottom land, free from overflow, must be understood as meaning that the land is such as is free from all except extraordinary overflow, according to the natural meaning attached to such terms in relation to Mississippi or other bottom lands, by those accus-

[1] Donovan v. Donovan, supra, Bigelow, C. J.

[2] Mizner v. Kussell, 29 Mich. 229. See Fisher v. Meister, 24 Mich. 447.

[3] Lee v. Jones, 17 Com. B. N. s. 482 ; s. c. 14 Com. B. N. s. 386.

tomed to speak of them ; unless, by the particular language used in connection with these terms, a different meaning would be more natural.[1] And, in determining whether the vendor misrepresented the character of such land, the condition of the land at the time of the contract is to be considered. Subsequent changes in its condition, produced by change of current, cut-off, or otherwise, are not to be regarded ; nor the state of overflow at any time, or under any circumstances, subsequent to the execution of the contract, only so far as the same may tend to show what the elevation of the land truly was when the contract was made.[2]

A party to a written contract may perpetrate a fraud upon the opposite party as well by false and fraudulent representations of the meaning of words used in the contract as in any other way. And if such words are material to a proper understanding of the agreement, and the other party, being ignorant of their true meaning, relies and acts upon such representation to his injury, he will have a good defence to an action upon the contract.[3]

The allegation of only part of the truth, with a view to deceiving the other party, and inducing him to act differently than he otherwise would do, is a fraud for which the contract may be repudiated, or an action for damages maintained.[4] Thus, the defendant in the case first cited, being desirous of purchasing certain stock of the plaintiff, of the value of which he knew she was ignorant, told her, for the purpose of misleading her and inducing her to sell the stock at less than its value, of a fact calculated to depreciate the value of the stock ; but he omitted to disclose other facts within his knowledge which would have given her correct information of such value, and by

[1] Yeates v. Prior, 6 Eng. (Ark.) 58.
[2] Ib.   [3] Calkins v. State, 13 Wis. 389.
[4] Mallory v. Leach, 35 Vt. 156; Snyder v. Mutual Life Ins. Co., 4 Big. 424.

this course he succeeded in obtaining the stock at much less
than it was worth. There was evidence also tending to show
a relation of confidence between the parties.[1] It was accordingly held that the conduct of the defendant was fraudulent,
entitling the plaintiff to damages for the loss sustained.
Hence, *a fortiori*, a representation that a party is owner of
certain buildings is false, if they belong to his wife, and he
have only a revocable license to use them.[2]

And the effect of a partial misrepresentation is not to
alter or modify a transaction *pro tanto*, but to destroy it
entirely, and to operate as a personal bar to the party
who practised it.[3] This is true, at least, where the aid
of equity is invoked to obtain the specific performance
of a contract.[4] If it were otherwise, — if a contract in
such case were only to be altered *pro tanto*, — there would be
great encouragement for fraud. If not found out, the party
would gain his object; and, if detected, he would have the
benefit of the contract in the same manner as if he had practised no deception. The Court of Chancery has therefore
settled the requirement that he must come into court with
perfect propriety of conduct. If he does not, that alone is a
sufficient answer to him.[5]

Further, the misrepresentation must be material; and
it is material if the transaction might not have taken
place without it. This, however, does not mean that
the particular misrepresentation complained of must have
been the sole inducement to the plaintiff's action. The
rule simply means that the particular representation in
question must have been necessary, even with other inducements, to cause the party to act as he did. And whether the

---

[1] *Quære* if this were material in such a case?
[2] Moore *v.* Cains, 116 Mass. 396.
[3] Clermont *v.* Tasburgh, 1 Jac. & W. 112.
[4] Ib.; Cadman *v.* Horner, 18 Ves. 10.
[5] Clermont *v.* Tasburgh, *supra.*

representation were in this sense material is a question for the jury.[1]

Whether the misrepresentation of a fact supposed at the time to be material, but which afterwards turns out to be immaterial, can be set up by the party to whom it was made, is a question of some interest. It would seem that it could; since a party's rights and duties are in general to be judged of, and properly so, by the motives operating at the time of the transaction. However, it has recently been decided that where, in the sale of a patent right, the vendor represented that a certain contrivance of the invention was one of great utility, when in fact it afterwards proved to be worthless, without, however, affecting in any way the general utility of the invention, the misrepresentation was not such an one as would entitle the purchaser to set aside the sale. But the court observed that there was no evidence that the purchaser was at all influenced by the misrepresentation referred to.[2] It would seem to be no answer to an allegation of this kind, in a suit *ex contractu*, that the article was just as good as it would have been had the representation been true; for though this would show that no damage had been suffered, and hence that an action for deceit could not be maintained, the purchaser still is entitled to what he contracted for. He may have regarded the fact as of the essence of his purchase; and that should be sufficient to enable him to return the property, and demand back the consideration.

In the next place, the matter misrepresented must, in general, be fact as distinguished from law. A representation of what the law will or will not permit to be done is a matter upon which the party to whom it is made cannot safely rely. If he does so, he cannot ask the courts to relieve him from the consequences. The truth

---

[1] McAleer v. Horsey, 35 Md. 439.

[2] Percival v. Harger, 40 Iowa, 286.

or falsehood of such a representation is matter of law which all parties are bound to know.[1] Hence, a stockholder in a corporation cannot be relieved of his connection with the concern on the ground that he was misinformed as to the legal effect of his contract.[2] Nor can a defendant, who could not by contract lawfully relieve himself from liability as a stockholder, accomplish that result by proof that it was fraudulently represented to him that he could so relieve himself.[3] And this rule prevails in equity as well as at common law.[4]

It is not, however, universally true that a misrepresentation of the law is not binding upon the party who made it. Thus, where a party, knowing that a promissory note was barred by limitation, stated to the representative of the maker that the note was unpaid and valid in law, and obtained a bond from such representative in consideration of an agreement to provide for part of the note, it was decided that the facts stated were a good defence to an action on the bond.[5]

Where one who has had superior means of information professes a superior knowledge of the law, and thereby obtains an unconscionable advantage of another who is ignorant, and has not been in a situation to become informed, the injured party in justice is as much entitled to relief as if the misrepresentation had been concerning matter of fact. And this principle has been applied to the case of an immigrant, who, having just arrived from abroad, meets an old citizen who professes familiarity with the land titles of the country, and proposes to sell him land, to which, he·

---

[1] Fish v. Clelland, 33 Ill. 243 ; Upton v. Tribilcock, 91 U. S. 45, 50; Grant v. Grant, 56 Maine, 573; Martin v. Wharton, 38 Ala. 637.

[2] Upton v. Tribilcock, *supra.*

[3] Ib. ; Ogilvie v. Knox Ins. Co., 22 How. 380.

[4] Upton v. Tribilcock.

[5] Brown v. Rice, 26 Gratt. 467.

assures the immigrant, he has a perfectly good title ; though the statement in reality was a misrepresentation of law.[1]

In transactions between parties in confidential relations towards each other, even innocent misrepresentations of the law may be fatal. Thus, where trust and confidence were reposed by a widowed sister in-law in her brother-in-law, and the former was led to believe that her title to certain property was invalid, and in this belief sold it to the latter at a low price, it was held that she could avoid the sale, though the misrepresentation was made in good faith.[2] So, too, if a party to a contract place a known trust and confidence in the other party in respect of a mixed question of law and fact, and the latter purposely mislead him, equity will grant relief.[3]

Where the purchaser of a note, knowing the ignorance of the seller, induced the latter to sign a guaranty that it was "good," upon the representation that the legal effect of that term was simply that the note was genuine and unpaid, the deluded party was held entitled to relief as against the purchaser.[4] But a misrepresentation as to the legal effect of a guaranty, in a matter of mere judgment equally open to the inquiries of both parties, does not constitute a fraud, unless some peculiar fiduciary relation exists between the parties, of which one knowingly avails himself to mislead the other by such misrepresentation, or knowingly takes advantage of the other's ignorance of law.[5]

The misrepresentation complained of should also be clear

---

[1] Moreland v. Atchison, 19 Tex. 303.

[2] Sims v. Ferrill, 45 Ga. 585.

[3] Peter v. Wright, 6 Ind. 183; Shaeffer v. Sleade, 7 Blackf. 178 ; State v. Holloway, 8 Blackf. 45 ; Cooke v. Nathan, 16 Barb. 342 ; 1 Story, Equity, §§ 130–133.

[4] Cooke v. Nathan, 16 Barb. 342. See Hirschfield v. London Ry. Co., Law R. 2 Q. B. Div. 1. See, however, Lewis v. Jones, 4 Barn. & C. 506 ; Edwards v. Brown, 1 Cromp. & J. 307.

[5] Townsend v. Cowles, 31 Ala. 428 ; Cowles v. Townsend, 37 Ala. 77.

and certain, otherwise the party to whom it is made will not be justified in acting upon it. Thus, a vendor, about to sell a tract of land, pointed out to the purchaser the *probable* western boundary ; the boundary having no marks to designate it, but being an open line, and its definite position not certainly known. Upon a survey of the line after the purchase, it was found further east than represented, and twenty-five acres were cut off which the purchaser supposed he was buying ; without, however, diminishing in the result the number of acres contract d for, or their quality. It was held that the misrepresentation was not of a character to justify a rescission of the contract.[1] It might have been otherwise, had the misrepresentation materially affected the subject of the purchase ;[2] for in such case, though an action for deceit could not have been maintained, the contract would have failed for want of identity between the premises as actually existing and those agreed upon.

A representation in regard to the existence of prior incumbrances to a party about to take a mortgage of premises, " that there was none, so far as he [the mortgagor] knew," is not a distinct statement of fact. The import of the language simply is, that the mortgagor did not know whether there was a prior incumbrance or not ; and this is enough to put the mortgagee upon inquiry to ascertain the fact for himself.[3] So, too, a mere statement that another is " a fine man, and the owner of a considerable estate and able to do well," is not such a representation of solvency as may safely be acted upon.[4]

It follows also from this rule, requiring the representation to be certain and definite, that it must relate to a present or past state of facts.[5] Relief as for deceit cannot

---

[1] Halls *v.* Thompson, 1 Smedes & M. 443.　　　　　[2] Ib.

[3] Bristol *v.* Braidwood, 28 Mich. 191.

[4] Savage *v.* Jackson, 19 Ga. 305.

[5] Gage *v.* Lewis, 68 Ill. 604 ; Morrison *v.* Kock, 32 Wis. 254 ; Hazlett

be obtained for the non-performance of a promise,[1] or of other statements looking to the future.[2] Even equity will not relieve against misrepresentations of facts yet to come into existence; representations based upon general knowledge, information, and judgment, as distinguished from representations which, from knowledge peculiarly his own, a party may certainly know whether they are true or false.[3]

The above doctrine, however, proceeds upon the supposition that the statement is an expression of an honest intention; and, such being the case, it is to be received with the understanding that the party making it may change his mind. But if the statement were not an honest one; if the party had no such intention at the time of the statement as he expressed; if in this sense it were fraudulently made, the injured party will be entitled to relief.[4]

Relief is sometimes given in equity on the ground of fraud, for a failure to observe the implied understanding of the parties to the sale of a good will.[5] But, if the right of redress rest upon the ground that the action is a breach of one of the implied terms of the contract of sale, it is clear that the application of the term "fraud" to the act of the defendant is not accurate. The "fraud upon the agreement" is simply a breach of the terms of the contract of sale. It is extremely doubtful if such an act would support an action of deceit. If, however, instead of being a

v. Burge, 22 Iowa, 535; State v. Prather, 44 Ind. 287; Fouty v. Fouty, 34 Ind. 433; Hartsville Univ. v. Hamilton, Ib. 506; Long v. Woodman, 58 Maine, 49; Pedrick v. Porter, 5 Allen, 324.

[1] Jordan v. Money, 5 H. L. Cas. 185; Citizens' Bank v. First National Bank, Law R. 6 H. L. 352, 360; Long v. Woodman, 58 Maine, 49.

[2] Pedrick v. Porter, 5 Allen, 324.

[3] Sawyer v. Prickett, 19 Wall. 146.

[4] Kimball v. Ætna Ins. Co., 9 Allen, 540.

[5] Shackle v. Baker, 14 Ves. 468; Harrison v. Gardner, 2 Madd. 198; Cruttwell v. Lye, 17 Ves. 346; Smith v. Gibbs, 44 N. H. 335.

mere breach of an implied undertaking, it should appear that,
when the defendant made the supposed representation that
he would not set up a rival business within the limits understood, he had no intention of keeping the same, proof of such
fact would be a fraud.[1]

Statements as to the operation and utility of an invention
must, in most cases, be mere matter of opinion; upon which,
therefore, a purchaser cannot safely rely. Thus, in a
recent case,[2] the defendant to a suit upon a note given
for the purchase of a patent right pleaded as follows:
That the plaintiff exhibited to him a model of the invention (a machine), and "claimed" that the machine, when
properly constructed, would cut a ditch for draining purposes; that the defendant had no means of knowing whether
it would do so or not; that, relying upon such representations, he made the purchase and executed the note; that,
when the machine was duly constructed, it failed to produce the result and was of no value; and that this was
known to the plaintiff at the time of the sale. On demurrer,
it was held that the plea was not an answer to the suit.[3] But
the purchaser of a patent may rely upon the representations
of the vendor as to what is covered by the patent; and, if
there should be no patent for a material part of that which
is exhibited by the vendor as an invention, the purchaser is
entitled to relief.[4]

In general, equity will set aside conveyances of property
on the ground of misrepresentation, only where the misrepresentation relates to the quantity, quality, or situation
of the property, or the pecuniary responsibility of the purchaser, or something of that nature. But the courts do
not limit themselves by set rules or precise definitions, par-

[1] See Kimball v. Ætna Ins. Co., 9 Allen, 540.
[2] Hunter v. McLaughlin, 43 Ind. 38.
[3] See Kernodle v. Hunt, 4 Blackf. 57 ; Gatling v. Newell, 9 Ind. 572.
[4] Rose v. Hurley, 39 Ind. 77.

ticularly in matters of fraud. Fraud is so multiform as
to admit of no such rules or definitions ; and hence equity
leaves the way open to punish frauds, and redress wrongs
perpetrated by means of them, in whatever form they
may appear. A misrepresentation producing confusion and
terror of mind, unsettling the judgment, and depriving the
party of the reasoning faculty, so that he cannot think or act
deliberately or with knowledge and calmness ; a misrepresentation made to produce such an effect on the mind, with
intent to take advantage thereby, is one which equity will
consider and redress in a suit to set aside a conveyance.[1]

Representations made by an agent of a railroad company
in regard to the value of a donation of land made to the company, and in regard to the amount of assets of the company,
and their ability to complete the road within a specified
time, and the probable cost and profits of the road, though
false and exaggerated, and intended to induce persons to
subscribe for stock in the company, are but expressions of
opinion. Subscribers for stock have no right to rely upon
them ; and, if they do, they cannot set them up as ground
for avoiding the contract of subscription.[2] So, too, advertise-
ments of the sale of town lots, in which the prospective
and present advantages of the town are set forth, and vague,
general representations in relation to the value of the lots,
will not, though false, be deemed fraudulent, so as to justify a court in granting rescission of contracts of sale made
by reason of such representations.[3]

A bill was filed in a recent case[4] to set aside the purchase of an interest in a certain mine in Utah, and for
the cancellation of a note given for the price, on the
ground of fraudulent misrepresentations of the quality and

[1] Knelkamp v. Hidding, 31 Wis. 503, Dixon, C. J.
[2] Walker v. Mobile & O. R. Co., 34 Miss. 245.
[3] Anderson r. Hill, 12 Smedes & M. 679.
[4] Tuck v. Downing, 76 Ill. 71.

prospects of the mine. It appeared that the vendor went
East to make sales of shares, and upon his representations procured capitalists to appoint a committee to go and
investigate, the purchaser acting with the rest in the appointment. The committee reported that the representations
were true; and the vendor made extravagant declarations of
the prospects of the mine, but made no warranty aside from
the nature of such representations. It was considered that
such declarations could only be regarded as the expression of
an opinion of a matter concerning which the committee could,
and were bound to, judge for themselves; and the sale was
accordingly decided to be valid.

A buyer, in general, is not liable for misrepresenting a
seller's chance of obtaining a good price for his property; but, if there be any peculiar relation between the
parties implying or leading to confidence, the contrary is
true.[1] Thus, in the case cited, the president of an insurance company, professing a desire to aid a stockholder
in selling his stock, advised and effected a sale thereof at
a price below the market value. He caused the transfer
to be made to a third person, whom the stockholder supposed
to be the purchaser, but who really took it for the president,
and afterwards transferred it to him. It was accordingly
held that the president was liable to the stockholder for the
difference between the price for which the stock was sold
and its real value.

An action cannot be maintained by the seller of his share
in a trade against the buyer for persuading him to sell it
at a certain price, by representing that certain partners whose
names he would not disclose were to be joint purchasers, and
that they would give no more than the particular sum; though
in truth they had authorized the defendant to purchase it
on the best terms he could, and though the defendant
charged them with a higher price than he gave.[2]

[1] Fisher v. Budlong, 10 R. I. 525.
[2] Vernon v. Keys, 4 Taunt. 488.

A person can rely upon the representations of another as to the location and nature of land about to be bought by him, lying at a distance from the parties; and it is not necessary that he should have in the deed a warranty upon the point.[1] And the same has been held true where the false representations related to the value of the land, the purchaser having been prevented from going to see the land by the strong assurances of the vendor that that was unnecessary.[2]

The honest expression of opinion, however, by the vendor as to the location of one of the boundary lines, even though erroneous, is not such a misrepresentation as constitutes a fraud on the purchaser, and is not available to him in abatement of the purchase-money.[3] But where the quantity of land is the inducement to a purchase, and there is fraud on the part of the vendor, the transaction is vitiated, and the purchaser may proceed to set aside the sale.[4] Thus, the vendor of a forty-acre tract of land, well knowing the location of the corners and lines, represented one of the lines so to run as to embrace nine or ten acres of cleared land, when in truth it contained much less, — the difference of value between the land pointed out and that conveyed amounting to almost one-third the purchase-money. Upon discovering the mistake, the purchaser proposed to the vendor to rescind the contract, or to be allowed to retain the land and be allowed a deduction for the purchase-money, or leave the matter to arbitration; which several propositions were rejected. It was decided that these facts showed a fraudulent misrepresentation, and entitled the purchaser to a rescission of the contract.[5]

[1] Maggart v. Freeman, 27 Ind. 531.

[2] Harris v. McMurray, 23 Ind. 9.

[3] Stow v. Bozeman, 29 Ala. 397.

[4] Hill v. Brower, 76 N. C. 124; Whitney v. Allaire, 1 Comst. 305; Clark v. Baird, 9 N. Y. 183; Wiswall v. Hall, 3 Paige, 313; Kelly v. Allen, 34 Ala. 663.

[5] Elliott v. Boaz, 9 Ala. 772.

If a tract of land be sold upon a representation that it contains a certain number of acres, and there be a deficiency in quantity, the purchaser is entitled to an abatement of the purchase-money for so much as the quantity falls short of the representation.[1] If the purchaser prefer to keep the land actually conveyed rather than to rescind, he is not entitled in any event to claim an abatement of more than the value of the land not conveyed.[2]

The purchaser of a flouring mill, unacquainted with milling, may rely upon the positive and unqualified representations of the vendor that the mill is capable of grinding a specific number of bushels of wheat per hour; and, if the representations be false and fraudulent, the vendor is liable for the deceit.[3] So, too, if positive and unqualified representations be made that the foundation of a sluiceway connected with a mill is firmly laid upon the sand rock, the same may be relied upon by a person purchasing the mill property and appurtenances.[4] These are matters of fact, capable of positive knowledge by the vendor.[5]

In Massachusetts and Maine, and perhaps elsewhere, it is held that misrepresentations as to what an article cost, or what it has been sold for, or of offers made for it, are not the subject of an action.[6] A statement, moreover, that certain lands had large deposits of oil, and were of great value for manufacturing oil, has in Maine been held to be a mere statement of opinion.[7] But a false and fraudulent statement

---

[1] Cox v. Reynolds, 7 Ind. 257; Cravens v. Kiser, 4 Ind. 512; Howk v. Pollard, 6 Blackf. 108; Earl v. Bryan, Phill. Eq. (N. C.) 278; Cullum v. Branch Bank, 4 Ala. 21.

[2] Ib.; Hill v. Buckley, 17 Ves. 394.

[3] Faribault v. Sater, 13 Minn. 223.   [4] Ib.   [5] Ib.

[6] Medbury v. Watson, 6 Met. 246, 260; Hemmer v. Cooper, 8 Allen, 334; Manning v. Albee, 11 Allen, 622; Mooney v. Miller, 102 Mass. 220; Cooper v. Lovering, 106 Mass. 79; Long v. Woodman, 58 Maine, 52; Martin v. Jordan, 60 Maine, 531; Holbrook v. Connor, Ib. 578; Bishop v. Small, 63 Maine, 12.

[7] Holbrook v. Connor, *supra*, two judges dissenting.

of the amount of hay cut upon a farm the previous year has, in the latter State and in New Hampshire, been held good ground for an action of deceit.[1] It would doubtless be otherwise as to representations of the amount of hay or wood *to be* cut on a farm.[2]

It is not, then, every false affirmation by the vendor of property that will give the purchaser an action, even though he may be deceived by it. If the buyer of goods trust to representations which were not calculated to impose upon a man of ordinary sagacity, or if he neglect to use means of inquiry directly before his eyes and pointed out to him,[3] he cannot recover. Hence, no action will lie, as a general rule, for a false affirmation by the vendor of property concerning the value of it, since it would be folly in the purchaser to rely upon statements as to value from that source.[4] Besides, value is generally matter of opinion merely, upon which men will widely differ. Possibly, also, an action will not lie for a false affirmation that a person bid a particular sum for the property, though the vendee was thereby induced to purchase, and was deceived as to the value of the property.[5]

It is considered as to such cases that the mere false affirmation, though knowingly and intentionally made, is not enough. The purchaser, it is said, should show that some deceit was practised " for the purpose of putting him off his guard."[6] It should rather be said that some deceit should

[1] Martin v. Jordan, 60 Maine, 531; Coon v. Atwell, 46 N. H. 510. See Irving v. Thomas, 18 Maine, 418.

[2] Mooney v. Miller, 102 Mass. 217.

[3] A plaintiff's claim in deceit is not repelled by mere evidence that the means of inquiry were open to him. David v. Park, 103 Mass. 501. See *post*, § 4.

[4] Harvey v. Young, Yelv. 20; Davis v. Meeker, 5 Johns. 354; Medbury v. Watson, 6 Met. 246; Noetting v. Wright, 72 Ill. 390.

[5] Page v. Parker, 43 N. H. 363; Van Epps v. Harrison, 5 Hill, 63, 69, *dicta*, and stated in a dissenting opinion in the latter case.

[6] Van Epps v. Harrison and Page v. Parker, *supra*. See Simar v. Cannaday, 53 N. Y. 298, holding that statements of value with intent

be shown *tending* to put the purchaser, as a man of ordinary intelligence, off his guard. A false affirmation of value, knowingly made, is always made for the *purpose* of putting the purchaser off his guard; but the proper question is, Should it have had that effect?

While it has been stated in cases just cited that no action can be maintained for a false affirmation, that a person bid a particular sum for property, a distinction is suggested in the same cases, founded on early decisions, as to false statements of the annual rental of property. A false representation, for example, that property to be sold was rented for £42 *per annum*, when the rent was much less than that, whereby the plaintiff was deceived and induced to pay a high price for the purchase, was considered actionable.[1] So, too, it was held, in one of the cases under consideration,[2] that a fraudulent representation that a piece of property cost the vendor $32,000, when in fact it cost him but $16,000, was ground for an action in deceit.[3] There is ground, therefore, for doubting the correctness of the proposition that an action cannot be maintained for a false representation of a sum bid for the property in question. Nor is it clear that an action will not lie, at least in equity, under some circumstances for

---

to deceive are actionable. To the same effect, Cruess *v.* Fessler, 39 Cal. 336; Gifford *v.* Carvill, 29 Cal. 589; Davis *v.* Jackson, 22 Ind. 233, of *invoice* value; Neil *v.* Cummings, 75 Ill. 170; Bradley *v.* Bosley, 1 Barb. Ch. 125. If a person be deceived in an exchange of lands as to the value of the property for which he exchanges, he has an equitable lien on his late estate for the deficiency in value. Bradley *v.* Bosley, *supra.*

[1] Page *v.* Parker, *supra*, citing Elkins *v.* Kesham, 1 Lev. 102; Lysney *v.* Selby, 2 Ld. Raym. 1118; s. c. 1 Salk. 214; Dobell *v.* Stevens, 3 Barn. & C. 623; Bowring *v.* Stevens, 2 Car. & P. 337.

[2] Van Epps *v.* Harrison, 5 Hill, 63.

[3] See also Green *v.* Bryant, 2 Kelly, 67 ; Morehead *v.* Eades, 3 Bush, 121 ; McFadden *v.* Robinson, 35 Ind. 24; McAleer *v.* Horsey, 35 Md. 439, to the same effect. *Contra*, Tuck *v.* Downing, 76 Ill. 71; Banta *v.* Palmer, 47 Ill. 99 ; Cooper *v.* Lovering, 106 Mass. 77; Hemmer *v.* Cooper, 8 Allen, 334; Manning *v.* Albee, 11 Allen, 520 ; Mooney *v.* Miller, 102 Mass. 217.

a false affirmation purely of value. It has been held, indeed, in New Hampshire, that where it was alleged that a party in negotiation with another had expressed his ignorance concerning the value of certain stock offered him by the owner, and declined to take it for that very reason, whereupon he was told that it was valuable, and was thereby induced to buy it, the allegation of ignorance of the value of the stock was material, and must be proved by the party making it, else the statement of the owner of the stock would not be an actionable misrepresentation.[1] And the language of the court indicates clearly that, if the statement of the purchaser had been shown to be true, the vendor would have been liable.[2] So, too, representations of value made by an expert, as to a matter of which the purchaser is ignorant, may afford ground of action, if false.[3] It should be added that specific performance of a contract for the sale of land will not be enforced, when there is any misrepresentation of the condition or value of the property.[4]

[1] Lawton v. Kittredge, 30 N. H. 500.

[2] "It is not," said the court, "that a representation of the quality or value of a thing sold must always follow an objection or inquiry on the part of the purchaser, in order to charge the vendor, if untrue; for the cases show the contrary [no cases, however, are mentioned], and there would be no reason in such a rule. But it is necessary for the party complaining of the deceit to prove that the language was used with an intent that it should be believed; that it was spoken, not for the purpose of suggesting a rumor, a general impression, or the speaker's private opinion on a subject as to which the listener had precisely the same means of information, but in the way of assurance, and for the express object of making a representation."

[3] Picard v. McCormick, 11 Mich. 68; Kost v. Bender, 25 Mich. 515. See McGar v. Williams, 26 Ala. 467.

[4] Powers v. Hale, 25 N. H. 145. See further Stover v. Wood, 11 C. E. Green, 417, where a vendor of stock was held liable for false representations of its value; Alexander v. Beresford, 27 Miss. 147; Bryan v. Hitchcock, 43 Mo. 527. A fraudulent assertion that a mistake has been made in an inventory of goods, making the valuation less than it really was, is not a mere false representation of value. Wilder v. DeCou, 18 Minn. 470.

False representations of the elements of *fact* going to make up value certainly should afford ground for an action of deceit, or of defence to an action upon the contract of purchase or of subscription. Aside from the cases above mentioned, this is clearly the rule as to the too common case of false representations made in prospectuses of companies and corporations.[1] The same has been held of representations concerning the age of a horse,[2] the number of feet of lumber a saw-mill can cut in a day,[3] and of the number of subscribers there are to a newspaper offered for sale,[4] and of the extent of sales of a patented article, in connection with the statements of agents in letters concerning the same;[5] and this, too, in a State in which it has been conceded that mere representations of value, such as the market value of a commodity, are not actionable.[6] It must be admitted, however, that the law upon this subject of misrepresentations of the value of property, is in great confusion.

Representations by the agent of a corporation that the stock of the company is not assessable beyond a certain percentage of its value constitute no defence to an action against the holder of the stock to enforce payment of the entire amount subscribed, where he has failed to use due diligence to ascertain the truth or falsity of such representations.[7] Nor does the word "non-assessable" upon the certificate of stock cancel or impair the obligation to pay the amount due upon

---

[1] Campbell *v.* Fleming, 1 Ad. & E. 40; Bagshaw *v.* Seymour, 4 Com. B. N. s. 873; Bedford *v.* Bagshaw, 4 Hurl. & N. 538; Clarke *v.* Dickson, 6 Com. B. N. s. 453 ; Bradley *v.* Poole, 98 Mass. 169; Bigelow's L. C. Torts, 25 *et seq.*

[2] Reid *v.* Flippin, 47 Ga. 273.　　[3] Sieveking *v.* Litzler, 31 Ind. 13.

[4] Harvey *v.* Smith, 17 Ind. 272.　　[5] Allin *v.* Millison, 72 Ill. 201.

[6] Cronk *v.* Cole, 10 Ind. 485.　See Foley *v.* Cowgill, 5 Blackf. 18.

The Roman law concerning the effect of puffing one's wares was thus stated : " Ea quæ commendandi causa, in venditionibus dicuntur, si palam appareant, venditorem non obligant, veluti, si dicat servum speciosum, domum bene ædificatam." — Digest, Lib. 18, tit. 1, § 43.

[7] Upton *v.* Tribilcock, 91 U. S. 45.

the shares, created by the acceptance and holding of such
certificate. Its legal effect, at most, is a stipulation against
liability from further assessment or taxation after the entire subscription of one hundred per cent. shall have been
paid.[1]

In an action against a surety upon a bond given by one
partner to another, to indemnify the latter against the partnership liabilities, false and fraudulent representations as to the
amount of these liabilities, made to the surety to induce him
to sign the bond, will (where equitable defences are pleadable
at law) constitute a good defence.[2] So, if a debtor procure
a composition of his debts with his creditors, by means of
false representations as to the amount of his property, the
composition is not binding, and a creditor may recover the
whole of his debt.[3] So, again, if a party be induced to become
surety of another for part of a sum for which the debtor has
compromised with his creditors, upon the false representation
by the debtor and creditors that such part is in full, the surety
cannot be held on his agreement.[4]

It is also held that the vendor of land, having a lien for the
purchase-money, does not lose his lien by taking other securities, if such securities are worthless, and known to be so by
the purchaser, and the vendor took them upon his representation that they were good.[5] So, if one get possession of the
property of another, by falsely and fraudulently representing
to him that a promissory note given in exchange for the property was good and would be paid, when the holder knew it
was worthless, he is not entitled to notice of non-payment.[6]
So, too, where one sells property for paper which is represented to be good, but which is worthless, and known to be so
by the holder, the injured party may treat the contract as a

---

[1] Upton v. Tribilcock, 91 U. S. 45.   [2] Fishburn v. Jones, 37 Ind. 119.
[3] Seving v. Gale, 28 Ind. 486.   [4] Weed v. Bentley, 6 Hill, 56.
[5] Tobey v. McAlister, 9 Wis. 463.
[6] Alexander v. Dennis, 9 Porter (Ala.), 174.

nullity, and bring trover for the property, or an action of deceit, where the measure of damages will be the injury sustained in consequence of the fraud.[1]

In this connection, it is proper to consider the subject of false representations concerning the pecuniary standing of parties. It has been held for nearly a century that a person may render himself liable for a false representation of the solvency of another (the other elements of deceit being present), notwithstanding a very urgent objection by some of the judges that such a representation was, in its nature, nothing more than an expression of opinion.[2] Such representations must certainly be very definite, and certain to carry any liability with them.[3] Hence, where, in answer to inquiries as to the circumstances and credit of a third person, the party questioned merely says that " *he* should be willing to give the person in question credit for any thing he wanted," this statement will not be sufficient to render the party making it answerable as for a fraudulent misrepresentation, though he knew that the person concerning whom the inquiry was made had previously been discharged under an insolvency act. There is a material difference between a man's stating that he himself is ready to give credit to another, and that such other person is fit to be trusted generally.[4] A representation, however, that a note is "good," is sufficiently certain to render

---

[1] Alexander *v.* Dennis, 9 Porter (Ala.), 174.

[2] Pasley *v.* Freeman, 3 T. R. 51. A further objection urged in later cases, that, if the false representations were oral, it would come within the intent of the Statute of Frauds, though generally repudiated by the courts (Bigelow's L. C. Torts, 39, 40), has been quite generally accepted by the Legislatures, and a special enactment passed requiring such representations to be in writing. See Browne, St. Frauds, App.

The statute requiring that representations of credit should be in writing has no application to the case of an indorsement of a note procured by the misrepresentation of the indorsee as to the solvency of the maker. Lenheim *v.* Fay, 27 Mich. 70.

[3] Haycraft *v.* Creasy, 2 East, 92 ; Gainsford *v.* Blachford, 7 Price, 549.

[4] Ib.

the party liable, if the maker of the note is not responsible and does not pay it.[1]

Where a marriage has taken place on the faith of representations made by a third person as to the circumstances of one of the parties to the marriage, such third person must make good his representations, even at the suit of a *particeps criminis*.[2] Thus, if a creditor suppress the fact of his debt, in order to promote a marriage, he will not be permitted to set it up even against the person in whose favor and at whose instance he made the suppression.[3] And, upon a similar principle, if one of the parties contracting for marriage be placed ostensibly in one situation by the articles, but in another and a worse situation by private agreement, the latter agreement cannot be enforced.[4]

When a person has been induced to take shares in a joint stock company by misrepresentation, either by the directors or by their officer as to the effect of taking the shares and as to the solvency and position of the company, the contract is voidable at the option of the holder of the shares.[5]

In order to make a misrepresentation concerning solvency ground for an action, it is said that there should be some indication in the representation or its circumstances of the extent to which the credit may go. If the representation do not point with reasonable certainty to the amount or bounds of the expected credit, it is thought that it ought not to serve as a foundation for any credit at all. In such case, a reasonable man would not act upon it.[6] But this is a local doctrine.

---

[1] Weeks *v.* Burton, 7 Vt. 67.

[2] Neville *v.* Wilkinson, 1 Brown, C. C. 546 ; De Manneville *v.* Crompton, 1 Ves. & B. 356; Thompson *v.* Harrison, 1 Cox, 346; Ainslie *v.* Medlycott, 9 Ves. 21.

[3] Dalbiac *v.* Dalbiac, 16 Ves. 125; Neville *v.* Wilkinson, *supra;* Estabrook *v.* Scott, 3 Ves. 461.

[4] Palmer *v.* Neave, 11 Ves. 167; Scott *v.* Scott, 1 Cox, 378.

[5] *In re* Ætna Ins. Co., Law R. 7 Irish Eq. 264.

[6] Glover *v.* Townsend, 30 Ga. 90; Hopkins *v.* Cooper, 28 Ga. 392.

It has been said also that an action cannot be sustained for false and fraudulent representations made by the defendant in respect of *his own* pecuniary responsibility and circumstances, whereby the plaintiff was induced to sell him property on credit.[1] The court, in the case referred to, considered the rule of liability for misrepresentations of pecuniary standing to apply only to cases in which the statements had been made by a stranger to the contract made under the influence of the fraud. It was, however, held, in an earlier case in the same court, that if a debtor, by false and fraudulent representations as to his pecuniary situation, induce his creditor to deliver to him his promissory note upon payment of part only of what is due, the creditor may, upon discovering the fraud, recover the balance of his debt in an action on the note.[2] Indeed, the doctrine of the above decision is difficult to understand. The matter of one's own solvency is a fact as capable of actual knowledge as any other, and there is no good reason for holding a representation concerning it to be of less effect than a representation concerning the solvency of a third person. The authorities generally are also opposed to the doctrine referred. We shall presently find it well-settled law that a purchaser of goods, for example, may be guilty of such fraud, by falsely representing himself to be solvent, as to enable the vendor to rescind the sale and retake the goods.[3]

In the case of a false representation of the solvency of another, it is not necessary for the injured party first to bring an action against the party intrusted, before he can sue the party guilty of the false representation.[4]

[1] Dyer *v.* Tilton, 23 Vt. 313.　　　[2] Reynolds *v.* French, 8 Vt. 85.

[3] *Post,* p. 37, and cases there cited.

[4] Kidney *v.* Stoddard, 7 Met. 252. The following are further cases on the subject of representations of solvency : Tapp *v.* Lee, 3 Bos. & P. 367 ; Eyre *v.* Dunsford, 1 East, 318; Hamar *v.* Alexander, 2 Bos. & P. N. R. 241; Evans *v.* Bicknell, 6 Ves. 174 ; Clifford *v.* Brooke, 13 Ves. 131 ; Venezuela Ry. Co. *v.* Kisch, Law R. 2 H. L. 99; Hutchinson *v.* Bell, 1 Taunt. 558 ; Upton *v.* Vail, 6 Johns. 181 ; Wise *v.* Wilcox, 1 Day,

It is not universally true that a party is not bound to make good an expression of opinion. If such opinion be fraudulently expressed, the party giving it will be bound by it;[1] as where a party puts forth, in the form of opinion, that concerning which he has positive knowledge at variance with such expression, to one supposing the opinion to be honest and acting upon it.[2] Thus, in the case first cited, the plaintiff, suing for the price of cattle sold the defendant, had expressed an opinion that the cattle would weigh 900 lbs. and upwards per head; and the defendant had bought them upon this statement. But it appeared that the plaintiff had already weighed the cattle, and had found that their average weight was considerably less than 900 lbs. It was accordingly held that the defendant was entitled to recoup against the purchase price the damage sustained by him through the plaintiff's fraud. And it was considered that the case was not affected by the fact that immediately after the purchase the defendant had weighed the cattle and ascertained their true average weight; inasmuch as he did not at that time know that the plaintiff had himself weighed the cattle, but supposed that he had given an honest expression of opinion on the subject. Under such circumstances, the defendant was not bound to tender the cattle back to the vendor.

Whether the false representation must in all cases be made upon a secular day, in order that the injured party may obtain relief, is not clear. The question must be decided upon the interpretation to be given to the Sunday law statutes of the different States. It is clear, however, that if the effect of the statement were to draw the injured party into a relation of

22; Ewins v. Calhoun, 7 Vt. 79; Newsom v. Jackson, 26 Ga. 241; Slade v. Little, 20 Ga. 371; Patten v. Gurney, 17 Mass. 182.

[1] But this proposition, as applied to statements of the value of property, must be taken in connection with what has just been said *supra*.

[2] Birdsey v. Butterfield, 34 Wis. 52. So held even in Massachusetts. Pike v. Fay, 101 Mass. 134.

contract with the alleged wrong-doer, and the object of the complaint be to obtain a release from the engagement or sale, the courts will not listen to the demand. But if a sale be effected on Sunday upon false representations made the day before, and the purchaser on Monday promise to pay for the property, he will be bound.[1]

It matters not whether a party who has made a false statement was under any obligation to speak or not. Though under no duty to speak, if he will speak, he must declare the truth, and not be guilty of making a fraudulent misrepresentation.[2]

Where an agreement has been made, and a term vested thereunder in a party, and he has been let into possession, the estate has so far passed that it cannot be defeated by a collateral fraud committed in making the agreement. The remedy for such a wrong is to sue for damages, not for the property itself. Thus, where a person obtained a lease of premises upon the false representation that he intended to carry on there the business of a perfumer, when he in fact intended to turn the premises into a brothel, and actually did so, it was held that the term had effectually passed, and that the lessor had no right to turn out the tenant; and, having forcibly done so, the latter was restored by ejectment to possession.[3] But the case must be distinguished where an action is brought upon the lease for rent. In such a case, it is a good defence that the lease was induced by false representations on the part of the plaintiff; and this, too, though possession was taken under the lease, provided the same was surrendered directly upon discovery of the fraud.[4]

The foregoing presentation of the law relating to the

[1] Winchell v. Carey, 115 Mass. 560. See Stebbins v. Peck, 8 Gray, 553; Hall v. Corcoran, 107 Mass. 251; Cranson v. Goss, Ib. 439.

[2] Kelly v. Rogers, 21 Minn. 146, 152 ; Pasley v. Freeman, 3 T. R. 51.

[3] Feret v. Hill, 15 Com. B. 207.

[4] Milliken v. Thorndike, 103 Mass. 382 ; Irving v. Thomas, 18 Maine, 418.

nature of actionable misrepresentations supposes that the representation was made to or for the complaining party. But there is another class of cases, with several branches, in which the situation is different. A representation may be made of a man or of his property, to his injury, as well as *to him;* and, though the exact relation of such cases to the general law of deceit has not been so accurately defined as might be desired, we have endeavored to show in another work, by a somewhat critical examination of the authorities, that this class of cases stands, in reality, upon the same footing as the class above considered.[1]

False representations of a person may consist either (1) in disparaging his credit, or the title to his property, or his property itself, or (2) in attempts to personate him or his badge of business. We have already considered the case of misrepresentations of credit made *to* the complaining party ; [2] and in principle there is no difference between such a case and the situation of the party himself whose pecuniary reputation may have been injured by the false representation. If he have suffered an actual damage, he will be entitled to redress.

If the misrepresentation relate to the plaintiff's title to property or to the quality of his property itself, the wrong done is termed slander of title ; if it be an attempt to personate him or the reputation of his goods in business, it will commonly be the case of an infringement of his trade-mark.[3]

---

[1] Bigelow's L. C. Torts, 54–59, 69–72.

[2] *Ante,* pp. 23–25.

[3] An infringement of a patent is not an attempt to obtain the benefit of another's reputation in business, but to make and vend the very same article, to do which an exclusive right has been given another. There is no attempt to deceive any one in the infringement of a patent; and the same is measurably true of infringements of copyrights. These subjects therefore do not belong to the law of deceit ; nor do they belong properly to any branch of the law of fraud. An invasion of a patent or a copyright is a simple invasion of a right of property, and is no more a fraud than is a trespass upon real estate. Indeed, the jurisdiction of

We cannot, however, treat at length of these subjects here without going over ground already occupied in our work on Torts; and we must therefore omit further reference to them.

The subject of warranty is so closely connected with that of fraudulent representations that it is proper to make some reference to it here. Indeed, a warranty in one aspect is but a species of representation. A warranty is simply a strong representation, so strong indeed that it is wholly unnecessary to prove, in the case of an action for a breach of it, that the statement (or representation) warranted true was false to the knowledge of the warrantor. In technical language, it is not necessary in such an action to prove the *scienter*. Aside from this, there is no difference from the standpoint from which we are now taking our observation between the action of deceit and the action for a breach of warranty. When, therefore, the complaining party's case is strong enough to establish a warranty, the preferable course for him is to sue in contract for the breach, since he will thus escape all danger from questions relating to the *scienter*.

A simple affirmation of soundness does not constitute a warranty, unless it be so intended and understood when made.[1] But, to constitute a warranty in the sale of personal property, it is not necessary that the word " warrant" should be used. It is sufficient if the language used import an undertaking on the part of the seller that the chattel is what he represents it to be.[2] For an auctioneer, about to sell a drove of sheep, to say, " Here is a nice lot of young, sound sheep," is not a warranty of their soundness, if the statement were reasonably supposed to be true.[3] Nor would it afford

equity as to statutory trade-marks is treated as resting on grounds of property, and not on fraud. Leather Cloth Co. *v.* American Leather Cloth Co., 4 DeG., J. & S. 137; Hall *v.* Barrows, Ib. 150.

[1] Lindsay *v.* Davis, 30 Mo. 406.

[2] Callanan *v.* Brown, 31 Iowa, 333; 1 Parsons, Contracts, 579, 580 (5th ed.).

[3] McGrew *v.* Forsythe, 31 Iowa, 179.

ground for an action in deceit. But the rule would perhaps be different for either species of liability, if the statement were made without reasonable ground. It would then be fraudulent.[1]

The rule that a general warranty does not extend to visible defects does not apply when the vendor uses arts to conceal, and succeeds in concealing, such defects.[2]

In the absence of warranty or actual fraud, the conveyance of property by one whose interest is merely that of a tenant will not entitle the grantee to relief against such grantor.[3] Indeed, it is held in Alabama that fraud as to the *title* to land is not a good defence at law to a note given for the purchase-money of land, when the purchaser has accepted from the vendor a deed with covenants of warranty.[4]

Fraud committed by a vendor in the sale of land, through the concealment of an incumbrance, created by himself, by means of which the purchaser is evicted, is relievable in equity by restraining the collection of the purchase-money to the extent of the injury, or by an entire rescission of the contract, although the incumbrance is of record, and the conveyance is with warranty, covering incumbrances generally. The fact that a covenant covering eviction was entered into by the vendor will not prevent the purchaser from insisting on the fraud, in order to rescind the contract.[5] Before eviction, however, in the *absence* of fraud, the remedy of the purchaser, so far as it relates to questions of title, must be found in an action upon the covenants of his deed.[6]

---

[1] *Post*, pp. 62, 63.

[2] Chadsey *v.* Green, 24 Conn. 562.

[3] Hastings *v.* O'Donnell, 40 Cal. 148.

[4] Patton *v.* England, 15 Ala. 69. But see *post*, p. 68.

[5] Cullum *v.* Branch Bank, 4 Ala. 21. Deceit is maintainable without an eviction, in case of fraud. *Post*, p. 68.

[6] The doctrine as to eviction has, of course, no application to the case of an action for fraud not relating to the title to the land; such, for example, as false representations of the condition and quality of the soil.

A purchaser of land who has received a deed with only a special, limited warranty may show, in defence of an action for the purchase price, or in a suit for rescission, that a fraud has been practised upon him with respect to the title. When, indeed, a purchaser of land accepts a quit-claim deed, or a deed with special warranty, he will ordinarily be presumed to have acted upon his own judgment and knowledge of the title, being put upon his guard in this particular. But it is held that when, in the negotiations preliminary to the execution of the contract, the purchaser stipulates for a perfect title, but is afterwards induced by the fraudulent misrepresentations of the vendor to accept a quit-claim or special warranty deed, in the belief that he is thereby acquiring a perfect title, he will be permitted to allege the deceit, and will be relieved.[1]

Next, as to *concealment*. We have said that the representation may consist in conduct as well as in words, and that relief may be granted in cases arising out of acts, even though no language were employed to deceive. It does not follow that fraud, in contemplation of the law, can be established out of pure passive concealment. Concealment may be of two kinds, and confusion sometimes arises from overlooking the fact. To tell half the truth only is to conceal the other half; but concealment of this kind is simply false statement, and differs in no respect, as we have already seen,[2] from the case of false representation above considered. Concealment of this kind we can then dismiss, as a subject already illustrated. But concealment may be of another kind: it may consist in mere silence; and this we have yet to treat of. However, we shall also find it necessary, or at least important, to consider in the same connection concealments in which something of active misconduct appears.

---

[1] Rhode *v.* Alley, 27 Tex. 443; Mitchell *v.* Zimmerman, 4 Tex. 75; York *v.* Gregg, 9 Tex. 85; Hays *v.* Bonner, 14 Tex. 629.

[2] *Ante*, p. 6.

The general proposition of law upon this point is that mere passive concealment, when not promoted by any active misconduct misleading the complaining party, is not fraudulent, and hence is not a subject of redress on grounds of fraud.[1] The buyer of goods is not bound to communicate intelligence of external circumstances which might influence the price of the commodity, and is exclusively within his knowledge.[2] Thus, it was held in the case cited that the purchaser of a quantity of tobacco was not bound to communicate to the vendor news of peace, which would have materially affected the price of the commodity. But each party, it was decided, must take care not to do or say any thing tending to impose upon the other.[3]

So, too, by the general law, mere silence on the part of the vendor of goods with respect to a latent defect therein of which the purchaser is ignorant, will not be ground for avoiding the sale; but the slightest active conduct tending to mislead the buyer should be permitted to go to the jury as evidence of fraud.[4] The putting up of goods, for example, in such a way as to make them present a fair exterior and to conceal defects within, is fraudulent.[5]

It is held, however, in Missouri, that if a person sell property having a latent defect of which he is aware, but which he fails to disclose to the purchaser, knowing that the latter is acting upon the supposition that no such defect exists, he is guilty of fraud; and the fraud may be pleaded as a defence to an action for the price of the property.[6]

---

[1] Laidlaw v. Organ, 2 Wheat. 178; Hanson v. Edgerly, 29 N. H. 343; Smith v. Countryman, 30 N. Y. 655; Kintzing v. McElrath, 5 Barr, 467; Fisher v. Budlong, 10 R. I. 525, 527; Hadley v. Clinton Importing Co., 13 Ohio St. 502; Williams v. Spurr, 24 Mich. 335; Law v. Grant, 37 Wis. 548; Mitchell v. McDougall, 62 Ill. 498; Frenzel v. Miller, 37 Ind. 1.

[2] Laidlaw v. Organ, 2 Wheat. 178.   [3] Ib.

[4] See Hadley v. Clinton Importing Co., 13 Ohio St. 502.

[5] Singleton v. Kennedy, 9 B. Mon. 225.

[6] Cecil v. Spurger, 32 Mo. 462; McAdams v. Cates, 24 Mo. 223; Barrow v. Alexander, 27 Mo. 530.

So, too, it has been said in Mississippi that in cases of latent defect, where the sale is for a full price, the seller is bound to disclose such defect if known to him, especially when the disclosure may so far influence the purchaser as to induce him to decline the purchase.[1] This observation was, however, *obiter*, and unnecessary to the decision of the case.

The rule by which a party to a sale of property is not bound to disclose all the circumstances within his knowledge which might affect the value of the property applies as well in favor of the purchaser as of the vendor.[2]

The rule excusing parties from making disclosure in sales of personalty applies equally in sales of real estate. A person, for example, who knows that there is a mine in the land of another, of which the latter is ignorant, may nevertheless buy it, without disclosing the existence of the mine.[3] But, if the purchaser do any thing to mislead the vendor, it is a fraud, and the sale is not binding.[4] Therefore, though a vendor of land, effecting a sale at an extravagant price, knew that the estimate of the value of the land formed by the purchaser was based upon his belief in the ability of a certain person to detect mineral veins by walking over the surface of the land, and though the vendor himself fix a high valuation upon the land by reason of such supposed condition of the soil, this alone will not relieve the purchaser from payment of the agreed price. The contract price is binding in the absence of any false representations or acts of the vendor tending to cause or strengthen the false opinion upon which the purchaser acted.[5]

It is not a fraud for a party to make a professed sale of

---

[1] Patterson v. Kirkland, 34 Miss. 423, 431.

[2] Laidlaw v. Organ, 2 Wheat. 178; Kintzing v. McElrath, 5 Barr, 467; Smith v. Countryman, 30 N. Y. 655, 670, 681; Fisher v. Budlong, 10 R. I. 525, 527.

[3] Harris v. Tyson, 24 Penn. St. 347; Williams v. Spurr, 24 Mich. 335. *Contra*, Williams v. Beazley, 2 J. J. Marsh. 578.

[4] Ib.   [5] Law v. Grant, 37 Wis. 548.

property, as a lot of hogs, *in præsenti*, to be thereafter delivered, without owning the subject of the contract, if he make
no representation of having it.[1] It will be proper for him in
such a case to purchase the property on the market, and the
purchaser will be bound by his contract. But it will be
otherwise if, at the time of making the contract, he falsely
represent that he has the property on hand.[2]

It is not a fraud for a party to remain silent as to the
correctness of an opinion expressed by a stranger to the
contract at the time parties are contracting, though such
opinion may influence the other party to the contract to his
prejudice.[3]

In regard to those incidents of a sale which materially affect
the quality and value of articles sold for a special purpose, the
rule excusing non-disclosure does not prevail. Not only will no
positive misrepresentation in such cases be permitted, but there
is also a degree of negative deceit which the recent cases do
not countenance. But negative deceit, like positive, must be
practised in such a manner and upon such a subject as to be
calculated to mislead and impose upon a person of ordinary
sagacity. And in general the guilty party must know at the
time that the other party is misled, and must intend that he
shall be misled, to the unjust advantage of the former.[4]

This negative deceit has more commonly been reached in
the English courts by engrafting successive exceptions to the
general rule of warranty, by way of implied warranties; as in
regard to provisions bought for consumption, that they are
wholesome. So, too, in regard to manufactured articles pur-

---

[1] Bales *v.* Weddle, 14 Ind. 349; Sanborn *v.* Benedict, 78 Ill. 309;
Wolcott *v.* Heath, Ib. 433.

[2] Bales *v.* Weddle, *supra*.   [3] Williams *v.* Beazley, 3 J. J. Marsh. 577.

[4] Paddock *v.* Strobridge, 29 Vt. 470, 477, Redfield, C. J.   Silence as
to a known defect in an article sold for a *specific purpose* is equivalent
to fraud. Van Bracklin *v.* Fonda, 12 Johns. 468; Emerson *v.* Brigham,
10 Mass. 197; Winsor *v.* Lombard, 18 Pick. 57, 62. And this is equally
true where the vendor has endeavored to remove the defect, and supposes
that he has succeeded. French *v.* Vining, 102 Mass. 132.

chased for a particular use known at the time to the vendor, it is held that there is an implied warranty that they are fit for such use, though nothing is said to the effect that the articles are fit for the use for which they were purchased. So, too, of articles contracted to be delivered in future for any specified use, and cases where the law implies a warranty that articles sold are of a merchantable quality. These cases are only exceptions, founded upon certain flagrant indications of fraud and deceit, which do not exist in ordinary cases.

Following out this idea, it appears to be settled law in Westminster Hall that there is an implied warranty on the part of the seller that the article sold is what it appears to be, so far as the vendor knows; in other words, that a defect in the article which changes its essential character, and renders it wholly unfit for the purpose for which it is purchased, will justify the purchaser in rescinding the sale or bringing suit for damages, at his election. It seems to be there considered that secret defects in the article sold, materially affecting its value, which the vendor supposes the purchaser would regard as an impossible barrier to the contract, must be disclosed, or the contract is not binding. To have this effect, the defect must be known to the vendor and wholly unknown to the purchaser; and there must be no external or sensible indication calculated to excite suspicion in ordinary observers. It must be of such a character as clearly to have formed an impassable barrier to the contract, and so understood by the seller at the time. Such a case is not what the law considers as a latent defect. There is no sound distinction between such a case and one where the party uses some device to mislead the other party in regard to a defect which he might otherwise have discovered, or where he makes a positive misrepresentation of a fact, with knowledge. But, if in any case the vendor sell "with all faults," this is equivalent to putting the purchaser upon his guard, and he buys at his own risk.[1]

[1] Ib.; Baglehole v. Walters, 3 Campb. 154; Pickering v. Dawson, 4 Taunt. 779; 2 Kent, Com. 482.

There are other cases of negative deceit, fatal to contracts effected through it.   Thus, where the defendant induced the plaintiff to accept an insolvent tenant in his stead, knowing his insolvency and not disclosing it to the plaintiff, it was considered that the mere fact of the defendant's offering such person to take his own place was equivalent to a representation of his solvency.[1]   And in another case it was held that suffering one to buy goods under a wrong impression as to their quality in an essential particular was a fraud, though the seller did nothing to induce the misapprehension.[2]   So, too, if in the sale of a horse there be an internal and secret malady of a fatal character, of which there are no external indications, but of which the vendor is aware, and of which he knows that the purchaser is wholly ignorant, such malady rendering the animal of no value, while the sale is for the apparent value, and the vendor understanding that he could not effect the sale if the true condition of the horse were known to the purchaser, the seller is guilty of an actionable fraud.[3]

A person who negotiates commercial paper payable to bearer, or under the blank indorsement of another warrants that he has no knowledge of any facts which prove the paper to be worthless, on account of the failure of parties, or of a previous payment, or otherwise to have become void or defunct.   Any concealment of this nature, it is said, would be a manifest fraud.[4]

The mere fact that the buyer of property is to his own knowledge insolvent at the time of his purchase is not ground for relief to the vendor.   But it is otherwise, if the purchaser

[1] Bruce v. Ruler, 2 Man. & R. 3.

[2] Hill v. Gray, 1 Stark. 434.

[3] Paddock v. Strobridge, 29 Vt. 470, containing a lucid opinion by Chief Justice Redfield, from which the substance of the above consideration of negative deceit is taken.

[4] Brown v. Montgomery, 20 N. Y. 287, 292 ; Story, Promissory Notes, § 118.

actively mislead the vendor ;[1] especially if he make any false statements as to his financial condition.[2] And the purchaser's knowledge of his own insolvency at the time is proper evidence, in connection with other facts, to support the charge of fraud.[3] But the mere non-disclosure of his own insolvency by the purchaser of goods does not amount to fraud ; nor will a consciousness in him of his inability to pay for the property amount to fraud, if the purchase be made in good faith, and without a design not to pay for them.[4] Nor does the mere fact that a person knows that he can no longer continue business, or that his property is liable to be attacked at any moment by his creditors, necessarily imply a knowledge of his insolvency.[5]

By the general current of authority upon this subject, a debt is created by fraud where one, intending not to pay for property, induces the owner to sell it to him on credit by falsely representing or causing the owner to believe that he intends to pay for it,[6] or by falsely concealing the intent not to pay.[7] Mere insolvency cannot be treated as fraud. There must be a fraudulent intent.[8]

[1] Bell v. Ellis, 33 Cal. 620, overruling Seligman v. Kalkman, 8 Cal. 207.

[2] Schweizer v. Tracy, 76 Ill. 345.

[3] Rodman v. Thalheimer, 75 Penn. St. 232.

[4] Redington v. Roberts, 25 Vt. 686 ; Irving v. Motley, 7 Bing. 543; Cross v. Peters, 1 Greenl. 376 ; Lupin v. Marie, 6 Wend. 83 ; Rowley v. Bigelow, 12 Pick. 307.

[5] Morrill v. Blackman, 42 Conn. 324.

[6] Stewart v. Emerson, 52 N. H. 301; Hovey v. Grant, Ib. 569; Dow v. Sanborn, 3 Allen, 181; Rowley v. Bigelow, 12 Pick. 307; Thompson v. Rose, 16 Conn. 71; Bidault v. Wales, 19 Mo. 36; s. c. 20 Mo. 546; Ash v. Putnam, 1 Hill, 302. See Nichols v. Pinner, 18 N. Y. 295; Mitchell v. Worden, 20 Barb. 253; Powell v. Bradlee, 9 Gill & J. 220; Wiggin v. Day, 9 Gray, 97 ; Jordan v. Osgood, 109 Mass. 457.

[7] Stewart v. Emerson, 52 N. H. 301 ; Hovey v. Grant, Ib. 569; Conyers v. Ennis, 2 Mason, 236, 239; Buckley v. Artcher, 21 Barb. 585; Durell v. Haley, 1 Paige, 492; Hall v. Naylor, 18 N. Y. 588. *Contra*, Smith v. Smith, 21 Penn. St. 367; Brackentoss v. Speicher, 31 Penn. St. 324; Bell v. Ellis, 33 Cal. 620, 630.

[8] McCracken v. Cholwell, 8 N. Y. 133; Nichols v. Pinner, 18 N. Y. 295; Hennequin v. Naylor, 24 N. Y. 139; Patton v. Campbell, 70 Ill. 72.

In Pennsylvania, however, it has been decided by a majority of the court that a purchaser's concealment of his insolvency and of his intent not to pay, without any fraudulent overt act or artifice, intended and fitted to deceive the vendor, is not fraudulent.[1] And in California it has been doubted whether the concealment of an intent not to pay is fraudulent.[2] In Missouri, it is held that, if the intent be not preconceived, it is not fraudulent so as to avoid the sale.[3]

It has, however, very recently been laid down by the Supreme Court of the United States as established by the weight of authority that a party not intending to pay, who induces the owner of goods to sell to him goods on credit by fraudulently concealing his insolvency and his intent not to pay for the property, is guilty of an act entitling the vendor, if no innocent third party has acquired an interest in them, to disaffirm the contract and recover the goods.[4] But in some cases a distinction, apparently sound, is taken between an intent never to pay for the goods and an intent not to pay for them at the time agreed upon, the latter case not being considered fraudulent.[5]

Failure to disclose that about which no inquiry is made is not, generally speaking, fraudulent,[6] unless agreed to be so,

[1] Smith v. Smith, and Brackentoss v. Speicher, *supra*. See Kline v. Baker, 99 Mass. 253.

[2] Bell v. Ellis, *supra*.

[3] Bidault v. Wales, 19 Mo. 36.

[4] Donaldson v. Farwell, 93 U. S. 631; Byrd v. Hall, 2 Keyes, 647; Johnson v. Monell, Ib. 655; Noble v. Adams, 7 Taunt. 59; Kilby v. Wilson, Ryan & M. 178; Bristol v. Wilsmore, 1 Barn. & C. 513; Stewart v. Emerson, 52 N. H. 301; Bidault v. Wales, 19 Mo. 36; s. c. 20 Mo. 546.

[5] Bidault v. Wales, 20 Mo. 546; Noble v. Adams, 7 Taunt. 59.

[6] Rawls v. American Life Ins. Co., 27 N. Y. 282; s. c. 1 Big. 558; Morrison v. Tennessee Ins. Co., 18 Mo. 262; Hill v. Lafayette Ins. Co., 2 Mich. 476; Hartford Ins. Co. v. Harmer, 2 Ohio St. 452; Laidlaw v. Liverpool Ins. Co., 13 Grant Ch. (Up. Can.) 377; Clark v. Manufacturers' Ins. Co., 2 Woodb. & M. 472; s. c. 8 How. 235; Keith v. Globe Ins. Co., 52 Ill. 518. The proposition, as the cases cited indicate, relates particularly to insurance.

or unless the fact be of a glaring character.[1]　If, for instance, a policy of life insurance should not make it a cause of forfeiture for the insured to die for crime at the hands of the law, and a person under sentence of death were to procure and forward an application answering every question truly, and the insurer should take a risk upon his life, not knowing that he was then under sentence of death, the insurer would not be bound by accepting the application and granting a policy.[2]　So, if a person, knowing that a conflagration was raging in the vicinity of his property, were to apply for insurance to an underwriter not aware of the fact, and obtain a policy, the contract would doubtless be invalid as against the latter.　Upon this point, the law of insurance seems to be at variance with the law of sales in similar cases.　The moral aspect of a non-disclosure by the purchaser of property of facts unknown to the vendor, which greatly enhance its value, as the existence of a mine in land to be sold, is quite as objectionable as the non-disclosure to an underwriter of the above facts; but, as we have seen, the seller is without remedy in such a case.

The only exception, perhaps, to this rule is found in the doctrine of concealment in marine insurance.　It is well-settled law that a marine policy is not binding if the assured or his agent fail to disclose any material fact, whether by design or not, and whether an inquiry is made such as would elicit the fact or not.[3]　The duty devolves upon the applicant for such insurance to disclose to the underwriter every thing he knows respecting the proposed adventure, and he cannot safely exercise his own judgment as to the materiality of any part of the information he may possess.　If he should not disclose the whole, and what is kept back should

---

[1] Bufe v. Turner, 6 Taunt. 338.

[2] Cheever v. Union Life Ins. Co., 4 Am. Law Rec. 155; s. c. 5 Big. 458, Yaple, J.

[3] See Hartford Ins. Co. v. Harmer, 2 Ohio St. 452, where the whole law of concealment in insurance is considered.

appear to the court to be material, the policy will not be valid, though the concealment was without fraudulent intention, and arose merely from error of judgment.[1]

A material fact in this connection is one which, if communicated to the opposite party, would induce him either to refrain altogether from the contract, or not to enter it on the same terms.[2] The duty of disclosure is not one merely binding upon the applicant: it is mutual. The marine underwriter as well as the applicant is bound to disclose all circumstances peculiarly within his knowledge in any degree affecting the risk; and therefore, if at the time of subscribing the policy he know that the ship has arrived in safety at its destination, the contract is void as against the insured, and the premiums may be recovered back.[3]

It is the duty of the assured, as we have said, to communicate to the underwriter all the intelligence he has that may affect the mind of the underwriter as to either of the two following points: 1st, whether he will take the risk at all; and, 2dly, at what premium he will take it. And this is a duty attaching at the time of effecting the insurance, and not in the least dependent upon subsequent events; for the effect of a concealment on the policy is determined not by its eventual relation to the nature of the risk, but with reference to its immediate influence upon the judgment of the underwriter. Hence, though the intelligence concealed turn out to be wholly unfounded, or the loss to arise from a cause totally unconnected with the fact concealed, the policy is void.[4]

If a carrier has given general notice that he will not be liable above a certain sum, unless the value of articles shipped is made known to him at the time of their delivery to him, and a premium for insurance paid, such notice, if brought

---

[1] Arnould, Marine Insurance, 512 (4th Eng. ed.).

[2] Arnould, p. 509.   [3] Ib. 511.

[4] Ib.; Seaman v. Fonnereau, 2 Strange, 1182; Lynch v. Hamilton, 3 Taunt. 37; s. c. 14 East, 494, in error.

home to the knowledge of the owner (and courts will generally infer such knowledge from the publication of the notice), is as effectual in qualifying the acceptance of the goods as a special agreement; and the owner must, at his peril, disclose the value of the goods and pay the premium. In such a case, the carrier is not bound to make inquiry; and if the owner omit to make known the value, and do not therefore pay the premium at the time of delivery to the carrier, the carrier is liable only to the amount mentioned in his notice, or not at all, according to the terms of the notice, if that be a proper part of the contract.[1]

It has very lately been laid down that, in cases of valid limitation of a carrier's liability to a specified amount, it is so important for the shipper to disclose the value of his goods that, if such value exceed the amount specified, silence alone on the part of the shipper, as to the value of the goods, is a fraud in law, discharging the carrier from liability for loss of the same occasioned by his negligence; and this, too, though no inquiry were made as to the value of the goods, and no artifice employed by the shipper to deceive the carrier.[2] Where, however, no limit is placed upon the carrier's liability, the shipper is not bound to disclose the value of the goods, unless he is asked thereof by the carrier.[3] The latter at the same time has a right to make inquiry, and is entitled to a true answer; otherwise, he will not be liable for a loss caused by negligence.[4] He would in any case be liable for losses caused intentionally. Thus, it is held to be no excuse for the *conversion* by a carrier of the property of a consignee that the consignor fraudulently misstated the weight of the goods, and that the consignee knew that the bill of lading

---

[1] Orange Co. Bank *v.* Orange, 9 Wend. 115; Oppenheimer *v.* United States Exp. Co., 69 Ill. 62; Western Transp. Co. *v.* Newhall, 24 Ill. 466.

[2] Maguire *v.* Dinsmore, 62 N. Y. 35. [3] Ib.

[4] Ib.; Crouch *v.* London Ry. Co., 14 Com. B. 255. See Batson *v.* Donovan, 4 Barn. & Ald. 21.

stated the weight at less than it was, and did not notify the carrier thereof.[1]

A distinction founded in justice exists between the effect of those notices by carriers which seek to discharge them from duties which the law has annexed to their employment, and those which are designed simply to insure good faith and fair dealing on the part of the consignor. In the former case, notice alone is not effectual : the consignor must assent to the restriction. In the latter case, notice alone, if brought to the knowledge of the shipper, will be sufficient.[2]

It is held that, independently of express stipulation, a consignor of goods cannot recover for the loss of valuable goods by the carrier, where, in order to secure their carriage at a low rate, he fails to inform the carrier of their value.[3] In a recent case,[4] a shipper delivered to a carrier for transportation a bundle having the appearance of bedding only, when in fact it contained within the bedding valuable clothing, such as a silk dress, a brocha shawl, and furs, of the value of $200. This was not disclosed to the shipper, and the bundle was sent at a low freight. The goods having been lost, it was held that the carrier was liable for the value only of what was properly to be treated as bedding.

By the rules of the common law, there are but two exceptions to the liability of a common carrier : first, the act of God ; secondly, that of the king's enemies. Many and persistent attempts, however, have been made by common carriers to add to these exceptions, and with varying success. It is conceded that a special contract with the shipper, properly entered into, may limit the carrier's liability ; but such a

---

[1] Wiggin v. Boston & A. R. Co., 120 Mass. 201.

[2] Oppenheimer v. United States Exp. Co., 69 Ill. 62.

[3] Oppenheimer v. United States Exp. Co., 69 Ill. 62 ; Chicago & A. R. Co. v. Shea, 66 Ill. 471. See Relf v. Rapp, 3 Watts & S. 21; Hollister v. Nowlen, 19 Wend. 234 ; Cole v. Goodwin, Ib. 251; Chicago & A. R. Co. v. Thompson, 19 Ill. 578.

[4] Chicago & A. R. Co. v. Shea, *supra*.

contract must be fair and open, to the terms of which it may reasonably be presumed the shipper's attention has been called, and his full assent obtained. The receipt, for example, by the consignor in person of a bill of lading in which the carrier stipulates against liability by fire or perils of the sea, without objection made by the consignor, constitutes in the absence of fraud a special contract, binding upon the consignor, whether he reads it or not.[1] But no binding contract is made out by the mere delivery of a card to a passenger by an express messenger, in exchange for his baggage checks, which contains limitations in fine print, not read by the passenger.[2] The object of such limitations is not honest, and the artifice by which the attempt is made to fix them upon the unwilling traveller will not succeed. Consent cannot be obtained by fraud.

The chief difficulty, however, has been found in considering the effect to be given to notices of the carrier not expressly entering into the contract of shipment. The English courts formerly allowed a serious innovation in this particular upon the old common-law doctrine ; but the interests of the public required a return to the former position, and the Carrier's Act was passed by which the steps taken by the courts were mostly retraced.[3] Great reluctance has always been felt in this country to introduce special limitations to the rigorous liability of common carriers. The courts have considered that the interests of the public demand that the carrier should be held to a strict accountability in view of the trust reposed in him and the opportunities for fraud and collusion afforded by his position. Exemption from or even restriction of liability, without express assent of the

---

[1] Grace v. Adams, 100 Mass. 505 ; King v. Woodbridge, 34 Vt. 571; Boorman v. American Exp. Co., 21 Wis. 152; Cincinnati R. Co. v. Pontius, 19 Ohio St. 222; Symonds v. Pain, 6 Hurl. & N. 709 ; Van Toll v. South-eastern Ry. Co., 12 C. B. N. s. 75.

[2] Blossom v. Dodd, 43 N. Y. 264.

[3] See 2 Story, Contracts, §§ 950, 951 (5th ed.).

shipper, is not admitted in this country.[1] In order to make a mere notice in any case binding upon the carrier, knowledge of it must be brought home to the shipper, and doubtless in such a way as to show that it has not operated as an imposition upon him. The mere fact that such a notice is exposed to view in the office of the carrier, or is published in a newspaper, or circulated in handbills, is not sufficient to charge the shipper. The carrier must show actual knowledge. It may be that the consignor cannot read, or that, though he can read, and in fact saw various notices upon the walls of the carrier's office, he did not read them, having no intimation that they concerned him. In such case, he is not bound. *A fortiori*, if there be any artifice on the part of the carrier, as if the limitations of liability be printed in very small letters, so as not to attract attention, while the advantages of carriage are conspicuously set forth, the object of the carrier will not be permitted to succeed.[2]

Where a person is induced to enter into a suretyship on a false representation of the state of circumstances, or where there are circumstances connected with the transaction which are purposely concealed by the creditor, the surety cannot be held liable. But the concealment must be a concealment of facts, which it was the duty of the person charged with it to reveal. If there was no duty incumbent upon him to reveal the particular circumstances, the surety cannot complain.[3]

It is not necessary that a creditor should disclose to a surety obligor every material circumstance of the situation. A surety is in general a friend of the principal debtor, acting at his request, and not at the request of the creditor; and it may be assumed that in ordinary cases the surety obtains from the principal all the information which he requires. At

---

[1] 2 Story, Contracts, § 952 (5th ed.); Judson *v.* Western R. Corp., 6 Allen, 486; Hollister *v.* Nowlen, 19 Wend. 234.

[2] Butler *v.* Heane, 2 Campb. 415; 2 Story, Contracts, § 956.

[3] Greenfield *v.* Edwards, 2 DeG., J. & S. 582.

the same time, when the creditor describes to the proposed surety the transaction proposed to be guaranteed, that description amounts to a representation, or at least is evidence of a representation, that there is nothing in the transaction that might not naturally be expected to take place between the parties to a transaction such as that described. And if a ʽrepresentation to this effect be made to the intended surety by one who knows that there is something not naturally to be expected to take place between the parties to the transaction, and that this is unknown to the person to whom he makes the representation, and that, if it were known to him, he would not enter into the contract of suretyship, this is evidence of such a fraudulent representation as will discharge the surety.[1] Thus, in the case cited, a surety for the faithful conduct of another alleged that the creditor had concealed from him the fact that the subject of the obligation was already heavily in debt to the obligee; and this was held upon the above principles a good defence to an action upon the obligation.

A creditor is not bound without inquiry to disclose to a surety that the principal debtor is indebted to him beyond the amount of the security signed by the surety. Thus, where a creditor received from his debtor the latter's promissory note, payable to a third party who indorsed the same as surety, in part payment of his demand, and the debtor's individual claim for the balance, it was decided that the creditor was not bound to communicate the existence of the latter security, unless inquiry was made.[2]

On the other hand, persons proposing to become sureties to a corporation for the good conduct and fidelity of an officer to whose custody its moneys and other valuables are to be intrusted have a right to be treated with the utmost good faith.

---

[1] Lee *v.* Jones, 17 Com. B. N. s. 482, *per* Blackburn, J., affirming s. c. 14 Com. B. N. s. 386.

[2] Booth *v.* Storrs, 75 Ill. 438.

If the directors are aware of secret facts materially affecting
the risk to be assumed by a person about to become a surety,
such person is entitled to a disclosure of the facts ; and, if
such disclosure be not made, the surety will not be liable.[1]
And this is true not only where the facts are actually known
to the directors, but also where by the proper discharge of
their duty they would be known. Thus, in the case just
cited, it appeared that the cashier of a bank, who had never
executed a bond, had been guilty of fraud and embezzlement
of the funds of the bank, the discovery of which might have
been effected by the exercise of slight diligence on the part of
the directors. They, however, published (in accordance with
law) a statement of the condition of the bank, from which
it appeared that its affairs were being prudently and honestly
managed, and from which the public had the right to believe
that the cashier was trustworthy. Afterwards, persons who
had seen this report became sureties upon the official bond of
the cashier ; but, when sued thereon, it was decided that they
had the right to believe that the directors, before publishing
the statement, had made an investigation of the condition
of the bank, and, being misled by the misrepresentations in
the published statement, they were not liable.

He is guilty of a fraud who secretly changes a state of
affairs, and then, without revealing this fact, procures another
to do an act into which the true state of affairs enters as
a motive. Thus, if a creditor, knowing that his debtor is in
failing circumstances, obtains from him, for part of his claim,
a mortgage substantially covering all of his property, and
gets the debtor to obtain the indorsement of another person
for another part, without revealing the fact of the mortgage,
this is a fraud upon the indorser, and discharges him from
liability.[2]

An action on the case is maintainable by a woman against

[1] Graves v. Lebanon Bank, 10 Bush, 23.
[2] Lancaster Co. Bank v. Albright, 21 Penn. St. 228.

a man for his deceit, whereby she is induced to contract a void marriage with him;[1] as where he has a wife living at the time, and the fact is concealed from the plaintiff.[2] There is some doubt, however, whether the right of action survives against the representative of the wrongdoer.[3] Under the statutes of Maine, it is held that the action survives. In Pennsylvania, on the other hand, it has been held that the action does not survive ; and the decision was based both upon common-law doctrine and upon the statute relating to actions against personal representatives.[4] It is clear, indeed, upon common-law principles, that if the woman knew, before the man's death, that he had a wife living, or was put upon inquiry as to the fact, and failed to institute suit in his lifetime, she could not maintain an action against his representative. But, upon the analogy of principles governing the operation of the Statute of Limitations, it may well be doubted if the same rule would prevail, even at common law, where the existence of the facts and consequent right of action were *actively* concealed by the wrongdoer throughout his lifetime. The common law has never been so unequal as to deprive a person of redress for wrongs the existence of which has by artifice, misrepresentation, or other fraud been concealed by the wrongdoer. And, further, it is to be remembered that the common-law doctrine of the non-survivorship of certain classes of actions appears to have been founded upon the long since (for the most part) abandoned notion that the heir or other party entitled to the succession is in some sort a purchaser of the estate for value.[5] Had the later position of such party been admitted and recognized in the early English law, the doctrine of non-survivorship could not have arisen.

[1] Blossom *v.* Barret, 37 N. Y. 434.

[2] Withee *v.* Brooks, 65 Maine, 14. See Proctor *v.* McCall, 2 Bail. 298; Sturge *v.* Starr, 2 Mylne & K. 195.   [3] Ib.

[4] Grim *v.* Carr, 31 Penn. St. 533.

[5] How much the rule of primogeniture had to do with the origination of this principle is an interesting question.

It certainly should not now be extended to cases as to which it is extremely doubtful if it ever was applicable.

It is to be observed in this connection that a deed is not invalidated against an innocent purchaser by the fraud of one of the grantors, if he have only a nominal interest in the property. The other grantors, though the fraud was perpetrated upon them and without their knowledge, cannot defeat the object of the deed, the grantee being innocent.[1] In the case cited, a man already married went through the ceremony of a marriage with G. W., and afterwards joined with her in executing to the plaintiff an assignment of a life interest owned by her in a trust-fund. The plaintiff filed a bill against the trustee and G. W., the object of which was to obtain the benefit of this assignment. He was an innocent purchaser for value, and G. W. was not aware of the fraud that had been practised upon herself when the assignment was executed. The bill was sustained, though the assumed husband of G. W. was not a party to the suit. The case, however, would have been different, had the defendant purchased with notice.[2]

No one is permitted to take advantage of a deed, which he has fraudulently induced another to execute, that the former may commit an offence against morality, to the injury or loss of the party by whom the deed is executed.[3] Thus, where a married woman obtains a separation deed from her husband, with pecuniary allowance, for the purpose of enabling her the more effectually to carry on an adulterous intercourse with another, a court of equity will, on the petition of the husband, decree that the deed be delivered up to be cancelled.[4] And proof of subsequent adultery with a person with whom the wife had had sexual intercourse before marriage, and had continued on terms of improper intimacy afterwards, seems to be sufficient evidence that such a deed

---

[1] Sturge v. Starr, 2 Mylne & K. 195.
[2] Proctor v. McCall, 2 Bail. 208.
[3] Evans v. Carrington, 2 DeG., F. & J. 481.   [4] Ib.

was obtained for the fraudulent purpose of promoting the adultery.[1] But such a deed will not be set aside for adultery previously committed; nor will a marriage settlement be annulled on the ground that the wife has concealed from her husband the fact of previous incontinence, though he allege that he would not have married her, had he known it.[2] The case may, however, be different where there is proof that an unchaste woman conspired with others, by fraudulent misrepresentations, to marry herself as a virgin.[3]

If a legacy be given to a person under a particular character which he has falsely assumed, and which alone can be supposed to be the motive of the bounty, the legacy fails. Thus, where a legacy was given by a woman to a man in the character of her husband, whom she supposed and described as such, but who at the time of the marriage ceremony with her had a wife living, the Court of Chancery held him not entitled to the bounty.[4] It was, however, thought that the rule would be different where, from circumstances not moving from the legatee himself, the description was inapplicable; as where a testator gives a legacy to a child from motives of affection, supposing it to be his own when it is not, and he has been imposed upon in that respect.

The burdens to which a husband becomes liable upon marriage are, at common law, the consideration for his marital rights in the wife's property; and hence fraud may be committed upon him in respect of such rights, as by a secret voluntary conveyance of her real estate. But a conveyance by a woman, as well as by a man, even the moment before marriage, is *prima facie* valid. The burden of impeaching its validity rests upon the husband, if he object to it.[5]

---

[1] Evans *v.* Carrington, 2 DeG., F. & J. 481.
[2] Ib. 　　　　　　　　　　　　[3] Ib.
[4] Kennell *v.* Abbott, 4 Ves. 802.
[5] Strathmore *v.* Bowes, 1 Ves. Jr. 22, 38.

Antenuptial settlements made by an intended wife are held voidable in England by the husband after marriage, provided it appear (1) that intermarriage was in the contemplation of the parties at the time ; (2) that the woman executed the settlement in contemplation of the future marriage ; (3) that she concealed it from her intended husband. If these facts be proved, the cases have established the principle that such a settlement cannot stand against the marital right of the husband.[1] And the same doctrine prevails at common law in this country.[2] The husband therefore cannot avoid the wife's settlement where, before the marriage, he had sufficiently early notice that it was intended to settle the wife's property, if nothing afterwards passed to justify a belief on the husband's part that, at the time of the marriage, no settlement had been made.[3]

In applying the principle upon which conveyances made by the intended wife, pending a treaty for marriage, are avoided on the ground of fraud upon the marital right, equity will take into consideration any meritorious object of such conveyances, and the situation of the intended husband in point of pecuniary means.[4] As to antenuptial conveyances by a woman after a treaty of marriage, Mr. Justice Buller considered that they were not invalid merely because the *feme* did not disclose the transaction to her intended husband. He said that in most of the cases the husband had actually made some settlement or provision on the wife, in the expectation of being admitted to the enjoyment of the property conveyed. In the case referred to, the husband had not only not made any provision for his wife, but avowed his intention not to do so. Relief was therefore denied him ; and, upon a rehearing

---

[1] Goddard v. Snow, 1 Russ. 485 ; Strathmore v. Bowes, 2 Cox, 28 ; s. c. 2 Brown, C. C. 345.

[2] Baker v. Jordan, 73 N. C. 145 ; Williams v. Carle, 2 Stockt. 543 ; Duncan's Appeal, 43 Penn. St. 67 ; Jordan v. Black, Meigs, 142.

[3] Wrigley v. Swainson, 3 DeG. & S. 458.

[4] St. George v. Wake, 1 Mylne & K. 610.

before the Lord Chancellor, the decision of Mr. Justice Buller was affirmed.[1]

In the same case, the learned judge last named said that the result of the cases as to conveyances by women not previously married, or by a widow without children, was, that if the wife were guilty of any fraud, professing to the husband that there was nothing to interfere with his rights, any deed executed by her in prejudice of such representation was void. But this was considered to be the extent of the cases. The mere non-disclosure of an antenuptial conveyance would not of itself render the transaction impeachable by the husband; nor, when provision was made by a widow for the children of a former marriage, would the deed be invalid.

Though a settlement, then, by an intended wife be voluntary, and not disclosed to the intended husband, it is not therefore necessarily fraudulent. The courts will consider the nature of the provision, the situation of the husband in point of pecuniary means, and any other facts which tend to show that no fraud was intended. The equity which arises in cases of this nature depends upon the peculiar circumstances of each case, as bearing upon the question whether the facts do or do not amount to fraud upon the intended husband.[2]

It is held in North Carolina, contrary to the English doc-

[1] Strathmore v. Bowes, 2 Cox, 28. Several of the old cases were doubted or explained by him. Carleton v. Dorset, 2 Vern. 17 ; Edmunds v. Dennington, cited in that case ; Howard v. Hooker, 2 Ch. Cas. 31. Mr. Justice Buller thought the circumstances of the marriage worthy of consideration also. "It is clear," said he, "that, down to the 16th January, Lady Strathmore meant to marry Mr. Grey [a third person]. The deed complained of was executed on the 10th. Mr. Bowes was a perfect stranger to Lady Strathmore till the 16th, and it is rather material to consider how he became acquainted with her. A sham duel is fought between Mr. Bowes and another gentleman, in which Mr. Bowes is supposed to be asserting the honor of Lady Strathmore. In consequence of this, she pays attention to him, which ends in a marriage on the next day. He who begins with such a stratagem is not entitled to much favor either in law or in equity."

[2] Gregory v. Winston, 23 Gratt. 102.

trine, that, if a widow during a treaty for a second marriage
convey her property secretly and with intent to deceive her
intended husband, he can avoid the conveyance, though it be
made to children of the widow by her former husband, and
they be innocent of the fraud.[1]

In order to establish the husband's right to have an antenuptial conveyance of the wife set aside, as in fraud of his
marital rights, it is not necessary that he should prove actual
deception; for deception will be inferred, if, after the commencement of a treaty of marriage, the wife should have
attempted to dispose of her property without the knowledge
of her intended husband.[2]

It is not a valid objection, it seems, to the husband's claim
against the validity of such an antenuptial conveyance of the
wife, that he was ignorant until after the marriage that the
wife owned the particular property.[3] Lord Eldon, indeed,
once made the observation that, in the absence of any representation by the wife as to her ownership of specific property,
no implied contract existed on the part of the lady, during
the treaty for marriage, that her property as it existed at the
commencement of the treaty should in no way be diminished.[4]
But this probably merely shows that in Lord Eldon's opinion
not every alienation of the wife's property during the treaty
can be regarded as fraudulent, where the husband is ignorant
of the transaction; which is certainly true, as we have
seen. The observation is not to be understood as going to
the extent of upholding cases in which every farthing of the
wife's property has, without the husband's knowledge of the
extent of the wife's estate, been withdrawn from him. Lord
Eldon is thought to mean simply this: that, there being no

---

[1] Tisdale v. Bailey, 6 Ired. Eq. 358 ; Goodson v. Whitfield 5 Ired.
163 ; Logan v. Simmons, 3 Ired. Eq. 487.

[2] Taylor v. Pugh, 1 Hare, 608.

[3] Taylor v. Pugh, 1 Hare, 608, 613.

[4] De Manneville v. Crompton, 1 Ves. & B. 354.

implied contract on the part of the lady that her property should not be in any way diminished, it is for the courts to determine whether, having regard to the condition in life of the parties, and the other circumstances of the case, a transaction complained of by the husband should be treated as fraudulent or not. And it was conceded that where the husband had by his conduct rendered retirement from the treaty of marriage impracticable, as where he had induced her to cohabit with him before the marriage, he would not be permitted to object to the antenuptial conveyances of the wife.[1]

---

[1] Wigram, V. C., in Taylor *v.* Pugh, *supra.* "Several circumstances," said this learned judge, "would certainly appear to have been sometimes thought material as negativing the imputed fraud; such as the poverty of the husband, the fact that he had made no settlement on the wife, the reasonable character of the settlement, as in the case of a settlement upon the children of a former marriage, and the ignorance of the husband that his wife possessed the property. Upon these, I am not called upon to say more than that I am glad to find other grounds upon which to decide the present case. I could not give my individual consent to the sufficiency of any of the reasons I have mentioned. The poverty of the husband, the absence of any settlement upon the wife, the reasonable manner in which she desires to deal with her property, may be very material considerations for the guidance of the parties in determining in what manner the wife's fortune should be settled; but why they should constitute a reason for concealing the arrangement from the husband I cannot comprehend. It might be very proper to bring these considerations to the attention of the intended husband. He might be told that the lady has a certain fortune, but, regard being had to the claims upon her and to his circumstances, the settlement ought to be made in a particular way; and upon this statement, if he does not approve of the proposed settlement, the marriage contract may be determined. But I cannot comprehend the reasoning which says that any one of the reasons suggested is a sufficient ground for practising concealment upon the husband, or treats such concealment as immaterial. So, also, with respect to the ignorance of the husband of the property of the wife: that, no doubt, materially lessens his disappointment at finding the wife's fortune has been withdrawn from his control; but the equity is not founded upon his disappointment, for, if that were so, it would follow that his ignorance of the existence of the property would always be an answer, however that ignorance was produced. The equity would never arise where the wife had contrived to conceal her property from the husband; but this is not

A secret settlement made by a woman pending a treaty for
marriage is not necessarily void in a court of law, though
liable to be set aside in equity; since on the marriage the
husband does not take (under the statute of 27 Eliz.) as a
purchaser.[1]

It is clear that an obligation founded on a valuable consideration, executed by a woman pending a treaty of marriage,
cannot be set aside merely because it is concealed from the
husband.[2] But the transaction must be accomplished *bona
fide:* if the wife meditate a fraud, and the other party be
aware of the fact, the obligation will be void as against the
husband.[3]

If a marriage settlement be set aside on the ground that
it is a fraud upon the *inchoate* marital rights of the husband,
or that it was obtained from the wife by undue influence,
the person at whose suggestion the settlement was made,
especially (though this appears to be unnecessary)[4] if he be

so, for the cases clearly show that practised concealment by the wife will
be treated as a fraud on the husband. . . . But, without calling any one
of these reasons to the aid of my judgment, there is one fact which determines me in refusing the relief which the husband asks in this suit;
and it is that the husband before the marriage put it out of the power
of the wife effectually to make any stipulation for the settlement of her
property. By his conduct towards her, retirement from the marriage was
on her part impossible. She must have submitted to a marriage with her
seducer, even although he should have insisted on receiving and spending
the whole of her fortune. The only way in which a woman can insist
upon a settlement is by making it a part of the marriage treaty that her
property shall be settled. The husband, by bringing the intended wife to
his house, and inducing her to cohabit with him before the marriage,
deprived her of the power to protect herself, and thereby precluded himself from telling this court with any effect that his wife had committed
a fraud upon him, because she has taken the precaution to have her
property secured to herself and her children.''

[1] Doe d. Richards v. Lewis, 11 Com. B. 1035.

[2] Blanchet v. Foster, 2 Ves. Sr. 264; Gregory v. Winston, 23 Gratt.
102, 123.

[3] Gregory v. Winston, *supra.*

[4] Harvey v. Mount, 8 Beav. 439 ; Baker v. Loader, Law R. 16 Eq. 49.

guilty of actual misconduct aside from suggesting the settlement, and defend the suit, may be ordered with the defendant to pay the costs.[1]

The rule at common law as to conveyances of the property of a woman or the giving of securities by her without value during the treaty for marriage, and without notice to the intended husband, is said to rest upon the peculiar right which a husband has in his wife's property. A wife has, it is held in Ireland, no similar equity to have a conveyance or security of the intended husband set aside on the ground of fraud upon her marital rights.[2] But circumstances may change this rule. In the case just cited, it appeared that upon the subsequent marriage of a son the father agreed to give up to him a farm and stock, in consideration of the wife's fortune being paid to the father; it being then stated that the intended husband was not indebted to any extent. A deed was drawn up and executed in pursuance of this agreement; and on the same day the intended husband gave his father a promissory note for £200. Upon the death of the son, it was held that this security could not be enforced against his estate, since, coupled with the statement that the son was not indebted to any extent, it was a fraud both upon the intended wife and upon her father, who had given the fortune.

An antenuptial conveyance by the intended husband for the purpose of defeating his intended wife of dower is invalid by statute in North Carolina.[3] And in Kentucky it is held that for the husband before marriage to convey the whole or a valuable portion of his property without the knowledge of his intended wife is a fraud on her rights, even when the property

---

[1] Prideaux v. Lonsdale, 4 Giff. 159; s. c. 1 DeG., J. & S. 433; Harvey v. Mount, 8 Beav. 439; Baker v. Loader, Law R. 16 Eq. 49; *In re* Clark, Law R. 4 Ch. Div. 515. See also Hugenin v. Baseley, 14 Ves. 273; Bridgman v. Green, 2 Ves. Sr. 627; Beadles v. Burch, 10 Sim. 332.

[2] McKeogh v. McKeogh, Law R. 4 Irish Eq. 338.

[3] Littleton v. Littleton, 1 Dev. & B. 327.

is given to children by a former marriage ;[1] the consideration being love and affection.[2]

The question of the right of a husband to defeat his wife's prospective interest in his real or personal property by a postnuptial conveyance does not depend upon the wife's knowledge of the transaction. The knowledge of a *wife* does not imply consent. Such conveyances, then, are good or bad, when not assented to by the wife, regardless of the question whether they were made secretly or openly. We therefore reserve the consideration of such cases for another and more appropriate place.

Wherever there is a special relation of confidence between the parties, the duty to communicate all facts of interest to the party whose situation prevents him from possessing full knowledge of the facts necessary to intelligent action is imperative. Any concealment in such a case, whether intentional or not, will be fatal ; and the burden rests upon the party in the superior situation to show that full communication of the facts was made. This branch of our subject must be reserved for full consideration in the chapter on Confidential Relations.[3]

§ 3. Of the Wrongdoer's Knowledge of the Falsity of the Representation.

We have now considered the nature of the representation necessary to relief on the ground of deceit. The next in order of the elements of such relief is that of the *knowledge*

---

[1] Leach *v.* Duvall, 8 Bush, 201, on authority of McAfee *v.* Ferguson, 9 B. Mon. 475, the case of an antenuptial conveyance by the *wife.* Petty *v.* Petty, 4 B. Mon. 216, however, is a direct authority for Leach *v.* Duvall; and in that case it was held that the wife was entitled to relief in the lifetime of the husband.

[2] See also Smith *v.* Smith, 2 Halst. Ch. 515.

[3] Ch. V. See also the chapter on Specific Performance, Ch. X.

on the part of the alleged wrongdoer of the falsity of the representation.

Generally speaking, an honest statement of fact, believed to be true by the party making it, though made with a view to being acted upon, and justifying action upon it from the standpoint of the conduct of the prudent man, will not, upon turning out to be false, create a liability for damages against the party making it ; nor will it afford the complaining party ground for relief from any contract which he may have made with the supposed wrongdoer under the inducement of such a misrepresentaion, so far at least as such relief is demanded on the ground of fraud. Fraud is not established, and redress or relief will not in general be granted, without proof that the party who made the false representation knew at the time that it was false.[1] The law raises no presumption of knowledge from the *mere* fact that the representation is false.[2]

There are, however, many cases in which the law does raise a presumption of the party's knowledge concerning the facts of which he has made a false representation ; or, more correctly speaking, there are many cases in which the law holds the party, from his special situation, bound to know of the truth of his representations. Such cases we have now to present. They may mostly be embraced under the general proposition, that a man is supposed and required to know all matters pertaining to his own business. If a person make a false representation of such a matter, he will not be allowed, as against an innocent man who has suffered by reason of

[1] Collins *v.* Evans, 5 Q. B. 820, 826; Ormrod *v.* Huth, 14 Mees. & W. 651, 664; Behn *v.* Kemble, 7 Com. B. N. S. 260; Barley *v.* Walford, 9 Q. B. 197, 208; Thom *v.* Bigland, 8 Ex. 725; Childers *v.* Wooler, 2 El. & E. 287; Mahurin *v.* Harding, 28 N. H. 128; Evertson *v.* Miles, 6 Johns. 138; Case *v.* Boughton, 11 Wend. 106, 108; Carley *v.* Wilkins, 6 Barb. 557; Edick *v.* Crim, 10 Barb. 445.

[2] Ib.; Barnett *v.* Stanton, 2 Ala. 181; McDonald *v.* Trafton, 15 Maine, 225.

such false representation, to say that he made it honestly, believing it to be true.

One of the most common illustrations of this proposition is to be found in the case of express or implied representations of agency. It is settled law that if a person, however honestly, assume to act for another in respect of a matter over which he has no authority, he renders himself liable, not merely to his principal, but to the person whom he has thus deceived. This action is sometimes said to be based upon a breach of warranty of authority, and sometimes upon deceit: in either form of action, the injured party is entitled to recover against the supposed agent, to the extent of the damage sustained.[1]

It has accordingly been decided that, in an action against a telegraph company for delivering a message never sent, and alleging that the defendants falsely represented that they were authorized to deliver such a message, and thereby caused the plaintiff to suffer damage, it is not necessary to allege that it was false, to the knowledge of the defendant. Such an action was considered as in the nature of a false warranty against one professing to act as agent, and representing that he has an authority which he has not.[2]

While, however, a person professing to be an agent, generally speaking, is liable in deceit in case he does not possess

---

[1] Collin v. Wright, 8 El. & B. 647; Randell v. Trimen, 18 Com. B. 786; Cherry v. Colonial Bank, Law R. 3 P. C. 24; Pow v. Davis, 1 Best & S. 220; Spedding v. Nevill, Law R. 4 Com. P. 212; Godwin v. Francis, Law R. 5 Com. P. 295; Richardson v. Williamson, Law R. 6 Q. B. 276; White v. Madison, 26 N. Y. 117, 124; Jefts v. York, 4 Cush. 371; Bartlett v. Tucker, 104 Mass. 336; Johnson v. Smith, 21 Conn. 627; McCurdy v. Rogers, 21 Wis. 197, 202. It is held in Maine that the proper remedy is by an action of deceit. Noyes v. Loring, 55 Maine, 408. It is, however, held in New York that an action *ex delicto* for deceit can be maintained though an express warranty was made, if deceit can be proved. Indiana R. Co. v. Tyng, 63 N. Y. 653.

[2] May v. Western Union Tel. Co., 112 Mass. 90. See Jefts v. York, 10 Cush. 392; Bartlett v. Tucker, 104 Mass. 336.

the authority professed, still, if he honestly and fully disclose all the facts touching the supposed authority under which he acts, he is not liable.[1] So, too, if the party act as a public officer, and in that capacity act honestly as to his powers, he will not be personally liable.[2] And, if his authority to act be defined by public statute, all who contract with him will be presumed to know the extent of his authority, and no one can allege his ignorance as a ground for charging him with acting in excess of his authority, unless he knowingly mislead such person.[3]

There is a difference between an agent's situation towards his principal and towards third persons. The latter can hold him liable as for a fraudulent representation of his authority, when the former could not. Mere proof, for example, that an agent has exceeded his authority, to the damage of his principal, will not render him liable to the principal in an action for fraud.[4] In such a case as this, it seems necessary to prove actual fraud in the agent.

This doctrine of the liability of a party who falsely represents the extent of his authority to act for another applies still more strongly to the case of a person professing to be a partner in a mercantile or other firm. Thus, it has recently been held that one who, by representing himself to be a partner in a firm, induces another to give credit to the supposed partnership, is liable to him as a partner, whether actually a partner or not.[5] And this is of course entirely immaterial of any supposed relation to the firm, making the party, in the mind of the wrongdoer, a partner in the firm.

Upon the same principle, one who professes to be an expert in any particular, and thus competent to give advice in mat-

---

[1] Newman *v.* Sylvester, 42 Ind. 106.

[2] Ib.; Belknap *v.* Reinhart, 2 Wend. 375; Hodgson *v.* Dexter, 1 Cranch, 345; Nichols *v.* Moody, 22 Barb. 611.

[3] Newman *v.* Sylvester, *supra.*

[4] Price *v.* Keyes, 62 N. Y. 378.

[5] Rice *v.* Barrett, 116 Mass. 312.

ters pertaining to his art, is liable as for deceit or false warranty in case he make any false statements of substance to
another, intending that the same should be acted upon, though
he believed them to be true. Thus, one who, during negotiations for the sale of lands, professes to have peculiar scientific
knowledge as to the probability of the value of the lands for
the production of oil, and falsely represents such value,
renders himself liable to the purchaser if he rely thereon and
is deceived.[1] So, too, if a party make a representation of
facts of which he assumes to have a definite knowledge,
superior to that of the party to whom he makes it, or as to
which the latter is entirely ignorant, though the same may
not relate to the party's own business, he will be liable as for
a fraud.[2] The facts, however, in such case should be sus-
ceptible of actual knowledge.[3] Nor need the *scienter* be
proved against one in possession of land who professes to be
familiar with its quality,[4] unless indeed the purchaser have
equal means of knowledge.

A director of a corporation who knowingly issues or sanc-
tions the issue of a prospectus containing false and fraudulent
representations of the condition of the company, which are
likely to deceive the public, is personally liable therefor.[5]
But the mere fact that a trustee allows his name and credit
to be used to bolster the stock of a corporation which afterwards turns out to be worthless, does not make him liable
to persons investing in reliance thereon. Knowledge of the
condition of the concern must be proved against him.[6]

It has often been laid down that if a party innocently and

[1] Kost *v.* Bender, 25 Mich. 515; Pickard *v.* McCormick, 11 Mich. 68.
See also McGar *v.* Williams, 26 Ala. 467; Eaton *v.* Winnie, 20 Mich. 156.

[2] See Indiana R. Co. *v.* Tyng, 63 N. Y. 653; Hazard *v.* Irwin, 18
Pick. 95; Fisher *v.* Mellen, 103 Mass. 503.

[3] Litchfield *v.* Hutchinson, 117 Mass. 195; Spaulding *v.* Knight, 116
Mass. 148.

[4] Goodwin *v.* Robinson, 30 Ark. 535.

[5] Morgan *v.* Skiddy, 62 N. Y. 319. See Eaglesfield *v.* Londonderry,
Law R. 4 Ch. Div. 693.   [6] Morgan *v.* Skiddy, *supra*.

by mistake misrepresent a material fact, upon which another
is induced to act, it affords as good a ground for relief for
fraud as a wilfully false assertion.[1] And the same rule is
laid down by Mr. Justice Story, the ground being that the
misrepresentation operates as a surprise and imposition upon
the other party.[2] This doctrine has sometimes also, though
rarely, been applied at common law. But it is apprehended
that the proposition is true only of relief sought on grounds of
mistake,[3] or cases in which the party making the misrepresentation was bound to know the truth of the matter; as where
the facts were peculiarly within his own knowledge, and not
so within the knowledge of the complaining party.[4] If the
party made the representation, not knowing whether it was
true or false, he cannot be considered as innocent; since a
positive assertion of fact is by plain implication an assertion
of knowledge concerning such fact. Hence, if the party have
no knowledge about it, he has asserted for true what he
knows to be false.[5] Such cases as this, then (and they are

[1] Smith *v.* Richards, 13 Peters, 26 ; Allen *v.* Hart, 72 Ill. 104 ; Lewis
v. McLemore, 9 Yerg. 206; Converse *v.* Blumrich, 14 Mich. 109, 123;
Rosevelt *v.* Fulton, 2 Cowen, 139; Miner *v.* Medbury, 6 Wis. 295;
Pearson *v.* Morgan, 2 Brown, C. C. 385; McKenon *v.* Taylor, 3 Cranch,
270; Davis *v.* Heard, 44 Miss. 50, 58 ; Rimer *v.* Dugan, 39 Miss. 477;
Glasscock *v.* Minor, 11 Mo. 655 ; Pulsford *v.* Richards, 17 Beav. 94–96;
Sankey *v.* Alexander, Law R. 9 Irish Ch. 259, 296.

[2] 1 Story, Equity, § 193, and note.

[3] Such as would amount to a misconception of the real subject of the
contract. In such cases, rescission will be granted, but on the ground of
the failure of the contract, not on the ground of fraud. Story, Equity,
§ 142.

[4] As in the case of a misrepresentation, honestly made, of one's authority to act for another, above noticed.

[5] Evans *v.* Edmunds, 13 Com. B. 777, 786 ; Beatty *v.* Ebury, Law R.
7 H. L. 102; Haycraft *v.* Creasy, 2 East, 92 ; Taylor *v.* Ashton, 11 Mees.
& W. 401 ; Lobdell *v.* Baker, 1 Met. 193, 201 ; Bennett *v.* Judson, 21
N. Y. 138; Thomas *v.* McCann, 4 B. Mon. 602 ; Woodruff *v.* Garner,
27 Ind. 4; Stone *v.* Covell, 29 Mich. 359 ; Converse *v.* Blumrich, 14 Mich.
109 ; Eaton *v.* Winnie, 20 Mich. 156 ; Foard *v.* McComb, 12 Bush, 723.
It is no defence to an action for positive misrepresentations that the de-

numerous), do not sustain the broad doctrine under consideration. But the case last put is to be distinguished from cases
in which a positive statement is made, in the belief that it is
true, such belief being based upon information which would
justify it. If under such circumstances the information upon
which the representation is based should turn out incorrect,
there clearly could be no liability in deceit;[1] and, if a bill for
rescission were based upon an allegation of *fraud*, it is impossible to understand how it could be maintained.[2] The
facts would not justify a finding of actual fraud; and the
doctrine of constructive fraud has no application to such a
case. This, however, is not to say that relief might not be
had in cases of contract; but relief in such case must proceed
upon the ground that the minds of the parties have not met
upon the subject of the contract, and not upon the ground of
fraud.[3] On the other hand, if a man make a positive repre-

---

fendant had no personal knowledge of the facts, but made the statements
upon the information of others. He should have so stated when he made
them. Fisher v. Mellen, 103 Mass. 503.

[1] Taylor v. Leith, 26 Ohio St. 428 ; Bird v. Forceman, 62 Ill. 212 ;
Botsford v. Wilson, 75 Ill. 132 ; State Bank v. Hamilton, 2 Ind. 457 ;
Brooks v. Hamilton, 15 Minn. 26 ; Faribault v. Sater, 13 Minn. 223,
231. But Bird v. Forceman, *supra*, went too far in holding a contract
binding which had been effected through mistake.

[2] Botsford v. Wilson, 75 Ill. 132.

[3] Brooks v. Hamilton, 15 Minn. 26, a case deserving of special mention; Rawle, Covenants, 573, note, 4th ed.; 2 Kent's Com. 471; 1 Story,
Equity, § 142.

It has sometimes been supposed, in cases arising on insurance policies, that a misrepresentation or a failure to mention a fact about
which inquiry is made must be known to be false, in order to defeat
the contract. Fitch v. American Life Ins. Co., 5 Big. 316; Mutual Bene-
fit Life Ins. Co. v. Robertson, 59 Ill. 123; s. c. 5 Big. 25, and note.
But both principle and the weight of authority are opposed to this view.
Campbell v. New England Life Ins. Co., 98 Mass. 381; s. c. 1 Big. 229;
Mutual Benefit Life Ins. Co. v. Cannon, 48 Ind. 264; s. c. 5 Big. 122 ;
Baker v. Home Life Ins. Co., 4 Thomp. & C. 582; s. c. 5 Big. 297;
Duckett v. Williams, 2 Cromp. & M. 348; s. c. 3 Big. 8; Vose v. Eagle
Life Ins. Co., 6 Cush. 42; s. c. 1 Big. 161; Abbott v. Howard, 3 Big.

sentation of fact, believing it to be true, without having any
information or any *adequate* information upon which to base
it, as where he acts upon mere rumor, he then acts, to his
own knowledge, falsely, for the reason above suggested, — that
a positive assertion implies actual knowledge. This view of
the subject will reconcile all of the cases in their *result*,[1] and
will, it is believed, furnish the true ground of decision.

By way of summary, the doctrine may be put thus : Deceit
or an action for relief in equity can be maintained (other elements being present) : (1) for a false representation, known by
the party making it to be false ; (2) for a false representation,
not believed to be either true or false ; (3) for a false representation, believed to be true, but the truth of which he was
bound to know ; (4) for a false representation, believed to be
true, but upon inadequate grounds, such as rumors. In the
same cases, a plea of such facts will be a good defence to
an action *ex contractu* by the party making the false representation. (5) Deceit cannot be maintained for a false representation, believed to be true, which is based on adequate
information ; nor will a plea of fraud, or a bill asking for relief for fraud, be supported by such evidence. But a plea

294; Hutton *v.* Waterloo Life Assur. Co., 1 Fost. & F. 735; s. c. 3
Big. 199. See Jeffries *v.* Economical Life Ins. Co., 22 Wall. 47 ; s. c.
5 Big. 572; Ætna Life Ins. Co. *v.* France, 91 U. S. 510; s. c. 5 Big.
587; Holabird *v.* Atlantic Ins. Co., 2 Dill. 166; s. c. 4 Big. 181; Macdonald *v.* Law Life Ins. Co., Law R. 9 Q. B. 328; s. c. 4 Big. 609.
If the misrepresentation, though innocent and honest, be such as to
affect the risk, making it different from the one actually existing, the
contract fails by reason of the fact that there is no such risk as the one
assured. The language of the policy, however, may be such as to
require the statements to be fraudulently untrue in order to avoid
the contract. Washington Life Ins. Co. *v.* Haney, 10 Kans. 525; s. c.
4 Big. 69.

[1] Unless there be cases which hold that deceit can be maintained for
a false affirmation of fact, believed on just information to be true. If
there be such cases, they are not trustworthy authorities. See Brooks *v.*
Hamilton, 15 Minn. 26; Faribault *v.* Sater, 13 Minn. 223, 231; Rawle,
Covenants, 573, note, 4th ed.

that no contract was consummated, or a bill for relief based upon the same ground, will be sustained by the evidence.

There is another situation deserving of mention in this connection. Where an action is brought against a party who is bound to indemnify the plaintiff for an act done by the defendant's authority upon a false representation made by him, as in the case of an action by a sheriff against an attorney who has required him to levy upon certain goods as the property of a judgment debtor when they were not his property ; or to take the body of such a person as being the one intended in a writ, when he was not the person intended, — in these cases, it is not necessary for the plaintiff to prove that the defendant knew that his statement was false.[1] But the action in such cases is for indemnification, and not for deceit.

§ 4. OF THE IGNORANCE OF THE COMPLAINING PARTY, AND HIS BELIEF IN THE TRUTH OF THE REPRESENTATION.

We have next in order to consider the rule that requires the party complaining of the deceit to have been ignorant of the truth of the matter concerning which the representation was made, and to believe that the representation was true. In general, both of these situations must be true of him ; he must be ignorant of the true state of facts, and may trust in the representation of them as made by the alleged wrong-doer. He must be deceived ; and if he have notice or knowledge of the truth, or if without notice or knowledge thereof he act upon independent information, and not in a belief of the truth of the *wrongdoer's* representation, he is in the one case not deceived at all,[2] and in the other is not de-

---

[1] Humphries v. Pratt, 5 Bligh, N. s. 154 ; Collins v. Evans, 5 Q. B. 820.

[2] Hagee v. Grossman, 31 Ind. 223; Tuck v. Downing, 76 Ill. 71 ; Halls v. Thompson, 1 Smedes & M. 443; Whiting v. Hill, 23 Mich. 399.

ceived by the person of whom he complains. And the
burden of proof in these particulars rests upon the party
making complaint.[1]

Should a purchaser of property choose to make investigation of his own as to the truth of representations made by
the vendor, he is not merely barred from alleging the express
misrepresentations of the vendor. In such a case, it will not be
allowed him to say that, besides making false representations,
the vendor concealed facts of importance to the purchaser,
provided he did nothing to prevent the purchaser from making as ample an investigation as he chose.[2] Thus, where the
vendor of a large tract of land represented the estate to contain only fifty or sixty acres of untillable soil, and the purchaser, before the sale, examined all of the land more than
once, it was held that he could have no relief upon subsequently discovering that the estate contained three hundred
acres unfit for cultivation.[3]

If a person believe at first that representations made to
him are untrue, but afterwards come to believe them to be
true by the assurances of the party making them, can he
claim relief in case he act upon the representations to his
injury? It would seem that he could. If, however, notwithstanding he acts upon them, he still believe them to be false,
the contrary will clearly be true.[4]

But as there are many cases in which the alleged wrongdoer, though in fact ignorant that he had made a false repre-

---

[1] It has recently been held in Vermont that it is not incumbent upon
a plaintiff suing for deceit in a sale, to allege want of knowledge in
himself of that which made the sale fraudulent, — in that case, a lien
upon the property sold. Patee v. Pelton, 48 Vt. 182. But this was a
case in which there was held to be a warranty of title; and in such cases
it may be that there is a presumption of the purchaser's ignorance of the
defect. This, however, is not clear.

[2] Halls v. Thompson, 1 Smedes & M. 443.

[3] Ib.

[4] Bowman v. Carithers, 40 Ind. 90.

sentation, and supposing the same to be true, is bound to know the facts, and is liable for his conduct, so there are many cases in which the party complaining of the alleged deceit, though actually ignorant of the true state of facts, and supposing the representation to be true, is considered by the law as fixed with knowledge of the facts, and is not allowed to complain of the deceit. These cases we are now to consider.

The first case we have to notice under this element of the law of deceit is that in which the party, having the means at hand of informing himself of the truth of the matter in question, refuses or fails to make inquiry concerning the same. Thus, it is laid down as a broad proposition of law that if the means of knowledge be at hand and equally available to both parties, and the subject of the transaction be open to the inspection of both alike, the injured party must avail himself of such means, if he would be heard to say that he was deceived by the representations of the other party,[1] unless there was a warranty of the facts. Hence, if the quality of goods bought be open to the observation of the buyer, and he have equal means of testing them, he cannot (in the absence of a warranty) set up their inferiority in an action for the price of them,[2] or bring an action for damages on such ground.[3] Nor can the purchaser of property complain that he was deceived in the quality of it, where it appears that he viewed it as far as he chose, but omitted to make full investigation,[4] the omission not being caused by the vendor.

Upon a not dissimilar ground, it is held that a divorce will not be granted a man from his wife on the ground that she falsely stated to him before the marriage that she was not pregnant, if he himself had already had sexual intercourse with her, though her pregnancy was by another man, and the

[1] Slaughter *v.* Gerson, 13 Wall. 379.
[2] Brown *v.* Leach, 107 Mass. 364.
[3] Salem Rubber Co. *v.* Adams, 23 Pick. 256.
[4] Buck *v.* McCaughtry, 5 T. B. Mon. 221.

child a bastard.[1] The complaining party is put upon notice
in such a case.

In another case, it appeared that a manufacturing establishment about to be sold by a trustee was represented by
him to have a water power of about fifteen feet fall. The
fall in fact was considerably less; but the purchaser had for
many years been one of the owners of the property, and had
united with the other owners in a deed conveying the property, and describing it as having about fifteen feet of water
power. He had ample means of knowing the truth, and it
was accordingly considered that he could not have relied
upon the trustee's representation.[2]

Every contracting party not in actual fault has a right,
however, to rely upon the express statement of an existing
fact, the truth of which is known to the contracting party
who made it, and unknown to the party to whom it is made,
when such statement is the basis of a mutual engagement.
He is under no obligation to investigate and verify the statement, to the truth of which the other party to the contract,
with full means of knowledge, has deliberately pledged his
faith.[3] Indeed, the law goes further than this. It is well

---

[1] Crehore v. Crehore, 97 Mass. 330. See Foss v. Foss, 12 Allen, 26.

[2] Ely v. Stewart, 2 Md. 408.

[3] Mead v. Bunn, 32 N. Y. 275, 280, Porter, J.; McClellan v. Scott,
24 Wis. 81, 87; Upshaw v. Debow, 7 Bush, 442; Walsh v. Hall, 66 N. C.
233; Hale v. Philbrick, 42 Iowa, 81; Oswald v. McGehee, 28 Miss. 340;
Spalding v. Hedges, 2 Barr, 240; Starkweather v. Benjamin, 32 Mich.
305. *Contra* in North Carolina, Lytle v. Bird, 3 Jones, 222; Fields v.
Rouse, Ib. 72; Fagan v. Newsom, 1 Dev. 20; Saunders v. Hatterman, 2
Ired. 32.

A surety upon a bond given by a deputy to a sheriff (the plaintiff),
applied to the plaintiff for a release as a favor, and, in order to induce the
plaintiff to give it, falsely and fraudulently made certain representations
concerning the performance of the conditions of the bond, and at the
same time stated that he had made inquiries on the subject of the official
liability of the deputy at the offices of certain attorneys, and had there
learned that the facts were as he had stated. It was held that to a plea
of the release, in an action upon the bond, the sheriff could reply the

settled that a party may act upon the *express* representation
of another, though the means of information be fully open to
him.[1]

The purchaser of land, for example, is entitled to relief
against the vendor for fraudulent misrepresentations as to
title, even though the existence of the title complained of as
making the representations false was on record at the time of
the purchase.[2] And this, too, though there has been no eviction of the purchaser. In the case of fraud, it is not necessary for a purchaser of land to rely upon the covenants of
his deed; and hence an eviction is not necessary in order to
the recovery of substantial damages.[3]

Upon the same principle, the buyer of a patent may maintain an action against the seller for false representations as to
what was covered by the patent, or what was not covered by
an earlier patent, though he might have ascertained the truth
by searching the records of the patent office.[4]

Where one induces another to abstain from seeking information, mere concealment of material facts may become
fraudulent. And relief will not be refused in such a case,
merely because a sharp business man might not have been
deceived. Where a person practises arts designed to over-
reach another, and the latter, without fault or unreasonable

above facts ; and it was not necessary for him to ascertain the truth of
the surety's statements. Nor was the sheriff in such a case presumed to
know the defaults of his deputy. Hoitt v. Holcomb, 32 N. H. 185.

[1] Matlock v. Todd, 19 Ind. 130.

[2] Parham v. Randolph, 6 How. (Miss.) 435 ; Kiefer v. Rogers, 19
Minn. 32; Upshaw v. Debow, 7 Bush, 442; Young v. Hopkins, 6 Marsh.
23; Campbell v. Whittingham, 5 J. J. Marsh. 96; Bailey v. Smock, 61 Mo.
213; Holland v. Anderson, 38 Mo. 55; Claggett v. Crall, 12 Kans. 393.

[3] Ib.; Gilpin v. Smith, 11 Smedes & M. 109; Abbot v. Allen, 2 Johns.
Ch. 522 ; Edwards v. McLeary, Coop. 308; Coke, Litt. 384, note 332 ;
2 Kent, Com. 470.

[4] David v. Park, 103 Mass. 501 ; Brown v. Castles, 11 Cush. 348 ;
Manning v. Albee, 11 Allen, 520 ; s. c. 14 Allen, 7 ; Watson v. Atwood,
25 Conn. 313.

neglect, is defrauded, redress will not be denied.[1] Nor is the
rule different where the vendor suggests examination to the
purchaser, but in such a way as to indicate that such a step
would be quite unnecessary. If, for example, the vendor
should suggest that the purchaser should go and look at the
property, " as their judgments might not agree, and if not
satisfied the vendor would pay his expenses, but if satisfied
the purchaser should himself pay them," it is held that such
a proposal asserts by implication the exercise by the vendor
of an intelligent judgment upon the subject, tends to dissuade
from inquiry, and renders him liable, if the statements prove
false, even though he believed them to be true.[2] So, too,
though a purchaser may on close inspection detect a vice in
the property sold, still, if the vendor make representations
upon which the purchaser relies, refraining for this reason
from close inspection, the sale may be avoided.[3] So, if a
party make a false and fraudulent explanation of a visible
defect in property to be sold by him, he is liable as well as if
he had made a false and fraudulent statement concerning the
latent condition of the property.[4] And the same principle
prevails, though the party making the false explanation was
ignorant of its falsity, if he assumed to know the nature of the
defects.[5] And in general, where a party put upon notice is
actually misled and induced not to prosecute investigation by
the opposite party, he will be entitled to relief.[6] The maxim
caveat emptor does not apply when the vendor of prop-

---

[1] Swimm v. Bush, 23 Mich. 99; Starkweather v. Benjamin, 32 Mich.
305; Oswald v. McGehee, 28 Miss. 340; Roseman v. Canovan, 43 Cal. 111.

[2] Webster v. Bailey, 31 Mich. 36.

[3] Oswald v. McGehee, 28 Miss. 340; Baker v. Seahorn, 1 Swan, 54.
It was said in Baker v. Seahorn that if the vendor of a horse merely
suggest a doubt as to the goodness of the animal's eyes, knowing that
they are defective, this is as much a fraud as if he had been silent.

[4] Gant v. Shelton, 3 B. Mon. 423.

[5] Phelps v. Quinn, 1 Bush, 375; Robertson v. Clarkson, 9 B. Mon. 507.

[6] Roseman v. Canovan, 43 Cal. 111.

erty resorts to any artifice to put the purchaser off his guard.[1]

Accepting and paying for goods upon delivery will not bar the purchaser from relief, though the goods were open to his inspection at the time, if such acceptance and payment were procured by fraudulent artifices on the part of the vendor. Thus, where the defendants, manufacturers and vendors of tobacco, had fraudulently used damaged tobacco in the manufacture, and had fraudulently used boxes of green lumber, and while the tobacco was being manufactured they exhibited to the plaintiff from time to time, in order to mislead him, specimens of tobacco as of the kind they were supplying him, when in fact they were making a different and inferior kind, it was held, notwithstanding acceptance and payment, the plaintiff was entitled to recover damages for the loss sustained.[2]

However, if a party assert that he relied upon the statement of another, instead of using the means of information at his hands, the burden of proof is upon him to establish the statement. For, where persons can see for themselves if they choose to look, it is a presumption of law that they do look and ascertain the fact for themselves; and this presumption must be overcome, if they would prevail. But proof that a party is diverted from looking for himself, by the intentional act or conduct of the opposite party, will rebut the presumption; for how, it has well been asked, can one who has been diverted from looking for himself be said to refuse to look?[3]

Even though a party sell at the risk of the purchaser, he will not be permitted to practise fraud upon him. Thus, it has been held that where a party, during a negotiation for the sale of property, stated that the other contracting party must take the property at his own risk, such statement would not

---

[1] Biggs v. Perkins, 75 N. C. 397; Baker v. Seahorn, 1 Swan, 54.

[2] McAvoy v. Wright, 25 Ind. 22.

[3] Wilder v. De Cou, 18 Minn. 470, 480; Bailey v. Smock, 61 Mo. 213.

exonerate the party from liability for a deceitful suppression of the truth or for the suggestion of a falsehood.[1]

Where the parties do not stand upon an equal footing, the objection to a plea or claim of false representations, that the party to whom they were made was negligent in not making inquiry or examination, will not be allowed.[2] This rule of law rests upon the just and salutary ground that the injured party in such a case is in the power, to a greater or less extent, of the wrongdoer, so as to be more easily imposed upon than if he were standing at arm's length, and acting upon an equal footing with him.

The injured party is doubtless bound to know the state of his own business, and the facts relating to his own property, just as truly as is the wrongdoer. This subject, however, need not be enlarged upon here, as it has been presented with sufficient fulness in treating of the similar position of the wrongdoer.[3] It may, however, be observed that a director of a corporation is not bound to know the true condition of the company, though he has usually attended the business meetings; and he may obtain relief from the purchase of stock of the corporation made through the fraudulent representations of the company's cashier.[4]

A subscriber to the stock of a corporation, who resists payment or assessment on the ground that he was deceived by the false and fraudulent representations of the corporation's agent in giving his subscription, will not escape liability, it is held, if such representations relate to matters controlled by the charter of the company; the same showing that the agent had no authority to make such representations.[5] In

---

[1] George v. Johnson, 6 Humph. 36.

[2] Wannell v. Kem, 57 Mo. 478.

[3] See *supra*, pp. 57–60.

[4] Lefever v. Lefever, 30 N. Y. 27.

[5] Selma R. Co. v. Anderson, 51 Miss. 829; Wight v. Shelby R. Co., 16 B. Mon. 4; Andrews v. Ohio & M. R. Co., 14 Ill. 169; Irvin v. Turnpike Co., 2 Penn. 466; Ellison v. Mobile & O. R. Co., 36 Miss. 572.

other words, the subscriber is bound, under this rule, to examine the company's charter, and cannot safely rely upon the representations of its agents, except in matters (within the scope of his authority) as to which the charter is silent. As to matters not controlled by the charter, false and fraudulent representations within the general limitations of the doctrine of deceit, will vitiate contracts or afford a ground of action as in other cases.[1]

A distinction has been laid down in New York between a statement of fact concerning matters the knowledge of which is general and easily attained, and matters the knowledge of which is rare and exceptional. As to the former, it is said that it may reasonably be expected to have been intended that the person to whom they have been made should understand their character. Evidence of a positive assertion in such a case is sufficient, and it is not necessary for the injured party to prove that the person making the statement knew it to be false. As to the other class of facts, the knowledge of the same being unusual, statements concerning them will usually be understood as amounting only to an expression of the candid conviction of the party. They are to be understood as expressions of opinion or judgment rather than as absolute representations of fact. In other words, though statements of this kind be made in positive form, they are to be treated as *prima facie* honest and proper, and express evidence of knowledge of their falsity must be given.[2] But the soundness of this distinction may be doubted. It is not recognized in other cases; and the difficulty in the way of its application must make it too often impracticable. A few widely separate facts might be thus divided, such, for exam-

---

[1] Selma R. Co. *v.* Anderson, *supra ;* Waldo *v.* Chicago R. Co., 14 Wis. 625; Crump *v.* United States Mining Co., 7 Gratt. 352; West *v.* Crawfordsville Turnp. Co., 19 Ind. 242; Crossman *v.* Penrose Bridge Co., 26 Penn. 69.

[2] Marsh *v.* Falker, 40 N. Y. 562, 567.

ple, as representations concerning the kind or amount of
timber upon a piece of land, and representations concerning
matters of science or skill; but the largest number of cases
by far would be found difficult of classification, and opinions
would greatly and justly differ upon the correctness of any
classification that could be made. And no case could be a
precedent for another, unless the subject of the statements
were identical. But, even as to those cases in which the rule
might be of ready application, there certainly is no sound
reason for holding that a positive statement of fact relating to
a matter within the knowledge of but few persons should be
placed upon a better footing than a statement of fact relating
to matters within the knowledge of many. The presumption,
if any were proper, should favor the latter; for, if the statement relate to a matter with which most persons have some
familiarity, it may be considered that the party who made it
was speaking of facts of common observation merely, and
hence should not be bound without proof of actual fraud. If,
on the other hand, a man of science or skill make an assertion of
fact in his special department of knowledge, his learning will
give him the ear of the people, and his word will be received
where that of others would be distrusted. And this is the
doctrine of express authority.[1]

A person in the full possession of all his faculties, and
able to read, is bound to know and understand the contents
of an instrument executed by him or in his possession as
a party to it,[2] unless indeed it contain technical or foreign
terms, and he has been misled as to their meaning by the
opposite party. Such a person therefore cannot say that he
did not read an instrument conferring rights upon him which

---

[1] Kost v. Bender, 25 Mich, 515; Picard v. McCormick, 11 Mich. 68;
McGar v. Williams, 26 Ala. 467; Moreland v. Atchison, 19 Tex. 303.

[2] Rogers v. Place, 35 Ind. 577; New Albany R. Co. v. Fields, 10 Ind.
187; Russell v. Branham, 8 Blackf. 277; Clem v. Newcastle R. Co., 9
Ind. 488; Starr v. Bennett, 5 Hill, 303.

he is seeking to enforce, and that the other party falsely stated its terms.[1]

If a man execute a solemn instrument, by which he conveys an interest, and sign on the back a receipt for money, he cannot affect not to know what he was doing; and it is not enough for him afterwards to say that he thought it was only a form. That merely amounts to saying that a misrepresentation was made to him, under which he executed a deed; and still the deed may have been exactly what he intended to execute, though he intended that it should be used for a totally different purpose. But this does not affect the deed. The fraud of the person who used the deed does not make it less the deed of the person who executed it.[2]

A person who cannot read should require a contract about to be signed by him to be read to him; and, if he do not, he cannot in principle complain that the contents of the writing were falsely stated to him, at least where the misrepresentation was not made by the opposite party to the contract.[3] But it has been held that one who could only read with great difficulty might rely upon the statements of the agent of the opposite party as to such of the contents of a printed instrument as were in very small type.[4] It is doubtless the practice in such cases merely to explain the contents; but it may be doubted if due diligence does not require of the party that he should insist upon having the contract read at length. Then, if there be fraud, he will clearly be entitled to redress.

In the case just referred to, it is observed that if a contracting party (able to read only with difficulty) may not rely upon the representations of the party with whom he contracts as to

[1] Ib.; Bacon v. Markley, 46 Ind. 116; Seeright v. Fletcher, 6 Blackf. 380; Hawkins v. Hawkins, 50 Cal. 558.

[2] Hunter v. Walters, Law R. 7 Ex. 75, Lord Hatherley.

[3] Craig v. Hobbs, 44 Ind. 363.

[4] Keller v. Equitable Ins. Co., 28 Ind. 170. See also Sims v. Bice, 67 Ill. 88.

the contents of a written instrument, but must examine the instrument for himself, it is at the same time implied that the party who represents the contents of the instrument shall not by his own act have rendered such examination of more than ordinary difficulty. This remark would be very decisive, if the only alternative for stating the contents were an examination by the complaining party himself; but that is not the case. The most natural course for a person regardful of his own rights would be to require the opposite party to read the instrument slowly and carefully, rather than to attempt the difficult task of reading it himself or to risk the danger necessarily involved in an attempt to state the contents of the paper, — a danger greatly increased, if the instrument be lengthy or complicated.[1] And the force of these remarks will be still more apparent if the complaining party, instead of being ignorant and illiterate, and hence naturally more ready to accept a statement of the contents, should be a blind person, in the possession of the intelligence generally manifested by such people. It would hardly be excusable in a blind man of intelligence to accept a statement of the contents of a writing in which he is interested. He should require it to be read.

Cases of this sort, however, are to be distinguished from those in which a person is by trick or artifice caused to sign a different instrument from that to which he intended to give his signature, as where one paper is surreptitiously substituted for another. The doctrine as to the necessity of reading or having read the paper signed has no application to such a case. Even a negotiable promissory note in the hands of a *bona fide* indorsee for value is void, when the defendant's signature has been thus obtained.[2]

---

[1] *Post*, p. 78. See Louchheim *v.* Gill, 17 Ind. 139; Sims *v.* Bice, 67 Ill. 88; Taylor *v.* Atchison, 54 Ill. 196, the last-named case being directly in point. See also Hawkins *v.* Hawkins, 50 Cal. 558; Rockford R. Co. *v.* Shunick, 65 Ill. 223; Spurgin *v.* Traub, Ib. 170; Pigot's Case, 11 Coke, 27; Estes *v.* Furlong, 59 Ill. 298; Richardson *v.* Schirtz, Ib. 313; Leach *v.* Nichols, 55 Ill. 273.

[2] Munson *v.* Nichols, 62 Ill. 111. *Secus*, if the defendant has been

The rule in this class of cases appears to be based upon the negligence of the party signing the instrument in question. It *may* be found however, as matter of fact or as matter of law, that the signer, though perfectly able to read the writing, was not guilty of negligence in failing to read it; and, if this should be the case, there is strong authority for the position that the signer may not be bound even in favor of a *bona fide* purchaser for value.[1] Thus, in the case first cited, it appeared that the defendant, a man far advanced in years, was induced to put his name upon the back of a bill of exchange, by the fraudulent representation of the acceptor that he was signing a guaranty. The defendant did not see the face of the bill at all; and it appeared that, at the suggestion of the same party who had made this false statement of the contents of the paper, he had previously signed a guaranty for the same amount and for the same object, upon which he had not been involved in any loss. The jury were instructed that if the indorsement was obtained upon a fraudulent representation that the contract was a guaranty, and the defendant signed it without knowing that it was a bill, and under the belief that it was a guaranty, and if the defendant was not guilty of any negligence in so signing the paper, he was entitled to a verdict. The jury found for the defendant; and, upon a motion for a new trial, the instruction was held correct. The verdict was, however, set aside, upon the

guilty of any negligence. Mead *v.* Munson, 60 Ill. 49. See also Richardson *v.* Schirtz, 59 Ill. 313; Elliott *v.* Levings, 54 Ill. 213; Clarke *v.* Johnson, Ib. 296.

[1] Foster *v.* Mackinnon, Law R. 4 C. P. 704; Gibbs *v.* Linabury, 22 Mich. 479; Whitney *v.* Snyder, 2 Lans. 477; Chapman *v.* Rose, 56 N. Y. 137; Kellogg *v.* Steiner, 29 Wis. 626. See also Putnam *v.* Sullivan, 4 Mass. 45; Ross *v.* Drinkard, 35 Ala. 434.

It has been held in Missouri that, where the signature of the maker of a note has been obtained by false representations of the object of the contract, the paper will be void even in the hands of a *bona fide* holder for value. Corby *v.* Weddle, 57 Mo. 452; Briggs *v.* Ewart, 51 Mo. 245; Martin *v.* Smylee, 55 Mo. 577. But this may well be doubted.

ground that the evidence in respect of the negligence of the
defendant was such as to call for further investigation. The
ground taken for sustaining the instruction was, that the
defendant never intended to sign the contract in question, or
any such contract. He never intended to put his name to
any instrument that then was, or thereafter might become,
negotiable. He was deceived not merely as to the legal
effect, but as to the actual contents of the instrument. And
this is in substance the *ratio decidendi* in most of the cases
above cited. Further than this, and with the distinct limitation that there was no negligence on the part of the person
giving his signature, it would be unsafe to go.

The principle of the above case would perhaps apply to the
validity of a negotiable note, where the signature of the maker
was given to a printed form or blank having the appearance of
an order for a particular article, but which is afterwards so filled
up as to constitute it (in form) a promissory note. Such an
instrument would not perhaps be valid even in the hands of a
bona fide indorsee for value.[1] This is probably the extent of
the exemption. If the blank were such in appearance that it
might as readily be converted into a promissory note as into
another contract, it is apprehended that a party signing it
should be held liable to a *bona fide* indorsee for value, notwithstanding any fraudulent misrepresentations as to the
object of the paper; unless, indeed, the circumstances were
such that he was prevented, without negligence of his own,
from reading the instrument by the opposite party, or was by
him caused to relax his diligence and scrutiny.[2]

---

[1] Compare Kellogg v. Steiner, 29 Wis. 626. *A fortiori*, a person cannot be made liable in any way by another's writing a contract over, or in
connection with, his blank signature upon a fly-leaf, or in an autograph
album, or upon a loose sheet or piece of paper. Caulkins v. Whisler, 29
Iowa, 495; Nance v. Lary, 5 Ala. 370.

[2] Gibbs v. Linabury, 22 Mich. 479; Chapman v. Rose, 56 N. Y. 137;
Shirts v. Overjohn, 60 Mo. 305; McDonald v. Muscatine Bank, 27
Ind. 319.

The presumption of negligence against a person able to read the instrument, in not doing so, is clearly strong enough to justify a verdict for the indorsee;[1] and it must therefore devolve upon him to satisfy the court or jury that his conduct was perfectly free from fault.

If it appear that a party's signature to an instrument was obtained (without negligence on his part) by any fraudulent artifice in the shifting and substitution of one paper not intended to be signed, for another to which the party supposed he was giving his signature, he will not be liable even to a *bona fide* purchaser for value. Such a case is in substance a forgery, and the rule requiring a person to see to the contents of the instrument signed has no application.[2] And the same rule prevails where, without any negligence on the part of the signer, or delivery by him, a paper is obtained by theft or other fraud from his premises without the intervention of any one standing in a relation of trust or confidence to such party.[3] But the rule is probably otherwise as to bank-bills.[4]

If, then, there be an intention to execute, accept, or indorse a negotiable note or bill, and the act be accompanied with a delivery thereof, actual or implied, or if without such intention there be negligence in the execution, acceptance, or indorsement, followed by a delivery, actual or implied, the party so giving his signature will be liable to a *bona fide* holder for value. But there must be a contract, and this can arise only from intention or negligence.[5] If both of these are

---

[1] Douglass *v.* Matting, 29 Iowa, 498; Shirts *v.* Overjohn, 60 Mo. 305; Chapman *v.* Rose, 56 N. Y. 137; McDonald *v.* Muscatine Bank, 27 Ind. 319.

[2] Nance *v.* Lary, 5 Ala. 370; Gibbs *v.* Linabury, 22 Mich. 479; *ante*, p. 75.

[3] Burson *v.* Huntington, 21 Mich. 415, denying Shipley *v.* Carroll, 45 Ill. 285, and Gould *v.* Segee, 5 Duer, 266; also *dicta* in Marston *v.* Allen, 8 Mees. & W. 494, and in Ingham *v.* Primrose, 7 Com. B. n. s. 82. The Wisconsin cases certainly go too far in support of the defendant. Chipman *v.* Tucker, 38 Wis. 43; Roberts *v.* McGrath, Ib. 52; Roberts *v.* Wood, Ib. 60. In these cases, the paper was put into circulation by a custodian.

[4] Burson *v.* Huntington, *supra;* Worcester Bank *v.* Dorchester Bank, 10 Cush. 488.

[5] In the absence of assent, negligence cannot in strictness generate a

wanting, there can be no liability; and the same is true if
either is wanting, unless there be an actual or implied
delivery.

Under this principle, that intention to execute, accept, or indorse *some* note or bill, or negligence in respect of such act, followed by delivery, is necessary, will be embraced all that class
of cases where a party has given his signature to an incomplete
negotiable bill or note for the use of another; and the cases are
in strict accord with the above principle, establishing the rule
that, notwithstanding a fraudulent breach of confidence in the
party intrusted with the signature, the signer will be liable
to a *bona fide* holder for value, at least to the extent of the
outlay made by the latter in the purchase of the bill or note.[1]

The above considerations, so far as they relate to signa-
tures given to completed contracts upon a misrepresentation
of their contents, proceed upon the ground that the party so
giving his signature was able to read the written instrument
before him. Different considerations prevail in cases in which
the party was ignorant and unable to read the writing at all, or
able to read it only with difficulty. The party in such a case
stands in a dependent situation, and has a right to consider
his liability to depend as well upon the good faith of the
party for whom he signs as upon his own exercise of care.
Or more accurately, such a party can insist upon a higher
approach to perfect honesty in the other party (the human law
is powerless to compel perfect honesty), and can himself be

contract, but in such a case as this the consequences of a contract may
well be visited upon the negligent party. He would be liable in tort, it
should seem, and to the same extent, if the contractual liability were
not held to arise.

[1] Michigan Bank *v.* Eldred, 9 Wall. 544; Fullerton *v.* Sturgis, 4 Ohio
St. 529 ; Huntingdon *v.* Branch Bank, 3 Ala. 186; Orrick *v.* Colston, 7
Gratt. 189; Russell *v.* Langstaffe, 2 Doug. 514; Van Duzer *v.* Howe, 21
N. Y. 531; Bigelow, Estoppel, 394 (2d ed.). See Swan *v.* North British
Co., 2 Hurlst. & C. 175 (Ex. Ch.), intimating that the estoppel arising
from executing instruments containing blanks is confined to negotiable
instruments, and does not apply to deeds.

excused for exercising a lower degree of diligence or care than the person who stands upon an equal footing with the wrongdoer. The difference is perhaps only one of degree, since even an unlettered man may be negligent; and, if negligent, there is no sufficient reason for preferring him to an honest purchaser for value. At all events, it is clear that if such a person, without negligence of his own, be induced to sign a negotiable bill or note by reason of a false reading of the contents of the instruments, he cannot be held liable even to a *bona fide* indorsee for value.[1]

Not to read a deed to a party, in the rough draft before the execution, or in the engrossment at the time of execution, has been held in England to be a badge of fraud.[2]

The duty of reading an instrument may be cast by statute upon the maker thereof or upon an officer of the law; and when this is the case it would seem that the opposite party could rely thereon, without himself reading it, or calling upon a friend or agent to do so in case of his inability.[3] If the party entitled to the reading should be a foreigner, not well acquainted with the language of the instrument, he should insist upon a translation; and the failure to do so would be evidence of negligence on his part, which, however, might be rebutted doubtless by showing that he had been imposed upon by reason of his own ignorance.

The duty of reading an instrument to the opposite party may also be assumed, even when not required by law, by the party drafting it; and it would seem that one who assumes such a duty should be required to perform it honestly, and that the opposite party might safely rely upon the reading.

---

[1] Walker *v.* Ebert, 29 Wis. 196; Puffer *v.* Smith, 57 Ill. 537; Whitney *v.* Snyder, 2 Lans. 477; Chapman *v.* Rose, 56 N. Y. 137; Putnam *v.* Sullivan, 4 Mass. 45. See Schuylkill Co. *v.* Copley, 67 Penn. St. 386; Foster *v.* Mackinnon, Law R. 4 Com. P. 704; 1 Daniel, Neg. Instruments, §§ 848, 849.

[2] Bennet *v.* Vade, 2 Atk. 324, 327.

[3] See Terry *v.* Tuttle, 24 Mich. 206, 211.

This, we apprehend, will clearly be the case when there exists any inequality or confidence between the parties, and the party reading stands in the superior position.

In the absence of such a duty in the opposite party to read, or of fraud, one cannot allege that he did not agree to the terms of a written contract to which he is a party.[1]

The omission to read a portion of a deed *may* be as fatal, where such duty of reading devolves upon or is assumed by one of the parties to a written contract, as the misreading of it. This will be the case whenever the effect of the omission is to mislead. Thus, where a lady supposed that she was executing a mortgage to A, when in fact the name of B was inserted, and the agent of the mortgagor (who assumed the duty of reading the deed to the mortgagor) omitted to read the name of the mortgagee, the court, while deciding the case upon other grounds, were inclined to the clearly sound opinion that the omission rendered the deed invalid.[2] However, it would seem that the mere omission to read parts of the instrument well understood (this being the reason for not reading them) could not be fatal.

In a suit to set aside a deed made by a person unable to read, for misrepresentation of its contents, its purport, and effect, the burden of proof is upon the defendant. In such a case, it is part of the necessary proof of the execution of the deed to show that it was read, or its contents made known to the grantor. But an acknowledgment before an officer according to law is equivalent to proof that the grantor had knowledge of the contents, if such acknowledgment certify that the officer made known the contents to the grantor.[3]

Besides the above situations in which the complaining

---

[1] Grace *v.* Adams, 100 Mass. 505; Rice *v.* Dwight Manuf. Co., 2 Cush. 80, 87.　　　　　[2] Terry *v.* Tuttle, 24 Mich. 206.

[3] Hyer *v.* Little, 5 C. E. Green, 443. See Pool *v.* Chase, 46 Tex. 207; Williams *v.* Baker, 71 Penn. St. 476.

party is precluded or not from alleging that he was ignorant of the truth of the matter concerning which the representation was made, there is another class of cases, fully considered in another place, to which allusion should here be made. This class of cases is that of misrepresentations of the law. Generally speaking, a party is bound to know the law, and cannot allege that he has been deceived by a false statement thereof; but there are important qualifications to this rule, and reference should be made to the examination of this subject elsewhere.[1]

§ 5. OF THE INTENTION THAT THE REPRESENTATION SHOULD BE ACTED UPON.

As to the rule which requires the party complaining of deceit to prove that the opposite party intended his representation to be acted upon, it is to be observed that, while the rule is probably inflexible, its force appears chiefly in cases in which the deceit was practised with reference to a negotiation with a third person, and not with the party of whom the complaint is made. In cases of this kind, an example of which is found in false representations to the complaining party of the solvency of a third person, it is plain that the transaction with the third person, though shown to have been caused by the false representation in question, affords no evidence of an intention in the party complained of that the representation should be acted upon by the party. It would be perfectly consistent with mere evidence that the plaintiff (using this term generically) acted upon the defendant's knowingly false representation in a transaction with a third person, to the plaintiff's injury; that the defendant, notwithstanding his knowledge of the falsity of his representation, and his consequent moral culpability,

---

[1] *Ante*, pp. 8–10.

did not know that the plaintiff was about to act upon his
representation. And this would be equally true, though it
appeared that the defendant had not volunteered his statements, but had made them only upon inquiry by the plaintiff;
for the plaintiff might have made the inquiry out of pure
curiosity, or indeed out of a mere general interest in the
affairs of the third person. Proof of all these facts would
therefore be insufficient to show that the defendant had
intended to injure the plaintiff. The representation might
still have been a mere idle falsehood, albeit told knowingly
and with actual malice. In such a case, the person who had
been slandered in his character, profession, or occupation
might maintain an action of slander against the party utter-
ing the language, or an action of slander of title (so called),
if false representations of the state of his property had been
made to his actual damage; but no right of action would
accrue to any bystander who might have acted upon the
representation (for example, by breaking a bargain then
negotiating with the third person) to his own injury.

It follows, therefore, that where a party complains of false
representations, whereby he was caused to suffer damage in a
transaction with some third person, it devolves upon him to
give express evidence that the alleged wrongdoer intended
that he should act upon the misrepresentation; and that it is
not enough to prove that the misrepresentation was made
with knowledge of its falsity.[1]

The existence of such a class of cases as this has been
recognized for nearly a hundred years.[2] And from the first
case in which it is clearly enunciated,[3] it has been settled law

[1] Though this proposition has not been distinctly reasoned out in the
cases, it is supported by Pasley v. Freeman, 3 T. R. 51; s. c. Bigelow's
L. C. Torts, 1, and note, 36; Thom v. Bigland, 8 Ex. 725, 731; Tapp v.
Lee, 3 Bos. & P. 367; Foster v. Charles, 6 Bing. 396; 7 Bing. 105; and,
indeed, by all of the authorities in which such a situation was presented.

[2] It dates from Pasley v. Freeman, 3 T. R. 51 A. D. 1789.

[3] Pasley v. Freeman.

that it is not necessary that the misrepresentation complained of should have been made with a corrupt motive of personal gain on the part of the person making the representation, in order to entitle the opposite party to relief.[1]

Where, however, the effect of the false representation was to bring the plaintiff into a business transaction with the party himself who made the representation, the case is quite different. Proof of such a fact shows at once the intent of the defendant to induce the plaintiff to act upon the representation; and it follows that express evidence of an intention to this effect is unnecessary. This is the meaning of the cases which hold it not incumbent upon the plaintiff in deceit (and it should be observed that the rule is the same of any party, plaintiff or defendant, who complains of deceit), after proof of the other elements of redress, to give express evidence of an intent to deceive. We proceed to illustrate the subject from the authorities.

Where, for example, evidence is given that a defendant, in the sale of a horse, knowingly made false representations to the plaintiff concerning the animal, and that the plaintiff has been induced thereby to buy the horse, the jury are bound to find that the defendant made the representations with intent to induce the plaintiff to buy the horse; and the plaintiff cannot be required to give any further evidence of such intent of the defendant.[2] Again, if a party sell a horse as sound, knowing that he is not sound, the existence of an intent to defraud is proved; and this is equally true where the vendor knew that the horse was sick at the time of the sale, but did not know what was the matter with him. Selling the horse as sound under such circumstances, it is not necessary to give other evidence of an intent to defraud.[3] And,

[1] Pasley v. Freeman, 3 T. R. 51; Foster v. Charles, 6 Bing. 396; s. c. 7 Bing. 105; Hubbell v. Meigs, 50 N. Y. 480.

[2] Collins v. Denison, 12 Met. 549.

[3] Johnson v. Wallower, 15 Minn. 474; s. c. 18 Minn. 288; Lindsay v. Davis, 30 Mo. 406.

in general, where the facts themselves show that the wrong-doer intended the fraud, evidence of want of such intention is inadmissible.[1]

It is important to observe that in one branch at least of this class of cases it is not necessary that it should appear that the party complained of should have intended to *injure* the other. We have already seen that a person honestly professing to have authority to act in behalf of another is liable as for fraud for the damages sustained, if he have not the authority.[2] And in such cases it is obvious that the representation may have been made for the benefit of the complaining party.[3]

§ 6. OF ACTING UPON THE REPRESENTATION.

It is fundamental that the representation should have been acted upon by the complaining party to his injury.[4] General fraudulent conduct or dishonesty of purpose, or a mere general purpose to deceive, will not afford ground of action or defence unless connected with the particular transaction complained of, and shown to be the very ground upon which the party acted and upon which the transaction took place.[5] And this is as true in equity as at law.[6]

In accordance with the rule that fraud unaccompanied by damage is not actionable, it has very lately been held that an action for inducing the payee of a negotiable note to indorse it in blank upon its transfer, by false and fraudulent representations, cannot be sustained before actual payment of the

[1] Dulaney v. Rogers, 64 Mo. 201.

[2] *Ante,* pp. 58, 59.

[3] See also Polhill v. Walter, 3 Barn. & Ad. 114.

[4] Pasley v. Freeman, 3 T. R. 51; Wells v. Waterhouse, 22 Maine, 131; Branham v. Record, 42 Ind. 181; Rogers v. Higgins, 57 Ill. 244; Lindsey v. Lindsey, 34 Miss. 432; Taylor v. Guest, 58 N. Y. 262.

[5] Rutherford v. Williams, 42 Mo. 18; Attwood v. Small, 6 Clark & F. 447.

[6] Rogers v. Higgins, 57 Ill. 244.

instrument by such indorser.[1] But it is held that a party
who has been induced to subscribe to the stock of an insolvent corporation, and to give his bond and mortgage to secure
the payment of his subscription, has been damnified, though
his subscription has not in fact been paid.[2]

A person who is prevented from effecting an attachment
upon property by the fraudulent representations of the owner
or his agent is considered to have suffered no legal damage
thereby, though subsequently another creditor attach the
whole property and sell it upon execution to satisfy his own
debt.[3] The person thus deceived, having acquired no right in
the property, cannot lose any by reason of the deceit. The
most that can be said, it has been observed, is that the party
intended to attach the property, and that this intention has
been frustrated.[4] And it could not be certainly known that
this intention would have been carried out.[5] Of course,
however, the case would be different where a party has been
induced by false representations to abandon an attachment
actually made.[6] So, too, it is laid down that no action can
be maintained for fraudulently preventing one from obtaining
an expected gratuity from a testator.[7] Again, where a person
falsely represents that he has authority to lease a store to the
plaintiff, and proceeds to grant him a verbal lease for two
years, no action will lie for the fraud, since the lease was void,
and hence no legal damage had been sustained.[8]

Every contracting party has a right to rely upon the
express statement of an existing fact, the truth of which is

---

[1] Freeman v. Venner, 120 Mass. 424.

[2] Hubbard v. Briggs, 31 N. Y. 518. The distinction between this
and the preceding case (Freeman v. Venner, 120 Mass. 424) seems to be
that in the former nothing but a conditional liability had been incurred,
while in the latter an actual present estate had been conveyed.

[3] Bradley v. Fuller, 118 Mass. 239 ; Lamb v. Stone, 11 Pick. 527 ;
Wellington v. Small, 3 Cush. 145 ; Randall v. Hazelton, 12 Allen, 412.

[4] Lamb v. Stone and Bradley v. Fuller, *supra*.

[5] Bradley v. Fuller.   [6] Ib.

[7] Hutchins v. Hutchins, 7 Hill, 104.

[8] Dung v. Parker, 52 N. Y. 494.

known, or presumed to be known, by the opposite party, and not known to him to whom it was made, as the basis of an engagement.[1] A vendor of property may, for example, put upon the purchaser the responsibility of informing him correctly as to the market value of the property, or any other fact known to him which affects its value, and if the purchaser answer untruly, in positive terms, the purchase may be avoided.[2]

The rule requiring a party to act upon the false representations prevails where the complaining party does not rely upon the misrepresentation, but seeks from other quarters means of verification of the statements made, and acts upon the information thus obtained. He cannot afterwards allege that he has been deceived by the party who originally made the false representations.[3] Thus, in the case first cited, which involved the validity of a contract for the purchase of a steamboat, it appeared that previously to the execution of the contract, and with a view to examining the vessel, the defendant went from Baltimore to New York, taking with him his son, who subsequently became captain of the boat, and two ship-carpenters, and a square to measure her draught of water. Every opportunity was afforded him to examine the vessel ; and a thorough examination was made. It was considered under these circumstances that the defendant could not set up the false representations of the vendor by way of impeaching the sale. The case, however, would doubtless be otherwise if the complaining party were prevented, in the course of his independent examination, from ascertaining the truth by the fraud of the other party. The fact that he had made an examination of his own under such circumstances would not preclude him from alleging the fraudulent representations.[4]

---

[1] Mead v. Bunn, 32 N. Y. 275.

[2] Smith v. Countryman, 30 N. Y. 655. See ante, pp. 17–21.

[3] Slaughter v. Gerson, 14 Wall. 379; Attwood v. Small, 6 Clark & F. 232.   [4] See post, p. 88.

Though a party to whom a false representation has been made attempt to ascertain for himself the truth of the matter, still, if he be prevented from accomplishing the purpose, though not by the other party, and act in fact upon the misrepresentation, the party making it is bound to make it good. Thus, in a recent case,[1] the plaintiff, negotiating for the purchase of a farm from the defendant, went upon the premises to verify for himself the statements made by the defendant as to the nature of the soil. The depth of snow on the ground prevented him from doing so; and the statements previously made were there repeated by the defendant. The plaintiff purchased the farm, relying upon the defendant's representations; which having proved false, it was held that equity would rescind the contract.

The misrepresentation must have been made at the time of or only shortly before the action taken and complained of: if made afterwards, it could not have influenced the party's conduct, and can afford, therefore, no ground for relief.[2] Hence, a purchaser who does not act upon the representations of the vendor cannot afterwards claim the benefit of them.[3]

It is not necessary to prove that the plaintiff relied solely upon the defendant's representations. It is sufficient if the representations were relied upon by the plaintiff as constituting one of the substantial inducements to his action.[4] It is indeed sometimes said that the false representations must have been such that without them the transaction complained of would not have taken place. But it has well been said it is not possible for any man, in the aggregate of inducements which led to the transaction, to determine whether the result would have been attained with some of the inducements wanting. Nor should the guilty party be permitted to allege

---

[1] Risch v. Von Lillienthal, 34 Wis. 250.

[2] Fogg v. Pew, 10 Gray, 409.

[3] Lindsey v. Lindsey, 34 Miss. 432.

[4] James v. Hodsden, 47 Vt. 127; Winter v. Bandel, 30 Ark. 362. See Cabot v. Christie, 42 Vt. 121.

in excuse that the innocent party might have acted as he did, if less deceit had been practised upon him. If a man resort to unlawful means and accomplish an unlawful purpose, the law will not stop to measure such inducements. If, for example, a party, induced by the several false and fraudulent declarations of two persons, different in time and character, purchase worthless property, it would not do to say that because the trade might not have been made if only one falsehood had been uttered, and the purchase not wholly induced by either, the party injured is without redress. If a fraud be accomplished, and the unlawful acts of the defendant contributed thereto, he is answerable. The fraudulent acts of the defendant must indeed have worked an injury; but if the wrong have been done, and the defendant have been a party to its commission, " the court will not apportion the penalties of guilt among offenders, nor divide spoil among highwaymen." [1]

Hence, if B conspire with A to defraud C, by inducing the latter to loan money to A upon the security of a forged note, the fact that C, in making the loan, relied also upon other securities, and upon verbal representations made by B of the ability of A to repay the loan, will not prevent his recovering from B, in an action for the conspiracy, if C relied upon the forged note as well.[2] It is enough, then, that the representations materially influenced the conduct of the plaintiff, though (being combined with other motives) they were not the sole or even predominant inducement to the party's action.[3]

Concerning the question who may act upon the representation, it may be answered that not only may the representation be intended for a particular individual alone (in which case he alone is entitled to act upon it), but it may be intended

---

[1] Redfield, J., in James v. Hodsden, *supra*.

[2] Spaulding v. Knight, 116 Mass. 148. It is no defence to such an action that the person so obtaining the money intended to pay it at the time. Ib.

[3] Safford v. Grout, 120 Mass. 20; Matthews v. Bliss, 22 Pick. 48.

for several or for many, or for any one of a particular class.
In such a case as this, any one who comes properly within
the number or class intended by the party making the representation will be entitled to relief or redress against him by
acting upon the misrepresentation to his damage.[1] Thus,
where directors of a company put forth a prospectus containing false representations for the purpose of selling shares of
stock, the false representations are deemed to have been made
to all who read the prospectus and become purchasers from
the *company* in reliance upon the statements there made.[2] But
the purchaser of shares in the *market*, upon the faith of a prospectus which he has not received from those who are answerable for it, cannot by acting upon it so connect himself with
them as to render them liable to him for the misrepresentation
contained in it, as if it had been addressed to himself personally.[3]

Upon the same principle, where a representation was made
to the plaintiff's father with the view to being acted upon by
the plaintiff, it was decided that by acting upon it the plaintiff
had acquired a right of redress.[4] So, also, a party may make

[1] Swift *v.* Winterbotham, Law R. 8 Q. B. 244 ; Barry *v.* Croskey, 2
Johns. & H. 21 ; Bedford *v.* Bagshaw, 4 Hurl. & N. 548; Bagshaw *v.*
Seymour, 29 Law J. Ex. 62, note ; Gerhard *v.* Bates, 2 El. & B. 476;
Clarke *v.* Dickson, 6 Com. B. N. s. 453 ; Cazeux *v.* Mali, 25 Barb. 583;
National Exchange Co. *v.* Drew, 2 Macq. 103 ; Peek *v.* Gurney, Law R.
6 H. L. 377.

[2] See the cases just cited.

[3] Peek *v.* Gurney, Law R. 6 H. L. 377, overruling upon this point
Bedford *v.* Bagshaw and Bagshaw *v.* Seymour, *supra.*

It is held, however, in New York, that a corporation is liable for the
fraudulent overissue of stock, not only to the person to whom the overissue is made, but also to any subsequent *bona fide* purchaser thereof.
Such acts are done with intent to defraud any and all purchasers, the
perpetrators well knowing that every person into whose hands the false
certificates of stock should come by fair purchase might be injured. New
York & N. H. R. Co. *v.* Schuyler, 34 N. Y. 30; Phelps *v.* Wait, 30 N. Y.
78 ; Suydam *v.* Moore, 8 Barb. 358 ; Bruff *v.* Mali, 36 N. Y. 200. And
the action may be maintained jointly or separately against the agent who
committed the fraud. Phelps *v.* Wait, *supra ;* Suydam *v.* Moore, *supra.*

[4] Langridge *v.* Levy, 2 Mees. & W. 519; s. c. 4 Mees. & W. 337.

inquiry, where such is the custom, through his banker (instead of personally) concerning the standing of a third person; and it is no objection to a claim for redress for a fraudulent answer given to the plaintiff's banker that the misrepresentation was not made to the plaintiff.[1]

Statements made to a witness in the presence of the purchaser of property in relation to the property are, it is held, of the same effect as if made to the purchaser.[2] But a vendor of property sold at auction is not bound by representations made by him privately to some of the bidders, and not heard by the purchaser.[3]

Where a letter is written, marked "confidential," concerning the pecuniary standing of a party, it is for the jury to say whether it was intended for the exclusive perusal of the person addressed.[4] It is also for the jury to say, on a thorough examination of letters of this kind, and the facts and circumstances connected with them, whether they were calculated to inspire, and did inspire, a false confidence in the pecuniary responsibility of the party to which the writer knew he was not entitled.[5]

[1] Swift v. Winterbotham, Law R. 8 Q. B. 244.
[2] Alexander v. Beresford, 27 Miss. 747.
[3] Lindsey v. Lindsey, 34 Miss. 432.
[4] Iasigi v. Brown, 17 How. 183. [5] Ib.

CHAPTER II.

SPECIAL FRAUDS IN PAIS.

§ 1. INTRODUCTORY.

WE have in the preceding chapter considered in detail the typical case of fraud. All fraud, properly speaking, involves something of deceit. A truly fraudulent act cannot be committed without the practice of deception ; though a few classes of cases have come to be treated under the head of fraud, to the accomplishment of which wrong no deception is necessary ; such, for example, as conveyances of debtors made to hinder or delay their creditors (a statutory subject not considered in this work), and conveyances by husbands in fraud of the rights of their wives. But there are also many classes of cases in which indeed the general element of deception is present and necessary, in which, however, deception plays no special part, the decision of the case turning upon the answer to other questions. These cases have no further connection with each other than is indicated by this fact. We have now to consider them ; and have divided them into two separate chapters, according as they are frauds *in pais* (that is, frauds not arising in the administration of justice), or frauds upon the administration of the law.

§ 2. OF FRAUDS BETWEEN HUSBAND AND WIFE.[1]

The statutory grounds of divorce, though not specifying fraud, do not exclude it. A series of cases has settled the

---

[1] *Deceit* by the wife is mainly considered in the preceding chapter. See pp. 4, 5, 49–56, 66. Husband's deceit, pp. 47, 48.

rule that (apart from statutory enactment to the contrary), if a marriage be brought about by fraud, the injured party may go into equity and obtain a decree of nullity ; and this is true whether the fraud was committed by the other party [1] to the marriage or by third persons.[2] Fraud, however, may not always be established by proof of false representations believed to be true, more than it is in the case of actions of deceit.   Thus, if a stranger were to present himself to a woman (especially to a widow) of mature years for marriage, representing himself to be a man of respectability and good standing in his own community, and propose marriage at once, and should finally, though after several refusals at short intervals on the ground of his being a stranger, be accepted, the courts would be slow to grant the lady a decree of nullity ; though it should turn out that she had been united to a jail bird of the worst character.[3]   The court would have great pity for the woman in such a misfortune, but not the regard for suffering which would be extended perhaps to a young girl, inexperienced in the world.

As to what will be sufficient to constitute fraud for which nullity will be granted, the following are examples : In a case in New York, it appeared that the parties were white persons, and that the defendant had previously charged the plaintiff with being the father of her bastard child.   The

---

[1] Scott v. Shufeldt, 5 Paige, 43 ; Ferlat v. Gojon, Hopk. 478 ; Burtis v. Burtis, Ib. 557, 568; Robertson v. Cole, 12 Tex. 356.   See also Wier v. Still, 31 Iowa, 107, where it was considered that the fraud was not made out.

[2] Keyes v. Keyes, 22 N. H. 553 ; Sloan v. Kane, 10 How. Pr. 66; Harford v. Morris, 2 Hagg. Con. 423 ; Portsmouth v. Portsmouth, 1 Hagg. Ecc. 355 ; Hull v. Hull, 15 Jur. 710; s. c. 5 Eng. Law & E. 589. It is held, however, in Delaware, that neither imbecility of mind nor intoxication at the time of the marriage, accompanied with circumstances of fraud, combination, or circumvention on the part of the friends of the wife to induce the husband to marry her, will give the courts jurisdiction to divorce the parties.   Elzey v. Elzey, 1 Houst. 308.

[3] Wier v. Still, 31 Iowa, 107.

plaintiff thereupon, believing the child to be his, had married
the defendant to obtain his discharge from proceedings in
bastardy. Subsequently, he ascertained the fact that the
child was a mulatto, and that the defendant knew the fact
when at the time she swore it to be his; she having already
been delivered and having seen the child. The plaintiff was
granted a decree of nullity.[1] The same was held in Texas
of a case where it appeared that the plaintiff was but eighteen
years old ; that the parents had not given their consent to
her marriage ; that the marriage license required by law had
been procured by fraudulent representations and false swear-
ing by the defendant ; and that the plaintiff immediately upon
learning these facts repudiated the ceremony, and refused to
cohabit with the defendant.[2] In a case in New Hampshire,
it appeared that friends of the defendant, with whom she
was living, had by artifice procured the plaintiff to marry her,
knowing that she was insane, and the plaintiff being kept in
ignorance of the fact. A separation was granted him.[3] The
same was granted in England by reason of a forcible or fraudulent abduction of a ward of tender age by her guardian.[4] So,
too, where a marriage was effected under clandestine circumstances, from which fraud and circumvention were inferred,
between a person of weak and deranged mind and the
daughter of his trustee and solicitor, who had great influence
over him.[5] And again a decree was granted the plaintiff,
where it appeared that the ceremony was procured at the
instigation of the parents of the defendant, and that the plaintiff was but fourteen years of age at the time, and was under
their custody and control.[6] Other cases further illustrating

[1] Scott v. Shufeldt, 5 Paige, 43.
[2] Robertson v. Cole, 12 Tex. 356.
[3] Keyes v. Keyes, 22 N. H. 553.
[4] Harford v. Morris, 2 Hagg. Con. 423.
[5] Portsmouth v. Portsmouth, 1 Hagg. Ecc. 355.
[6] Hull v. Hull, 15 Jur. 710; s. c. 5 Eng. Law & E. 589.

the meaning of the term "fraud" in this connection are cited in the note.[1]

A distinction is sometimes suggested between cases of suits for nullity instituted before the marriage has been consummated by cohabitation, and the contrary;[2] but in principle it cannot be material whether the suit is brought before or after co-habitation, provided cohabitation was terminated as soon as the fraud was discovered, except perhaps in case of pregnancy or long lapse of time.[3] The fact that the wrongdoer has succeeded in gratifying passion, instead of making the situation permanent, should only aggravate his offence, and afford still stronger ground for obtaining a decree of separation.

It matters not how fraudulent may be the motives prompting the parties to marry, or what may be the consequences resulting from such marriage as affecting third persons : if the marriage be in compliance with the forms of law, and with the consent of the parties, they being capable of contracting marriage, no court has power, upon the application of a third person, either to dissolve the bonds of matrimony or to relieve against any of the consequences which result from the marriage.[4]

A gift whereby a husband actually and openly divests himself of his property, and of the enjoyment of it in his lifetime, in favor of children and others, making, according to the circumstances of his family, a just and reasonable present provision for persons having meritorious claims, and not with a view to defeat or diminish his wife's dower, is not invalid as being in fraud of her dower rights. The intent to defeat the widow must exist and operate at the time the conveyance

---

[1] Jolly v. McGregor, 3 Wils. & S. 85; Clark v. Field, 13 Vt. 460; Respublica v. Hevice, 3 Wheel. C. C. 505 ; Dalrymple v. Dalrymple, 2 Hagg. Con. 54, 104; s. c. 4 Eng. Ecc. 485.

[2] See Bishop, Marriage and Div., § 166.

[3] Cohabitation after knowledge would, of course, be evidence of assent to the fraud. See Robertson v. Cole, 12 Tex. 356, 365.

[4] McKinney v. Clarke, 2 Swan, 321.

is made.[1] To make gifts of real estate to children fraudulent
against a widow's right of dower, there must be a specific
intent to defraud in the making of such grants. Reasonable
advancements to children by a former wife are not fraudulent.[2]

Indeed, it is held by many authorities that a husband may
sell or give away his *personal* property, even with the avowed
purpose of preventing his wife from acquiring an interest
therein upon his death.[3] But such a sale or gift must be
bona fide and perfected. If the transfer by the husband be a
mere device or contrivance by which the husband, not parting with the absolute dominion over the property during his
life, seeks at his death to deny his widow her rights under the
law in such property, then it is invalid and ineffectual as to
her, so long as the property remains in the hands of the
donee or grantee, or in a purchaser with notice.[4] And if the
fraudulent donee or grantee has parted with the property to an
innocent purchaser for value, the widow may proceed against
the vendor for the proceeds of the sale. But a deed of trust,
it is held in Virginia, if it be not revocable by the grantor,
will not be treated as a will in disguise, by reason that all the
grantor's personal estate is thereby conveyed, and that he
reserves to himself the possession and control of the property
during his life.[5]

It has been decided in New York, notwithstanding some
dicta to the contrary,[6] that as between a wife and any other

[1] Reynolds *v.* Vance, 1 Heisk. 344 ; McIntosh *v.* Ladd, 1 Humph.
459 ; Littleton *v.* Littleton, 1 Dev. & B. 330.

[2] McIntosh *v.* Ladd, 1 Humph. 459.

[3] Smith *v.* Hines, 10 Fla. 258; Ford *v.* Ford, 4 Ala. 145; Griffith *v.*
Griffith, 4 Har. & McH. 101; Coomes *v.* Clements, 4 Har. & J. 481; Holmes
v. Holmes, 3 Paige, 363; Hays *v.* Henry, 1 Md. Ch. 337; Stone *v.* Stone,
18 Mo. 390; Davis *v.* Davis, 5 Mo. 183. See also Cameron *v.* Cameron,
10 Smedes & M. 398.

[4] Smith *v.* Hines, *supra.*

[5] Lightfoot *v.* Colgin, 5 Munf. 42.

[6] Moore *v.* New York, 8 N. Y. 110.

than the state, or its delegates or agents exercising the right of eminent domain, an inchoate right of dower in lands is a subsisting and valuable interest, for the protection of which she may resort to the courts.[1] And it has accordingly been held that, where a party had become the purchaser of dowable land by means of fraud, a right of action for such fraud was given, not only to the husband, but also to the wife, for the damages sustained by her in the loss of her inchoate right of dower.[2]

§ 3. OF CONFUSION OF GOODS.

The person whose property another has fraudulently mingled with his own has the right to take possession of the whole mass, for the purpose of separating and securing, or of disposing of, the portion belonging to himself.[3] By the rule of the Roman law, this was the extent of the injured party's rights. He was entitled to retain the whole or the proceeds in case of a sale, only upon making satisfaction for the value of the other party's share. The English law and the law of America go further, and give the entire property in such cases, without any account, to him whose property was originally invaded.[4] But, to produce such a result, the intermingling must be something more than intentional: it must be wrongful or fraudulent.[5] And the rule itself applies only to cases in which a separation is impossible or difficult. If the

---

[1] Simar v. Cannaday, 53 N. Y. 298.

[2] Ib. And it was held that the husband and wife might sue jointly for their respective damages.

[3] Stephenson v. Little, 11 Mich. 433; Wooley v. Campbell, 8 Vroom, 163; Ward v. Ayre, Croke Jac. 366; Ryder v. Hathaway, 21 Pick. 298; Buckley v. Gross, 3 Best & S. 566; 2 Kent, Com. 365; 2 Black. Com. 405.

[4] Hart v. Ten Eyck, 2 Johns. Ch. 62 ; 2 Kent, Com. 364.

[5] Ryder v. Hathaway, 21 Pick. 298; Spence v. Union Ins. Co., Law R. 3 C. P. 427, 437 ; Moore v. Bowman, 47 N. H. 494, 502; Hasseltine v. Stockwell, 30 Maine, 237; Bryant v. Ware, Ib. 295; Stephenson v. Little, 10 Mich. 433, 441.

goods can be easily distinguished and separated, as in the case of a mixture of articles of furniture,[1] no change of property takes place. So, too, if the articles, being alike, are of equal value, the injured party takes his given quantity, and not the whole. If, however, the articles be of different value or quality, and the original value be not distinguishable, the injured party takes the whole. It is for the party guilty of the fraud to distinguish his own property satisfactorily or lose it. The courts will not identify his property for him.[2] So, too, one who mingles the funds of another in his hands, put there to be loaned for the owner in the owner's name, and loans the same with his own money in his own name, commits a fraud in law, and in case of loss is bound to make the sum good to the injured party, though no actual fraud was intended.[3]

§ 4. OF ALTERATION OF WRITTEN INSTRUMENTS.

Where there has been an alteration or suppression of instruments which might have thrown light upon a suit, every thing will be presumed against the party by whom or by whose agent such alteration or suppression has been practised ; and every presumption will be made in favor of the *prima facie* rights of the other party.[4] In accordance with this principle,

---

[1] It is not necessarily evidence of a fraudulent intermingling of goods that a person occupying premises with another, upon which both have goods, refuses to designate to an officer (seeking to attach the latter's goods) which are his and which are not. Davis *v.* Stone, 120 Mass. 228. See Shumway *v.* Rutter, 8 Pick. 443, 448; Smith *v.* Sanborn, 6 Gray, 134.

[2] 2 Kent, Com. 365; Hart *v.* Ten Eyck, 2 Johns. Ch. 108; The Odin, 1 Ch. Rob. 248; Brackenridge *v.* Holland, 2 Blackf. 377; Willard *v.* Rice, 11 Met. 493; Beach *v.* Schmultz, 20 Ill. 185; Moore *v.* Bowman, 47 N. H. 494, 501.

[3] Cock *v.* Van Elten, 12 Minn. 522.

[4] Bowles *v.* Stewart, 1 Schoales & L. 222; Eyton *v.* Eyton, 1 Brown Parl. Cas. 153; Hampden *v.* Hampden, Ib. 252; Sepalino *v.* Twitty, Cas. in Ch. 76.

if a written agreement, whether under seal or not, be altered in a material part by the person claiming under it, he can neither recover upon the altered instrument nor avail himself of the true original form of the instrument.[1] Hence, a vendor of property, who has fraudulently and materially altered a promissory note given him for the price thereof, cannot resort to the original consideration, whether the note was received in payment or not.[2] But, further, if a bill or note be complete, any alteration in a material part, without the consent of the parties to it, renders it invalid even in the hands of an innocent holder for value.[3]

The fact that an altered note has been restored by the use of chemicals to its original form and amount, in the presence and without objection of the maker, does not revive its validity; and the maker may plead the alteration in bar of all liability on the note, even against a *bona fide* indorsee, since the note sued upon in such a case is not the note which the plaintiff purchased.[4] As to what constitutes such a material alteration of the instrument, the cases furnish many illustrations.

The addition of a promise to pay interest to a bill or note by a party thereto, without the consent of the acceptor or maker, renders the instrument invalid even in the hands of a *bona fide* holder for value; and there can be no recovery against the acceptor or maker, even for the amount of the paper as originally executed.[5] And it is not material that the altera-

---

[1] Pigot's Case, 11 Coke, 27; Newell v. Mayberry, 3 Leigh, 250.

[2] Smith v. Mace, 44 N. H. 553; Martindale v. Follett, 1 N. H. 95; Wheelock v. Freeman, 13 Pick. 164; Arrison v. Hamstead, 2 Barr, 101; White v. Huss, 32 Ala. 430; Whittier v. Frye, 10 Mo. 348.

[3] Wade v. Withington, 1 Allen, 561; Citizens' Bank v. Richmond, 121 Mass. 110; Holmes v. Trumper, 22 Mich. 427; Bank of Newark v. Crawford, 2 Houst. 282; Sudler v. Collins, Ib. 538; Woolfolk v. Bank of America, 10 Bush, 504, 517; Morehead v. Parkersburg Bank, 5 W. Va. 74; Burchfield v. Moore, 3 El. & B. 683.

[4] Citizens' Bank v. Richmond, 121 Mass. 110, citing Fay v. Smith, 1 Allen, 477, 479; Belknap v. National Bank, 100 Mass. 376; Draper v. Wood, 112 Mass. 315; Wood v. Steele, 6 Wall. 80.

[5] Holmes v. Trumper, 22 Mich. 427.

tion consisted merely·in filling a blank left for the *rate* of interest, if the sum inserted be larger than the paper would otherwise have carried.[1]

If the payee of a note without authority insert in it the words "to bear legal interest," this is a fraudulent alteration as to parties who signed it before the act, and no recovery can be had against them ; and in an action against a surety it has been held that the subsequent erasure of such words will not revive the contract.[2] The defendant's liability having once been discharged, it could not be revived without his consent.

So, too, an alteration of the date of a bill made after acceptance avoids the contract,[3] even as to a *bona fide* holder for value.[4] If, however, there be proof that the alteration was made with the assent of the acceptor, or of a subsequent assent by him, the bill will be good as to him, though invalid as to all other non-assenting parties.[5] Nor will it avoid the instrument to correct a mistake in the date.[6]

The effect of adding a place of payment to a bill of exchange payable generally, or at a different place from that added after acceptance, has been the subject of diverse rulings in England. In several of the earlier cases, it was

[1] Holmes *v.* Trumper, 22 Mich. 427. The instrument is complete notwithstanding the fact that it may end with the words " with interest at." The last word is to be disregarded in such a case; or, at all events, it authorizes the insertion only of the implied rate of interest. Ib. See Warrington *v.* Early, 2 El. & B. 763; Waterman *v.* Vose, 43 Maine, 504. The cases of Visher *v.* Webster, 8 Cal. 109, and Fisher *v.* Dennis, 6 Cal. 577, were somewhat doubted in Holmes *v.* Trumper.

[2] Lochnave *v.* Emmerson, 11 Bush, 69.

[3] Langton *v.* Lazarus, 5 Mees. & W. 629; Bowman *v.* Nicholl, 5 T. R. 537; Bathe *v.* Taylor, 15 East, 412; Kennedy *v.* Lancaster Bank, 18 Penn. St. 347.

[4] Master *v.* Miller, 4 T. R. 320; s. c. 2 H. Bl. 141; 5 T. R. 637 in Ex. Ch.

[5] Paton *v.* Winter, 1 Taunt. 420; Tarleton *v.* Shingler, 7 Com. B. 812. See Walter *v.* Hastings, 2 Chit. 121; s. c. 4 Campb. 223.

[6] Brutt *v.* Picard, Ryan & M. 37.

held that such an alteration was not material.[1]   Later authorities, however, are opposed to this view ;[2] and it is now held
in that country that such an alteration destroys the bill even
in the hands of a subsequent indorsee for value, without
notice of the fact.[3]   It is also settled law in this country that
if the holder of a bill of exchange alter the general acceptance
thereof by the addition of a place of payment, the instrument is vitiated as to all parties not consenting to the alteration.[4]   But if an accommodation indorser deliver an accepted
bill to the acceptor to enable him to raise money by its negotiation, and the acceptor change a general into a qualified
acceptance by designating a particular place of payment, the
indorser will still be liable to an innocent holder for value.[5]
So, too, if the maker of a note have express or implied
authority to consent for the other parties, as where they are
his partners, and the whole transaction is firm business, the
case will be different.[6]

It is held that the owner of a note or bill payable "at"
——, with a blank for the place of payment, has authority to
supply the name of such a place ; and, though this is done
contrary to the agreement of the parties, the paper, if negotiable, is good in the hands of a *bona fide* holder for value.

It has been held that the alteration of a contract which will

---

[1] Jacobs *v.* Hart, 6 Maule & S. 142; Stevens *v.* Lloyd, Moody & M.
292.

[2] Cowie *v.* Halsall, 4 Barn. & Ald. 197 ; Calvert *v.* Baker, 4 Mees. &
W. 417; Burchfield *v.* Moore, 3 El. & B. 683.   If the alteration be made
with the consent of the acceptor, he of course cannot afterwards object.
Walter *v.* Cubley, 2 Cromp. & M. 151; s. c. 4 Tyrwh. 87.

[3] Burchfield *v.* Moore, *supra.*

[4] Whitesides *v.* Northern Bank of Kentucky, 10 Bush, 501; Oakey
v. Wilcox, 3 How. (Miss.) 330; Alden *v.* Barbour, 3 Ind. 414; Pahlman
v. Taylor, 75 Ill. 629.

[5] Todd *v.* Bank of Kentucky, 3 Bush, 626 ; Rogers *v.* Poston, 1 Met.
(Ky.) 643 ; Whitesides *v.* Northern Bank of Ky., *supra.*

[6] Pahlman *v.* Taylor, 75 Ill. 629.

[7] Redlich *v.* Doll, 54 N. Y. 234.

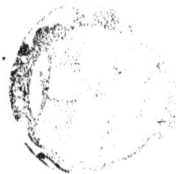

vitiate the agreement need not prejudice the party sought to
be charged.   An erasure of a seal, for example, after the
name of a surety, will operate to discharge the surety.   The
reason is that the identity of the instrument is thereby ob-
scured ; and the substitution of another in its place might be
possible, if the rule were not rigidly inforced.[1]   It has accordingly been decided that, if the holder of a note add the
name of another party to a note as surety, he cannot recover
thereon against the other parties.[2]   But it is held in England
that an addition of a signature to a note in the nature of an
indorsement, though put upon the face of the instrument, does
not invalidate it.[3]

If a note signed by several, in which it is declared that
" I promise to pay " be so altered by the payee without the
consent of the parties as to read " *We* promise to pay," it is
rendered invalid.[4]   So, also, it is a good defence to a note
originally made payable to order that it was subsequently
altered and made payable to bearer.[5]

Recovery can be had on a promissory note as originally
drawn, the original form being clear, notwithstanding an
alteration, if the alteration were not fraudulent, and the
rights of other parties have not intervened.   But if the alteration be made fraudulently or with an illegal intent, or if
any party has become interested in it or affected by it since
the alteration, the party who has changed it loses his right to
claim upon the original form of the instrument.[6]

---

[1] Organ *v.* Allison, 9 Chicago L. N. 250; 1 Greenleaf, Evidence,
§ 565.   See Crockett *v.* Thomason, 5 Sneed, 345; Blair *v.* Bank of Tennessee, 11 Humph. 84; Wood *v.* Steele, 6 Wall. 80.

[2] Shipp *v.* Suggett, 9 B. Mon. 5; Bower *v.* Briggs, 20 Ind. 139.

[3] *Ex parte* Yates, 2 DeG. & J. 191.

[4] Humphreys *v.* Guillow, 13 N. H. 385; Southwark Bank *v.* Gross,
35 Penn. St. 80.

[5] See Sherman *v.* Rollberg, 11 Cal. 38.   In this case, however, there
was a further defence of payment with constructive notice to the plaintiff.

[6] Kountz *v.* Kennedy, 63 Penn. St. 187.

When blanks are left in a bill or note, the party affixing his signature to such paper must suffer the loss, if his confidence should be violated and the blanks fraudulently filled.[1] So, too, if the paper has been so negligently drawn as by the leaving of spaces unfilled that alterations can be made without exciting suspicion, the loss must fall upon the party guilty of the negligence;[2] though of course the party committing the fraud would be liable both civilly and criminally.

A subsequent holder for value without notice can recover upon a negotiable instrument, notwithstanding an alteration of the same by a prior party, fraudulently made, if the alteration be immaterial;[3] though as against the wrongdoer the rule is otherwise.[4]

It has recently been held that the tearing off a condition written below a negotiable promissory note, on the same piece of paper, and referring to the note, was such an alteration of the whole contract as to render the note void in the hands of a *bona fide* holder for value.[5] Aside, however, from the two cases cited, the authorities do not support this proposition; and the subject deserves further consideration. As against the party who committed the act, or subsequent holders with notice, it is quite proper to treat the act as vitiating the note.[6] Further than this it is dangerous to go.

In regard to the fraudulent alteration of written instruments, a distinction has been taken between the effect of the act upon an executory and upon an executed contract. In the former case, the contract becomes null; in the latter case,

---

[1] Johnson v. Blasdale, 1 Smedes & M. 20; Clopton v. Elkin, 49 Miss. 95; Van Duzen v. Howe, 21 N. Y. 531; Ward v. Allen, 2 Met. 53; Bigelow, Estoppel, 394 (2d ed.), and cases cited.

[2] Young v. Grote, 4 Bing. 253; Trigg v. Taylor, 27 Mo. 547; Woolfolk v. Bank of America, 10 Bush, 504, 517.

[3] Commonwealth v. Emigrant Sav. Bank, 98 Mass. 12.

[4] Ib.; 1 Greenl. Evidence, § 568.

[5] Gerrish v. Glines, 56 N. H. 9; Benedict v. Cowden, 49 N. Y. 396.

[6] See Shaw v. First Meth. Soc., 8 Met. 223; Barnard v. Cushing, 4 Met. 230; Makepeace v. Harvard College, 10 Pick. 298; Fletcher v. Blodgett, 16 Vt. 26; Johnson v. Heagan, 23 Maine, 329.

at least in conveyances of real estate, the rule is otherwise. By the execution of the deed of grant, the property passes and vests in the grantee; and the destruction of the deed does not defeat the estate.[1] Hence a mortgagee may foreclose a mortgage, notwithstanding the fact that since the execution of the deed he has fraudulently added the signature of the grantor's wife in token of her relinquishment of dower.[2] But the contrary of this doctrine has been held in Illinois and New York.[3] And it has been held in Vermont that, if a lessee fraudulently alter his lease in a material part subsequently to its execution, he thereby destroys all his future rights under the lease, either to retain possession of the premises or to preclude the lessor from re-entering upon them.[4]

In order to render an instrument void on account of a material alteration, it is not necessary for all purposes to prove that the alteration was made with a fraudulent intent. The alteration after execution, without consent of the other party, avoids the instrument. It is only of moment to show that the alteration was done fraudulently, when there is a claim to a right of resort to the original indebtedness. If in such a case it appear that the instrument was fraudulently altered in a material particular, there can be no recovery either upon the instrument itself or upon the original debt for which it was given.[5]

Where the alteration of a writing is of such a character as to entirely defeat its operation for any purpose, as in the case of the erasure of the signature and seal to a deed, so that, admitting all to be true that appears upon the instrument, when produced it would be void in law, it should be explained to the court in the first instance, before being permitted to go

---

[1] Kendall v. Kendall, 12 Allen, 92 ; Hatch v. Hatch, 9 Mass. 307 ; Cheesman v. Whittemore, 23 Pick. 231; 1 Greenl. Evidence, § 568.

[2] Kendall v. Kendall, supra.

[3] Vogle v. Ripper, 34 Ill. 100 ; Waring v. Smith, 2 Barb. Ch. 135.

[4] Bliss v. McIntyre, 18 Vt. 466.

[5] Booth v. Powers, 56 N. Y. 22.

to the jury. In other cases, the instrument should be given in evidence, and go to the jury upon proof of its execution, notwithstanding the alteration; leaving the parties to such explanation and denial as may be offered.[1]

As to the time when an alteration of an instrument was made, it is material to know whether it was made before or after its execution by the party sought to be charged. Only in the latter case can the alteration defeat a recovery upon it, unless the defendant was blind or illiterate, and the alteration was made after reading.[2] And in any case the alteration, to affect the validity of the instrument, must be material.[3] In several of the States, it is held that there is a presumption, in the absence of evidence tending to show the facts, that the alteration was made before the execution of the instrument.[4] Elsewhere, it is held in the like case that the presumption is that the alteration was made at the time of the execution.[5] In New York, it is considered that where nothing appears but the fact of an erasure or interlineation in a material part of the instrument, of which no notice is taken at the time of the execution of the instrument, it is a suspicious circumstance, requiring explanation from the party producing it; and it is for the jury to say whether the explanation is satisfactory,[6] though by one of the cases this is not sufficient to exclude the instrument when offered in evidence.[7] In Massachusetts, it is held that there is no presumption either way as to the time when the alteration was made, but that

---

[1] Storer v. Ellis, 6 Ind. 152. See Newcomb v. Presbrey, 8 Met. 406.

[2] It is no defence to the acceptor of a bill against a *bona fide* holder for value that the same was fraudulently altered *before* the acceptance. Ward v. Allen, 2 Met. 53.

[3] Burnham v. Ayer, 35 N. H. 354; Cole v. Hills, 44 N. H. 227.

[4] Gooch v. Bryant, 1 Shep. 390.

[5] Beaman v. Russell, 20 Vt. 205.

[6] Jackson v. Osborn, 2 Wend. 559; Jackson v. Jacoby, 9 Cowen, 125; Herrick v. Malin, 22 Wend. 388.

[7] Smith v. McGowan, 3 Barb. 404.

the burden of proof is on the plaintiff offering the paper to
show that it was altered before the execution and delivery of
instrument.   The alteration may be such as to raise an inference that it preceded delivery, or slight evidence will be
received to show such fact.[1] It is held in Connecticut that
the burden of accounting for an erasure or alteration is not
necessarily upon the party producing the instrument.   Each
case, it is said, must depend upon its own circumstances.[2]

In New Hampshire, it is said to be the proper rule, in regard
to the alteration of a written contract, that the instrument,
with all the circumstances of its nature and history, the
appearance of the alteration, the possible or probable motives
to the alteration, or against such act, on the part of all persons connected with it or in whose possession it may have
been, and the effect of the alteration upon the rights and
obligations of the parties respectively, ought to be submitted
to the jury ; who should find from all these facts whether the
alteration was made before or after its execution, and consequently whether it rendered the instrument invalid or not.
Whether the handwriting of the alteration is the same with
that of the body of the instrument, whether it is the same
with that of the signature, whether the ink is the same or
different, whether from the appearance the body of the
instrument and the alteration were made at the same or at a
different time, whether the party claiming or the party sought
to be charged is to be benefited by it, whether the alteration
was made before or after its execution, and if after by whom
and for what purpose, — these are all questions for the consideration of the jury.[3] Upon the usual proof of the execution
of the instrument, it should, under this practice, be admitted
in evidence, without reference to the character of any alteration upon it, leaving all testimony relating to such alteration

[1] Ely v. Ely, 6 Gray, 439; Wilde v. Armsby, 6 Cush. 314.
[2] Hayden v. Goodnow, 40 Conn. 164; Bailey v. Taylor, 11 Conn. 541.
[3] Cole v. Hills, 44 N. H. 227, 234.

to be given to the jury with proper instructions upon the facts.[1] But if the jury cannot satisfactorily find when the alteration was made upon such facts, or if there be an entire absence of evidence and of circumstances, both in the instrument and in the evidence *aliunde*, from which an inference can be legitimately drawn as to the time when the alteration was made (an improbable condition of things), then, according to the rule in New Hampshire, the presumption arises that the alteration was made *after* the execution of the instrument.[2]

An alteration of a written instrument by a stranger, without the privity of a party interested, is a mere spoliation, and does not affect the rights or liabilities of the parties.[3]

That a portion of an indorsement signed by the defendant is written in different ink and handwriting from the rest does not afford sufficient evidence of a fraudulent alteration to require the plaintiff to explain the same.[4] Nor is a mere disfigurement or blot upon a writing, the result of accident, a material alteration.[5]

A contract may be evidenced by several writings, each constituting part of the whole undertaking; and, where this is the case, the material alteration of any of the writings, without consent, avoids the whole.[6]

§ 5. OF RESULTING TRUSTS.

Equity will relieve against a fraudulent purchase by converting the purchaser guilty of the fraud into a trustee for

[1] Cole *v.* Hills, 44 N. H. 227, 234; Beaman *v.* Russell, 20 Vt. 205; ailey *v.* Taylor, 11 Conn. 531.

[2] Cole *v.* Hills, *supra;* Hills *v.* Barnes, 11 N. H. 395 ; Burnham *v.* Ayer, 35 N. H. 354.

[3] State *v.* Berg, 50 Ind. 496 ; Cochran *v.* Nebeker, 48 Ind. 459 ; 1 Greenl. Evidence, § 566.

[4] Wilson *v.* Harris, 35 Iowa, 507 ; Jones *v.* Ireland, 4 Iowa, 63; Auld *v.* Fleming, 7 Iowa, 143.

[5] Organ *v.* Allison, 9 Chicago L. N. 250 (Sup. Court, Tenn , 1877).

[6] Meyer *v.* Huncke, 55 N. Y. 412.

the person injured.[1] Thus, one who procures and puts on
record a deed of land in fraud of the rights of a prior grantee
whose deed is not recorded becomes a trustee of the legal
title for him. And if such title, after a transfer to an innocent purchaser, revests in such fraudulent grantee, the trust
reattaches.[2]

Where one person advances the purchase-money for land,
and a deed is taken in the name of another, a resulting trust is
created by operation of law in favor of the party advancing the
purchase-money, and parol evidence may be received to prove
these facts ; which, when established, take the case out of the
operation of the Statute of Frauds.[3] In accordance with this
principle, a bill to set aside a conveyance obtained from a
third person, or to compel the defendant to convey the title
acquired from such third person, will be upheld where it appears that the title acquired by the defendant was in fraud
of the plaintiff's rights and contrary to the duty owed to the
plaintiff by the defendant. Thus, in the case cited,[4] the defendant had assigned to the plaintiff for value a contract for
the purchase of land from a railroad company. Subsequently,
by false representations that he had not parted with his rights
under this contract, the defendant obtained a conveyance of
the land from the railroad company. The plaintiff now filed
a bill praying that this conveyance be set aside, or that the
defendant be compelled to convey to him ; and on demurrer
the bill was sustained.

The ground of the doctrine of resulting trusts in the purchase of real property is that the party in whose favor such
trust arises has paid his money for the property in question,
and an attempt is made to defraud him of the fruits of it. If,
therefore, the party who sets up a resulting trust made no

[1] Jenckes v. Cook, 9 R. I. 520.
[2] Troy City Bank v. Wilcox, 24 Wis. 671.
[3] Hays v. Hollis, 8 Gill, 357, and cases cited *infra, passim.*
[4] Blakeslee v. Starring, 34 Wis. 538.

payment, he cannot be permitted to show by parol evidence that the purchase was made for his benefit or on his account. Nor would a subsequent advance of money to the purchaser, after the purchase is complete, alter the case.[1] But it is suggested that the case may be different when a verbal agreement is clearly proved between two persons to make a joint purchase, though no part of the price be actually paid at the time by him whose name is not in the articles or deed, but subsequent payment of his share is made. In such case, it is possible that the fulfilment of the bargain will cause relation back to the original agreement, and raise a trust.[2]

Of course, no resulting trust can arise where there is no agreement or understanding between the person effecting the purchase and him whose money is used that the purchase is to be made for the latter; and a *fortiori* where such purchaser uses part of his own money in the transaction.[3]

In order to raise a resulting trust, the principal's money must have been used at the time of the purchase.[4] After the legal title has been conveyed to one who agreed to buy for another, the application of the latter's money to pay notes for the purchase-money creates no resulting trust in favor of the other. The trust must attach, if ever, at the time of the conveyance; for it is the money which has gone to the vendor as the inducement for the title with which he parts that creates the equity in favor of him who advances it.[5]

The payment of *money* on the part of him who claims the existence of a trust is not necessary. If he be already entitled to a conveyance and employ another to procure it for him, and such person takes it in his own name, he will be

[1] Botsford v. Burr, 2 Johns. Ch. 405; Nixon's Appeal, 63 Penn. St. 279.

[2] Nixon's Appeal, *supra*.   [3] Coppage v. Barnett, 34 Miss. 621.

[4] Hollida v. Shoop, 4 Md. 465.

[5] McCarroll v. Alexander, 48 Miss. 128; White v. Carpenter, 2 Paige, Ch. 238 ; Botsford v. Burr, 2 Johns. Ch. 405; Alexander v. Tams, 13 Ill. 325; Walter v. Klock, 55 Ill. 362.

treated as trustee for the other. Thus, where a person entitled to soldiers' bounty land employed the defendants' grantor to obtain the warrant for him, and he procured the land to be located in his own name, he was considered as holding in trust for the person employing him.[1]

If only part of the purchase-money be paid by the agent, there will result a trust only *pro tanto*.[2] Property conveyed to one, in consideration of funds belonging jointly to himself and another, is held in trust for the latter to the extent of his part of the funds.[3]

The doctrine that a resulting trust may arise upon payment of part of the purchase price prevails only where the part-payment was made for some specific part or distinct interest in the estate; that is, for a specific share, as a tenancy in common, or a joint-tenancy of one-half, one-quarter, or other particular fraction of the whole; or for a particular interest, as a life estate or tenancy for years, or remainder in the whole. A general contribution of a sum of money toward the entire purchase is not sufficient.[4]

A trust will result in favor of one for whom the actual purchaser agreed to buy and hold, though the money paid for the land was loaned by the trustee to the *cestui que trust* for the purpose of the purchase. And, upon a dispute between the two as to whose money was used in effecting the purchase, the *cestui que trust* may show by parol that though the money, or part of it, was paid over to the grantor by the grantee, the sum so paid was paid on a loan for the alleged *cestui que trust*.[5]

---

[1] Smith v. Wright, 49 Ill. 403.

[2] Cecil Bank v. Snively, 23 Md. 261 ; Case v. Codding, 38 Cal. 191 ; Buck v. Swazey, 35 Maine, 41.   [3] Buck v. Swazey, *supra*.

[4] McGowan v. McGowan, 14 Gray, 119 ; Buck v. Warren, Ib. 122, note; Crop v. Norton, 2 Atk. 74 ; Sayre v. Townsends, 15 Wend. 647 ; White v. Carpenter, 2 Paige, 217 ; Perry v. McHenry, 13 Ill. 227; Baker v. Vining, 30 Maine, 121. The case of Jenkins v. Eldridge, 3 Story, 181, was doubted and distinguished.

[5] McDonough v. O'Niel, 113 Mass. 92 ; Kendall v. Mann, 11 Allen,

While proof of payment of money as between strangers will generally suffice to raise a presumption that a trust was intended, no such presumption arises where the title is taken in the name of a wife or child; and this principle extends to cases where, without legal relationship, the person paying the money stands, or assumes to stand, *in loco parentis* to the grantee. The presumption in such a case is that, in paying for the land to be granted to the child so situated, the grant is intended as a donation or as an advancement;[1] and the burden will rest upon the person seeking to establish the trust to overcome the presumption in favor of the legal title.[2] A wife, contributing of her own means to the purchase of land by her husband, who takes the title in his own name, she not insisting upon any agreement for repayment, or the conveyance of any interest in the land to her, will, however, upon her husband's death, be conclusively presumed to have intended the amount of her contribution as a gift to her husband.[3]

If a person hold out inducements to another whose estate is largely encumbered that he will furnish the means for him to redeem, and thereby prevent him from looking elsewhere, and in the mean time purchase such incumbrances himself and cut off the redemption, he will not be allowed to retain his advantage.[4] So, too, if a party whose property is sold under a right of redemption within a certain time be prevented from redeeming within the time by the fraud and artifice of the purchaser, a court of equity will permit him to redeem.[5]

15; Blodgett *v.* Hildreth, 103 Mass. 484; Jackson *v.* Stevens, 108 Mass. 94. See Burleigh *v.* White, 64 Maine, 23.

[1] Waterman *v.* Seeley, 28 Mich. 77.

[2] Cotton *v.* Wood, 25 Iowa, 43; Livingston *v.* Livingston, 2 Johns. Ch. 540; Guthrie *v.* Gardner, 19 Wend. 414; 2 Story, Equity, § 1203.

[3] Campbell *v.* Campbell, 21 Mich. 438.

[4] Wilson *v.* Eggleston, 27 Mich. 257. See Laing *v.* McKee, 13 Mich. 124.

[5] Guinn *v.* Locke, 1 Head, 110.

Upon a similar principle, when a sale under a mortgage or deed of trust made to secure payment of a debt is effected by the creditor's lulling the debtor into security through a promise not to sell without first making demand, equity will set aside the sale as against the creditor and purchasers with notice, and permit the debtor to redeem.[1] So, likewise, a resulting trust arises in favor of a lady whom a relative offers to attend at a public sale, where he fails to do so, but informs other relatives of the lady that he will attend and bid for her, and then bids in the property for himself. And, if the lady offer to comply with the terms of the sale, he will be bound to convey to her.[2]

A resulting trust will not arise where the effect would be to accomplish a violation of law. Thus, if A cannot by law acquire title to certain property, the law will not raise a trust in his favor if he put money into the hands of B with which to buy the property in the latter's name, which B does so buy.[3]

The authorities relating to secret trusts in favor of charities have established the rule that if an absolute estate be devised, but upon a secret trust assented to by the devisee, either expressly or impliedly, by knowledge and silence before the death of the testator, a court of equity will fasten a trust upon him upon the ground of fraud ; and consequently the Statute of Mortmain (where the testator dies within the period limited by that statute) will avoid the devise, if the trust be in favor of a charity. But if the devisee have no part in the devise, and no knowledge of it until after the death of the testator, there is no ground upon which equity can fasten such a trust upon him, even though, after it comes to his knowledge, he should express an intention of conforming to the wishes of the testator.[4]

[1] Clarkson v. Creely, 40 Mo. 114; s. c. 35 Mo. 95.

[2] Rives v. Lawrence, 41 Ga. 283.

[3] Alsworth v. Cordtz, 31 Miss. 32.

[4] Schultz's Appeal, 80 Penn. St. 396. "Equity raises a trust for the

A bill charging that the defendant, by false representations and other fraudulent means, had prevailed upon a party to convey to him a valuable copper mine, which party had by parol, to the defendant's knowledge, agreed to convey it to the plaintiff, cannot, it is held, be maintained.[1] The parol agreement was invalid by the Statute of Frauds; and hence the defendant had not interfered with any of the plaintiff's rights. But it may be doubted if a right of action does not accrue against a party who fraudulently prevents a third party from carrying out with the plaintiff an agreement which was not binding upon him. It is clear that no one but a creditor has a right to interfere with another's bestowing a gratuity upon a party.[2]

The trust will follow the estate into the hands of all purchasers with notice, and of volunteers. A father having made a voluntary gift to his daughter afterwards sought to defeat the same, and to this end had the property levied upon and sold for his debts. It was bought in by his agent, and under the father's direction was conveyed to other children of his. Such children were declared trustees for the daughter.[3] A resulting trust, further, will survive against an heir of the trustee, and the heir may be compelled to convey.[4]

It has been laid down in Pennsylvania that if one of two contracting parties insist upon a certain stipulation, and desire it to be made part of the written agreement, and the other, by his promise to conform to it as if inserted in the written agreement, prevent its insertion, this is a fraud, and chancery will enforce the agreement as if the stipulation had been inserted.[5] On the other hand, it has been held in the

purpose of preventing a fraud upon the statute precisely upon the same conditions as a trust is raised to prevent a fraud upon an individual." Ib. p. 403, opinion of auditor, adopted by the court.

[1] Lee v. McKenzie, 3 Jones, Eq. 232.   [2] Bigelow's L. C. Torts, 303.
[3] Uzzle v. Wood, 1 Jones, Eq. 226.
[4] Brown v. Dwelley, 45 Maine, 52.
[5] Overton v. Tracey, 14 Serg. & R. 326; Thompson v. White, 1 Dall.
8

same State that, where there is nothing more in the transaction than is implied from the violation of a parol agreement,
equity will not decree the purchaser a trustee.[1] It is said in
explanation of these latter cases that the element was wanting in them of a promise at the time to execute a declaration
of trust in writing, upon the faith of which promise the main
contract was made.[2] We must then understand the court of
Pennsylvania as holding that the breach of a parol promise
made contemporaneously with the execution of a contract of
which it is intended to be part, and to which it is a principal
inducement, is a fraud, justifying a court of equity in de-
creeing a specific execution of such oral agreement under
the Statute of Frauds.

The rule in England appears to go quite as far. Thus, it
has there been held that where a deed (purporting to have
been executed for a valuable consideration) was made on the
faith of an oral promise that the grantee should hold the land
for the grantor, a trust arose thereby, which would be enforced in equity.[3] So, too, it is there held that if an agent,
instructed to buy land for his principal, purchase in his own
name for himself, equity will compel a conveyance to the
principal, though the engagement between the agent and his
principal was verbal.[4] But it is otherwise if a conveyance
has already been executed by the vendor to the agent.[5] The

424; Christ v. Diffenbach, 1 Serg. & R. 464; Oliver v. Oliver, 4 Rawle,
144 ; Robertson v. Robertson, 9 Watts, 34; Wolford v. Herrington, 74
Penn. St. 311.

[1] Jackman v. Ringland, 4 Watts & S. 149 ; Barnet v. Dougherty, 32
Penn. St. 371.

[2] Wolford v. Herrington, 74 Penn. St. 311, 315. See further Sei-
christ's Appeal, 66 Penn. St. 237; Beagle v. Wentz, 55 Penn. St. 374;
Hoge v. Hoge, 1 Watts, 163; Lingenfelter v. Richey, 58 Penn. St. 485.

[3] Haigh v. Kaye, Law R. 7 Ch. 473; Childers v. Childers, 4 DeG. &
J. 482; Davies v. Otty, 35 Beav. 208.

[4] Heard v. Pilley, Law R. 4 Ch. 548.

[5] Ib.; Bartlett v. Pickersgill, 4 East, 577, note. See Pember v.
Mathers, 1 Brown C. C. 54; Clarke v. Grant, 14 Ves. 519, 524.

distinction taken is between executed and executory contracts between the agent and the vendor, — a distinction not easily understood. If the conduct of the agent be fraudulent in the one case (so as to take the agreement out of the statute), it is equally so in the other; since it consists in the same action, with the additional wrong, in the second case, of consummating the bargain with the vendor.

There is strong authority for the position that, if the principal or employer were already interested in the land bought in the name of the agent, the former shall be entitled to the benefit of the latter's purchase, if such be the agreement, even though the agent furnish the entire purchase-money. Such a case stands upon as good a footing as the case of a purchase by the agent of land for himself out of money furnished by the principal, when the principal had no previous interest in the premises. In either case, a different rule would permit the agent to make use of his employer's property, in order to get a title to property with little or no outlay of his own. In the one case, the agent would be permitted to seize upon and retain to his own use the property (that is, the equitable interest, which might be very large) of his principal against the latter's will; in the other case, he merely converts the principal's money voluntarily placed in his hands. The former is certainly none the less a fraud than the latter. Accordingly, we find it laid down in New York that if a purchaser under a foreclosure sale undertake to purchase for the benefit of the mortgagor, and thus acquire the title at a price greatly below its value, he will be deemed the trustee of the party for whom he has undertaken the purchase; and, on tender to him of the purchase price paid and interest, he will be compelled to convey the property to the mortgagor, though the undertaking to purchase was verbal.[1]

---

[1] Ryan v. Dox, 34 N. Y. 307; Brown v. Lynch, 1 Paige, 147; Sandford v. Norris, 4 Abb. App. Cas. 144; Levy v. Brush, 45 N. Y. 589, 596; Glass v. Hulbert, 102 Mass. 24, 39; Church v. Kidd, 3 Hun, 254, 265.

It has also been held by most of the courts of this country
that parol evidence is admissible to show that an absolute
conveyance was in reality intended as a security for a sum of
money loaned or other obligation incurred or due at the time
the deed was executed; and that equity will compel the grantee
to respect this intention, and to reconvey the premises upon
tender of the amount of the debt.[1] And this is true whether
the omission was by fraud on the part of the grantee, or by design, upon confidence reposed by the grantor in the grantee;[2]
though this position has not been accepted by some of our
courts,[3] and, so far as it may be looked upon as the generally
established law, should probably be treated as an admitted
(though not very intelligible) exception to the rule concerning the exclusion of parol evidence varying the terms of
a written contract, rather than as an exception to the operation of the Statute of Frauds. For the breach of a parol
agreement to reconvey premises (granted absolutely) upon
payment of the debt thus secured is as much a fraud as

See, further, Carr v. Carr, 52 N. Y. 251 ; Cipperly v. Cipperly, 4 Thomp.
& C. 342 ; Soggins v. Heard, 31 Miss. 426.

[1] Hodges v. Tennessee Ins. Co., 8 N. Y. 416 ; Despond v. Walbridge,
15 N. Y. 374 ; Taylor v. Luther, 2 Sum. 228 ; 4 Kent, 143.

[2] Taylor v. Luther, 2 Sum. 228.

[3] It is held in several of the States that in order to convert a purchaser
who takes a deed absolute on its face into a trustee for another, and
to convert the conveyance into a mere security for money loaned or
advanced, it must be alleged and proved that the clause of redemption
was omitted by reason of ignorance, mistake, fraud, or undue advantage ;
and the intention must be established by facts *dehors* the conveyance,
which are inconsistent with an absolute conveyance. Glisson v. Hill,
.2 Jones, Eq. 256. Brothers v. Herrill, Ib. 209 ; Cook v. Gudger. Ib. 172 ;
Lowell v. Barrett, Busb. Eq. 50 ; Brown v. Carson, Ib. 272 ; Clement v.
Clement, 1 Jones, Eq. 184 ; Briggs v. Morris, Ib. 193 ; Lamb v. Pigford,
Ib. 195 ; Taylor v. Taylor, Ib. 246 ; Thomas v. McCormick, 9 Dana, 108 ;
Franklin v. Roberts, 2 Ired. Eq. 560 ; Kelly v. Bryan, 6 Ired. Eq. 283,
See Shay v. Norton, 48 Ill. 100 ; Kent v. Lasley, 24 Wis. 654. An abso-
lute bill of sale of goods cannot at law be shown to have been intended as
a mortgage or other security. Harper v. Ross, 10 Allen, 332. *Secus*, of
a bill of parcels. Ib. ; Hildreth v. O'Brien, Ib. 104.

exists in the case of a refusal by an agent to convey to his principal whose money he has used in the purchase, or where the agent has bought under a foreclosure for the benefit of a mortgagor.[1] The latter case especially is like the case under consideration. To refuse relief to the party claiming the equitable right to the property would be to allow the grantee, against his express promise, to confiscate the grantor's property. This is the only element of fraud in any of the cases against agents.

Aside from cases of the above character, where the party claiming the existence of the trust had an interest cognizable by a court of equity or of law, prior to the parol engagement, we apprehend that the true rule is, that the mere breach of a parol agreement cannot be regarded as a fraud so as to take the case out of the statute.[2] If the rule were otherwise, and were then to be carried to its legitimate result, one of the vicious consequences would be that the salutary rule against the admission of parol evidence to vary the terms of a written contract would in a great measure be overturned. Fraud in one of the parties to a contract is everywhere recognized as a ground for opening the terms of a written agreement to parol proof, even when not wholly defeating the existence or binding force of the contract. But, under the above rule, it would only be necessary for one of the parties to prove the existence of a contemporaneous parol agreement which was one of the inducements to the written contract, and the breach of such parol agreement, to make out a case of fraud sufficient to overturn or modify the written contract. The unsoundness of the proposition itself, in the presence of the rule as to parol evidence, is apparent upon a moment's reflection. Evidence of fraud opens the terms of a written contract to the proof (in the case under consideration) of a parol contemporaneous agreement which has been broken by

---

[1] Compare Glass v. Hulbert, 102 Mass. 24, 39.

[2] Rogers v. Simmons, 55 Ill. 76; Merritt v. Brown, 6 C. E. Green, 401.

the opposite party ; or, in other words, evidence of this parol
agreement is only admissible upon proof of fraud. But, to
prove this fraud, this parol undertaking and its breach are
alone offered in evidence. That is, the very thing to be
proved is offered in evidence as the means of establishing
its own admissibility as evidence.[1]

This view is sustained by the most of our authorities.[2]
Indeed, few if any, when carefully examined, will be found,
apart from the *dicta* of the judges, to be opposed to it. A
deed in common form, containing a declaration of the use to
the grantee and his heirs in the *habendum*, will conclude the
parties, and exclude evidence of any resulting trust to the
grantor.[3] And the authorities generally are equally clear
that, in cases in which parol evidence would not be excluded
to prove the oral agreement (as where there has been no con-

[1] " It is not enough,'' says Mr. Hare, in 2 Lead. Cas. in Eq. 1015
(4th Am. ed.), " that the complainant was induced to change his
position for the worse by a promise which has not been fulfilled. It must
appear that the promise was used as a means of imposition or deceit.
If the case taken as a whole is one of fraud, the promise may be received
in evidence as one of the steps by which the fraud was accomplished.
But, until the fraud appears, there is no room for the admission of the
promise. To deduce the fraud from the contract, and then give effect
to the contract on the score of fraud, is obviously reasoning in a vicious
circle; or, as the rule has been stated in Maryland, the parol evidence
must show that the contract had its inception in the fraudulent contrivance of the party against whom the relief is sought, and not merely
that he is making an unjust use of the contract to keep an advantage
obtained through the reliance of the opposite party on his good faith and
fair dealing. Lamborn v. Watson, 6 Har. & J. 252; Wilson v. Watts,
9 Md. 461.'' See, further, Montecute v. Maxwell, 1 P. Wms. 618; Mc-
Donald v. May, 1 Rich. Eq. 91; Schmitt v. Heywood, 2 Rich. Eq. 162;
Johnson v. La Motte, 6 Rich. Eq. 356.

[2] Blodgett v. Hildreth, 103 Mass. 484; Walker v. Locke, 5 Cush. 90.

[3] Blodgett v. Hildreth, *supra;* Squire v. Horder, 1 Paige, 494; Phil-
brook v. Delano, 29 Maine, 410; Farrington v. Barr, 36 N. H. 86;
Graves v. Graves, 29 N. H. 129 ; Rogers v. Simmons, 55 Ill. 76 ; Merritt
v. Brown, 6 C. E. Green, 401. The 7th section of the English Statute of
Frauds as to trusts was not in force in Pennsylvania when Murphy v.
Hubert, 7 Barr, 420, was decided.

veyance between the parties to the alleged trust), the fraud
which will give jurisdiction to compel a performance of the
parol trust must consist in something more than a mere breach
of the parol undertaking in question.[1]

Where a gift or bequest to a volunteer is procured through
a promise to hold the premises in whole or in part for a third
person whom the giver desires to benefit, a trust will arise
ex maleficio, if the promise be not fulfilled.[2] But the grantee
or devisee is charged with the trust not by reason merely of the
oral promise, but because of the fact that by means of such
promise he has induced the transfer of the property to himself.[3]

That a devisee taking property upon a parol promise to
hold for the benefit of a third person may be compelled, at
the suit of such third person, to convey the intended interest,
is clear.[4] A more difficult question arises where with such
devisee there is associated another devisee, who claims that
he had no knowledge or intimation at the time of the execution of the will, or before the death of the testator, of such
intended trust. Parol evidence, however, though amounting
to no more than strong inference of knowledge of the trust,
has been held admissible in a case in which the will had been
advised and drawn upon the suggestion of the other devisee,
who fully admitted the trust.[5] The case does not go to the
extent of allowing evidence of a trust as to the refusing
devisee, where there was *no* evidence of his knowledge of the
alleged intention of the testator. It might well be doubted
if evidence could be received in such a case. The act of the

---

[1] Merritt *v.* Brown, 6 C. E. Green, 401; Marshman *v.* Conklin, Ib.
546 ; Rogers *v.* Simmons, 55 Ill. 76, and cases above cited.

[2] Russell *v.* Jackson, 10 Hare, 206; Tee *v.* Ferris, 2 Kay & J. 357;
Jones *v.* Badley, Law R. 3 Ch. 362; McCormick *v.* Grogan, Law R 4
H. L. 82; Glass *v.* Hulbert, 102 Mass. 24; Gaither *v.* Gaither, 3 Md. Ch.
158; Hooker *v.* Axford, 33 Mich. 453; 2 Lead. Cas. in Eq. 978 (4th Am.
ed.); Cipperly *v.* Cipperly, 4 Thomp. & C. 342.

[3] Glass *v.* Hulbert, 102 Mass. 24, 39.

[4] Hooker *v.* Axford, 33 Mich. 453 ; *post*, pp. 126, 127.   [5] Ib.

devisee in claiming to hold the property, notwithstanding the admission of his co-devisee, would not be a fraud. Fraud in such cases arises only when the devisee has consented to hold in trust; such consent being presumed to be the reason for omitting the declaration of trust from the will.

§ 6. OF WILLS.

Any person possessed of capacity sufficient to enable him to attend to his ordinary business is capable of making a valid will.[1] Mere weakness of understanding, indeed, if not excessive,[2] will not be sufficient of itself to invalidate a will. If the testator be capable of comprehending the nature of the dispositions made, he has the testamentary capacity.[3] It is not necessary that the testator should possess a knowledge sufficient for the transaction of general business: the ability to comprehend the ordinary routine of his own business is all at most that can be required.[4] Indeed, if the testator understand fully what he is doing when making his will, — that is, when he executes it, and (if such be the fact) that he has a family, and the relations in which he stands to it in fact and in law, that he has property and that he knows of what it consists, — it is said that he can make a will.[5] It is even held that long-continued habits of drunkenness do not raise the presumption of incompetency in a testator;[6] and that a will made by an habitual drunkard, who is under the influence of

---

[1] Ford v. Ford, 7 Humph. 92; Coleman v. Robertson, 17 Ala. 84.

[2] Capacity to make a will may accompany a great degree of mental imbecility. Daniel v. Daniel, 39 Penn. St. 192.

[3] Dornick v. Reichenback, 10 Serg. & R. 84; Elliott's Will, 2 J. J. Marsh. 340; Weir v. Fitzgerald, 2 Bradf. 42; Abraham v. Wilkins, 17 Ark. 292.

[4] Kinne v. Kinne, 9 Conn. 102; Stubbs v. Houston, 33 Ala. 555.

[5] Cordrey v. Cordrey, 1 Houst. 269. See also Stancell v. Kenan, 33 Ga. 56.

[6] Gardner v. Gardner, 22 Wend. 526.

intoxicating liquor at the time of its execution, is not void, unless he is under such a degree of excitement as to vitiate his judgment.[1] Indeed, it is held in New York that mere weakness of mind in a testator will not avoid his will, unless there is a total want of understanding.[2] And it is laid down in Kentucky that it is not necessary that a testator should have such strength of mind as would be necessary to enable him to traffic with and mortgage his property.[3] In Vermont and South Carolina, it is held that there need not be as high intellectual power in a testator as is necessary for a person making a contract;[4] while in Maryland, on the other hand, it is declared by statute that a person who has not the capacity to make a contract cannot make a will.[5] But this subject need not be further pursued. It involves the construction of various and diverse statutes, and is introduced here as merely introductory to what follows.

When it has been proved that a will has been executed with due solemnities by a person of competent understanding, and apparently a free agent, the burden of proving that it was executed under undue influence rests upon the party who alleges it;[6] or at least he must show facts from which the court would be justified in treating the circumstances attending the bounty as suspicious. Further, in order to set aside the will of a person of sound mind, it is not sufficient to show that the circumstances attending its execution are consistent with the hypothesis that it was obtained by undue influence. It must be shown that they are inconsistent with a contrary hypothesis.[7]

A will obtained by fraud is invalid; and fraud in this con-

---

[1] Peck v. Cary, 27 N. Y. 9. But see Nussear v. Arnold, 13 Serg. & R. 323.

[2] Blanchard v. Nestle, 3 Denio, 37.

[3] Howard v. Coke, 7 B. Mon. 655.

[4] Converse v. Converse, 21 Vt. 168; Kirkwood v. Gordon, 7 Rich. 474.

[5] Davis v. Calvert, 5 Gill & J. 269.

[6] Boyse v. Rossborough, 6 H. L. Cas. 2, 49.   [7] Ib. p. 51.

nection is used both in the sense of deceit, whether of words
or of artifice, and of undue influence. With regard to what
deceit is necessary to annul a testament, the question is left
to the judgment of the court upon comparing the deceit with
the capacity or understanding of the testator.[1] Thus, on an
issue to try the validity of a will impeached on the ground
of imposition upon and imbecility of the testator, evidence
was admitted of the false representations of the principal
devisee as to the character of the wife of another who was
equally entitled by relationship to the testator's bounty.[2]

Fraud and imposition upon weakness are sufficient ground
for setting aside a will, whether of real or of personal property.[3] As to imposition, it is laid down that though a man
may have a mind of sufficient soundness and discretion to
manage his own affairs in general, still, if such a dominion or
influence be obtained over him as to prevent his exercising
that discretion in the making a will, he cannot be considered
as having such a disposing mind as will give it effect.[4]

In cases of weakness of mind arising from the near approach
of death or otherwise, strong evidence may be required that
the contents of the will were known to the testator executing
the will at such time,[5] and that the execution was his spontaneous act.[6] A suspicion is justly entertained of a will conferring large benefits on the person by whom or by whose
agent it was prepared,[7] or of a will in favor of a medical attendant in whose house the testator resided.[8] But it seems
that such suspicion goes no further than to necessitate some-

[1] 1 Wms. Executors, 38 (2d Am. ed.).

[2] Dietrick v. Dietrick, 5 Serg. & R. 207.

[3] 1 Jarman, Wills, 30 (3d Eng. ed.).

[4] Mountain v. Bennett, 1 Cox, 355; Jarman, ut supra.

[5] Mitchell v. Thomas, 6 Moore, P. C. 137; s. c. 12 Jur. 967; Durnell
v. Corfield, 8 Jur. 915. But see Reece v. Pressey, 2 Jur. N. s. 380.

[6] Tribe v. Tribe, 13 Jur. 793.

[7] Paske v. Ollat, 2 Phillim. 323; Durling v. Loveland, 2 Curt. 225;
Baker v. Batt, 2 Moore, P. C. 317.

[8] Jones v. Godrich, 5 Moore, P. C. 16.

what stricter proof as to the testator's *capacity*, though not as to his knowledge of the contents of the will.[1] Where, however, the capacity of the testator is duly proved, he will be presumed cognizant of the contents of the will.[2]

Proof of previous instructions corresponding with the contents of the will, or a complete recognition of every part of it, as the free act of the decedent, is, it is held, indispensable in every case of diminished mental power, accompanied by suspicious circumstances as to the origin and execution of the instrument. Mere acknowledgment of the will is not sufficient: it must appear to be the result of the decedent's own suggestions, free from any influence.[3]

With regard to the matter of control and undue influence, a manifest distinction exists between them. Control is more easily capable of a description approaching to a definition, because it necessarily imports something of the nature of duress or fear. On the question of undue influence, especially in the case of a wife, very little of exact statement is to be found in the books, or could be expected to be found. Some accepted *dicta*, however, are given by the courts. For example, it has been observed that importunity, in its correct legal acceptation, must be in such a degree as to take away from the testator his free agency ;[4] and, again, that the influence to vitiate an act must amount to force and coercion, destroying free agency.[5] In still another case, it has been said that undue influence, in order to render a will void, must be an influence which can justly be described by a person looking at the matter judicially to have caused the execution of a paper pretending to express a testator's mind, which

---

[1] 1 Jarman, Wills, 30 (3d Eng. ed.) ; Barry v. Butlin, 2 Moore, P. C. 480.

[2] Browning v. Budd, 6 Moore, P. C. 435.

[3] *In re* Welsh, 1 Redf. 238.

[4] Kinleside v. Harrison, 2 Phillim. 551.

[5] Williams v. Goude, 1 Hagg. 577; Huddlestone v. Armstrong, 1 Moore, P. C. 478. See Stulz v. Schaeffle, 16 Jur. 909.

really did not express his mind, but expressed something else, — something which he did not really mean.[1]

It is observed by the Lord Chancellor, in the case just cited, that in a popular sense we often speak of a person exercising undue influence over another, when the influence certainly is not of a nature which would invalidate a will. And he illustrates his meaning thus: A young man is often led into dissipation by following the example of a companion of riper years, to whom he looks up, and who leads him to consider habits of dissipation as venial and perhaps even creditable. The companion is then correctly said to exercise an undue influence. But if in these circumstances the young man, influenced by his regard for the person who had thus led him astray, were to make a will and leave him every thing he possessed, such a will certainly could not be impeached on the ground of undue influence. Nor would the case be altered merely because the companion had urged, or even importuned, the young man so to dispose of his property; provided, only, that in making such a will the young man was really carrying into effect his own intention, formed without either coercion or fraud.[2]

The difficulties of defining the point at which influence exerted over the mind of a testator becomes so pressing as to be properly described as undue are greatly enhanced when the question is one between husband and wife. It is both difficult to inquire, and impolitic to permit inquiry, into all that may have passed in this intimate relation. But the difficulty is one of fact. The criterion for determining the question of influence is doubtless the same as in other cases; and it has been laid down in a case of this kind by the House of Lords that influence, to be undue within the meaning of any

---

[1] Boyse v. Rossborough, 6 H. L. Cas. 2, 34.

[2] 6 H. L. Cas. 48. But the burden of proof as to the fairness of the will would, in such case, probably be upon the party claiming the bounty.

rule of law which would make it sufficient to vitiate a will, must be an influence exercised either by coercion or by fraud. And, as to the latter (with which this work is alone concerned), it was observed that if a wife, by falsehood, raise prejudices in the mind of her husband against those who would be the natural objects of his bounty, and by contrivance keep him from intercourse with his relatives, to the end that these impressions which she knows he had thus formed to their disadvantage may never be removed, such contrivance may perhaps be equivalent to positive fraud, and may render invalid any will executed under false impressions thus kept alive.[1]

A will cannot be set aside on account of any persuasions or representations of the testator's wife, while the testator is at the point of death, to induce him to make a more liberal provision than he is disposed to make, though it should appear that such persuasions had prevailed upon him to comply with her wishes; provided it appear that the testator was of sound mind, and was not imposed upon by false representations, and that the provision made for the wife is not greatly disproportionate to that of others near of kin, and unreasonable.[2] It is not indeed, in any case, unlawful for a person, by honest intercession and persuasion, to procure a will in favor of himself or of another person. Nor is it unlawful to induce the testator to grant the bounty by fair and flattering speeches. Persuasion, if not accompanied by fraud, may be employed to influence the dispositions in a will, and does not amount to undue influence in the legal sense of that term.[3]

To invalidate a will on the ground of fraud and undue influence, it must be shown that such were practised with respect to the will itself, or so contemporaneously with the will or connected with it as by almost necessary presumption

[1] Boyse v. Rossborough, 6 H. L. Cas. 2, 48, 49.
[2] Lide v. Lide, 2 Brev. 403. See Small v. Small, 4 Greenl. 220.
[3] Calvert v. Davis, 5 Gill & J. 301.

to affect it. Other frauds committed against a testator are
only evidence to raise suspicion against any act done under
the superintendence or by the interference of those committing it.[1] But this principle must not be carried too far.
Where a jury see that, at and near the time when the will
sought to be impeached was executed, the alleged testator
was, in other important transactions, so under the influence
of the person benefited by the will that, as to him, he was
not a free agent, but was acting under undue control, the
circumstances may be such as fairly to warrant the conclusion,
even in the absence of evidence bearing directly on the execution of the will, that in regard to that also the same undue
influence was exercised.[2]

The alteration of a pecuniary legacy in a will, whether by
a stranger or by a legatee, will not avoid the will as to other
bequests.[3] Nor will fraud or undue influence in procuring
one legacy invalidate other legacies which are of the free will
of the testator;[4] but if the fraud or undue influence affect
the whole will, though practised by but one legatee, the
whole is void.[5]

A prohibition in a will against questioning the acts and
decisions of the executors on penalty of forfeiture of the
devise will not prevent the devisee from impeaching the executors' conduct for fraud and collusion.[6]

Should a testator be induced to omit the insertion in his
will of a formal provision for any intended object of his
bounty upon the faith of assurances given by the heir or
any other person whose interest would be affected by the
insertion of such a bequest in the will, that the testator's
wishes and intention shall be executed as punctually and

[1] Jones v. Godrich, 5 Moore, P. C. 16, 40.
[2] Boyse v. Rossborough, 6 H. L. Cas. 2, 51; Rossborough v. Boyse, 3
Irish Ch. 489, 510.
[3] Smith v. Fenner, 1 Gall. 170.
[4] Florey v. Florey, 24 Ala. 241.   [5] Ib.
[6] Lee v. Colston, 5 T. B. Mon. 246.

fully as if the bequest were formally made, this promise will raise a trust, which, though not available at law, will be enforced in equity, on the ground that a breach of it would be a fraud.[1] And an engagement of the kind referred to may be entered into not only by words, but by silent assent to such a proposed undertaking.[2] Of course, the case will be much stronger if the insertion of the provision be prevented by physical interference on the part of an interested person.[3]

Besides the foregoing cases of actual fraud arising from deceit or undue influence, there are other cases in which, from the peculiar circumstances under which the will was executed, a *presumption* of fraud arises, or at least a suspicion of unfairness or imposition sufficiently strong as matter of law to require the party claiming the bounty to prove the perfect fairness of the transaction and the freedom of action of the testator. Such a case occurs where a will is written or procured to be written by a person benefited by its provisions. Such circumstance is sufficient to excite close scrutiny, and to require strict proof of volition and capacity in the testator. However, the only effect of such a situation is to require the draftsman to make such proof of volition and capacity. But this subject belongs more properly to another division of our work, to wit, to Constructive or Presumptive Fraud ; and the reader is referred to the chapter on Confidential Relations[4] for a further consideration of the subject and a citation of the authorities. And the same chapter should be consulted for other ques-

---

[1] Russell *v.* Jackson, 10 Hare, 206; Jones *v.* Badley, Law R. 3 Ch. 362; McCormick *v.* Grogan, Law R. 4 H. L. 82; Chamberlain *v.* Agar, 2 Ves. & B. 262; Mestaer *v.* Gillespie, 11 Ves. 638; Stickland *v.* Aldridge, 9 Ves. 519; Barrow *v.* Greenough, 3 Ves. 154; Chamberlaine *v.* Chamberlaine, 2 Freem. 34; Oldham *v.* Litchford, Ib. 285; Glass *v.* Hulbert, 102 Mass. 24; Hooker *v.* Axford, 33 Mich. 453 ; *ante*, p. 119.

[2] Byrn *v.* Godfrey, 4 Ves. 10; Paine *v.* Hall, 18 Ves. 475.

[3] Dixon *v.* Olminus, 1 Cox, 414.   [4] Ch. V.

tions arising as to beneficiaries in relations of confidence with the testator.

Equity has no jurisdiction to set aside the probate of a will.[1] But it has been held that a will which has been fraudulently destroyed or suppressed may be set up in chancery.[2]

§ 7. OF BILLS AND NOTES.

In general, fraud in obtaining a bill of exchange or a promissory note will render the instrument invalid as between the parties to the fraud; or, more correctly, the innocent party can set up the fraud as against the party who committed it upon him.[3] But, if there be a sufficient consideration to support the contract, the mere fact of fraud committed by the payee in obtaining it, where the case is such that the fraud can work no injury to the defendant, will not be ground for refusing to pay.[4] It has accordingly been held to be no defence to an action against the maker of a note that the plaintiff obtained the note from the defendant, for a debt already due, by false and fraudulent promises to supply him with goods for a specified future time.[5]

As in other cases, fraud in obtaining a bill or note is a personal defence given the injured party alone: other parties cannot avail themselves of it, unless it go to the extent, as in case of a forged signature, of showing that the plaintiff has no title to the instrument. It is therefore no defence to an

[1] Broderick's Will, 21 Wall. 503.

[2] Buchanan v. Matlock, 8 Humph. 390; Tupper v. Phipps, 3 Atk. 360. *Contra*, Myers v. O'Hanlon, 13 Rich. 196.

This subject will be found more fully presented in the chapter on Jurisdiction, Ch. VII.

[3] Barber v. Kerr, 3 Barb. 149; Sides v. Hilleary, 6 Har. & J. 86; Simmons v. Cutreer, 12 Smedes & M. 584; Fisk v. Collins, 9 Mo. 137; Price *r.* Lewis, 17 Penn. St. 51. See Marion Co. v. Clark, 94 U. S. 278.

[4] Austell v. Rice, 5 Ga. 472.   [5] Overdeer v. Wiley, 30 Ala. 709.

action upon a promissory note by an indorsee against the
maker that the note was obtained from the payee by means of
fraudulent representations, of which the indorsee had knowledge when he received the note.   Payment to the plaintiff in
such a case is a good discharge to the defendant.[1] So, too,
it is no defence to an action by the indorsee against the
maker of a note that the plaintiff procured the indorsement
of the payee by undue influence when he was of unsound
mind and incapable of making a valid indorsement, if the
payee or his legal representatives have never disaffirmed it.[2]
Such an act, though fraudulent as to the payee, does not render the instrument absolutely void ; and the indorsee has a
title to the note until the indorsement is legally annulled.
Nor is it a defence to the maker of a negotiable note that the
plaintiff took it overdue, after it had been obtained by a fraud
committed by one indorser against another.[3]

On the other hand, a party sued upon a note or bill cannot
set up in defence the fraud practised upon him by a third
person, though the latter be also a party to the instrument, if
the plaintiff, being a holder for value, had no knowledge or
notice of the fraud when he took the instrument; unless, as
in the above case, the fraud be of such a character as to
show that no title to the paper could ever have passed to the
plaintiff.[4]   For example, it is no defence to a surety on a note
that the principal debtor obtained his signature by fraud, if
the payee was ignorant of such fact when he took the note.[5]

As against an indorsee of a bill of exchange or a promissory
note, it is not a defence (as we have seen) for the acceptor or
maker that the instrument was obtained from the defendant
by fraud, not going to the very existence of the contract.   A
plea of such fact, however, is not without some effect.   The

---

[1] Prouty v. Roberts, 6 Cush. 19.   [2] Carrier v. Sears, 4 Allen, 336.
[3] Parker v. Stallings, Phill. (N. Car.) 590.
[4] *A fortiori*, where the defendant himself was *particeps criminis*.
Warren v. Lynch, 5 Johns. 239.
[5] Robb v. Halsey, 11 Smedes & M. 140.

presumptions of law, indeed, are all in favor of the right of action of the holder, when there is no circumstance of suspicion upon the face of the paper. But a plea that the instrument was obtained from the defendant by fraud, or that it was fraudulently put into circulation, puts the plaintiff to proof that he took the paper for value and without notice of the fraud ; [1] or at least that some holder before him did so.

Fraud, however, may in some cases go to the existence of the contract ; and a plea of fraud of this kind — that is, of such fraud as shows that no contract was in reality ever made by the defendant, and not merely that a voidable contract was executed by him — will of course bar all right of recovery by any person, even a *bona fide* indorsee for value. There is a difficulty, however, in determining what state of facts will constitute a fraud of this kind. We have elsewhere considered the subject.[2]

The general result of the authorities may be thus stated : Where the evidence shows that, without negligence on the part of the defendant, he was imposed upon by the fraudulent representations or artifice of another party to the paper, as to the contents of the instrument which he was signing, and the defendant signed it without knowing that it was a bill or note, and under the belief thus caused that it was an instrument of a different purport ; [3] or where, having signed the instrument with knowledge of its character, he has never made any delivery of it, but it has been obtained from his premises by theft or other fraud not participated in by any one in whom he has reposed a trust or confidence,[4] — in either of these

[1] Bailey *v.* Bidwell, 13 Mees. & W. 73 ; Hall *v.* Featherstone, 3 H. & N. 284; Smith *v.* Braine, 16 Q. B. 244; Harvey *v.* Towers, 6 Ex. 656; s. c. 15 Jur. 544; Smith *v.* Sac Co., 11 Wall. 139 ; Kesson *v.* Stanberry, 3 Ohio St. 156; Vallett *v.* Parker, 6 Wend. 615; Hamilton *v.* Marks, 63 Mo. 167; Carrier *v.* Cameron, 31 Mich. 373.   [2] *Ante*, pp. 75–80.

[3] Foster *v.* Mackinnon, Law R. 4 Com. P. 704; Gibbs *v.* Linabury, 22 Mich. 479; Chapman *v.* Rose, 56 N. Y. 137.

[4] *Ante*, pp. 76–78; Burson *v.* Huntington, 21 Mich. 415.

cases there can be no recovery against him by any person. If, however, he were in either case guilty of any negligence, the effect of the fraud practised upon him will be overturned, and he will be liable to a *bona fide* indorsee for value.[1]

If a bill or note given for accommodation be fraudulently diverted by the party accommodated from the purpose for which it was agreed the paper should be used, this is *prima facie* a defence to an action against the accommodation party. But such defence may be rebutted by evidence that the plaintiff took the paper for value and without notice of the fraud,[2] or that he took it from some prior holder, who was a *bona fide* indorsee for value.

The fraudulent diversion, notice of which will preclude a plaintiff's right of recovery against an accommodation party, must be one which can be reasonably presumed to be material; such a one as it is reasonable to presume might not have been assented to by the defendant. The mere fact that it was used, to the knowledge of the plaintiff, in some slightly different manner from that contemplated, will not be a good defence. Thus, where the defendant accommodation party indorsed a note for the purpose of being discounted at a bank, and upon the refusal of the bank to take the note it was discounted by the plaintiff with notice of these facts, it was held that he was entitled to recover.[3]

The fact that bank-notes were fraudulently issued, and were void at law, is no defence *per se* to a suit to collect the debt constituted by giving such notes to the defendant as a loan of money. It may appear that the notes were actually current at the time the defendant received them, that they had not proved worthless in his hands, and that he was not bound to take them back from the persons to whom he had passed them; and in such a case the defendant will be liable.[4]

[1] See the above cases and the fuller discussion, pp. 75–80.
[2] Small *v.* Smith, 1 Denio, 583; Wardell *v.* Howell, 9 Wend. 170.
[3] Powell *v.* Waters, 17 Johns. 176.   See Mohawk Bank *v.* Corey, 1 Hill, 513; Wardell *v.* Howell, *supra*.   [4] Orchard *v.* Hughes, 1 Wall. 73.

§ 8. Of Fraud on Powers.

A fraud upon a power must be committed either on the
donor of the power or on the objects of it. It is committed
on the former when a power to create a burden on the estate
in settlement is used for a purpose not intended. It is committed on the latter when a power to control the devolution
of the estate is used to give a benefit to some one not an
object of it.[1] But of course when all the objects on whom
alone such fraud can be committed concur in or confirm the
transaction, and no imposition or undue influence is used in
the matter, the fraud is waived.[2]

If the donee of a power appoint the fund to one of the
subjects named in the power, upon an understanding that
the appointee will lend the fund to the donee, the appointment is bad, though the fund was to be loaned on good
security.[3] In such case, the party entitled in default of
appointment obtains the fund.[4]

An appointment made with the object of giving an exclusive advantage to the appointor is invalid; but, if the object
of the appointment be to secure a benefit for all the objects
of the power, the appointment is good, though the appointor
may to some extent participate in such benefit.[5] Thus, in
the case cited, it was urged that certain appointments (made
by a tenant for life acting under a power given by a marriage
settlement), the object of which was to effect building leases,
were for the benefit of the appointor, and therefore, not
being authorized by the settlement, were invalid. But the
Master of the Rolls considered that this principle should give

---

[1] Rowley v. Rowley, Kay, 258; Skelton v. Flanagan, Law R. 1 Irish
Eq. 362, 369.
[2] Skelton v. Flanagan, *supra*.
[3] Arnold v. Hardwick, 7 Sim. 343.   [4] Ib.
[5] *In re* Huish's Charity, Law R. 10 Eq. 5.

way, where, as in this case, the benefits of the appointment
extended to parties in interest. The building leases had,
indeed, benefited the tenant for life ; but they had also benefited the other interested parties in the improved value of
the property, which they would lose if the appointment were
declared void. To hold otherwise would be to strain a rule
intended to benefit the objects of the power to a rigid exact-
ness, which would inflict manifest injury to them.[1]

It is not necessary that an appointment under a power
should be directed (contrary to the intent of the power) to
the exclusive benefit of the appointor, in order to make it
invalid. Where the donee exercises a power of appointment
in favor of one of several objects of the power with a view
to the benefit of a stranger, the appointment is considered
fraudulent; and this, too, though the appointee be ignorant
of the fraud, and though the motive of the donee be not
morally wrong.[2] In the case cited, a married woman having
a power to appoint a fund (of which she was to receive the
income during her life) among her children, appointed the
whole fund at her death to her eldest daughter. The object
of this was that the daughter should, out of the fund, benefit her father. The daughter was not informed of her
mother's intention until after the mother's death ; but the
appointment was held invalid.[3]

---

[1] See McQueen v. Farquhar, 11 Ves. 467; Cockcroft v. Sutcliffe, 25
Law J. Ch. 313; Topham v. Portland, 1 DeG., J. & S. 517; s. c. 11 H. L.
Cas. 32, Law R. 5 Ch. 40; Vane v. Dungannon, 2 Schoales & L. 118;
Warde v. Dixon, 28 Law J. Ch. 315; Cooper v. Cooper, Law R. 8 Eq.
312; s. c. Law R. 5 Ch. 203; In re Marsden's Trust, 4 Drew. 594.

[2] In re Marsden's Trust, 4 Drew. 594.

[3] " In some of the cases which have been cited," said the court, " there
has been a direct bargain between the donee of the power and the person
in whose favor it is exercised, under which the donee of the power was
himself to derive a benefit; and certainly there has been nothing of that
kind in this case. In my opinion, however, it is not necessary that the
appointee should be privy to the transaction, because the design to defeat
the purpose for which the power was created will stand just the same,

The same general principles which are applicable to discretionary trusts in general are applicable to this particular species of discretionary trust. Unless it can be shown that the trustee having the discretion exercises the trust corruptly or improperly, or in a manner which is for the purpose not of carrying into effect the trust, but of defeating the purpose of the trust, the courts will not control or interfere with the exercise of the discretion. Though there be a suspicion that the trust has been exercised in a particular manner and from a motive which, if proved, would be held fatal, still, if there be nothing but suspicion (though this would be occasion for jealous investigation), and nothing amounting to a judicial inference or conviction from the facts, the courts will not act upon it. On the other hand, if it can be proved to the satisfaction of the court that the power has been exercised either corruptly, or for a purpose which would defeat rather than carry into effect the object of the trust, the courts will not permit such an exercise of the power to prevail.[1]

If real estate be conveyed by a husband to a trustee, for the sole and separate use of the grantor's wife, with power to sell and convey, the proceeds of sale to be reinvested as the wife may direct, it is the duty of both the trustee and the purchaser, in the event of a sale, to see that the fund is paid over to the former, and reinvested by him for the benefit of the wife. If, in violation of the terms of the trust, the

whether the appointee was aware of it or not; and the case of Wellesley v. Morrington, 2 Kay & J. 143, shows that it is not necessary, in order to bring the case within the scope of the jurisdiction in which this court acts, that the appointee should be aware of the intentions of the appointment, or of its being actually made. Neither is it necessary that the object should be the personal benefit of the donee of the power. If the design of the donee in exercising the power is to confer a benefit, not upon himself actually, but upon some other person not being an object of the power, that motive just as much interferes with and defeats the purpose for which the trust was created, as if it had been for the personal benefit of the donee himself."

[1] *In re* Marsden's Trust, 4 Drew. 594, 599.

purchaser contract with the husband, pay him the purchase-money, and then, though upon authority of the wife, receive a conveyance from the trustee, the transaction is a fraud upon the power, and upon the wife's application it will be set aside.[1] But the case would be otherwise where the purchaser had no notice of the breach of trust.[2]

If a parent, having a power of appointment amongst his children, purchase the share of one child, it would be a plain fraud for him to attempt, by the exercise of his power, to entitle himself to more than the share which that child would have taken in default of appointment.[3] It would be equally fraudulent if a father were to appoint to a child who was deceased, intestate and without issue, or who, though living, was an infant in a hopeless state of health.[4] Such an appointment would in reality be an appointment to the father himself.

Where the legal estate is outstanding in trustees, a bill by a purchaser for valuable consideration and without notice, under a fraudulent appointment of property in settlement, will be dismissed as against the persons who, in default of a valid appointment, are entitled. The payment of a money consideration cannot make a stranger become the object of a power created in favor of children. He can only claim under a good appointment. An appointment, at first impeachable as voluntary, may indeed be sustained by a consideration *ex post facto;* as, for instance, where the subject of appointment is purchased for a valuable consideration from the appointee. But that is only where a valuable consideration was all that was wanting to make the appointment good *ab initio.*[5] Where there has been fraud in the concoction of a

---

[1] Cardwell *v.* Cheatham, 2 Head, 14.   See Wormley *v.* Wormley, 8 Wheat. 421; Champlin *v.* Hoight, 10 Paige, 274; s. c. 7 Hill, 245.

[2] Cardwell *v.* Cheatham, *supra.*

[3] Smith *v.* Camelford, 2 Ves. Jr. 714.

[4] McQueen *v.* Farquhar, 11 Ves. 479; Hinchinbroke *v.* Seymour, 1 Brown C. C. 395.   [5] George *v.* Milbank, 9 Ves. 190.

bargain, payment of money cannot make an appointment in pursuance of such bargain fair, though the appointment may cease to be voluntary.[1]

But though, under circumstances similar to those above stated, the whole transaction is void, there is a distinct class of cases in which the execution of powers is void only in part; as where a parent, having power to appoint amongst children only, appoints (without their consent[2]) a part to grandchildren. This is a fraud only to the extent in which it deprives the true objects of the power of the benefit intended for them by the party creating the power; the execution of which, therefore, is held void only for the excess.[3] And, in general, the rule, that where an appointment is made for a bad purpose, the bad purpose affects the whole instrument, does not apply to cases in which the evidence enables the court to distinguish what is attributable to an authorized from what is attributable to an unauthorized purpose.[4]

§ 9. Of Inadequacy of Consideration.

It is established law that when parties understand fully what they are doing, and there is no fiduciary relation between them, mere inadequacy of price will not suffice to impeach a sale, though there be also the absence of professional assistance. And the mere circumstance that one of the parties is in poverty and distress, and the other wealthy, will not take a case out of this rule.[5] He who, standing in

[1] Daubeny v. Cockburn, 1 Meriv. 626; Cadogan v. Kennett, Cowp. 434; 2 Hovenden, Fraud, 222.

[2] White v. St. Barbe, 1 Ves. & B. 399.

[3] Adams v. Adams, 2 Cowp. 651; Pitt v. Jackson, 2 Brown C. C. 51; Bristow v. Warde, 2 Ves. Jr. 350; Palmer v. Wheeler, 2 Ball. & B. 28; Crompe v. Barrow, 4 Ves. 685.

[4] Topham v. Portland, 1 DeG., J. & S. 517.

[5] Harrison v. Guest, 1 DeG., M. & G. 424; s. c. 8 H. L. Cas. 481;

an independent relation, would impeach a sale for fraud, must establish the fact that the transaction is invalidated by some of the elements, the presence of which renders what is in form a contract inoperative in equity. The term "fraud," however, in such case, is not to be understood in its popular sense. In the sense in which it is understood in equity, it comprises the use of undue influence and unfair means. But while inadequacy of consideration and the absence of professional advice, added to the presence of distress, do not come within this extended signification of fraud, they are all material facts, and may exist to such an extent in connection with other facts as to be proof of fraud.[1] In the case cited, a purchase deed was set aside under the following circumstances : The vendor received as a consideration for the sale less than half the value of the property. He was a person of reckless and improvident habits, greatly embarrassed, indebted to the purchaser, and to some extent dependent upon him. He had acted without professional advice ; and there was evidence of management and contrivance on the part of the purchaser in procuring the vendor's signature to the contract of sale, and of his having depreciated the title and having deterred others from purchasing, though he was himself aware of counsel's favorable opinion as to the title, and did not inform the vendor of the fact.

If there be such inadequacy as to show that the person whom it affects did not understand the bargain he was making, or was so oppressed that he was glad to make it, knowing its inadequacy, this will show a command over him which may amount to fraud.[2]

It is held in Pennsylvania that gross inadequacy, though sufficient to shock the judgment of the court, is insufficient

---

Knight *v*. Majoribanks, 11 Beav. 322; s. c. 11 Macn. & G. 10; Butler *v*. Miller, Law R. 1 Irish Eq. 195, 210.

[1] Butler *v*. Miller, Law R. 1 Irish Eq. 195, 210.

[2] Heathcote *v*. Paignon, 2 Brown, C. C. 167.

ground of itself to set aside an *executed* contract between parties standing on an equality, though it might be otherwise
of an executory contract.[1] The general language of the
authorities, however, is that inadequacy so great as to shock
the conscience will suffice to avoid any contract. This, however, must be admitted to be a very uncertain standard of
relief. We add several illustrations of the subject from the
decisions of the courts.

A bid of $100 at a fair public sale for property worth $1,500,
but upon which there were liens amounting to $800, is not, of
itself, so grossly inadequate as to show fraud.[2] But where
property worth $12,000 was bid off at judicial sale for $400,
it was held that such inadequacy, of itself, afforded strong

[1] Davidson *v.* Little, 22 Penn. St. 245. " Such gross inadequacy as
there was in this case," said Black, C. J., " is very well calculated to fix
upon the transaction a serious suspicion of its fairness. It is contrary to
all our usual experience that a man should part with his property at five
per cent. of its value, unless he was excessively weak or ignorant, or under
the influence of some deception. But if the vendor was thoroughly
acquainted with every fact which it was necessary for him to know; if
he was twenty-one years of age and of sound mind; if there were no
circumstances which gave the vendee an improper control over him,
amounting to mental imprisonment; if, in short, the vendee behaved
honestly, and the vendor was able to act like a free man, with his eyes
open, then the one had a right to sell, and the other to buy, on any terms
they saw proper to agree upon. The law will never interfere between
the parties themselves to set aside an honest contract which they have
voluntarily made. When creditors complain, the case is totally different.
. . . The court should have charged the jury that, if there was no actual
fraud committed by the vendee, the conveyance could not be disturbed;
that the inadequacy of the price, gross as it was, could be regarded only
as evidence of fraud; that, this being the case of an executed contract,
the inadequacy is not sufficient to prove the fraud without some additional
evidence; that all the facts connected with the transaction must be considered together; and, if by this means it should appear to be honest,
the verdict ought to be for the vendee." The decision expressly excepts
similar transactions with expectant heirs, and doubtless would except all
cases where the parties do not stand upon an equality.

[2] Weber *v.* Weetling, 3 C. E. Green, 441.

ground for equitable relief.[1] So, too, it has been held that
the sale of property worth $800 for $200 is not evidence of
fraud.[2] The fact that at sheriff's sale a lot of land sold for $5,
and another lot for $10, is not evidence of fraud, when the
value of the land is not stated.[3] The agreement, however,
of a county to sell and transfer stock to the amount of $20,000
in a railroad company for $2, is held to be unconscionable and
fraudulent *per se*, there being no evidence of an intention to
make a gift of the stock.[4] Where, in a suit for partition, a
sale of lands worth $1,500, in which infants were interested,
was directed, and an agent was directed to be present at the
sale to see that the property was not sacrificed, and owing to
his (accidental) failure to attend the land was sold for $50,
it was held that the sale should be set aside.[5]

Where a sale is set aside for inadequacy, or for any other
matter which renders it fraudulent by construction of law
only, the courts act upon the principle of redemption, and the
conveyance will stand as a security for principal and interest.[6]

In the case of a charity estate, the security of rent is the
first object to be regarded ; and hence the inadequacy of the
rent reserved in such cases is less indicative of fraud than in
almost any other situation. Thus, a tenant, though he may
appear to be in possession of a lease of charity estates at a
very low rent with reference to the value of the property,
will not be turned out, if he have acted fairly and honestly.
There must be some evidence or a presumption of collusion
or improper conduct as ground for so dealing with him. If,
for example, the tenant happen to be a relative of the trustee
who granted the lease, this will be a circumstance justly cal-

---

[1] Hodgson *v.* Farrell, 2 McCarter, 88. There is perhaps a distinction
between private and judicial sales upon this matter of inadequacy, the
latter being involuntary.

[2] Feigley *v.* Feigley, 7 Md. 537.

[3] Foster *v.* Pugh, 12 Smedes & M. 416.

[4] Macoupin Co. *v.* People, 58 Ill. 191 ; Madison Co. *v.* People, Ib. 456.

[5] Mitchell *v.* Jones, 50 Mo. 438. [6] 1 Story, Equity, § 344.

culated to excite suspicion.[1] And when the undervalue is considerable, and not accounted for by circumstances rendering the terms substantially reasonable, a lease of charity estates may be set aside upon the mere ground of undervalue.[2]

If a lease of charity estates for ninety-nine years be obtained, it is incumbent upon the lessee who takes a term of that duration to show such a consideration as will make it a proper lease ; since such a letting would be out of the ordinary course of provident management. Nor can trustees make a lease with covenants for perpetual renewal unless a consideration be received equivalent to the value of the inheritance, which by such a lease is virtually alienated.[3]

Upon principles adopted for the purpose of guarding against possible fraud, one of the governors of a charity cannot become a lessee of the lands which, as governor, it was his duty to let to the greatest possible advantage. It will be no sufficient justification of such a transaction to show that there was no inadequacy or other circumstance of suspicion imputable to the lessee or the other governors.[4]

A person who with his eyes open purchases property at a price greatly *exceeding* its value cannot obtain relief in equity on that ground.[5] But, when the purchase at such price is a mere condition to the obtaining a loan, equity may grant relief.[6]

<hr>

[1] *Ex parte* Skinner, 2 Meriv. 457; Attorney-Gen. *v.* Backhouse, 17 Ves. 291; Attorney-Gen. *v.* Mawgood, 18 Ves. 315; 2 Hovenden, Fraud, 326.

[2] Attorney-Gen. *v.* Cross, 3 Meriv. 541; Attorney-Gen. *v.* Gore, Barnard, 152; s. c. 9 Mod. 229.

[3] Attorney-Gen. *v.* Brooke, 18 Ves. 326; Attorney-Gen. *v.* Wilson, Ib. 519; Attorney-Gen. *v.* Owen, 10 Ves. 560; Attorney-Gen. *v.* Green, 6 Ves. 452; Attorney-Gen. *v.* Warren, 1 Wils. C. C. 412; s. c. 2 Swanst. 304; Watson *v.* Hempsworth Hospital, 14 Ves. 333; 2 Hovenden, 326.

[4] Attorney-Gen. *v.* Clarendon, 17 Ves. 500.

[5] Abbott *v.* Sworder, 4 DeG. & S. 448.

[6] Marshall *v.* Billingsly, 7 Ind. 250; Collett *v.* Preston, 15 Eng. L. & E. 101; Lawley *v.* Hooper, 3 Atk. 278.

§ 10. OF PUBLIC SALES.

Public sales may be invalidated either for fraudulent combinations or artifices among the bidders to obtain the property on sale at a price within certain limits, or for fraudulent acts and artifices of the vendor to advance the price. In the former case, the vendor is the sufferer, and he alone can complain of the wrong ; in the latter case, the purchaser is the sufferer, and objection must come from him. A sale effected by such means is void even at law ; and a deed executed in pursuance of it conveys no title.[1]

In accordance with this principle, a partition sale will be set aside where the evidence shows any collusion or contrivance to enable the purchaser to obtain the land at a price below its value.[2] Thus, where it appeared that at such a sale the bidders, for the purpose of obtaining the property at a sacrifice, agreed that one should become the purchaser and the others refrain from bidding in consideration of sharing the benefits of the purchase, the sale was annulled.[3] So, too, a combination between a commissioner appointed by court to sell property, whereby the commissioner becomes a partner with others in the purchase of the property sold by him, is fraudulent ; and the commissioner and his partners are liable for the profits realized by them from the transaction.[4]

Where lands of a decedent are sold by an officer of court, and part of the distributees combine and agree not to bid against each other, and they prevent competition at the sale by promising to divide the fruits of their purchase with others intending to bid, if they will not bid, and thus become purchasers of the land at a price far below its value, the case

---

[1] Den d. Smith *v.* Greenlee, 2 Dev. 126.
[2] Neal *v.* Stone, 20 Mo. 294; Wooton *v.* Hinkle, Ib. 290.
[3] Wooton *v.* Hinkle, *supra*.
[4] Chatham *v.* Pointer, 1 Bush, 423.

affords sufficient ground for a refusal by the court to confirm
the sale.[1] So, also, if a bidder at auction offer to one proposing to bid that, if he will desist, the former will divide the
property with him, this is a fraud upon the vendor.[2] So
where the parties agreed that if the defendant would not bid
upon a note against the plaintiff at an auction sale thereof, the
plaintiff would discharge a demand against the defendant,
the agreement was considered void, and the demand held
enforceable.[3]

When a purchaser bids off property at a public sale, the
fact that a combination existed to prevent certain lands from
being sold to other bidders, to which he was not a party,
and of which he was ignorant, will not invalidate his
purchase.[4]

Parties may purchase jointly at public sales, if all be open
and fair. A combination of interests is not necessarily corrupt. It is the end to be accomplished which determines
whether a combination is lawful or otherwise. If it be to
depress the price of the property by artifice, the purchase
will be void; if it be to raise money for payment, or to divide
the property for the accommodation of the purchasers, it will
be valid.[5]

Agreements, therefore, concerning biddings at public sales
are not *per se* illegal. Whether they are invalid or not depends
upon the intention by which the parties are governed, and
the object sought to be accomplished. If the object be fair,
if there be no indirection or purpose to prevent the competition of bidders, and such is not the necessary effect of the

---

[1] Swofford *v.* Garmon, 51 Miss. 348.

[2] Whitaker *v.* Bond, 63 N. C. 290.

[3] Gardiner *v.* Morse, 25 Maine, 140.

[4] Case *v.* Dean, 16 Mich. 12.

[5] Small *v.* Jones, 1 Watts & S. 128; Breslin *v.* Brown, 24 Ohio St.
565; Phippen *v.* Stickney, 3 Met. 388; Den d. Smith *v.* Greenlee, 2 Dev.
126; McMinn *v.* Phipps, 3 Sneed, 196; James *v.* Fulcrod, 5 Tex. 512. But
see Atcheson *v.* Mallon, 43 N. Y. 147.

arrangement, the agreement will be sustained.[1] In the case cited, there was an agreement that the defendants in error should procure judgments against certain parties, levy on their property, expose the same to sale, and that the plaintiff in error should bid the amount of the judgments for it. The agreement did not declare that the other party should not bid ; and it was sustained. In another case,[2] there was an agreement between two persons that one of them only should bid, and that, after buying the property, he should sell part of it to the other upon such terms as the witnesses to the agreement should decide to be just and reasonable. This agreement was upheld. It was agreed in another case [3] that a party should bid a certain amount for a steamboat, about to be sold under a mortgage, and transfer to the mortgagor an undivided interest of one-third, upon his paying a corresponding amount of the purchase-money. The contract was held valid. In still another case,[4] an agreement was made between a senior and a junior mortgagee. The former agreed to bid the amount of his debt for a specific part of the mortgaged property ; and this bargain was held a proper one.

So, also, a simple agreement between two or more persons, each of whom wished to purchase a part only of certain land offered at a chancery sale, that they would purchase the whole jointly, and afterwards make division among themselves, does not constitute such a combination to stifle the biddings as will vitiate the sale.[5]

It is not necessary that the restraint upon competition should be effected by the bidders. If the auctioneer fraudulently prevent competition, the sale is equally invalid. Thus, where an auctioneer, on seeing a party approach, who, as he

---

[1] Wicker v. Hoppock, 6 Wall. 94.

[2] Phippin v. Stickney, 3 Met. 384.

[3] Bame v. Drew, 4 Denio, 290.   [4] Garrett v. Moss, 20 Ill. 549.

[5] McMinn v. Phipps, 3 Sneed, 196. See Den d. Smith v. Greenlee, 2 Dev. 126.

knew, was likely to bid, knocked down the premises before such party could bid, the sale was set aside.[1] But if the auctioneer give all buyers a fair chance to purchase, only refusing to assure the title to the property, his own purchase is not fraudulent, however inadequate the price.[2]

From considerations of public policy, courts are strongly inclined to uphold judicial sales; but these considerations will not induce them to sustain them, when they have been conducted with bad faith. Hence, if a purchaser at execution sale falsely appeal to the benevolence of the bidders by giving out that he is buying for the benefit of the debtor or his family, this will be a circumstance which, with other slight evidence, may be sufficient to justify a court in setting aside the sale as fraudulent. And the same result will follow when the representations are made privately, and persons are thereby kept away who otherwise would have attended the sale for the purpose of bidding.[3]

A scheme was entered into by the widow and the administrator of a decedent to procure a foreclosure sale of the intestate's lands, at which the administrator was to buy them in at an inadequate price by giving out at the sale that he was purchasing for the widow, thus dissuading others from bidding. Under these circumstances, the administrator purchased the lands at sheriff's sale, and agreed to convey them to the widow for the price at which they were struck off to him. On his refusal to do so, the widow and the intestate's only child filed a bill to redeem; and it was held that the widow was barred by her participation in the fraud. But, as to the child, the administrator was decreed a trustee for her.[4]

If it appear that no one was influenced by the false repre-

[1] Jackson v. Crafts, 18 Johns. 110.

[2] Brotherline v. Swires, 48 Penn. St. 68.

[3] Stewart v. Severance, 43 Mo. 322. See McNew v. Booth, 42 Mo. 189.

[4] Johns v. Norris, 12 C. E. Green, 485; s. c. 7 C. E. Green, 103.

sentations of a bidder that he was bidding in the interest of the owner and his family, or that only the attorney for the execution plaintiff was so influenced, and it do not appear that he would have bid more than the amount of the debt, a sale for the amount of the debt will be valid.[1]

The employment of a puffer at an auction sale is a fraud upon the bidders; and equity will set aside the contract,[2] or direct a bond, given by a bidder for property bought under such circumstances, to be delivered up.[3] But evidence that the plaintiff requested the defendant to bid on the property as an under-bidder, and told her that she would not be bound to take the property, but might take it if her husband desired, does not show any fraud practised upon third persons, or any illegal contract between the plaintiff and the defendant.[4] A purchaser of land is not entitled to relief because the price was run up by the apparent competition of a person in reality insolvent and unable to comply with the terms of the sale, who bid upon the known special desire of the purchaser.[5] Nor is it any objection to a sale of mortgaged property, that the mortgagee bid and ran up the price to a high figure, provided it appear that the auctioneer gave distinct notice at the sale that the parties were at liberty to bid.[6]

If property be advertised to be sold without reserve, such advertisement excludes any interference, direct or indirect, by the vendor, which can under any possible circumstances affect the right of the highest bidder, whatever be the amount of his bid, to be declared the purchaser. And any evasion of that duty on the part of the vendor will disentitle him to

[1] Gilbert v. Carter, 10 Ind. 16.
[2] Veazie v. Williams, 8 How. 134; McDowell v. Simms, 6 Ired. Eq. 278; Morehead v. Hunt, 1 Dev. Eq. 34.
[3] Woods v. Hall, Ib. 411.
[4] Faucett v. Currier, 115 Mass. 20.
[5] Williams v. Bradley, 7 Heisk. 54.
[6] Dimmock v. Hallett, Law R. 2 Ch. 21.

the aid of equity to enforce the sale.[1] Thus, where the vendor, previously to the sale of a life interest, advertised to be without reserve, entered into a private agreement with another person that the latter should bid a certain sum at the auction, and be the purchaser at that sum unless a higher sum were bid, a bill by the vendor for specific performance against another who had been declared the purchaser at the auction, though for a much higher price, was dismissed.[2]

§ 11. OF PARTNERSHIP.

An appropriation of partnership assets by one partner without the assent of his copartners, in satisfaction or for security of his private debt, is presumed to be fraudulent as against the other members of the firm, and may be set aside by them. The presumption of fraud, however, is not always conclusive, and may sometimes be rebutted.[3] In the case cited, the sole acting member of a dissolved partnership, having full power to dispose of its property and to pay its debts, became himself a creditor of the firm by advancing his own funds in payment of its debts, and then in good faith, and with no intention to defraud the firm, disposed of the partnership property to an amount less than the sum due himself in satisfaction of a debt due from himself to a third person ; and this person received the same in good faith, supposing that the sale was authorized by the firm. It was held that this disposition of the property could not be avoided by another member of the firm, as it appeared that all of the outside debts of the firm had been paid or secured, and that there was nothing due to such other member from the firm.

A person dealing with a firm through a member of it, and having no actual knowledge, suspicion, or cause of suspicion,

---

[1] Robinson v. Wall, 2 Phill. Ch. (Eng.) 372.   [2] Ib.

[3] Corwin v. Suydam, 24 Ohio St. 209.

of any fraud practised upon the partnership in the transaction, may hold the firm upon any contract thereby entered into on behalf of the partnership. The agency of the partner in such a case cannot be disputed.[1]

Courts of equity will grant relief where a partnership has been entered into by one partner under circumstances of fraud or gross misrepresentation by the others. In such cases, equity will not only decree the partnership to be void, but will also interpose and restore the injured party to his original rights and property as far as practicable.[2] On the other hand, equity will also grant relief where a retiring partner has been induced to sell his interest to his copartners at an inadequate consideration, in consequence of the fraudulent concealment and misrepresentation of the condition of the firm property by one of the firm whose special and peculiar business it is to know the state of such property.[3]

Equity will not grant the dissolution of a partnership for every trivial violation of duty by one of the partners; but where there is gross misconduct, such as abuse of known authority, or gross want of good faith, such as must, if continued, be disastrous to the interests of the other partners, equity will interfere and grant a dissolution.[4] To justify such extraordinary interposition, however, the court always requires strong and clear evidence of positive or meditated abuse. It is not enough to show that there is a temptation to such misconduct, abuse, or bad faith: there must be an unequivocal demonstration by overt acts or gross departure from duty that the danger is imminent, or that the injury

[1] Blodgett v. Weed, 119 Mass. 215.

[2] Story, Partnership, § 232 ; Fogg v. Johnson, 27 Ala. 432; Tattersall v. Groote, 2 Bos. & P. 131; Oldaker v. Lavender, 6 Sim. 239; Jones v. Yates, 9 Barn. & C. 532; Rawlins v. Wickham, 3 DeG. & J. 304.

[3] Maddeford v. Austwick, 1 Sim. 89; Perens v. Johnson, 3 Smale & G. 419.

[4] Story, Partnership, § 287; Story, Equity, § 673; 3 Kent, Com. 60, 61.

is already done.[1] For minor acts of misconduct, equity will ordinarily go no further than to grant an injunction against the partner.[2]

Though a fraudulently concerted commission of bankruptcy will not be supported, it is not necessary that the sole motive for issuing it should be the distribution of the bankrupt's estate among his creditors. There may be other legitimate grounds upon which it may be supported; for instance, it may not only be prudent, but it may also be perfectly consistent with good faith, to get the bankrupt partner out of the partnership, which might otherwise be ruined by his misconduct. And if this appear to have been, *bona fide*, the object of the commission, it cannot be vitiated thereby. To do this, it is not enough that there has been a bye-motive for taking out the commission, if there has been no fraud.[3]

If two partners enter into a contract for the purpose of defrauding their joint creditors, the one permitting the other to withdraw money out of reach of the creditors, such a contract is void as to such creditors.[4] But the mere fact that at the time when it was determined to dissolve a partnership both partners knew that the joint effects were insufficient to pay the joint debts will not, of itself, be enough to invalidate a dissolution of the firm, if honestly made; though it be one of the terms of the dissolution that the retiring partner shall receive a premium for relinquishing his share in the business. If there be no actual fraud in the case, it is competent to partners to make such a bargain, however advantageous or disadvantageous it may be to either party.[5]

A retiring ostensible partner who conceals his withdrawal, and allows the remaining members of the firm to contract in

---

[1] Story, Partnership, § 287; Story, Equity, § 673; 3 Kent, Com. 60, 61.   [2] Ib.

[3] *Ex parte* Wilbeam, Buck, 461; 2 Hovenden, Fraud, 160.

[4] Anderson *v.* Maltby, 2 Ves. Jr. 255.

[5] *Ex parte* Peak, 1 Madd. 354.

his name, is guilty of a fraud upon persons who may in ignorance of the withdrawal still give credit to the firm on the
faith of the continuance of the old partnership.[1] Such a
retiring partner will moreover be liable to creditors of the
firm as it existed before the change (they dealing in ignorance), notwithstanding any private arrangement between
the partners relative to his liability. The fact of his having
been a partner may have been the chief inducement to dealing
with the firm; and parties may well suppose that the firm
remains unchanged until notice is given to the contrary.
And this principle will apply equally to persons dealing for
the first time with the firm after the partner's withdrawal, if
he allow the remaining members to continue to hold him out
to the world as a partner.[2] A retiring ostensible partner should
then give notice of his withdrawal to his old customers, and
as to new ones be careful that he is no longer held out as a
member of the firm; though of course, if the new customers
have notice of his withdrawal, they cannot claim that he has
committed a fraud upon them by the act of his (late) partners
in keeping his name among those of the firm. And, if such
person be a dormant partner, he need not give notice of his
withdrawal, because, having never been held out as a partner,
credit cannot be supposed to have been given to him.[3]

A partner who has been recognized as such by his associates
cannot be deprived of participation in the profits of the concern, because the funds which he carried into the partnership,
as his equal contribution to the capital stock, had been procured by a gross fraud, perpetrated by him on one of his
copartners in another and distinct partnership.[4] It is no
defence to an action for breach of a contract to form a partnership with the plaintiff that the plaintiff had defrauded a

---

[1] Buffalo Bank v. Howard, 35 N. Y. 500.
[2] 2 Story, Contracts, § 313 (5th ed.).
[3] Ib.
[4] Ingraham v. Foster, 31 Ala. 123.

previous partner, and that the circumstances of the affair had
been concealed from the defendant.[1]

§ 12. OF SURETIES.[2]

If a person be induced to become surety in a contract in
which his principal and the obligee, without the surety's
knowledge, adopt terms and conditions of an illegal nature
and prejudicial to the surety's interests, the surety is entitled
to a discharge ; and relief will not be refused on the ground
that the principal has allowed the matter to stand. This
seems to be true, though there was no combination or collusion against the interests of the surety.[3] Whether the
rule would apply, however, to a mere personal fraud practised upon the principal by the obligee, which the former
had seen fit to overlook or waive, is matter of doubt.[4] An
agreement between a creditor and principal debtor that the
former shall not notify the surety of the default of the latter
is not a fraud upon the surety.[5]

A surety in a promissory note may avoid the same as against
the payee, on the ground that the payee induced him to sign
through deception.[6] And in order to enable the sureties on a
note to avoid their contract on the ground that the note was
obtained by fraud, it is not necessary that the principal should
have joined in the fraud.[7] But it is held that the fact that
a person was induced to become a surety upon a recognizance
by fraudulent representations does not affect his liability
to a conusee not a party to the fraud.[8]

[1] Andrewes v. Garstin, 10 Com. B. N. S. 444.
[2] As to certain questions of *deceit*, see *ante*, pp. 22, 44–46, 67, note.
[3] Denison v. Gibson, 24 Mich. 187.   [4] Ib. p. 202.
[5] Grover v. Hoppock, 2 Dutch. 191.
[6] Trammell v. Swan, 25 Tex. 473.
[7] Clopton v. Elkin, 49 Miss. 95.
[8] Martin v. Campbell, 120 Mass. 126.

While an agreement with a principal debtor, whereby the nature of his contract is changed without the consent of the surety, will in general operate to discharge the latter, the principle requires that such an agreement shall be valid. If, for example, a new agreement were to be substituted for the old upon a representation by the debtor that the signature of the surety to the contract offered as a substitute is genuine, when in fact it is a forgery, the creditor, on discovering the fraud, may repudiate the new contract and maintain an action against the surety upon the original agreement.[1] So, too, a release given by the obligee of a bond to the principal obligor, if obtained by fraud, will not discharge a surety in the bond. And, in an action against such surety, evidence of the principal's fraud upon the plaintiff is admissible, though the surety was not privy to the fraud.[2]

If a sheriff after taking a forthcoming bond prevent the surety in such bond from delivering the goods on the day named, a court of equity on a bill exhibited by the surety will require the sheriff and all parties concerned to answer a charge of fraud and combination, and, whether fraud be established or not, will perpetually enjoin a judgment against the surety upon the bond as unconscionable against him. The plaintiff in that judgment will be left to his remedy against the sheriff; and the sheriff, if innocent, to his remedy against the parties indemnifying him, if there be any.[3]

§ 13. OF CORPORATIONS.[4]

A majority of the corporators have no right to exercise the control over the corporate management which legitimately belongs to them, for the purpose of appropriating the corpo-

---

[1] Kincaid v. Yates, 63 Mo. 45.
[2] Gordon v. McCarty, 3 Whart. 407.
[3] Lusk v. Ramsay, 3 Munf. 417.
[4] As to *deceit*, see *ante*, pp. 9, 14, 21, 24, 60, 71, 72, 90.

rate property or its avails or income to themselves or to any of the shareholders, to the exclusion or prejudice of the others. And if any such unfair advantage have been obtained by fraud or abuse of the trust confided to them as officers or agents of the corporation, it is not in the power of a majority to ratify or condone the fraud and breach of trust, so far as it affects the rights of the others, without reasonable restitution. This is not only true as to formal transactions, such as assessments of capital or dividends of income,[1] but also as to indirect appropriations of the common property, profits, or means of profit, to their own benefit by any portion of the corporators, in fraud of their associates. No act of the majority can purge such fraud. If it were otherwise, the minority would be without the means of protection or redress against inequality and injustice.[2]

If the charter of a corporation provide that stockholders only shall be elected directors, persons having no interest in the stock, but fraudulently and collusively receiving the transfer of a share to qualify them, are not eligible; and the stockholders combining in such fraud have no power to confer upon them authority to do corporate acts. And such fraud and combination will prevent those participating in it from claiming any protection under its provisions to escape personal responsibility.[3] So, also, if the directors of a railway

---

[1] Preston v. Grand Collier Dock Co., 11 Sim. 327; Hodgkinson v. National Ins. Co., 26 Beav. 473.

[2] Wells, J., in Brewer v. Boston Theatre, 104 Mass. 378, 395; Gregory v. Patchell, 33 Beav. 595; Atwool v. Merryweather, Law R. 5 Eq. 464, note.

[3] Bartholomew v. Bentley, 1 Ohio St. 37; s. c. 15 Ohio, 666. "A valid act of incorporation," said the court, in 15 Ohio, "or an invalid and pretended right to exercise corporate functions, is alike powerless to secure the guilty from the consequences of their fraudulent conduct where it has been knowingly resorted to as the mere means of chicane and imposition, and used to facilitate the work of deception and injury. . . . If the defendants, with the design to defraud the public generally, have knowingly combined together, and held forth false and deceptive

company give away certificates of stock, a major part of the whole issue, to contractors building the road, for the purpose of giving them a controlling influence in the election of officers and in the management of the road, equity will declare the gift void, especially if part of the directors are interested in the contract with the contractors.[1]

The officers of a corporation are chargeable with fraud, if they receive in payment for stock property at a valuation known to be in excess of its real worth, and thereon issue paid-up certificates of stock. But such a fraud is greatly aggravated when the officers deal with themselves as stockholders, and accept such a conveyance in payment of their own stock.[2]

Private arrangements between an agent of a corporation procuring subscriptions of stock, by which peculiar privileges or exemptions from payment are accorded to certain subscribers, are a fraud upon the other subscribers; and it is held that they cannot be set up in defence to an action upon the subscription.[3] But it has been decided that the condition of a subscription paper by which a signer bound himself to pay $500, providing $5,500 more should be raised in C, is not performed unless the amount is subscribed in good faith or is actually paid by residents of C. The condition is not performed by subscriptions to that amount of responsible residents of C, if it was understood between the payee and any of the subscribers that they should pay nothing, and that

colors, and done acts which are wrong, and have thereby injured the plaintiff, they must make him whole by responding to the full extent of that injury; and they cannot place between him and justice with any success the charter of the German Bank of Wooster, whether it be valid or void, forfeited or *in esse*. Neither a good nor a bad thing may be falsely used for purposes of deception, and made a scapegoat for responsibility."

[1] Gilman R. Co. *v.* Kelly, 77 Ill. 426; People *v.* Logan Co., 63 Ill. 374.

[2] Osgood *v.* King, 42 Iowa, 478.

[3] New Albany R. Co. *v.* Fields, 10 Ind. 187; New Albany R. Co. *v.* Slaughter, Ib. 218.

understanding has been carried out; though the payee might have compelled them to pay the whole amount of their subscriptions.[1] So, too, it appears to be considered in Mississippi that if an agent for procuring subscriptions of stock to a corporation obtain a party's signature by means of a colorable signature already given by a well-known and influential citizen, stated by the agent to be well acquainted with such matters, he can avoid his contract of subscription. The subscription, however, will be binding upon him, if he were not induced to give it by such colorable subscription.[2]

If a corporation secure subscriptions of stock, to be binding only when a sufficient sum shall be subscribed to secure the completion of a certain work, the directors have no right to pass a resolution that the subscriptions are sufficient for the purpose, when they are obviously not so. Such action would be evidence of fraud, and the subscribers would not be liable for payment of the stock.[3]

The members of the governing body of a corporation are the agents of the corporation; and if they exercise their functions for the purpose of injuring its interests, and improperly alienating its property, they are personally liable for any loss caused thereby.[4]

Fraud in the organization of a municipal corporation is ground for annulling the franchise.[5] But the charter of a corporation cannot be declared void in a collateral proceeding, and evidence of fraud in the procurement of the charter is therefore inadmissible in a suit by the corporation against an individual.[6] Nor can fraud be collaterally shown in order to avoid an act of a municipal body.[7]

---

[1] New London Inst. v. Prescott, 40 N. H. 330.

[2] Walker v. Mobile & O. R. Co., 34 Miss. 245.

[3] Cass v. Pittsburgh Ry. Co., 80 Penn. St. 31.

[4] Attorney-Gen. v. Wilson, Craig & P. 1.

[5] State v. Ford Co., 12 Kans. 441.

[6] Duke v. Cahawla Nav. Co., 16 Ala. 372.

[7] Jersey City & B. R. Co. v. Jersey City & H. R. Co., 5 C. E. Green, 61.

§ 14. OF ILLITERATE, WEAK-MINDED, AND DRUNKEN PERSONS.

If an illiterate man execute a deed which is falsely read to him, or the sense declared to be different from the truth, it does not bind him. Nor does it bind him, if the false reading be by a stranger any more than if it be by the party to whom the deed is given. So, too, though it be by a friend of him who executes it, and without covin.[1] The same is true of an instrument signed by a blind man, if falsely read to him.[2] So, too, if a deed be falsely read to a grantor weak-minded or too infirm to read it himself, or if the contents be untruly stated to him, it may be avoided at law. But, if he be simply misinformed as to its legal effect, it must stand at law; and the party's remedy is in equity, where the deed can be corrected.[3]

Equity will set aside a conveyance made to a person while intoxicated, if advantage be taken of his situation by another to sell him property at a price greatly exceeding its value, and no time be allowed the purchaser to become sober before the bargain is closed.[4] Indeed, where the facts show that the plaintiff, an intemperate man, with his faculties much impaired, has been the victim of a gross imposition in the purchase of goods, equity will grant relief, though it is not clear that at the time of the purchase the plaintiff was absolutely drunk.[5]

[1] Thoroughgood's Case, 2 Coke, 9b; Simons v. Great Western Ry. Co., 2 C. B. N. s. 620, 624, Willes, J.; Stacy v. Ross, 27 Tex. 3. See *ante*, pp. 73–81.

[2] 2 Rolle's Ab. 28, l. 20; Willes, J., *ut supra.*

[3] Eaton v. Eaton, 8 Vroom, 108.

Chancery will correct a written instrument where through the fraud of the opposite party it does not conform to the intention of the parties. Goodell v. Field, 15 Vt. 448.

[4] Hotchkiss v. Fortson, 7 Yerg. 67.

[5] Freeman v. Dwiggins, 2 Jones, Eq. 162.

There may also be such contrivance or management of one party to draw another into drink, and then to take advantage of his intoxication, as will justify the interposition of equity on the ground of fraud, even when the drunkenness is not so great as to wholly deprive the party of his power of reason and will.[1] Indeed, we shall hereafter see that all transactions with illiterate, weak-minded, and drunken persons to their disadvantage, are looked upon with suspicion by the courts; and the burden of proof rests upon the opposite party, if he will establish the fairness of the same.[2] A deed obtained from a drunken man by fraud and imposition may, however, be subsequently ratified by him and thereby made binding ; as where, after becoming sober, he gives a bond or other instrument in pursuance of the one obtained by fraud.[3]

In transactions connected with the transfer of property, the non-intervention of a disinterested third party or independent professional adviser, when the donor, from age, weakness or other disabling circumstance, is likely to be imposed upon, or the statement of a consideration when there was none, or great improvidence in the transfer, will be circumstances which furnish a probable, though not always a certain, test of undue influence.[4]

§ 15. OF DELIVERY OF DEEDS.

A deed stolen from the grantor, or the delivery of which is obtained from him by fraud, without his knowledge, consent, or acquiescence, and without negligence on his part, does not pass the title to the property embraced in it, even as against a subsequent purchaser for value, without notice.[5]

[1] Mansfield v. Watson, 2 Iowa, 111; Wood v. Pindall, Wright, 507 ; 1 Story, Equity, § 231.

[2] Chapter V. § 21.   [3] Moore v. Reed, 2 Ired. Eq. 580.

[4] Cadwallader v. West, 48 Mo. 483.

[5] Fisher v. Beckwith, 30 Wis. 55; Everts v. Agnes, 4 Wis. 343; s. c. 6 Wis. 453. See Burson v. Huntington, 21 Mich. 415.

Fraud in obtaining delivery of a deed the execution ˸of which was obtained *bona fide* affects it as much as if practised to obtain the execution.[1] And a similar rule prevails as to the delivery of a negotiable promissory note. If the instrument were obtained without negligence in the maker, under the circumstances above stated, the title to it cannot be passed so as to bind the maker.[2] And the same doctrine prevails where a deed, or a note and mortgage, deposited in escrow, are afterwards purloined from the depositary, before the terms of the deposit have been complied with.[3]

If a grantor, upon making his conveyance, fraudulently retain possession of the deed, when it was the intention of the parties that there should be a delivery, such facts will be deemed to constitute a delivery, even for the purposes of an action at law for possession of the land.[4] But the intention to deliver is essential. Hence, where a deed was executed by the grantor when the grantee was not present and did not know of the transaction, and the grantor caused it to be recorded, and then took it away and retained possession of it, it was held that this was not sufficient evidence of a delivery. The grantee should have shown further an intention to deliver.[5]

§ 16. OF POSSESSION OF TITLE–DEEDS.

In the absence of registration, a prior encumbrancer of an estate can be postponed to a later, on the ground that he has left the title-deeds in the possession of the mortgagor only where the possession of the title-deeds is legally incident to the estate of the first encumbrancer. The possession of title-

[1] Abingdon *v.* Butler, 1 Ves. Jr. 206.

[2] Burson *v.* Huntington, 21 Mich. 415. As to the effect of negligence on the part of the maker, see the same case; also *ante*, pp. 76–78.

[3] Ib.; Andrews *v.* Thayer, 30 Wis. 228; Powell *v.* Conant, 33 Mich. 396.

[4] See Hayes *v.* Davis, 18 N. H. 600.   [5] Ib.

deeds as between the trustees of an estate and an annuitant to whom they have charged the estate for a term of years is not a legal incident to the estate of the annuitant; and it follows that he will not be postponed to a later encumbrancer who, through the fraud of the trustees, loaned money on a mortgage of the estate, finding the title-deeds in possession of the trustees.[1]

§ 17. OF LIEN OF INNKEEPER OR CARRIER.

By the acceptance of a draft from a guest, in payment of board and lodging, and thereupon relinquishing possession of the goods of the guest, an innkeeper probably loses his lien, supposing no fraud to have been practised upon him. But, if the draft be accepted under fraudulent representations, the innkeeper will not be deemed to have lost his lien upon the goods of the guest.[2]   Nor does a common carrier lose his lien upon goods for their carriage by delivering them to the consignee, if the delivery was obtained by fraud. In such a case, the carrier may disaffirm the delivery, and sue the consignee in replevin.[3]

§ 18. OF SUPPRESSION OR DESTRUCTION OF WRITINGS.

If an heir suppress a deed or will of his ancestor, in order to prevent another party, as a grantee or devisee, from obtaining the estate vested in him thereby, equity will grant relief upon due proof by other evidence, and perpetuate the possession and enjoyment of the estate in such grantee or devisee.[4] And in general, where the contents of a suppressed or destroyed instrument are satisfactorily proved, the party will,

---

[1] Harper v. Faulder, 4 Madd. 129.
[2] Manning v. Hollenbeck, 27 Wis. 202.
[3] Bigelow v. Heaton, 6 Hill, 43.
[4] 1 Story, Equity, § 254.

in equity at least, receive the same benefit that he would otherwise have received.[1] In Pennsylvania, indeed, it is held that an obligee of a bond, from which a clause was omitted by the fraud of the obligor, can sue upon the same as if the clause had been inserted.[2] But this is perhaps to be explained upon the system of law there in vogue of blending law and equity in the same court. Equity will consider that as done which should have been done ; and hence, if a man be fraudulently prevented from doing an act, equity will treat the act as performed.[3]

§ 19. OF RELEASING JUDGMENT.

A judgment creditor who has been fraudulently induced to release his judgment for an unavailable security may proceed to enforce the judgment, unless the judgment debtor will remove the obstacle to the enforcement of the security.[4] Thus, in the case cited, a judgment creditor agreed with his debtor to resort for payment to a fund created by a deed of trust, which, without the knowledge of the creditor, contained a limitation of time for parties to come in, which time had expired. The creditor now proceeded upon his judgment ; and it was held that he could not be enjoined from so doing, unless the debtor would so modify the terms of the deed of trust as to let him in.

§ 20. OF REPEAL OF USURY LAWS.

The repeal of the usury laws does not affect the power of a court of equity to review and set aside usurious transactions

---

[1] 1 Story, Equity, § 254.   [2] Partridge v. Clarke, 4 Barr, 166.
[3] Middleton v. Middleton, 1 Jac. & W. 94.
[4] Mechanics' Bank v. Lynn, 1 Peters, 376.

when they are founded in fraud. Upon this principle, a series of deeds, charging sums advanced by a money-lender with exorbitant interest on the borrower's estates, which were ample security, were sought to be set aside. The deeds contained unusual clauses, such as clauses authorizing a sale without notice, and empowering the lender to pay off existing charges, which bore a low interest, and to charge 20 per cent. thereon, and others of a like character. The bill was upheld; the court being of the opinion that the clauses were introduced by the fraud of the money-lender without the knowledge of the borrower, who was unprotected by proper professional advice.[1]

§ 21. OF SURPRISE.

Cases of surprise are to be classed under the head of fraud. These are cases in which an undue advantage is taken of a person under circumstances which mislead, confuse, or disturb the just result of his judgment. But it is not every surprise which will render a man's act invalid; since a man may be said to be surprised in every action which is not done with so much discretion as it ought to be.[2] The surprise here referred to must be accompanied with fraud and circumvention, or at least with such circumstances as demonstrate that the party had no opportunity to use suitable deliberation, or that there was some sinister influence or management to mislead him. If proper time is not allowed to the party, if he is importunately pressed, if those in whom he places confidence make use of strong persuasion, if he is not fully aware of the consequences and is suddenly drawn in to act, if he is not permitted to consult disinterested friends or counsel before he

---

[1] Howley v. Cook, Law R. 8 Irish Eq. 570. See Miller v. Cook, Law R. 10 Eq. 641; Croft v. Graham, 2 DeG., J. & S. 160.

[2] 1 Fonblanque, Equity, bk. 1, c. 2, § 8.

is called upon to act in circumstances of sudden emergency: in these and the like cases in which he has been caused to suffer loss or to make an unequal bargain, relief will be granted.[1] Thus, in an English case, a deed was set aside on the ground of surprise; the evidence showing that it had been obtained for an inadequate consideration from persons in low circumstances, who were unaware of their right until the very time of the conveyance. No misrepresentation or fraud was proved ; but the Master of the Rolls considered the case one of surprise. The plaintiff, he observed, had not had sufficient time to act with caution ; and therefore, though there was no actual fraud, there was something like fraud, in that an undue advantage had been taken of his situation.[2]

§ 22. OF ACTS OF THIRD PERSONS.

A contract can seldom be avoided by either party thereto for fraud, unless the fraud was committed by the other party, or by his authorized agent or servant. If committed by a third person, it cannot ordinarily be alleged in defence of an action upon the contract.[3] Thus, a sheriff in obtaining a forthcoming bond against a debtor whose property is levied upon is not considered for such purpose as the agent of the creditor to whom the bond is payable, and his (the sheriff's) fraud in obtaining the bond is not imputable to the obligee.[4]

A contractor cannot allege that he was drawn into the contract by the fraud of a third person, or even by that of a

---

[1] 1 Story, Equity, § 251; Evans v. Llewellyn, 1 Cox, 439; s. c. 2 Brown, C. C. 150 ; Irnham v. Child, 1 Brown, C. C. 92 ; Townshend v. Stangroom, 6 Ves. 338 ; Pickett v. Loggon, 14 Ves. 215.

[2] Evans v. Llewellyn, 1 Cox, 333.

[3] Gordon v. Jeffery, 2 Leigh, 410.

[4] Ib. But, in giving notice on the forthcoming bond, the sheriff acts as agent of the creditor, and the creditor is bound by any fraudulent conduct of the sheriff in that matter. Ib.

co-contractor on the same side of the undertaking with himself, unless such party be the agent of the contractee. He can
complain of fraud only when practised by the opposite party.
It is accordingly held in Indiana that, where a person is induced by the false representations of a judgment defendant to
become replevin bail, he is still bound ; but that it is otherwise, if the misrepresentations be made by the judgment
plaintiff, or by any one properly acting for him.[1]

Upon the same principle, a person who voluntarily executes
a deed, though induced to do so by fraud, can avoid it only
as against the party who exercised the unlawful influence, or
against one who took title under the deed with participation in
or notice of the fraud, and not against one who took a title
apparently good from those having capacity to convey.[2]
Hence, a married woman whose acknowledgment to a release
of dower or to a conveyance has been properly taken cannot
afterwards allege against the grantee that her signature was
procured by fraud or undue influence on the part of her
husband, unless she can show that the grantee participated
in the same.[3] It seems, however, that fraud practised by a
cestui que trust will avoid a sale honestly made by the trustee.[4]

If goods be furnished to a wife while living apart from her
husband, under circumstances that might not make the husband liable, but the husband afterwards take the goods home
and agree to pay for them, he will be bound by his promise,
though he may have been induced to make it by the deception of his wife. But the case will be otherwise, if the vendor
participated with the wife in the fraud.[5]

Where, however, a third person has had an interest in the
contract, he may, while in such a position, have committed

[1] Lepper v. Nuttman, 35 Ind. 384; Harshman v. Paxson, 16 Ind. 512;
Burge, Suretyship, 218.

[2] White v. Graves, 107 Mass. 325; Somes v. Brewer, 2 Pick. 184.

[3] White v. Graves, supra; Pool v. Chase, 46 Tex. 207; Williams v.
Baker, 71 Penn. St. 476; See Loudon v. Blythe, 16 Penn. St. 532.

[4] Cheshire v. Booe, 1 Dev. Eq. 22.   [5] Allen v. Aldrich, 29 N. H. 63.

a fraud of such a character as to render the contract wholly void, so that no action can afterwards be maintained thereon by any one. Thus, if the payee of a negotiable bill or note were to make a material alteration of the same without the consent of the other parties, the instrument would be rendered absolutely void as to all parties except such payee, even against a *bona fide* indorsee for value.[1]

Where a certificate as to the completion and character of work, necessary to entitle the party performing the work to pay, is withheld by collusion between the person by whom it is to be given and the employer, the party may still recover for the materials furnished and labor done.[2] But it is considered necessary in such cases to prove that the refusal to give the certificate was grossly and palpably perverse, oppressive, and unjust; so much so that the inference of bad faith would at once arise when the facts were known. Having stipulated to submit to the decision of a skilled arbiter the question whether his work conforms to the contract, the party cannot in general substitute the judgment of a jury on that question.[3] And the refusal must be shown to have been the wrongful or fraudulent act of the defendant or opposite party to the contract as well as of the superintendent or other party whose certificate is to be obtained.[4] If the certificate of a third person agreed upon to examine and report upon the plaintiff's work, and the sum due therefor, be fraudulently made out, the plaintiff is not bound; and he may recover for the real value of his work.[5]

A creditor, it is held, is not responsible for communications between the debtor and his surety, unless he has himself been

[1] Wade *v.* Withington, 1 Allen, 561; *ante*, p. 99.

[2] Bannister *v.* Petty, 35 Wis. 215. See Hudson *v.* McCartney, 33 Wis. 331.

[3] Hudson *v.* McCartney, *supra;* Baasen *v.* Baehr, 7 Wis. 521.

[4] Clarke *v.* Watson, 18 Com. B. N. S. 278 ; Batterbury *v.* Vyse, 2 Hurl. & C. 42.

[5] Baltimore & O. R. Co. *v.* Polly, 14 Gratt. 447.

guilty of some fraudulent practice, or unless he has authorized the communication. The fact, for example, that the
surety may be falsely told by the debtor that a note indorsed
by the latter would be taken in full satisfaction of the creditor's claim, will not release the surety from his indorsement,
unless the creditor had knowledge of the statement, and
did not deny it.[1]

[1] Booth *v.* Storrs, 75 Ill. 438.

CHAPTER III.

FRAUDS ON THE ADMINISTRATION OF THE LAW.

HAVING now considered frauds arising *in pais*, we come next to the consideration of frauds upon the administration of the law.

§ 1. OF ATTACHMENTS, ABUSE OF PROCESS, &C.

It is established by the authorities that a valid and lawful act cannot be accomplished by any unlawful means, such as the use of fraud; and, whenever such unlawful means are resorted to, the law will interfere and afford some suitable remedy, according to the nature of the case, to the party injured.[1] The authority of a sheriff, for example, is given upon condition that it shall not be colorably used to effect an unlawful purpose. The law will operate retrospectively to defeat all acts thus done under color of lawful authority; and, *a fortiori*, will it operate prospectively to prevent the acquisition of any lawful rights by the abuse of an authority given for useful and beneficial purposes.[2] Thus, it would be dangerous to allow rights to be acquired by an attachment procured through violence or fraud.[3] Hence, if upon pretence of search for stolen goods, but in reality for the purpose of levying an attachment upon goods, an officer open a trunk

---

[1] Ilsley v. Nichols, 12 Pick. 270; Wells v. Gurney, 8 Barn. & C. 769; Pomroy v. Parmlee, 9 Iowa, 140; Respass v. Zorn, 42 Ga. 389; Graham v. Warner, 3 Dana, 148; Wanzer v. Bright, 52 Ill. 35; Stein v. Valkenhuysen, El., B. & E. 65. See Lehman v. Shackelford, 50 Ala. 437. But it is said that no act can be in fraud of the law, when the act is intended and calculated to carry out the law. Sanford v. Huxford, 32 Mich. 313.

[2] Ilsley v. Nichols, *supra*.   [3] Ib.; and other cases, *supra*.

any levy upon the contents for such purpose will be void.[1]
So, too, if a person should be arrested on Sunday under criminal process, and held until Monday, that he might then be
arrested on civil process, he would be entitled to a discharge.[2]
Indeed, jurisdiction of the person obtained by fraud, as by entic-
ing a party to come within the limits of a particular jurisdiction on false pretenses, is, if followed by damage, actionable,[3]
and judgment thereunder is invalid.[4]

The fraudulent antedating of an attachment is void as to
innocent parties suffering by reason of it. Thus, if a person
procure an attachment upon real estate to be antedated, so
that it falsely appears of record as prior to a conveyance
made by the owner to a third person, and such third person,
not knowing that the attachment was antedated, pay the
creditor, for the purpose of dislodging it, the amount which
the attachment purported to secure, he may recover back the
same, though the money was paid to the defendant by the
hand of his debtor without any disclosure that he was paying it as the agent of the plaintiff.[5]

A collusive attachment cannot confer any right as against
a subsequent *bona fide* attachment. Thus, a member of a
firm in failing circumstances made a firm-note to his sister
for a personal debt of his own to her, a debt barred by the
Statute of Limitations, and procured her to sue the firm upon
it, and attach the firm property. The brother advanced the
costs of suit, and had the property bid off in her name; and
it was clear that the whole scheme was collusive, the firm
owing the lady nothing. It was accordingly held that the
attachment could not stand as against an attachment subsequently made by *bona fide* creditors of the firm.[6] But collu-

[1] Pomroy v. Parmlee, 9 Iowa, 140.
[2] Wells v. Gurney, 8 Barn. & C. 769.
[3] Wanzer v. Bright, 52 Ill. 35 ; Stein v. Valkenhuysen, El., B. & E.
65 ; Williams v. Bacon, 10 Wend. 636; Snelling v. Watrous, 2 Paige,
314; Carpenter v. Spooner, 2 Sandf. 717; Leaver v. Robinson, 3 Duer, 622.
[4] *Post*, p. 171.   [5] Handly v. Call, 30 Maine, 9.
[6] Briody v. Conro, 42 Cal. 135.

sion between a garnishee and the plaintiff in the garnishment process, in order to secure to the latter his claim against the principal debtor, is not a fraud upon such debtor, and constitutes no valid reason for vacating the garnishment proceedings. The law compels the garnishee to make payment to the plaintiff in that process ; and it matters not that he may be anxious to do so.[1] So, too, one about to pay money due from himself may inform those to whom his creditor is indebted, and aid them in attaching it after it shall be paid and become the property of his creditor. Such a proceeding is neither a fraud nor a legal wrong.[2]

It is a disputed question whether equity will exert its jurisdiction, in favor of an attaching plaintiff,[3] to set aside a fraudulent transfer of property by the defendant, executed before judgment, or enjoin any disposition which he may then choose to make of it. Some of the courts have held that a plaintiff who has attached the property of another upon whom he has a claim has a sufficient lien thereon to entitle him to file a bill in equity to remove an incumbrance or obstruction to a levy or sale, placed upon the property by fraud on the part of the defendant.[4] Other courts of equal respectability have denied the existence of such rights, and have refused altogether to exert any such jurisdiction before judgment. They have held that a plaintiff could not restrain or question the disposition of the defendant's property until he had completed his title at law by judgment and execution. And the reason given is this : that, until the plaintiff has established his title and recovered judgment, it does not appear that he has any right to interfere with any disposition of property which the defendant may make ; that, although he may have

---

[1] Barber v. Walker, 26 Wis. 44.   [2] Root v. Ross, 29 Vt. 488.

[3] The cases are generally those of creditors' attachments, but they doubtless apply equally to attachments by plaintiffs suing *ex delicto.*

[4] Tappan v. Evans, 11 N. H. 311 ; [Kittredge v. Emerson, 15 N. H. 227 ; Stone v. Henderson, 26 N. H. 506 ; Hunt v. Field, 1 Stockt. Ch. 36.

commenced an attachment suit and levied upon property, still
the justice and extent of his claim are yet to be settled by
judicial investigation; that he may never recover judgment,
and, if he should not, his interference with the exercise of
the defendant's rights would be unwarranted and oppressive;
that, when he has recovered judgment and exhausted his legal
remedies, he may then invoke the power of a court of equity
to remove any embarrassment which may exist in the collection of his debt; but, until he has done this, he has no concern
with the defendant's frauds, or ground for controlling him in
the exercise of the power of alienation.[1]

A pardon from the executive procured by fraud is invalid.[2]
And this is true, though it appear that the prisoner had
nothing to do with the fraud.[3]

§ 2. OF DOMICIL.

A dwelling-house is a protection from arrest upon civil
process to the occupant, his children, and domestic servants,
and to all who have for the time being a legal residence in
the house.[4] But a residence obtained by fraud affords no
protection. Thus, where the plaintiff removed to another
town from that of her real residence to the house of her son-
in-law, in order to avoid the payment of taxes, it was held
that the collector might lawfully open the outer door to make
an arrest.[5]

---

[1] Almy v. Platt, 16 Wis. 169, *per* Cole, J., where, however, the point
was not decided; Wiggins v. Armstrong, 2 Johns. Ch. 144 ; Brinkerhoff
v. Brown, 4 Johns. Ch. 671 ; Williams v. Brown, Ib. 681 ; McDermott v.
Strong, Ib. 687 ; Day v. Washburn, 24 How. 352 ; Dodge v. Griswold, 8
N. H. 425; Neustadt v. Joel, 2 Duer, 530; Reubens v. Joel, 3 Kern. 488;
Melville v. Brown, 1 Harrison, 349; Mills v. Black, 30 Bosw. 550.

[2] Dominick v. Bowdoin, 44 Ga. 357; Commonwealth v. Ahl, 43 Penn.
St. 210; State v. McIntyre, 1 Jones, 61.   [3] Ib.

[4] Foster's C. L. 320; 2 Hale, P. C. 117; Oyster v. Shed, 13 Mass.
520; Still v. Wilson, Wright, 505.

[5] Gordon v. Clifford, 28 N. H. 402.

In several of the States, statutes have been passed, providing in effect that where a party removes to another State or country for the purpose of getting such a residence there as to enable him or her to sue for a divorce, no decree granting divorce in such State shall be binding; and these statutes have often been enforced. [1]

§ 3. Of Sales and Knowledge of Intended Fraud.

Mere knowledge on the part of a vendor of goods that the purchaser intends to make a fraudulent or illegal use of them, as in contravention of a statute, will not bar him from recovering the price of the goods from such purchaser.[2] It would, however, be otherwise, if the vendor, besides having such knowledge, sold the goods with reference to the fraudulent or illegal purpose, and to enable the purchaser to effect it.[3] Thus, if a vendor should forward prohibited goods to the purchaser in a disguised form, erasing marks upon the casks, and packing the goods in an unusual manner to avoid detection, or should do any other unlawful act in aid of the unlawful purpose, his conduct would be a fraud upon the law, and the courts would not aid him in recovering the price of the goods.[4]

In accordance with the above rule of law, a sale of lottery tickets, effected in one State where such sale is lawful to a citizen of another State where the sale is unlawful, is a valid transaction, though the seller knew that the purchaser bought for the purpose of illegal sale in the latter State.[5] But

---

[1] See Cooley, Const. Lim. 400, 401 (3d ed.).

[2] Webber v. Donnelly, 33 Mich. 469; Tracy v. Talmage, 14 N. Y. 162; Hill v. Spear, 50 N. H. 253.

[3] Webster v. Munger, 8 Gray, 584; McIntyre v. Parks, 3 Met. 207; Aiken v. Blaisdell, 41 Vt. 655.   See Ely v. Webster, 102 Mass. 304; Adams v. Coulliard, Ib. 167.   [4] Ib.

[5] McIntyre v. Parks, 3 Met. 207; Adams v. Coulliard, 102 Mass. 167.

it is otherwise if the sale be made in the State in which such transactions are forbidden.[1]   And if a party having delivered goods or paid money to another for an illegal and fraudulent purpose subsequently, before the rights of others intervene, repudiate the transaction, he can recover the goods or their value or the money from the bailee.   Such an action is not founded upon the illegal agreement.[2]   But, if the agreement has been executed, the action cannot be maintained.[3]

§ 4. Of Judgments and Awards.

It is well-established law that a judgment may during the term or (in the absence of statute) afterwards be set aside for certain kinds of fraud.   But this does not mean that the merits of a question involving a fraud put in issue in the case can be reopened in equity or by motion (except for a new trial) after the rendition of the judgment, so as to retry the matter of fraud.   Such a proceeding is not allowed.[4] The fraud referred to must consist either in facts relating to the manner of obtaining jurisdiction of the cause, to the mode of conducting the trial, or to the concoction of the judgment, or in facts not actually or necessarily in issue at the former trial.[5]

[1] Adams v. Coulliard, supra; Cannan v. Bryce, 3 Barn. & Ald. 179; Pearce v. Brooks, Law R. 1 Ex. 213.

[2] Taylor v. Bowers, Law R. 1 Q. B. Div. 291; Symes v. Hughes, Law R. 9 Eq. 475.

An action for money had and received will lie at common law against a person who has received the proceeds of a lottery ticket which he had fraudulently caused to be drawn as a prize.   Catts v. Phalen, 2 How. 376.

[3] Taylor v. Bowers, supra; Hastelow v. Jackson, 2 Barn. & C. 221; Bone v. Eckless, 5 Hurl. & N. 925.

[4] Sample v. Barnes, 14 How. 70; Emerson v. Udall, 13 Vt. 477; Atkinsons v. Allen, 12 Vt. 619.

[5] " The frauds for which courts of equity will interfere to set aside or stay the enforcement of a judgment of a court, having juris-

In regard to the manner of obtaining jurisdiction of an action, it is held that if a judgment be obtained in a cause, jurisdiction of which was acquired by the fraud of the prevailing party, the fact may be collaterally shown.[1] Thus, if a person residing in one jurisdiction be induced under false pretences or representations to go into another for the real purpose of getting service of process upon him, the jurisdiction and the judgment rendered thereunder will be deemed to have been fraudulently obtained ; and such fact will be a sufficient ground for proceedings to set aside the judgment, or, if it were rendered in another State or country, for denying its validity in a collateral action brought to enforce it.[2] In the case of a foreign proceeding, no mode of vacating the judgment would exist ; but an injunction against proceeding to enforce it,[3] or a plea of the fraud in obtaining the jurisdiction in a suit to enforce the judgment, would be allowed, or an action could be maintained for the fraud by which jurisdiction was acquired.[4]

diction of the subject-matter and the parties, must consist of extrinsic collateral acts not involved in the consideration of the merits. They must be acts by which the successful party has prevented his adversary from presenting the merits of his case, or by which the jurisdiction of the court has been imposed upon." Field, J., in United States v. Flint, U. S. Circ. Court, Cal. Sept. 1876. "It is true that a decree may be avoided, by showing that it was obtained by fraud. But this must be fraud in its concoction [2 Story, Equity, § 1575], such as corruption of the court, collusion between the parties, or other circumstances which would establish that what seemed a decree was in fact no decree; that it was *fabula, non judicium.*" Hoffman, J., in s. c. This, it should be observed, was said of an attempt to open the merits of a former decision, which had there been necessarily passed upon. The court nowhere speak of anterior fraud in obtaining the claim sued upon, when such fraud was not actually or necessarily in issue at the trial. See the consideration of this subject further on in the present chapter.

[1] Dunlap v. Cody, 31 Iowa, 260. See *ante*, p. 166.

[2] Dunlap v. Cody, 31 Iowa, 260. So of the effect of fraudently obtaining service of a cross-petition. Pfiffner v. Krapfel, 28 Iowa, 27.

[3] See Price v. Dewhurst, 8 Sim. 279.

[4] Wanzer v. Bright, 52 Ill. 35. See, however, Luckenbach v. Ander-

If through the instrumentality of one party to an action,
the witnesses of his adversary be forcibly and illegally de-
tained, or bribed to disobey its subpœna, or if the testimony
of his adversary be secreted or purloined,[1] or if the citation
to him be given under such circumstances as to defeat its
purpose, a fraud is committed for which relief will be granted
in equity, if it produce injury to the innocent party.[2] So, if
the litigation be collusive, if the parties be fictitious, if real
parties affected be falsely stated to be before the court, the
judgment may be set aside, or its enforcement restrained.[3]

Fraud may also be shown in equity for the purpose of
impeaching and vacating a judgment, if not also in a collateral
action,[4] where the fraud consists in deceit practised upon the
court in which the former suit was tried ; the injured party
being absent, and having no notice of the acts resorted to.
For example, obtaining judgment in violation of an agreement
between the parties, and without the knowledge of the opposite party, is ground for relief in equity.[5] And this is true,

son, 47 Penn. St. 123, where it is held that the justice of the claim thus
sued upon must also be denied.

  [1] Shedden Case, 1 Macq. 535.
  [2] United States v. Flint, U. S. Circ. Court, Cal. Sept., 1876, Field, J.
  [3] Ib.
  [4] Of course, if evidence of fraud, going to the very existence of the
judgment, appear upon its face, the judgment may be impeached for such
fact in a collateral suit at law as well as in equity. Mason v. Messenger,
17 Iowa, 261, 274. But it is considered in some of the States that, if
such fraud do not appear upon the face of the record, it cannot be shown
in a collateral action. The remedy is by suit to vacate the judgment.
Ib.; Kelley v. Mize, 3 Sneed, 59. Contra, Jackson v. Summerville, 13
Penn. St. 359; Edgell v. Sigerson, 20 Mo. 494; Hall v. Hamlin, 2 Watts,
354; State v. Little, 1 N. H. 257; Smith v. Keen, 26 Maine, 411; Thouve-
nin v. Rodriques, 24 Tex. 468; Hartman v. Ogborn, 54 Penn. St. 120.

  [5] Ochsenbein v. Papelier, Law R. 8 Ch. 695 (case of a foreign judgment); Johnson v. Muversaw, 30 Ind. 435; Stone v. Lewman, 28 Ind.
97 ; Jarmin v. Saunders, 64 N. Car. 367 ; Chambers v. Chambers, 28
Conn. 552; Holland v. Trotter, 22 Gratt. 136 ; Broaddus v. Broaddus, 3
Dana, 536; Pelham v. Moreland, 6 Eng. 442; Hibbard v. Eastman, 47
N. H. 507; Rogers v. Gwinn, 21 Iowa, 58; Dobson v. Pearce, 12 N. Y.
165.

though the agreement was made on the Sabbath.[1] A judgment, however, cannot be collaterally impeached because false testimony was given in the case, unless it be on the ground of fraudulent practices in procuring it by the party in whose favor it was rendered.[2] Nor can a cross-action be maintained for damages by a judgment obtained by fraud and perjury, when the suit involves an impeachment of the judgment.[3] So, also, while a judgment remains unreversed, the defendant against whom it was obtained cannot, it is held, maintain an action for conspiracy against the plaintiff, his officers, or attorney, where the question of fraud was tried in the former action.[4] But it has been held that, in an action upon a judgment obtained against several defendants, one of them may show that the judgment was obtained by conspiracy between the plaintiff and the other defendants.[5]

In regard to fraud in the concoction of a judgment, if a party's own counsel should prove false to him, and by collusion with counsel for the other side, or perhaps by materially violating his instructions, to the knowledge of the opposite party, and has then consented to the judgment in question, these facts would afford ground for vacating the judgment. And, if the judgment were rendered in a foreign court, such facts would doubtless be admissible in defence to an action

---

[1] Blakesley v. Johnson, 13 Wis. 530.

[2] Fisk v. Miller, 20 Tex. 579; Hartman v. Ogborn, 54 Penn. St. 120. See Field v. Flanders, 40 Ill. 470; Dilling v. Murray, 6 Ind. 324.

A decree of the probate court, rendered on the final settlement of an administrator's account, will be opened and set aside in equity, at the instance of non-resident distributees who had no actual notice of the proceedings, on proof that the administrator claimed and was allowed credit for a payment which he must have known he had never made. Morrow v. Allison, 39 Ala. 70.

[3] Demeritt v. Lyford, 27 N. H. 541; Hillsborough v. Nichols, 46 N. H. 379; Dunlap v. Glidden, 31 Maine, 435; Smith v. Abbott, 40 Maine, 442.

[4] Smith v. Abbott, 40 Maine, 442; Demeritt v. Lyford, 27 N. H. 541.

[5] Spencer v. Vigneaux, 20 Cal. 442.

upon the judgment. So, too, where a trustee in violation of duty to his *cestui que trust*, or a guardian in violation of his duty to his ward, or several of the parties to a cause in violation of the rights of their fellows on the same side, should consent to a collusive judgment: in all of these and the like cases, it is apprehended that the facts would constitute a ground for vacating the judgment, and, at least in the case of a foreign judgment, of collaterally impeaching the same.[1]

Cases of this kind are more common where the fraud is sought to be practised upon a third person. It is often laid down in general terms that third persons are not bound by judgments, not being parties to them, and may impeach them for fraud.[2] Lord Chief Justice Grey long since laid it down that in civil suits all *strangers* might falsify for covin either fines or real or feigned recoveries, and even a recovery by a just title, if collusion were practised to prevent a fair defence ; and this whether the covin were apparent upon the record, as in not assigning or not demanding the view, or by suffering judgment by confession or default, or extrinsic, as in not pleading a release, collateral security, or other matter of advantage.[3] This doctrine as to strangers whose right or title is directly affected by the judgment has been uniformly followed.[4]

---

[1] See Bigelow, Estoppel, 169 (2d ed.); Ochsenbein *v.* Papelier, Law R. 8 Ch. 695.

[2] De Armond *v.* Adams, 25 Ind. 455 ; Callahan *v.* Griswold, 9 Mo. 775; Vanderveere *v.* Mason, 4 Zab. 818; Humphries *v.* Bartec, 10 Smedes & M. 282; Annett *v.* Terry, 35 N. Y. 256; Great Falls Co. *v.* Worster, 45 N. H. 110; Atkinson *v.* Allen, 12 Vt. 619; Sidensparker *v.* Sidensparker, 52 Maine, 481; Philipson *v.* Egremont, 6 Q. B. 587; Parkhurst *v.* Sumner, 23 Vt. 538.

[3] Duchess of Kingston's Case, Bigelow, Estoppel, 134 (2d ed.).

[4] Perry *v.* Meadowcroft, 10 Beav. 122; Meadowcroft *v.* Huguenin, 4 Moore, P. C. 386 ; Bandon *v.* Becher, 3 Clark & F. 479 ; Gaines *v.* Relf, 12 How. 472; Hall *v.* Hamlin, 2 Watts, 354; Dougherty's Estate, 9 Watts & S. 189 ; Thompson's Appeal, 57 Penn. St. 175; Bigelow, Estoppel, 135–137 (2d ed.).

But this rule needs some explanation. Third persons are bound by judgments *inter alios*, and, it is apprehended, cannot allege that they were obtained by fraud or collusion, except in so far as they have at the *time* of the judgment a legal right to insist upon its fairness. The fact that they have no *present* right of this kind, or a present right that is only remotely and indirectly affected by the judgment, will not enable them to attack it for the fraud. But third persons who have a present interest either in the amount of the judgment, or in the property concerned, are permitted to complain that the judgment was concocted in fraud of their rights. For example, judgment creditors may attack a judgment where it is a fraud upon them, as where there has been collusion between the debtor and the creditor; but they cannot object to it merely because it is a fraud upon the debtor.[1] They can attack the judgment for collusion, but not for matter of defence, original or subsequent.[2] That is a matter of defence personal to the debtor.[3] Under the like circumstances, a surety can allege that a judgment against the principal debtor, now sought to be enforced against him (the surety), was obtained by collusion between the principal debtor and his creditor, in fraud of the surety.[4]

Concealment of facts which, had they been known, would have prevented a judgment, affords ground for relief;[5] and that, too, even after the term in which the judgment was

[1] Thompson's Appeal, 57 Penn. St. 175.

[2] Lewis v. Rogers, 16 Penn. St. 18.

[3] Sidensparker v. Sidensparker, 52 Maine, 481; Candee v. Lord, 2 Comst. 269; Voorhees v. Seymour, 26 Barb. 569, 585.

[4] Annett v. Terry, 35 N. Y. 256; Great Falls Co. v. Worster, 45 N. H. 110; Parkhurst v. Sumner, 23 Vt. 538. See further, as to the right of third persons to allege fraud in obtaining the judgment, De Armond v. Adams, 25 Ind. 455; Vanderveere v. Mason, 4 Zab. 818; Humphries v. Bartec, 10 Smedes & M. 282; Philipson v. Egremont, 6 Q. B. 587; Bandon v. Becher, 3 Clark & F. 479.

[5] Fish v. Lane, 2 Hayw. 342; Noyes v. Loeb, 24 La. An. 48; Ocean Ins. Co. v. Fields, 2 Story, 59.

rendered.[1] Mere suspicion of fraud, however, in obtaining a judgment is not sufficient ground for annulling a judgment, if the facts were known during the trial, or might have been known by the exercise of reasonable diligence.[2]

The distinction between fraud as a ground of impeaching a judgment and fraud not such ground lies in the consideration whether the fraud were such as to render the judgment void (that is, liable to be treated by the injured party as a nullity[3]), or such as to render it merely voidable (that is, erroneous, or as being based upon a verdict contrary to evidence). The existence of fraud of the first kind, whether it consist in the preliminary steps necessary to obtaining jurisdiction of the cause, or in the subsequent proceedings down to the rendition of the judgment, is good ground for relief in equity, and, according to some cases, may be pleaded in an action upon the judgment at law. Fraud of the second kind is not available in equity or at law, except by motion for a new trial or in arrest of judgment, or by writ of error or appeal.

On the other hand, fraud is always a ground of action where the proof of it does not necessarily involve an impeachment of the previous judgment. But, if the object of the proceeding be to impeach the validity of the judgment, the remedy must be sought in equity. And even then it is not clear that jurisdiction will be assumed, unless the fraud were unknown to the complaining party at the time the judgment was rendered, or soon enough thereafter to enable him to

---

[1] Edson v. Edson, 108 Mass. 590; Allen v. McClellan, 12 Penn. St. 328; Jennison v. Haire, 29 Mich. 207.

[2] Smith v. Nelson, 62 N. Y. 286.

[3] A judgment is a judicial determination of a cause agitated between real parties, upon which a real interest has been settled. In order to make a judgment, there must be a real interest, a real argument (if there be any argument at all), a real prosecution of the suit, a real defence (if any), and a real decision. The absence of any of these makes the judgment a nullity as to innocent parties, as was laid down in the House of Lords in Bandon v. Becher, 3 Clark & F. 479.

open the judgment by motion in the court in which it was rendered. The only safe course, therefore, in such cases is to bring a cross action at law or in equity, according to the nature of the remedy sought, accepting the judgment as binding, but claiming damages for the fraud by which the claim put in judgment was obtained.

Recovery of judgment upon a contract, if fraud be not pleaded, is no bar to an action for the deceit practised to induce the plaintiff to make it. And this principle not only permits a cross action by the defrauded party after judgment upon the contract by the wrongdoer (in the absence of a plea of fraud), but it permits the injured party to sue upon the contract, and then to sue for the fraud by which that contract was obtained.[1] The plaintiff in such a case has simply affirmed the contract (which, as the innocent party, he may do), and brought suit for the fraud by which he was induced to enter into it. If in the second suit he were to seek a recovery of specific goods sold under the contract after judgment upon the contract for their value, the case would probably be different. It would be an answer to the second action, that the first suit had been an affirmance of the sale.[2] But the case put is not a repudiation of the sale.[3] The two actions are therefore consistent with each other; they are distinct, and may both be the subject of an action.[4]

It has been laid down in New York, upon thorough consideration, that money received by one party from another by means of a judgment or other judicial proceeding, which was obtained through fraud, falsehood, and imposition of the successful party upon the tribunal by which it was adjudged, where the money so recovered was paid before the discovery of the fraud by the party paying it, can be recovered by the thus defrauded party.[5] So, likewise, if an attachment of

[1] Wanzer v. DeBaun, 1 E. D. Smith, 261.   [2] Ib.   [3] Ib.   [4] Ib.
[5] Michigan v. Phœnix Bank, 33 N. Y. 9, 25; Cadaval v. Collins, 4 Ad. & E. 858.

property be obtained by fraud, and the property, after judgment, bought by the creditor on execution, the debtor can maintain an action of deceit against the creditor, but not trover.[1]

Judgments of courts of foreign powers, whether *in rem* or *in personam*, may be impeached for fraud; that is, it may be shown that the judgment was obtained by fraud or collusion. This does not mean, however, at least in a collateral proceeding, that the injured party may show that the judgment was obtained by the production of false testimony. Parties are probably allowed to impeach foreign judgments only in the particulars in which the privilege is granted as to the domestic judgments. Aside from the above case, it would seem that the plea of fraud must be directed to the mode of obtaining the jurisdiction, or to the concoction of the judgment. And even as to the plea of fraud in obtaining the jurisdiction, it is held necessary to show further that the claim itself is invalid.[2]

The rule in this country as to the right to impeach for fraud a judgment rendered in a sister State has never been fully settled. Some of the courts have asserted that the right exists,[3] while others have denied its existence.[4] The apparent conflict in these cases may be partly reconciled in the fact that several of the cases which assert the right of impeachment for fraud were proceedings in equity; and most of the authorities admit that the plea of fraud is good in equity.[5] Thus, it has been held in several cases that equity will enjoin

---

[1] Whitaker v. Merrill, 28 Barb. 526.

[2] Luckenback v. Anderson, 47 Penn. St. 123.

[3] Holt v. Alloway, 2 Blackf. 108; Borden v. Fitch, 15 Johns. 121; Andrews v. Montgomery, 19 Johns. 162; Shumway v. Stillman, 4 Cowen, 292; Pearce v. Olney, 20 Conn. 544; Engel v. Scheuerman, 40 Ga. 206; Rogers v. Gwinn, 21 Iowa, 58. See Dobson v. Pearce, 12 N. Y. 156.

[4] Anderson v. Anderson, 8 Ohio, 108; Bicknell v. Field, 8 Paige, 440; Christmas v. Russell, 5 Wall. 290. See Bigelow, Estoppel, 214–217 (2d ed.).   [5] *Contra*, Bicknell v. Field, *supra.*

proceedings upon a judgment rendered in a sister State, if it was obtained by fraud.[1]

The question has never been fully determined by the Supreme Court of the United States; and to this court alone can we look for a settlement of the same, since it involves the construction of the constitutional provision and act of Congress concerning the effect of judgments of the sister States.[2] As a question of equity, the subject has not appeared in that court. In its legal aspect, the court have lately expressed the opinion that fraud is not a valid ground for impeaching a judgment rendered in a sister State;[3] and this is probably a final decision of the question, so far as it goes. It may be doubted, however, if this case goes any further than to decide that fraud cannot be alleged at law where the facts show that the judgment is voidable only. It would be to put the judgments of the courts of a sister State above those of the domestic courts to hold that the allegation of fraud is inadmissible even where the facts pleaded show that the judgment was actually void. We apprehend that the Supreme Court of the United States would not refuse to allow the allegation of fraud in either of the three following cases: first, where the jurisdiction of the court was obtained by fraud, and the claim sued upon was palpably without foundation;[4] secondly, where the judgment itself or some material step leading to it was concocted in fraud; and, thirdly, where the allegation is not attended with any impeachment of the judgment, as where the injured party, accepting the judgment as binding, sues for damages for the fraud by which the opposite party obtained the claim passed into judgment.[5]

An award not made a rule of court cannot be set aside for

---

[1] Pearce v. Olney, 20 Conn. 544; Engel v. Scheuerman, 40 Ga. 206; Rogers v. Gwinn, 21 Iowa, 58. See Dobson v. Pearce, 12 N. Y. 156. *Contra*, Bicknell v. Field, *supra*.

[2] See Bigelow, Estoppel, 179, 180 (2d ed.).

[3] Christmas v. Russell, 5 Wall. 290.

[4] Luckenback v. Anderson, 47 Penn. St. 123.

[5] Wanzer v. De Baun, 1 E. D. Smith, 261; *ante*, p. 177.

fraud in a court of law. The only remedy is by bill in equity. This is true, however gross the misconduct or even corruption of a party or of the arbitrator.[1] The reason of this is that in such cases there is no ground upon which a court of law can entertain jurisdiction for such purpose.[2]

It is equally true that, after an award under a rule of court has been entered as the judgment of the court, it cannot be set aside at common law for fraud except under a practice applicable to judgments generally. The fraud should have been alleged before the award became the judgment of the court, or before the close of the term. At that time, the court would have vacated the award on motion of the injured party, or upon plea of the facts in opposition to a motion by the opposite party to have the award entered as the judgment of the court.[3] Afterwards the remedy is by bill in equity.[4]

It follows that in cases of awards of this kind (under a rule of court), if an action be brought upon the arbitration bond for non-performance of the award, or in an action upon the award itself, the defendant cannot, in the absence of statute, plead fraud on the part of the plaintiff or of the arbitrator in defence to the action.[5] For, the award having become a judgment of court, to allow such a plea would be to allow the party to impeach a judgment in a collateral action; at least, if the plea were a plea in bar of the right of action, and not in the nature of a cross-claim to damages by reason of the fraud. In principle, it would seem doubtful therefore if the same rule would apply to awards neither made under a rule of court nor entered as judgments thereof. The award in such a case is but an ordinary contract,[6] simple or special accord-

---

[1] Fletcher v. Hubbard, 43 N. H. 58; Veale v. Warner, 1 Wms. Saund. 327 c; Greenhill v. Church, 3 Rep. in Ch. 49; Russell, Awards, 50 (4th ed.).

[2] Russell, *ut supra.* [3] Morse, Awards, 611.

[4] See Emerson v. Udall, 13 Vt. 477.

[5] Morse, Awards, 542, citing many cases.

[6] Russell, Awards, 50 (4th ed.).

ing to its form ; and it should seem that, when sued upon, it should be subject to the same kinds of defence as may be made in other cases of contract. And so it has been decided, even in a case in which the submission was upon agreement that there should be no appeal.[1]

It would seem on principle that, whether the award has become a judgment of court or not, an action can be brought by the injured party for the fraud whereby the claim upon which the award was based was obtained, provided no issue as to such fraud were raised in the arbitration ; since such a proceeding does not impeach the award. In such a case, the party adopts the award, but seeks damages for the original fraud of the plaintiff in the award. The case is precisely like the common one of a party drawn into a contract by fraud accepting the bargain, and then suing for the fraud.[2] Whether such a cross action can be maintained for perjured evidence introduced by the opposite party does not appear to have been decided. If the award was made under a rule of court and has passed into judgment, it is at least very doubtful if such an action could be maintained. The authorities concerning ordinary judgments are opposed to such actions.[3] Nor is it clear that equity will set aside an award of this kind on such grounds, if the award has become a judgment of court ;[4] though, before the award has been adopted by the court, equity would doubtless entertain a bill to set it aside for perjury of the opposite party's witnesses. And, *a fortiori*, would this be true of an award out of court. This, indeed, would seem to be the preferable mode of proceeding for such a case, instead of bringing a cross action.

A common law or statutory award, subject to the foregoing qualifications, is assailable for corruption or misbehavior of the arbitrators, notwithstanding that the parties may have

[1] Speer *v.* Bidwell, 44 Penn. St. 23.
[2] *Ante*, p. 177.   [3] *Ante*, p. 173.
[4] Emerson *v.* Udall, 13 Vt. 477.

agreed that there shall be no appeal.[1] And the same would
doubtless be true in respect of fraud in the opposite party
alone ; for it cannot be presumed that the agreement against
exceptions or appeal was intended to cover any fraudulent
practice that might be resorted to. Such an agreement merely
bars the parties from setting up mistakes of law or of fact by
the arbitrators.[2]

As to what constitutes evidence of fraud or corruption, no
general rule can be laid down : each case must be judged by
its own facts. However, it is held that the fact that the damages assessed are much larger than a court would probably
give, and that they are divided very disproportionably and to
appearance arbitrarily between two defendants, will not
constitute evidence of fraud or improper conduct in the
arbitrator ; at least, not so decisively alone as to be ground
for setting aside the award.[3] But, if the amount of damages
assessed be grossly extravagant, it seems that the award may
be treated as fraudulent.[4]

Strong evidence is required to impeach a result on which
the arbitrators heard the parties and exercised their judgment,
if there was no actual concealment of facts. Something more
is necessary than a mere showing by an accountant that the
statement of account presented to the arbitrators by the
opposite party was, for example, in a form not according to
the rules of book-keeping, when it is apparent that the statement as made out could not have misled, if compared with
other papers in the case, to which it must be presumed that
all the parties looked for information.[5]

---

[1] Speer v. Bidwell, 44 Penn. St. 23.

[2] Ib. ; McCahan v. Reamey, 33 Penn. St. 535.

[3] Burchell v. Marsh, 17 How. 344. A very excessive award may be
considered erroneous, however. South Carolina R. Co. v. Moore, 28
Ga. 398.

[4] Van Cortlandt v. Underhill, 17 Johns. 405 ; Rudd v. Jones, 4 Dana,
229 ; Tracy v. Herrick, 25 N. H. 381 ; In re Hall, 2 Man. & G. 847 ;
Morse, Awards, 539.   [5] Beam v. Macomber, 33 Mich. 127.

Where an award is procured by false and fraudulent pretences and testimony, equity will restrain the collection of the award, where the complainant could not make a successful defence in a court of law; and the fact that the award was confirmed by the Circuit and Supreme Courts will not prevent equity from enjoining the collection of the judgment.[1] The whole award, however, need not be disturbed where the fraud complained of can be discriminated and settled by itself.[2]

In some cases, if not in all, arbitrators may open and retry a judgment or decree upon the matter submitted to them, if they find that it was obtained by artifice, trick, or other fraudulent practice. Thus, it has been held that if the plaintiff in a suit in equity has been induced by fraud to settle the same, and his bill has thereupon been dismissed without an entry that it was without prejudice, and if then, without applying to the court for a correction of the decree, an agreement is made to submit to arbitration "all claims, whether in law or in equity, existing between the parties," the arbitrators may receive evidence that the settlement was obtained by fraud, and proceed to retry the subject-matter of the equity suit.[3]

[1] Chambers v. Cook, 42 Ala. 171.
[2] Champion v. Wenham, Ambl. 245; Beam v. Macomber, 33 Mich. 127.
[3] Mickles v. Thayer, 14 Allen, 114.

CHAPTER IV.

WAIVER AND CONFIRMATION.

It is well established that if a party, with knowledge that a fraud has been perpetrated upon him in a particular transaction, confirm the transaction by making new agreements or engagements respecting it, or by retaining and using the subject of it after knowledge,[1] or otherwise recognize it as binding, he thereby waives the right to treat it as invalid, and abandons his right to rescind if it be a case of contract, or to redress if it be a tort not attended with a contract with the wrongdoer.[2] If the fraud result in a contract, performance of the same, after discovering that it was fraudulently obtained by the opposite party, does not preclude a person from suing for damages on account of the fraud.[3] The injured party may retain the benefits of the contract, confirm its validity, and still recover damages for the fraud by which he was induced to make it;[4] or he may recoup any damages which he has sustained, if the opposite party sue him for money due on the contract, or for other failure to perform it.[5]

A contract tainted with fraud, being merely voidable, may be confirmed or ratified without a new contract founded upon a new consideration,[6] unless the fraud be committed upon a third person. In such a case, the parties to the wrong cannot

[1] Dunks v. Fuller, 32 Mich. 242.

[2] Edwards v. Roberts, 7 Smedes & M. 544.

[3] Parker v. Marquis, 64 Mo. 38. See Chap. XVI. § 2.   [4] Ib.

[5] Goodwin v. Robinson, 30 Ark. 535.

[6] Pearsoll v. Chapin, 44 Penn. St. 9, overruling Miller's Appeal, 30 Penn. St. 478, and, it seems, Stuart v. Blum, 28 Penn. St. 225.

in any way ratify it so as to make it binding upon the person intended to be defrauded.[1]

In order to show a valid confirmation of a contract tainted with fraud against one of the parties, very strong facts must be proved, particularly that he had full knowledge of the truth.[2] Fraud cannot be condoned, unless there be full knowledge of the facts and of the rights arising out of those facts, and the parties are at arm's length.[3] The confirmation, for example, of a bond obtained by undue influence, the ratifying act being made under pressure (though not duress), and in ignorance that the original obligation was not valid in law, is not binding.[4] To constitute a binding confirmation in such a case, it is necessary that there should be knowledge of the invalidity of the obligation; and, though this be a matter of law, the court will not presume it.[5] So, where a person agrees to give up his claim to property in favor of another, such renunciation of right will not be supported if, at the time of making it, he was ignorant of his legal rights and of the value of the property renounced, especially if the party with whom he dealt possessed and kept back from him better information on the subject.[6]

The compromise of a matter founded in fraud, without knowledge of the commission of such wrong, is not binding, though the injured party may have had suspicions of the fraud, if his suspicion were not founded upon facts or upon investigation.[7]

In general, the compromise of a doubtful right is valid, especially where a cause is ended by it; and where a plaintiff is fully apprised of his rights, and understands what he is doing, he may compound a demand on what terms he will.

[1] Pearsoll v. Chapin, supra.
[2] Juniata Bank v. Brown, 5 Serg. & R. 226.
[3] Moxon v. Payne, Law R. 8 Ch. 881.
[4] Kempson v. Ashbee, Law R. 10 Ch. 15.   [5] Ib.
[6] McCarthy v. Decaix, 2 Russ. & M. 614.
[7] Baker v. Spencer, 47 N. Y. 562.

Nor will inequality be sufficient ground for setting aside the
transaction. But, as follows from what has just been said,
the compromise itself must have been fairly obtained. Fraudulent compromises, it has been strongly said, should be broken
through, though made over and over again. It was accordingly held in a case before Lord Hardwicke that the confirmation of an unconscionable purchase of a seaman's prize-
money would be set aside, the confirmation being no more
just than the purchase.[1] So, where a contract is clearly
fraudulent by reason of misrepresentation, a second contract
annulling the first, made while under the influence of such
misrepresentation, and a repetition thereof, is a continu-
ation and not a confirmation or condonation of the first
fraud.[2]

In order to make the receipt of the consideration of a sale
operate as a waiver of the right to rescind the same for fraud,
it must clearly appear that, at the time the consideration was
received, the vendor was free from the influence and control
of the fraudulent acts, and that the act set up as a waiver
was knowingly done by the vendor or by some one specifically
authorized by him. The mere receipt of money from his
general agent, paid to the agent by the wrongdoer, is not
sufficient, unless it appear that the vendor knew he was
thereby accepting the money of the purchaser upon the contract.[3] A compromise of fraud, however, is good, though the
party was compelled to consent to it by a strong pressure of
pecuniary difficulty.[4]

To have effect as a confirmation of a contract obtained by
fraud, a subsequent transaction must appear to have been
entered into with that intention, or that portion of it alleged
to be a confirmation must have been with such intention,

[1] Taylour v. Rochfort, 2 Ves. 281.
[2] Davis v. Henry, 4 W. Va. 571.
[3] McLean v. Clark, 47 Ga. 24.
[4] Craig v. Bradley, 27 Mich. 353.

where the party confirming was not under the influence of
the previous transaction.[1]   Where a confirmation of fraud is
relied on as a defence to a suit for relief from a fraud clearly
established, the confirmation must stand upon the clearest
evidence.[2]   The confirming act must be so disconnected with
the previous transaction as to leave the defrauded party the
complete power of determining, as upon an original act,
whether he will do it or not.[3]   The parties must be at arm's
length and stand on equal terms.[4]

No one except a purchaser for value, without notice, can
hold an interest obtained through the fraud of another, any
more than he could if the fraud were committed by himself.
By receiving and retaining a benefit procured by the fraud of
another, he is bound by that fraud.[5]   It follows that, after a
party has obtained knowledge that he has been led into an
executory contract for the purchase of property by false
representations made by the vendor, he cannot accept of a
conveyance of the property without waiving the fraud.[6]
Hence, he cannot then set up the fraud in defence to an
action for the purchase-money.[7]   So, where a party, with full
knowledge of the alleged fraudulent circumstances, recog-
nizes or confirms a contract made in his name by an agent,
he cannot afterwards, when sued upon the contract, set up
the fraud or want of authority in that agent.[8]

A fraudulent act should in certain cases be repudiated by
the subject of it promptly upon its discovery, if ever. A
party, for example, who has paid money in pursuance of a

---

[1] Montgomery v. Pickering, 116 Mass. 227.

[2] Ib.; Morse v. Royal, 12 Ves. 355, 373.   [3] Ib.

[4] Moxon v. Payne, Law R. 8 Ch. 881.

[5] Bowers v. Johnson, 10 Smedes & M. 169; Cobb v. Hatfield, 46
N. Y. 533.

[6] Vernol v. Vernol, 63 N. Y. 45; Saratoga & S. R. Co. v. Row, 24
Wend. 74.   [7] Vernol v. Vernol, supra.

[8] McGowen v. Garrard, 2 Stewart (Ala.), 479; Fitzsimmons v. Joslin,
21 Vt. 129.

contract for a speculative purpose cannot recover the money
on the ground that he was led into such contract and payment by fraud, where, after discovering the fraud, he has
continued to claim and exercise his rights under the contract
until the enterprise has proved unsuccessful.[1] But this rule
proceeds on the principle of protecting the rights of others,
which may have intervened ; and mere delay in repudiating
a fraud, where no such rights have been acquired, will not
bar an action for the fraud, or preclude a defence to a contract obtained by fraud. There must be something more than
mere delay in repudiating fraud, even in the case of a subsisting contract. There must be something equivalent to a
ratification of the contract after discovery of the fraud ; and
this may be either by acts of express recognition of its binding force, or by allowing the other party to proceed upon it
and change his position, or by the intervention of the rights
and interests of third innocent persons. But such facts as
these merely preclude the injured party from *repudiating* the
contract : he may still bring an action for the damage sustained by being drawn into the contract,[2] even though the
contract has passed into judgment,[3] unless he has compromised his claim.[4]

A failure by an underwriter to return premiums after discovering that the contract of insurance was obtained through
fraud is not a ratification of the undertaking. The underwriter cannot be compelled to return the premiums paid in
such cases.[5]

A waiver or confirmation of fraud can of course be made
only by the injured party, or by his duly authorized agent.
An agent, however, can never ratify a fraud of his own.

---

[1] Grannis v. Hooker, 31 Wis. 474.   [2] *Ante*, p. 184.
[3] Wanzer v. De Baun, 1 E. D. Smith, 261 ; *ante*, p. 177.
[4] *Ante*, pp. 185, 186.
[5] Harris v. Equitable Life Assur. Soc., 6 Thomp. & C. 108; s. c.
5 Big. 342.

Hence, an arrangement made by persons who are directors of a railroad company with a contractor, by which such persons are to share in the profits of the contract for the construction of the road, can only be confirmed by the stockholders.[1]

If a party who has been induced by the fraud of another to give him a security (upon a false representation of indebtedness, for example) bring an action on the case for the fraud so practised upon him, he will be allowed to recover the value of the security. But the plaintiff thereby affirms the validity, it is said, of the security, and cannot afterwards contest his liability thereon.[2]

[1] Paine *v.* Lake Erie R. Co., 31 Ind. 283.
[2] Fenemore *v.* United States, 3 Dall. 357.

II. PRESUMPTIVE OR CONSTRUCTIVE FRAUD.

CHAPTER V.

CONFIDENTIAL RELATIONS AND THE LIKE.

§ 1. INTRODUCTORY.

IN the preceding chapters, we have had under consideration the subject of Actual Fraud, as to which we have seen, sometimes by direct statement and at other times by plain inference, that it is universally necessary for the party bringing forward the allegation of such a wrong to support his charge by express evidence. We come now to a branch of fraud of a quite different type. Instead of finding the burden of proof resting upon the complaining party, we shall hereafter find the law, upon the appearance of certain relations between the parties, termed relations of confidence, raising a presumption of fraud, — a presumption that the transaction brought to the notice of the court was effected through fraud or (what is the same thing in law) undue influence by the opposite party, by reason of his occupying a position affording him peculiar opportunities for taking advantage of the complaining party. Having special facilities for committing fraud upon the party whose interests have been intrusted to him, the law, looking to the frailty of human nature, requires the party in the superior situation to show that his action has been honest and honorable.

A confidential relation arises wherever a continuous trust is reposed in the skill or integrity of another, or the property or pecuniary interest, in whole or in part, or the bodily custody, of one person, is placed in charge of another. For the protection of the former, the law raises a presumption that any transaction between such parties has been effected through undue and illegal means by the latter, — that the party in the superior position has used that position to the injury of the party in the inferior situation ; and this presumption must be overcome, if the transaction be impeached, before the superior party in the confidential situation can succeed.

It is a well-established principle of equity that persons standing in a confidential relation towards others cannot hold benefits which those others may have conferred upon them, unless they can show to the satisfaction of the court that the persons by whom the benefits have been conferred had competent and independent advice, or at least a full disclosure from themselves of all facts affecting the bounty. Nor does the age or capacity of the person conferring the benefit, or the nature of the benefit conferred, affect the principle. Age and capacity are considerations which may be of great importance in cases in which the principle does not apply ; but they are of little, if of any importance, in cases in which the principle is not applicable.[1] And, as to the nature of the benefit, the injury to the party by whom the benefit is conferred cannot depend upon its nature.[2]

This principle, however, admits, it is thought, of some limitation. It cannot be said that a mere trifling gift to a person standing in a confidential relation, or a mere trifling liability incurred in favor of such a person, ought to stand in the same position as would the gift of a man's whole property, or a liability involving it. In such cases of mere trifling benefits, equity will not interfere to set them aside, upon the mere fact of the proof of a confidential relation and the absence of proof of competent and independent advice. Before the court would undo such a benefit, it would require proof of *mala fides* or of undue exercise of influence.[3]

---

[1] Rhodes *v.* Bate, Law R. 1 Ch. 252.   [2] Ib.   [3] Ib., Turner, L. J.

The relief granted in these cases of confidential relations stands upon a general principle, applying to all the variety of relations in which dominion may be exercised by one person over another.[1]　And, when a confidential relation is once established between parties either by act of law or by agreement, the rights incident to that relation continue until the relation terminates; and time will not operate as a bar during the existence of such relation.[2]

§ 2. OF ATTORNEY AND CLIENT.

The relation of attorney to client is one of close confidence, and at the same time one in which the attorney stands at a great advantage. For this reason, courts of equity often interpose to declare transactions void which in other relations would be held unobjectionable. By the law both of England and of America, a gratuity, or a security for a gratuity, given during the pendency of a suit, and with reference to the litigation, will seldom be upheld ; and, if services have been actually rendered, the security or gift will be valid in most cases only in so far as just services have been the consideration for it ; and *a fortiori* if the client be a person of weak mind. Thus, in a case before Lord Hardwicke, a bill was filed to set aside a deed by which the plaintiff's wife, while separated from her husband, had made an absolute conveyance to the defendant, a solicitor, of £1,000. The consideration expressed in the deed was for services done and favors shown. It appeared also that the woman was of weak mind. Lord Hardwicke decreed that the deed should stand as a security only for such sum as was justly due the defendant.[3]

---

[1] Huguenin v. Baseley, 14 Ves. 273, 285; Dent v. Bennett, 4 Mylne & C. 269, 277.

[2] Blount v. Robeson, 3 Jones, Eq. 73; Northcott v. Casper, 6 Ired. Eq. 303.

[3] Sanderson v. Glass, 2 Atk. 296. See also Walmesley v. Booth, Ib.

The same doctrine has been held in much more recent cases.[1] In the case first cited, a question arose as to the validity of a conveyance of real estate to the defendant, a solicitor by the plaintiff's intestate, his client. It appeared that the defendant was the son of one for whom the client had for many years entertained feelings of great regard and respect, and that after the father's death the client had induced the defendant to commence practice as a solicitor, with promises of support and patronage from himself. Under these circumstances, and entertaining personal regard for the defendant, the client had conveyed to him the land in question by a deed, on its face a purchase-deed, the consideration of which was recited to be the payment of £100. The real value of the property was £1,200. The defendant produced evidence to show that no money passed ; that the transaction was not intended to be a purchase, but was intended as a gift for his services and for affection. The defendant had prepared the deed, and the client had had no other advice. The deed was set aside, many authorities being cited to support the decision.[2]

In another recent case, a claim was preferred by a solicitor against the estate of his client, deceased, for a sum of money alleged to have been advanced to the client on loan. In fact,

27 ; Newman v. Payne, 2 Ves. Jr. 199 ; Plenderleath v. Fraser, 3 Ves. & B. 174 ; Wood v. Downs, 18 Ves. 20 ; Rose v. Mynatt, 7 Yerg. 30 ; Berrien v. McLean, Hoff. Ch. 420 ; Miles v. Ervin, 1 McCord, Ch. 524 ; Bibb v. Smith, 1 Dana, 580 ; Starr v. Vanderheyden, 9 Johns. 253 ; Mott v. Harrington, 12 Vt. 199.

[1] Tyrrell v. Bank of London, 10 H. L. Cas. 26 ; Tomson v. Judge, 3 Drew. 306 ; Holmes's Estate, 3 Giff. 337 ; O'Brien v. Lewis, 4 Giff. 221 ; Walker v. Smith, 29 Beav. 394 ; and see American cases cited in preceding note.

[2] Holman v. Loynes, 18 Jur. 839 ; Welles v. Middleton, 1 Cox, 112 ; Hatch v. Hatch, 9 Ves. 292 ; Morse v. Royal, 12 Ves. 371 ; Ormonde v. Hutchinson, 13 Ves. 47 ; Wood v. Downes, 18 Ves. 127 ; Montesquieu v. Sandys, 18 Ves. 302. Lord Eldon's ruling in Harris v. Tremenheere, 15 Ves. 31, was doubted, and said to be inconsistent with other decisions here cited of the learned chancellor.

the money formed the proceeds of a bond debt due to the
testator, and received by the solicitor at the client's direction;
the solicitor alleging that his client had given the same to
him by an agreement prepared by the solicitor, at the client's
expense, which, however, contained no recital of intended
bounty, and that the money had been then loaned to the
client. The claim was refused. The court said that such a
transaction was very unusual; and, considering that it was a
transaction between solicitor and client, that circumstance
created a great difficulty in the way of the claim. The law
of the court was well established; and the principle was that
the relation of solicitor and client was one of such high confidence on the part of the client that the solicitor was considered
to have an amount of influence over the mind and action of
his client, which, while that influence remained, rendered it
almost impossible that the gift should prevail.[1]

A fortiori, in the absence of clear evidence of circumstances
sufficient to remove the pressure of influence presumed to
exist over the client, a mere parol direction by a client to his
solicitor to retain, as a present, money of the former afterwards
to come into the hands of the latter, cannot amount to such
a gift or act of bounty as cannot be set aside.[2]

Relief may be afforded even when the plaintiff claims as
a mere volunteer under the client. Thus, in an Irish case, it
appeared that the plaintiff was a daughter of the defendant's
client, and that she was entitled to a moiety under a provision
by her father, charging certain real estate for the benefit of
children by a previous marriage (of whom the plaintiff was
one); provided later conveyances to the defendant of the
same premises, annulling the charge, were void. The court
found that these conveyances were made by the plaintiff's
father while in prison for debt; that the defendant was his
solicitor at the time; and that there was no consideration for

---

[1] Holmes's Estate, 3 Giff. 337.   [2] O'Brien *v.* Lewis, 4 Giff. 221.

the same at the time when they were made. They were accordingly set aside ; the court saying that the plaintiff was in as good a position as an heir-at-law, and that nothing was more common than for the court to afford relief to an heir-at-law against frauds committed upon his ancestor.[1] In another case, a gift by a client was declared invalid at the instance of a residuary legatee of the client.[2]

The relationship, however, creates no absolute incapacity on the part of the attorney to receive a gratuity from his client. He may not only receive a gift made without reference to a particular litigation or to particular services, as an expression of affection or admiration merely, but he may also receive a valid gift made in view of special pending or prospective services. As to past legal services, there never has been any doubt that the client can bind himself by a gratuity to his attorney. In cases of this kind, the relationship *in hac re* for which the gift was made having terminated, the attorney stands in the same position which any other person regarded as a benefactor would occupy ; and the transaction will stand or fall upon the general doctrines of law pertaining to gifts.

As we have stated, a client may make an irrevocable gift to his attorney with reference to particular services, pending or prospective ; but this is true only in cases where it is made to appear that the attorney has divested himself of the advantage of his position, and put himself, with reference to the gratuity, on the footing of a third person. He must have disclosed every fact within his knowledge with regard to the property given him which might have an influence upon the client, and have abstained from bringing to bear any pressure for the bestowment of the gratuity. He must have put the client at arm's length. But, if facts of this nature appear, the client's act will be binding.[3]

[1] Falkner *v.* O'Brien, 2 Ball & B. 214.
[2] Walker *v.* Smith, 29 Beav. 394.
[3] See cases, *infra*.

The mere existence of the relation of attorney and client raises a presumption against the validity of the gratuity ; and the burden of proof is upon the attorney to show the total absence of any pressure, unfairness, or concealment on his part. He must show by express evidence that the act proceeded from the free volition and desire of the client. It is not incumbent upon the client in the first instance to prove the exercise of undue influence or other impropriety by the attorney.[1] The learned commentator on equity jurisprudence, after stating that the burden of establishing the perfect fairness, adequacy, and equity of the transaction is thrown upon the attorney, adds that this proceeds upon the ground that he who bargains in a matter of advantage with a person who places confidence in him is bound to show that a reasonable use of that confidence has been made ; [2] quoting a familiar remark of Lord Eldon in a case of sale by the client to his attorney.[3]

---

[1] Tomson v. Judge, 3 Drew. 306 ; Holmes's Estate, 3 Giff. 337 ; Walker v. Smith, 29 Beav. 394 ; Nesbit v. Lockman, 34 N. Y. 167 ; Jennings v. McConnell, 17 Ill. 148. So, too, in the case of sales, which, according to Tomson v. Judge, are not so strong against the attorney, because the parties there are more at arm's length. Gibson v. Jeyes, 6 Ves. 266 ; Montesquieu v. Sandys, 18 Ves. 302; Bellew v. Russell, 1 Ball & B. 104, 107 ; Harris v. Tremenheere, 15 Ves. 34, 39 ; Cane v. Allen, 2 Dow, 289, 299 ; Edwards v. Meyrick, 2 Hare, 60 ; Hesse v. Briant, 6 DeG., M. & G. 623; Savery v. King, 5 H. L. Cas. 627; Barnard v. Hunter, 2 Jur. N. s. 1213; Rhodes v. Bate, L. R. 1 Ch. 252 ; Moore v. Prance, 9 Hare, 299 ; Hawley v. Cramer, 4 Cowen, 717 ; Evans v. Ellis, 5 Denio, 640 ; Howell v. Ransom, 11 Paige, 538 ; In re Post, 3 Edw. Ch. 369 ; Kisling v. Shaw, 33 Cal. 425 ; Poillon v. Martin, 1 Sandf. Ch. 569 ; Haight v. Moore, 37 N. Y. Superior, 161; McMahan v. Smith, 6 Heisk. 167 ; Brock v. Barnes, 40 Barb. 521 ; Condit v. Blackwell, 7 C. E. Green, 481 ; Harper v. Perry, 28 Iowa, 57 ; Dunn v. Record, 63 Maine, 17 ; Savery v. Sypher, 6 Wall 157.   [2] Story, Equity, § 311.

[3] Gibson v. Jeyes, 6 Ves. 266, 278. It is a corollary to the above presumption against the attorney, that the attorney cannot rely on the securities given him by the client to prove the existence of a debt due by the latter. He must, irrespective of such securities, prove the debt for which they were given. Lawless v. Mansfield, 1 Dru. & War. 557.

The presumption of influence, however, may sometimes be rebutted by circumstances short of the total dissolution of the relation of solicitor and client. That relation is only regarded as creating the influence ; and, if evidence is given of circumstances which remove all effect of the influence, there will remain no incapacity on the part of the solicitor to become the object of the client's bounty, and to be the recipient of a gift, valid both at law and in equity.[1] The burden of proof, however, always rests upon the recipient of the bounty to show that a gift was intended to be made ;[2] and also, as the cases above stated, and others[3] show, that it was made without undue influence.

Whatever the rebutting evidence is, it is said that the testimony of the recipient himself should not be considered, but the gift should be established by separate and independent evidence. No such evidence being adduced in the case referred to, a gift *inter vivos* was held void ; though there was no express evidence of undue influence. It was said that if the client had called in a third person, who had no interest in the matter, and had said that he had made the particular gift to the solicitor for the solicitor's own benefit, or for the benefit of himself and family, the transaction would have been upheld.[4] The question, moreover, whether undue influence is to be inferred from the nature of the transaction, as well as the question whether the transaction itself is contrary to the policy of the law, is a question of law, and should not be sent to a jury.

It seems that testamentary provisions in favor of a man's solicitor stand upon somewhat more favorable ground than gifts *inter vivos*. In a case in the English Court of Appeal in

[1] Holmes's Estate, 3 Giff. 337.
[2] Walker *v.* Smith, 29 Beav. 394.
[3] Hoghton *v.* Hoghton, 15 Beav. 275, 298; Cooke *v.* Lamotte, Ib. 234; Gibson *v.* Jeyes, 6 Ves. 266.
[4] Hoghton *v.* Hoghton, 15 Beav. 278, 298.
[5] Casborne *v.* Barsham, 2 Beav. 76.

Chancery, it appeared that a testator had made a provision in his will in favor of his solicitor to the extent of £1,000, by which he wished to confirm a gift he had already made to him. There was evidence that before signing the will, which had been drawn by the client, a third person, an old friend of the testator, had attended and read over the will, and had then asked if the disposition of property was such as he wished; to which he replied that it was, and that he would have done more for his solicitor, if the latter would have permitted. The provision was upheld. The Lord Justice Turner said that there was a great distinction between the jurisdiction of the Court of Chancery, as applied to contracts and as applied to testamentary dispositions. In the case of a written contract, chancery could direct the instrument to be delivered up to be cancelled, but it had no such jurisdiction with respect to a will. When a will was tendered for probate, a court of competent jurisdiction decided whether the document expressed the will and intention of the testator; and, if any fraud affecting the will or intention of the testator could be proved in the Ecclesiastical Court, that court could rectify the instrument, and take out of it the particular clause to which the objection applied.[1]

In a somewhat later case, however, the Master of the Rolls expressed the opinion that gifts of legacies do not stand upon any different principle from gifts *inter vivos*. He observed at the same time that in all cases of legacies where the testator or testatrix has the will clearly read over and explained, and gives directions to prepare it, and has it executed in the presence of the required number of witnesses, there is the best and most conclusive evidence that the testator intended the bounty to the legatee. And the question then arose whether the influence exercised by the legatee were such that the testator could not fairly be considered to have been

---

[1] Hindson v. Weatherill, 5 DeG., M. & G. 301, distinguishing Segrave v. Kirwan, 1 Beatt. 157.

a free agent, by being under any undue influence of the
person to whom the legacy was made. He accordingly proceeded to consider the question whether undue influence had
in fact been used in the case before the court; his conclusion
being that the legacy was free from any such taint.[1]

A bequest in favor of an attorney who writes a will is not
necessarily void.[2] The *onus probandi*, indeed, lies in every
case upon the party propounding a will. He must satisfy
the conscience of the court that the instrument propounded
is the last will of a free and competent testator. And, if
a party writes or prepares a will under which he takes a benefit, that is a circumstance which ought generally to excite
the suspicion of the court, and calls upon it to be vigilant
and zealous in examining the evidence in support of the
instrument; in favor of which it ought not to pronounce,
unless the suspicion is removed, and the court satisfied that
the paper propounded does express the true will of the deceased.[3] But the most that has been required in such cases
is satisfactory evidence that the testator was of sound mind
and clearly understood the contents of the will, and was at
the time under no restraint. No case has gone so far as to
overthrow a will duly executed, where it was shown that the
party executing it was of sound mind and clearly understood
its contents, though it was drawn by the person taking the
estate.[4] Thus, in a case just cited,[5] it appeared that one

[1] Walker *v.* Smith, 29 Beav. 394.
[2] Riddell *v.* Johnson, 26 Gratt. 152 ; Billinghurst *v.* Vickers, 1 Phill.
187 ; Paske *v.* Ollatt, 2 Phill. 323 ; Barry *v.* Butlin, 1 Curt. Ecc. 637 ;
Baker *v.* Batt, 2 Moore, P. C. 317 ; Hitchins *v.* Wood, Ib. 355, 436 ; Wilson *v.* Moran, 3 Brad. 172 ; Crispell *v.* Dubois, 4 Barb. 393 ; Cramer *v.*
Crumbaugh, 3 Md. 491; Watterson *v.* Watterson, 1 Head, 1 ; Adair *v.*
Adair, 30 Ga. 104; Nexsen *v.* Nexsen, 3 Abb. App. Dec. 360. The cases
of Meek *v.* Perry, 36 Miss. 256, and Garvin *v.* Williams, 44 Mo. 465, are
explained in Riddell *v.* Johnson, *supra.*
[3] Barry *v.* Butlin, *supra, per* Parke, B.; Riddell *v.* Johnson, *supra.*
[4] Wilson *v.* Moran, *supra ;* Riddell *v.* Johnson. See *post,* § 12.
[5] Riddell *v.* Johnson.

Johnson had died an unmarried man, with a large property, including a considerable sum in bonds. Bocock had been his counsel for years, and the deceased had for him a strong attachment. In February, 1867, Bocock wrote Johnson's will, by which he gave the most of his real estate to certain illegitimate children. He did not at this time dispose of the bonds, which were and remained in the hands of Bocock. In the summer following, Johnson requested Bocock to draw a codicil to his will; and by this codicil he gave to Bocock all that remained of the bonds after the payment of certain debts and expenses. Johnson had a number of next of kin, among them two sisters, to none of whom he gave any thing. It appeared that the testator was perfectly competent to make a will; that he dictated the bequest in favor of Bocock, without any suggestion from Bocock or from any one else; that the codicil was read to him, and that he clearly understood it, and intended that it should stand as written; and further that he had been on bad terms with his family for years, and had more than once expressed his determination not to leave any part of his estate to any of them. It was accordingly held that the bequest to Bocock must stand.

While the courts will scrutinize more closely the circumstances under which a gift has been made by a client to his attorney, than in the case of a sale, the rules of law governing these classes of transactions appear to be the same, except in so far as a gift differs in nature from a sale. The presumptions in both cases are against the attorney, and they are of the same character. In the case of a gift, as we have seen, the attorney, by reason of his position, rests under the opprobrious presumption of having exercised undue influence and of having suppressed facts concerning the property which should have been disclosed to the client; and, in order to maintain the validity of the gift, he must remove the effect of this presumption. The authorities about to be considered show that the same is true of sales by the client to his attorney;

and, further, that these presumptions are not removed by recitals of the client in a deed of conveyance.[1] And purchasers from the attorney with notice of his fiduciary relation towards the property stand in the same situation as the attorney himself.[2]

Sales and contracts between attorney and client will of course be upheld, where the attorney was not, to use the expression of the books, attorney *in hac re*, and derived no information from the client. In other words, a sale by a client to his attorney will be upheld, when the circumstances are not such as to put the latter under the duty of advising the former.[3]

But even this rule is to be taken with caution. Thus, in a case just cited,[4] the relation of attorney and client was held to continue, notwithstanding the attorney had not acted as such for the client for more than a year previously to the purchase in question, though he had prepared the purchase agreement and charged for the same. The sale in this case was set aside on the ground that the consideration, an annuity, ought to have been considerably greater by reason of the intemperate habits of the client and vendor, though he had acted under the advice of an auctioneer, had named the price, and pressed the attorney to purchase.[5] The principle of this case seems to require the annulling of purchases

[1] *Post*, p. 204 ; Moore *v.* Prance, 9 Hare, 299.

[2] Trotter *v.* Smith, 59 Ill. 240; Alwood *v.* Mansfield, Ib. 496.

[3] Montesquieu *v.* Sandys, 18 Ves. 302 ; Edwards *v.* Meyrick, 2 Hare, 60 ; Holman *v.* Loynes, 18 Jur. 839 ; s. c. 4 DeG., M. & G. 270. See Jones *v.* Thomas, 2 Younge & C. 498 ; Hunter *v.* Atkins, 3 Mylne & K. 113 ; Howell *v.* Baker, 4 Johns. Ch. 118 ; Devinney *v.* Norris, 8 Watts, 314 ; 1 Story, Equity, § 313.

[4] Holman *v.* Loynes, *supra*.

[5] See also Gibbs *v.* Daniel, 4 Giff. 1 ; Carter *v.* Palmer, 8 Clark & F. 657 ; Galbraith *v.* Elder, 8 Watts, 81 ; Reid *v.* Stanley, 6 Watts & S. 326; Hockenbury *v.* Carlisle, 5 Watts & S. 348. Where this confidential relation is once proved to exist, the courts will presume its continuance, unless there be clear evidence of its determination. Rhodes *v.* Bate, Law R. 1 Ch. 252.

made to the disadvantage of the client, so long as it may be
assumed that the attorney stands in a situation in which he
is likely to be called upon for advice by the vendor. If the
situation have so far changed that the vendor has employed
another attorney intermediate the last transaction with the
purchaser and the sale in question, and has not employed the
purchaser since, it would appear that in most cases they
would now be considered as strangers to each other. But
even such a change of situation would not always be conclusive: a man may have two attorneys, and the purchaser may
still stand *pro hac vice* in a confidential relation to the vendor.
And it is certain that where the relation of attorney and
client has once existed, and *a fortiori* where to any extent it
is still in active exercise, the circumstances must clearly show
either that that relation does not subsist in respect of the
subject of the sale, or, if it does subsist, that the purchaser
has given the vendor the same information and advice that
he would have given him in a transaction between the client
and a third person,[1] and that upon the information pos-

---

[1] Cane *v.* Allen, 2 Dow, 289 ; Gibson *v.* Jeyes, 6 Ves. 266, 278; Edwards *v.* Meyrick, 2 Hare, 60 ; Rhodes *v.* Bate, *supra.* In Gibson *v.*
Jeyes, Lord Eldon said: " With respect to the case of the attorney, I have
no difficulty in saying Jeyes might have dealt for this annuity. But he
had two ways of proceeding, which this court must have held it quite
incumbent upon him, dealing with this lady [who was aged and of weak
mind] to attend to. If she proposed to him to buy it, he would have
done well to have said to her that Gibson would give more than any one
else ; that it was his interest to do so ; that he would secure it upon real
estate ; that it was more fit for her to deal with her relation than her
attorney ; and the transaction would have a better appearance in the
world. It was natural enough that she should answer she would not
deal with Gibson, but would consider herself only and her own comforts,
according to Benyon's advice to her. Then it would have been right for
the defendant to have declined it. Suppose she had insisted that he
should be the person : it would be too much for the court to proceed
upon delicacies such as these, and to say, he should not permit himself
to contract with her. Therefore, I say, he might contract : but then he
should have said, if he was to deal with her for this, she must get another
attorney to advise her as to the value ; or, if she would not, then out of

sessed by him at the time he has paid a fair price for the property.[1]

The courts of this country will not annul a sale by a client to his attorney by reason merely of the existence of a confidential relation between the parties, nor even where, added to this, it is proved that undue influence was exercised by the attorney ; provided it appear that the client received an adequate consideration in the transaction. Courts of equity will not interfere in favor of the client, in cases in which no damage was sustained by him by reason of the transaction.[2] The general doctrine that fraud without damage gives no ground of action either at law or in equity [3] limits the rights of the client. The relation of attorney and client differs in this respect from that of trustee and *cestui que trust*. Transactions between these latter may, it is said, be set aside at will by the beneficiary.[4] But between attorney and client

that state of circumstances, this clear duty results from the rule of this court, and throws upon him the whole *onus* of the case, — that, if he will mix with the character of attorney that of vendor, he shall, if the propriety of the contract comes in question, manifest that he has given her all that reasonable advice against himself that he would have given her against a third person. It is asked, Where is that rule to be found? I answer, in that great rule of the court that he who bargains in matter of advantage with a person placing confidence in him is bound to show that a reasonable use has been made of that confidence ; a rule applying to trustees, attorneys, or any one else."

There is, however, no positive rule of law requiring the intervention of another attorney in cases of dealings between attorney and client. Cutts *v.* Salmon, 21 Law J. Ch. 750 ; Jones *v.* Price, 20 Law T. 49 And even the actual intervention of another attorney who, with the knowledge of the purchaser, neglects or fails to properly discharge his duty, is not sufficient to support a purchase by an attorney from his client. Gibbs *v.* Daniel, 4 Giff. 1.

[1] Edwards *v.* Meyrick, *supra*.

[2] Kisling *v.* Shaw, 33 Cal. 425 ; Hawley *v.* Cramer, 4 Cowen, 717 ; Miles *v.* Ervin, 1 McCord, Ch. 524; *post*, p. 205. See Edwards *v.* Meyrick, 2 Hare, 60, 71. The English rule in bankruptcy appears to be different. See *post*, p. 209.

[3] Story, Equity, § 203.　　　　　　　　[4] Ib. § 311.

mere inadequacy of consideration, though not so gross as to
show fraud, will suffice to obtain the intervention of equity
on behalf of the client.[1] The burden of proving the adequacy of the consideration is, further, upon the attorney;
since he is bound to prove the general fairness of the transaction.[2] The statement of consideration in a conveyance between such parties is not enough to support the deed, even
where no evidence is produced against it.[3]

If none of these circumstances exist, the sale will be upheld, even though it appear that the purchase was one of
speculation on the part of the attorney, and by the develop-
ment of other facts turned out afterwards to have been greatly
to his advantage. Thus, in one of the cases above cited,[4] it
appeared that a sale of mineral lands had been made by a
client to his attorney for a fair price according to the existing
state of things; the transaction being also free from undue
influence or of concealment of facts. A railroad which was
in contemplation at the time of the sale was afterwards
constructed through the neighborhood, enhancing the value
of the minerals; but the court upheld the transaction.[5] Perhaps had the fact of the intended construction of the railroad

[1] Holman v. Loynes, 18 Jur. 839 ; s. c. 4 DeG., M. & G. 270.

[2] *Ante*, p. 200; Champion v. Rigby, Taml. 421; s. c. 9 Law J. Ch. 211;
De Rose v. Fay, 4 Edw. Ch. 40.
But this doctrine concerning the burden of proof does not apply to
cases where the solicitor or attorney is in the hostile attitude of an urgent
creditor. Johnson v. Fesemeyer, 3 DeG. & J. 13. Or, generally, where
it appears that he had put his client at arm's length before the transaction was effected. See Pearson v. Benson, 28 Beav. 599.

[3] Gresley v. Mousley, 3 DeG., F. & J. 433. See Morgan v. Higgins,
1 Giff. 270, 280 ; Moore v. Prance, 9 Hare, 299 ; Morgan v. Lewes, 4
Dow, 46 ; Morgan v. Evans, 3 Clark & F. 195 ; Lawless v. Mansfield, 1
Drew. & War. 557.

[4] Edwards v. Meyrick.

[5] It is proper to state that there was some question whether the
attorney were such *in hac re;* but the court proceeded upon the
view that he was, or rather that it mattered not whether he was or
not.

through the neighborhood been known only to the attorney, and not disclosed by him to the vendor, the result would have been different; though the opinion of the court throws doubt even upon that position.[1] The prospect of a railroad, however,

[1] Shadwell, V. C., in giving judgment, said : " The material fact upon which any question of value is raised is this, — that it is proved, and indeed admitted, that the estate is worth more than £2,100 at the present time ; and I think I may add that it became worth much more very soon after the purchase was made. But to what do the parties attribute this? The whole of the evidence shows that, up to the time of the purchase, the formation of a railroad had never been taken into account in the valuation of estates in that district; and that sales and purchases were made with reference only to the surface value. The purchase was made in February, 1825. In May, 1825, a bill for making a railroad through that part of the country received the royal assent; and, in consequence of the railroad being made, there arose a probability of coal being worked at a period less remote than there was previously reason to anticipate ; and therefore coal speculators would give a higher price for the property than they otherwise would have done. The question then comes to this : whether I could, as against the defendant, hold that the relation in which he stood as the plaintiff's attorney, in the suits I have referred to, imposed on him the obligation to prove that he gave the plaintiff notice that a railroad might be made, and that by possibility there might be an opportunity for working the coal under the land with advantage, and that, if it was worked, the land would be of greater value ; the whole of these considerations being purely of a speculatory character. Now, certainly, looking at the relation in which these parties stood, I have no ground for supposing that this would be more likely to be present in the mind of Meyrick than of any other person. He had nothing to do with these farms. The advantage to be derived from the proposed undertaking was a point as much open to one party as to the other, and was a merely speculative result, the communication of which I think I ought not now to require the defendant to prove, unless in fact the land had at that time become of an improved value, owing to that circumstance. This, however, would be in the knowledge of the plaintiff ; and he has not suggested any such case. The fact relating to the railroad is not to be found in the pleadings: it comes out casually in the evidence that a railroad bill was at that time in contemplation ; and then an argument is raised upon an assumption that Meyrick knew it, and took advantage of that knowledge. It is true that the *onus* lies on the defendant to show that the treaty was fairly conducted; but I do not think that in this case I can reasonably hold the possibility of a speculative and consequential advantage of this kind to fall within those circumstances which an attor-

had gone no further than to reach the point of legislative contemplation. No bill had as yet passed. Had the bill been
passed and a company formed and actually about to begin
work, it would probably have been considered necessary for
the attorney to advise his client on the point, at least if the
matter was not notorious.

There is some intimation in a case before Lord Eldon [1] that,
where the claim of the client proceeds solely on the ground
of inadequacy of price, the inadequacy should be so gross as
to shock the conscience, or the transaction will be upheld.
Such, he said, had been stated by Lord Thurlow to be the law;
and, though he (Lord Eldon) considered it loose enough, he
thought that courts of equity had felt bound by it, and occasionally had acted upon it. But this doctrine appears to have
been departed from in the later authorities,[2] and it is probably
to be confined to cases of non-confidential transactions. In
order to set aside a purchase at an undervalue, made by an
agent from his principal, it is not necessary that fraud, in the
broad sense of the term, should be proved.[3] Part of the
evidence necessary in such case is, in other words, supplied
by presumption from the relationship of the parties; and
hence the case is often called one of *constructive* fraud.

The nature and extent of the consideration are matters,

---

ney is bound to prove he disclosed to his client. I cannot on this part of
the case, from any thing which is before me, form any conclusion whether
this possible improvement ought or ought not to have been in the mind
of any person dealing with the property. Considering, as I do, that the
court is bound to watch strictly transactions between attorney and client,
I do not think that this court is bound to allow a contingent advantage,
which may or may not have been in the contemplation of the parties at
the time, to afford ground for imputing fraud or improper concealment
to the attorney, because he does not prove that he communicated it to
his client.''

[1] Gibson v. Jeyes, 6 Ves. 266, 273.

[2] Holman v. Loynes, 18 Jur. 839; s. c. 4 DeG., M. & G. 270. Compare
also Peacock v. Evans, 16 Ves. 512 ; Lowther v. Lowther, 13 Ves. 95.

[3] Medlicott v. O'Donnel, 1 Ball & B. 156, 165.

however, in respect of which the courts exercise a watchful interest over the client; [1] though it would be extremely difficult to draw any line by which to express the limits of the law in this particular. Doubtless, if the property have a definite market value, or a value capable of definite ascertainment,[2] and the purchase be effected at a price so much below it as to show that the client has suffered an actual, and not a mere possible loss, the transaction will be avoidable. But if the property have no certain value, or if its value be estimated differently by competent and disinterested persons, and the amount paid be equal to some though not to the highest estimates, and the court cannot certainly say that the client has lost money by the transaction, it would seem that the purchase would be valid. Even in a case like this, however, if it should appear that another party had been willing to give more for the property than the attorney gave, and that this fact was known to the attorney and not disclosed to the client, the sale could be set aside, upon principles already stated. And, if the value were known by the attorney to be placed by any respectable person at a higher figure than the sum about to be accepted from him, his proper course would be to disclose the fact.[3]   .   .   .   .

Upon similar principles to those pervading the authorities above considered, attorneys rest under at least a *prima facie* incapacity to purchase, adversely, the property of their

---

[1] De Rose v. Fay, 3 Edw. Ch. 369; s. c. 4 Edw. Ch. 40.

[2] As in the case of an annuity or a life insurance policy. See Holman v. Loynes, *supra*. It is held in Ireland that the mere (intentional) misstatement of the consideration will be sufficient to avoid a conveyance by a client to his attorney. Uppington v. Bullen, 2 Dru. & War. 184. Even in the absence of evidence to show the recital untrue, the statement of the consideration will not be accepted as true, or the conveyance upheld, without further proof. Gresley v. Mousley, 3 DeG., F. & J. 433. See Morgan v. Higgins, 1 Giff. 270, 280; Moore v. Prance, 9 Hare, 299.

[3] Compare the high standard of morality held necessary by Lord Eldon in Gibson v. Jeyes, *ante*, pp. 202, 203. As to the nature and extent of the consideration, see, further, Mills v. Mills, 26 Conn. 213.

clients, at judicial sales. The position of an attorney in the
management of a litigation is considered as inconsistent with
such a right of purchase.[1] If an attorney do so purchase, at
least if the price paid by him be inadequate, the act will be
considered as done in trust for the client, or the sale will be
set aside on equitable terms upon proper application of the
client.[2] Even after the confirmation of a judicial purchase
made by the attorney (acting under an assumed name), the
Court of Equity will open the transaction, and order the
property to be offered again at the price agreed to be paid by
the attorney. But, in case no higher bid is made, the purchase
by the attorney will be held binding.[3] The proper course for
the attorney in such cases is to obtain the consent of court to
bid.[4]

Whether this incapacity of the attorney to purchase, at
judicial sales, without the client's consent,[5] be absolute or
merely *prima facie* is not quite clear. Lord Chancellor Thurlow has said that " no attorney can be permitted to buy in
things in the course of litigation, of which litigation he has
the management."[6] But the case in which this was laid down

---

[1] Hall *v.* Hallet, 1 Cox, 134; *Ex parte* Hughes, 6 Ves. 617; *Ex parte*
James, 8 Ves. 337; Howell *v.* Baker, 4 Johns. Ch. 118; Smith *v.* Thomp-
son, 7 B. Mon. 305; Foreman *v.* Hunt, 3 Dana, 614; Howell *v.* Mc-
Creery, 7 Dana, 388; Busey *v.* Hardin, 2 B. Mon. 407; Hawley *v.* Cramer,
4 Cowen, 717; Leisenring *v.* Black, 5 Watts, 303 ; Byers *v.* Suget, 19 How.
303; Cowan *v.* Barrett, 18 Mo. 257; Wheeler *v.* Willard, 44 Vt. 640;
Alwood *v.* Mansfield, 59 Ill. 496; Trotter *v.* Smith, Ib. 240; Stockton *v.*
Ford, 11 How. 246; Wade *v.* Pettibone, 11 Ohio, 57.

[2] See cases just cited. But an attorney engaged merely to prevent the
condemnation of land on execution is held not barred from purchasing
the land for himself at sheriff's sale. Devinney *v.* Norris, 8 Watts, 314.

[3] Sidney *v.* Ranger, 13 Sim. 118; Owen *v.* Foulkes, 6 Ves. 630, note.

[4] Sidney *v.* Ranger; Nelthorpe *v.* Pennyman, 14 Ves. 517.

[5] We are not now speaking of purchases directly from the client, and
the like cases, in which assent is implied, but of purchases from third
persons, or at judicial sales, adversely to the client, and without his
consent. We have seen that the former case presents no absolute incapacity against the attorney.

[6] Hall *v.* Hallet, 1 Cox, 134, 140.

was one of great inadequacy of consideration, — a fact prevailing, it may be observed, in all of the American cases. Later, Lord Eldon appears to have so ruled of a purchase "perfectly fair, the solicitor bidding openly in the presence of very respectable persons concerned for mortgagees and creditors, and declaring it was for himself."[1] This case was soon followed by another in which the same great judge said that "the purchase is not permitted in any case, however honest the circumstances; the general interests of justice requiring it to be destroyed in every instance, as no court is equal to the examination and ascertainment of the truth in much the greater number of cases."[2] The question was also suggested by a case before Chancellor Kent, but no opinion was expressed.[3] The court of Kentucky seem to regard the incapacity as absolute, though the case referred to was one of inadequacy of consideration; and the court therefore add: "Particularly ought a purchase under such circumstances to be regarded invalid, when it results in a sacrifice of the property."[4] Chancellor Walworth has given the subject elaborate examination; and his opinion is that the incapacity is not absolute. The English cases, admitted to be opposed to this view, were distinguished as being rulings in bankruptcy.[5] Other cases were also distinguished.[6]

[1] Owen v. Foulkes, 6 Ves. 630, note, and other cases there briefly stated. See Sidny v. Ranger, 12 Sim. 118. But see In re Bloye, 1 Macn. & G. 488, 494. [2] Ex parte James, 8 Ves. 337, 346.

[3] Howell v. Baker, 4 Johns. Ch. 118.

[4] Smith v. Thompson, 7 B. Mon. 305, 309.

[5] A fact alluded to by Chancellor Kent also, in Howell v. Baker. The language of English cases not in bankruptcy implies that the incapacity is not absolute. In re Bloye, 1 Macn. & G. 488, 494.

[6] Beardsley v. Root, 11 Johns. 464; Nelthorp v. Pennyman, 14 Ves. 517.

A purchase by an attorney at sheriff's sale, under an execution of which he has control, has been said to be "in the twilight between legal fraud and fairness, and will be deemed fraudulent or in trust for the parties concerned in the sale upon slight additional facts." Jones v. Martin, 26 Tex. 57; Howell v. McCreery, 7 Dana, 388.

It is held in England that, if a solicitor purchase his client's property at

The learned Chancellor laid down the following rule: An
attorney while retaining that character may contract with his
principal, where the principal is acting in his own right, and
not as agent or trustee for another; or he may purchase at
public auction or private sale in cases where his client is
interested in the proceeds of such sale, provided the purchase
is made with the knowledge and consent of the client. But
in all cases where the relation of attorney and client exists,
referable in any manner to the subject of the purchase,
whether such purchase be made by the attorney on his own
account or as agent or for the benefit of others, the purchaser
must be subject to the *onus* of making it fully manifest that
no advantage has been taken of the client. But, even testing
the case before the court by this rule, the transaction was not
upheld; the purchase having been made at a great undervalue.[1]

There appear to be no American cases opposed to this
doctrine; but there are no express decisions of the point except the above ruling of Chancellor Walworth. There can
be little objection to regarding the incapacity as only *prima
facie*, under the restrictions laid down by the learned Chancellor. The burden of proof, however, is upon the attorney;
and if, on the facts, the court be not "equal to the ascertainment of the truth," as Lord Eldon has stated to be generally
the case, the burden is not sustained, and the client must
prevail. But if the facts clearly bring the case within the
principle of Chancellor Walworth, the law should be with the

auction sale in a fictitious name, the sale will be opened for further bids;
the solicitor's purchase to stand, if no higher bid be obtained. Sidny *v.*
Ranger, 12 Sim. 118; Owen *v.* Foulkes, 6 Ves. 630, note. See *Ex parte*
Lacey, Ib. 625.

[1] The Supreme Court of California have (*obiter*) also said: "Even in
the case of a purchase of the suit by the attorney, the client may set it
aside at his pleasure, unless the attorney show by clear and conclusive
proof that no advantage was taken, that every thing was explained to the
client, and that the price was fair and reasonable." Valentine *v.* Stewart, 15 Cal. 387, 401.

attorney. It is not a promising matter for him, however; and he can rarely succeed.

The situation of an attorney also disables him from purchasing an outstanding title to property claimed by the client, either from the State or from a third person, and holding the property adversely to the client.[1] The nature of the incapacity in such cases is probably like that above noticed, except that the sum paid for the outstanding title, where the whole transaction is fair towards the client, and is effected with his full consent, is perhaps not material. If the client, upon full knowledge of the facts, request his attorney to buy in the outstanding title for his own benefit (as in a case where he intends to give or sell the property to the attorney), and the attorney act thereupon, it would seem that the client would be bound.[2] But such cases are probably more rare than those above considered, and should be very narrowly scrutinized. The presumptions must be strongly against them.

Fraud will not be imputed in the purchase of property by a party's attorney, at a sale under execution in favor of his client, when the latter has announced his inability to pay the costs and taxes, and has instructed his attorney to bid it off in his own name in order to reimburse himself for advances of money and costs.[3]

The same principle operates against the attorney in the purchase of equitable interests or choses in action (such as judgments and notes[4]) of the client, and of property levied upon in execution against the client's debtor.[5] The client may, if he elect

[1] Galbraith v. Elder, 8 Watts, 81; Hockenbury v. Carlisle, 5 Watts & S. 348; Cleavinger v. Reimar, 3 Watts & S. 486; Henry v. Raiman, 25 Penn. St. 354; Smith v. Brotherline, 62 Penn. 461; Case v. Carroll, 35 N. Y. 385; Harper v. Perry, 28 Iowa, 57; Davis v. Smith, 43 Vt. 269; Hatch v. Fogerty, 10 Abb. Pr. N. s. 147.

[2] See Hatch v. Fogerty, *supra*. The language of Galbraith v. Elder also implies this. Compare Wade v. Pettibone, 11 Ohio, 57.

[3] Page v. Stubbs, 39 Iowa, 537.

[4] Stockton v. Ford, 11 How. 246; Jones v. Thomas, 2 Younge & C. 498.

[5] Wade v. Pettibone, 11 Ohio, 57.

within a reasonable time,[1] and, before the rights of innocent
third persons have intervened, treat all such transactions as
effected in his interest and for his benefit. But this privilege
of the client is attended also with certain limitations in favor
of the attorney. The law will not permit the client to take
the benefit of a purchase made by an attorney without reim-
bursing the latter to the extent of the sum paid in making the
purchase,[2] including probably interest. And it has also been
held that where an attorney, in the exercise of a diligence
beyond that required of him against a debtor of his client,
has realized a fund due himself out of the debtor, he is not
bound to apply it to his client's claim against the common
debtor.[3]

Similar rules of law apply to the case of property sold *to*
the client, either directly by the attorney as owner, or by a
third person through the influence of the attorney. In cases
of the latter kind, the attorney must make a full disclosure to
his client of any interest he may have in the property, on pain
of losing the same or becoming a trustee for his client, according to the nature of the case.[4] In the case just cited, it appeared that the defendant, as solicitor, had had a private arrangement with R., by which he was to receive from him a
share in certain property then belonging to R., and to share
in the profit to be obtained in any sale of the same. In his
character of solicitor, the defendant had acted for the plain-

---

[1] As to the effect of lapse of time in cases of transactions between
attorney and client, see Gresley v. Mousley, 4 DeG. & J. 78. "During
the continuance of the relation, the same weight ought not to be given to
the lapse of time as is justly due to it when no such relation exists." Ib.,
per Lord Justice Turner. See s. c. 3 DeG., F. & J. 433; Lyddon v.
Moss, 4 DeG. & J. 104; Clanricarde v. Henning, 30 Beav. 175; Blagrave
v. Routh, 8 DeG., M. & G. 620; Moss v. Bainbrigge, 6 DeG., M. & G.
292; Macdonald v. Macdonald, 1 Bligh, 315; Savery v. King, 5 H. L.
Cas. 627.

[2] Davis v. Smith, 43 Vt. 269; Giddings v. Eastman, 5 Paige, 561.

[3] Cox v. Sullivan, 7 Ga. 144.

[4] Tyrrell v. Bank of London, 10 H. L. Cas. 26.

tiffs in the purchase of a large portion of that property, without communicating to them the fact that he had an interest in it. It was held by the House of Lords that the defendant was to be treated as a trustee for his clients, in respect of his share of the property so purchased.[1]

In like manner, where a security has been obtained by the attorney from his client, either for the payment of fees or to indemnify him for acts done on behalf of the client, the nature, purposes, and consideration[2] of the security will be narrowly scrutinized.[3] The attorney will not be permitted to make any undue gain out of it, or to use it in any way to the disadvantage of the client, further than is necessarily implied in making it available for the object for which it was given. When that object is accomplished, the security must be surrendered.[4] *A fortiori*, where a bond of indemnity has been obtained by the attorney to save him harmless from acts for which the client was in no way responsible, though performed in the prosecution of business for the client, the Court of Chancery will decree that the bond be given up to be cancelled.[5] And even where a security improperly obtained has

---

[1] *Per* Lord Westbury: "A solicitor shall not in any way whatever, in respect of the subject of any transaction in the relations between him and his client, make gain to himself at the expense of his client, beyond the amount of the just and fair professional remuneration to which he is entitled."

[2] The attorney must prove the consideration. Jones *v.* Thomas, 2 Younge & C. 498. However, it is held that a confession of judgment by a client to his attorney, if made fairly and with full knowledge of all circumstances, cannot be avoided on the mere ground that the value of the consideration is not equal to the amount of the judgment. Wise *v.* Harden, 5 S. Car. 325.

[3] See Jones *v.* Roberts, 9 Beav. 419. It is said that a solicitor cannot, under any circumstances, take security from his client as to *future* costs. Kerr, Fraud, 167 (Am. ed.) ; Jones *v.* Tripp, Jac. 322 ; Williams *v.* Piggott, Ib. 598; Boothe *v.* Creswicke, 13 Law J. Ch. 217 ; Coleman *v.* Mellersh, 2 Macn. & G. 309. See Pitcher *v.* Rigby, 9 Price, 79.

[4] See Ford *v.* Harrington, 16 N. Y. 285; Mott *v.* Henderson, 12 Vt. 199.   [5] Gray *v.* Emmons, 7 Mich. 533.

been assigned by the client to another person without notice of the inequitable character of the original transaction, the latter will be compelled to surrender to the client the security.[1] So, if the security contain unusual stipulations, to the great disadvantage of the client, they cannot be enforced.[2]

It is held that an attorney is not at liberty to deal with his client for a security for debt due to him by a third person, without giving to his client all the information he possesses connected with his demand, and informing him of the nature of the security.[3] In the case cited, a solicitor took from his client a security executed by him on a sum of money charged upon the estate of the principal debtor, for the recovery of which the client was then prosecuting a suit in equity, and did not disclose to him the circumstances known by him to be connected with that estate, or that he (the solicitor) had other demands affecting it. Having afterwards filed a bill to enforce the security against his client, the bill was dismissed with costs.

An attorney, moreover, who will contract with his client during the pendency of litigation, must not only not be guilty of undue influence and false representations, but is bound to advise his client of the falsity of any misrepresentations (concerning the contract) made to the client by others, to the knowledge of the attorney.[4]

There are many other cases in which chancery will interfere for the protection of the client, without requiring proof of actual fraud. Thus, where the attorney has assigned bonds and mortgages to his client, as security for money loaned,

---

[1] Poillon *v.* Martin, 1 Sandf. Ch. 569.

[2] Cowdry *v.* Day, 1 Giff. 316.

[3] Higgins *v.* Joyce, 2 Jones & L. 282. The duty of disclosure of the legal aspects of transactions between attorney and client is so strong that sales and contracts will be set aside for the non-disclosure of legal consequences of which the attorney claims to have been ignorant. Bulkley *v.* Wilford, 2 Clark & F. 102; s. c. 8 Bligh, N. s. 111. See *ante*, pp. 9, 10.

[4] Smith *v.* Thompson, 7 B. Mon. 305.

without putting him on his guard as to the character of the securities, and especially where he recommends them as good, he will be compelled to take back the securities and repay with interest the money loaned, if any of the securities turn out worthless. And this, too, however upright may have been his conduct in the matter.[1]

Releases and compromises obtained from clients in respect of services rendered probably stand upon a different footing from gifts, sales, and the like. An attorney is entitled, *prima facie*, to payment for services rendered ; and a release or compromise, especially if under seal, is evidence of services rendered and also of the value of such services. While therefore the Court of Chancery will readily listen to charges of unfairness, exorbitance, or fraud, preferred by clients against their attorneys,[2] it would seem that the burden of impeaching the validity of snch transactions would be upon the client. The presumptions must be on the side of the attorney.

It is not essential to the creation of the relation of attorney and client that the attorney should be employed in a litigation. It is enough that he is engaged professionally, to exercise his skill or to give his advice as a lawyer. Hence an attorney, who is employed and consulted as such to draw a deed, or to make application for an original title to land, becomes thereby, *in hac re*, the attorney of the party so engaging him, so as to be precluded, for example, as we have seen, from buying in for his own use any outstanding title to the property about which he was employed,[3] and from buying from the client except upon terms of scrupulous fairness.[4] So, too, the mere obtaining by an attorney of a power of attorney to collect a judgment, under an agreement by which the collector was to have a large share of the proceeds of the

---

[1] Lewis *v.* J. A., 4 Edw. Ch. 599.

[2] Barry *v.* Whitney, 3 Sandf. 696; Strange *v.* Brennan, 15 Law J. Ch. 389 ; Pince *v.* Beattie, 32 Law J. Ch. 734.

[3] Smith *v.* Brotherline, 62 Penn. St. 461; *ante*, pp. 208–210.

[4] Payne *v.* Avery, 21 Mich. 524.

judgment, is said to be sufficient to bring the parties within
the relation of attorney and client, and to enable the latter
to avoid the contract in case of a suppression of facts.[1] But
a mere proposition by a former attorney, who had not recently
been employed professionally by the person to whom it was
made, the proposition being rejected, does not renew the
relation of attorney and client.[2] So the mere consulting of
legal counsel, and directing him to prepare a conveyance,
which, however, is not done, owing to a failure of the negotiation with the intended grantee, will not prevent the attorney
from purchasing adversely to the party who employed him,
provided he acquired no information from him relative to the
property.[3] Nor, as we have seen, will the actual existence
of a limited relationship of attorney and client prevent the
attorney from acting adversely (in the legal sense of that
term) to the client in matters beyond the limits of such relationship, where he has derived no information from the
client.[4]

Where an attorney is employed to collect a claim secured
by mortgage, his relation to his client ceases after foreclosing
the mortgage and, under his client's directions, bidding off
the land at the sale thereunder. If afterwards the same land
should be put up for sale, as for non-payment of taxes, the
attorney may purchase, provided he has not been further
retained by the client. And his retention of the deed executed by the sheriff under the foreclosure sale, to secure his
fees, would not be a continuance of the relation of attorney
and client.[5]

Similar rules appear to apply to cases in which the attorney
has improperly obtained a grant to a third person, out of

[1] White v. Whaley, 3 Lans. 327.
[2] Taylor v. Boardman, 24 Mich. 287.
[3] Porter v. Peckham, 44 Cal. 204.
[4] Devinney v. Norris, 8 Watts, 314; ante, pp. 195, 201, 202.
[5] Baker v. Davis, 35 Iowa, 184.

which the former is to derive a benefit. If the grant be greatly to the disadvantage of the client, it seems that it may be set aside as to both the grantee and the attorney. This will clearly be the case if the grantee participate in the improper conduct of the attorney.[1]

An attorney in a cause cannot, by purchasing the interest of the *opposite* party, acquire a right against his client that he can enforce by judicial proceedings against him; and the client may treat the purchase as made for himself.[2] In the case first cited, it appeared that, while the plaintiff was acting as the defendant's solicitor and legal adviser in a foreclosure suit in favor of the defendant against one Putnam, the plaintiff purchased of Putnam his interest in the premises, and then tendered the defendant the amount due, with costs, in the foreclosure suit. The defendant declined to receive the same, and claimed the benefit of the purchase, offering to pay the plaintiff what he had paid to Putnam. The plaintiff then brought the present suit in chancery, praying for an order on the defendant to convey the premises to the plaintiff upon payment of the sum tendered. The court, however, held that the defendant was entitled to the benefit of the plaintiff's purchase by paying him the amount which the plaintiff paid.

The same principles which govern transactions between attorney and client apply between persons who stand in a similar relation to litigation, though the relation be not in strictness that of attorney and client. Thus, a party who acts as the confidential adviser of a litigant, though not an attorney-at-law, is bound to the same circumspection of conduct in his transactions with the litigant, and acts under the same limitations as if he were actually his attorney. Gifts and sales to him will be voidable under the same circumstances that would render them invalid in cases of attorney

---

[1] Robinson *v.* Proctor, 35 Beav. 329.

[2] Davis *v.* Smith, 43 Vt. 269; Smith *v.* Brotherline, 62 Penn. St. 461.

and client.[1] The same is true of one who has constituted
himself the legal adviser of another,[2] or has offered legal advice,[3] and also of a clerk of an attorney who has gained the
confidence of a client of his employer.[4] Where, however,
the relation between the parties to a transaction was that of
friendship only, though the one habitually relied on the advice of the other, and employed him in some sort of business,
it is for those who impugn the transaction to prove that an
undue advantage was taken of the influence arising out of
this transaction.[5]

The principle of all these cases is a plain one. The doctrine is that in respect of acts done pending litigation or other
matters involving legal advice, or in expectation thereof, the
Court of Chancery will protect the client from unfortunate
contracts or gratuities, obtained by undue influence, suppression of facts, or the failure to give such advice as would be
given by a disinterested attorney in the matter. The rule
bears against transactions made with reference to present or
future legal business alike. If the transaction be intended
as compensation for legal services, or for security of the same,
the court, as we have seen, will see that the compensation is
a reasonable one.[6] If it be intended as a gratuity, it will only
be upheld upon affirmative proof on the part of the attorney

[1] Buffalow v. Buffalow, 2 Dev. & B. Eq. 241; Purcell v. Macnamara,
14 Ves. 91; McCabe v. Hussey, 2 Dow & C. 440; s. c. 5 Bligh, N. s. 715;
Carter v. Palmer, 8 Clark & F. 657, 707; Brown v. Kennedy, 33 Beav.
133.

[2] Tate v. Williamson, Law R. 1 Eq. 528; s. c. Law R. 2 Ch. 65. See
Wyse v. Lambert, 16 Irish Ch. 379.

[3] Davis v. Abraham, 5 Week. R. 465.

[4] Hobday v. Peters, 28 Beav. 349; Nesbitt v. Berridge, 32 Beav. 284;
Parnell v. Tyler, 2 Law J. Ch. 195; Poillon v. Martin, 1 Sandf. Ch. 569;
Kerr, Fraud, 171 (Am. ed.).

[5] Hunter v. Atkins, Coop. temp. Brough. 464.

[6] The rule therefore does not preclude the attorney from contracting
in advance as to the value of his services, or even receiving his entire fee
in advance. It simply requires that the sum shall be a reasonable one,
when so paid or contracted for.

or *quasi* attorney that the parties stood in the position of strangers; that is, that the attorney had so far divested himself, *pro hac vice*, of the advantage of his position as to leave the client upon an equal footing with himself.

But after the litigation or other legal business has been completed, the parties are considered as standing, with reference to such *past* business, in the situation of strangers; or, to use the common expression of the books, they are now supposed to be at arm's length. The client may now make such disposition of his property in favor of his attorney, whether by way of gratuity or of a measure of compensation for services at their agreed value, as he will;[1] and the transaction will be subject to impeachment only as other transactions between persons not in confidential relations are impeachable. And, even in cases in which the principle under consideration might have been invoked, the right to set aside the transaction may become barred by acquiescence after the relation of attorney and client has come to an end, especially if there be great delay in bringing suit.[2]

In a contest between an attorney and his client with regard to counsel fees, it is held that the burden rests upon the attorney to show that the contract for his services was free from all fraud, undue influence, and exorbitancy of demand.[3] And, if an attorney having special information concerning the condition of an estate propose to heirs to undertake a settlement of it, he is bound to divulge his knowledge, so that the heirs may be able to agree intelligently upon the value of his services. If he does not, such an agreement as to his fees, if they are large and the services rendered are slight, will be presumptively fraudulent; and it will be incumbent upon the

---

[1] Walmesley *v.* Booth, 2 Atk. 27.

[2] Lyddon *v.* Moss, 4 DeG. & J. 104; Champion *v.* Rigby, Taml. 421; s. c. 9 Law J. Ch. 211.   See Proctor *v.* Robinson, 35 Beav. 329.

[3] McMahan *v.* Smith, 6 Heisk. 167; Planters' Bank *v.* Hornberger, 4 Cold. 578.

attorney to remove the presumption to entitle him to recover the sum agreed upon.[1] Thus, in the case cited, it appeared that one Ashton had died, leaving an estate in Iowa of the value of $12,000, and a wife and children in Illinois. After his death, one of the plaintiffs, who resided in the same county in Iowa with Ashton, went to Illinois, and entered into a contract with the heirs-at-law, whereby the plaintiffs were to receive twenty-five per cent. of the value of the estate for effecting a settlement of it. No litigation was involved in the undertaking, and the debts were small; and it was accordingly held, in the absence of satisfactory explanation from the plaintiffs, that the contract was not binding upon the heirs.[2]

While an attorney is not permitted to acquire his client's property in bad faith, still the attempt of the latter to defraud him of reasonable compensation will authorize the attorney to sever the relation between them, and act for his own protection. Thus, where a client refused for four years to pay his attorney for services and to reimburse him for expenses incurred in an action to foreclose a mortgage, and the mortgaged land was afterwards purchased by the attorney at a tax-sale, the client having been informed of the sale and failing to pay the amount thus advanced, it was held that the client would not be permitted, seven years afterwards, to set aside the tax-sale.[3]

Accounts between attorney and client stand upon different grounds from those between parties treating at arm's length. That which between others would be a conclusive settlement is not so between them. Settlement and payment of a bill, even though a long period may since have elapsed, is not conclusive, and will not bar an examination of the fairness of the demand. If the settlement were made during the pendency

---

[1] Ryan v. Ashton, 42 Iowa, 365.
[2] See Greenfield's Estate, 14 Penn. St. 489.
[3] Eckrote v. Myers, 41 Iowa, 324.

of the suit, the client must have been in some degree under the control of the attorney, and a settlement under such circumstances may be opened.[1]

Should an attorney advise a bill to be filed for the administration of the assets of a testator whose sole executor he is, and continue to act as the attorney of the plaintiff in such suit, but, abusing the confidence reposed in him, neglect for an unreasonable length of time to put in his answer to the bill filed upon his own recommendation, such conduct would be considered strong evidence of a scheme to retain in his own hands the personal estate of his testator. Equity will not permit such an abuse of its practice ; and, on motion, the party will be ordered to file his answer within a time stated, or stand committed.[2]

An agreement between the counsel of parties who have submitted their claims to reference, that the arbitrators shall have no instructions in writing, is very like a fraud, and relief might be had even at law. But the fact that the award was prepared by the counsel for one of the parties is no ground of itself for setting aside the award.[3] For, though Lord Eldon has declared that a general rule forbidding a solicitor by himself or his partner to be employed on both sides would be extremely beneficial, still it has not been deemed convenient to put an end to the practice. And the reasons for its continuance are strong ; for, if every creditor or legatee were bound to employ a different solicitor, the costs would eat up the estate.[4] It is, however, clear that whenever a person intrusted to act as attorney for all parties abuses the confidence placed in him, this is a fraud which gives ample ground for the interference of equity.[5]

[1] Crossley v. Parker, 1 Jac. & W. 462; Aubrey v. Popkin, 1 Dick. 404; Langstaffe v. Taylor, 14 Ves. 263; Lewes v. Morgan, 5 Price, 56.

[2] Mootham v. Hale, 3 Ves. & B. 92.

[3] Featherstone v. Cooper, 9 Ves. 68.

[4] Dyott v. Anderton, 3 Ves. & B. 178.

[5] Costigan v. Hastler, 2 Schoales & L. 165; 1 Hovenden, Fraud, 49.

In the case of a contract by an attorney to purchase his client's property, a confirmation which shall entitle the attorney to a specific performance of the contract must be strong and plain, and with full knowledge of the infirmity of the contract. And this is the case even where the property, the subject of the contract, being one of many lots to be sold at auction, the buyer (the attorney), openly became a bidder, in competition with others, and had the particular property knocked down to him in the usual manner; provided, of course, he was concerned in the auction professionally, as attorney of the vendor. And even in such a case, in order to affect the vendor with the usual consequences of acquiescence or confirmation, it is necessary to show that, when acting in the manner alleged against him, he was free from the attorney's influence, and aware of every thing affecting his interest.[1]

It need scarcely be said that the right of the client against his attorney, in cases such as we have been considering, is a personal one only, pertaining exclusively to the client, and to his assignees and representatives. Other persons cannot take advantage of it, even though the case be one of clear fraud upon the rights of the client;[2] except, indeed, in cases of conveyances obtained in fraud of creditors or purchasers under the statutes of Elizabeth.

§ 3. OF PRINCIPAL AND AGENT.

Agents also occupy a relation of trust, with peculiar opportunities for fraud upon their principals; and the rules of law, in respect of transactions between them concerning the interest in trust, are in some particulars more unfavorable to the

---

[1] Salmon v. Cutts, 4 DeG. & S. 125.

[2] Marshall v. Joy, 17 Vt. 546; Leach v. Fowler, 22 Ark. 143; Cowan v. Barret, 18 Mo. 257.

agent than the rules relating to attorney and client are to the attorney.

There is, however, no rule prohibiting an agent from dealing with his principal in respect of the trust. At the same time, the presumptions of law, as in the case of the dealings of an attorney with his client, are against him. If an agent seek to uphold a transaction between himself and his principal, or a principal to avoid a transaction between himself and his agent, the burden is upon the agent to show that he gave to his principal the same advice in the matter as an independent disinterested adviser would have done; and that he made a full disclosure of all he knew respecting the property, and that the principal knew with whom he was dealing, and made no objection, and finally that the consideration was fair and just.[1]

The position of an agent differs from that of an attorney, in that it appears to be unnecessary that the principal should have suffered injury from the agent's action, or would suffer injury if the transaction were upheld.[2] In the case first cited, Lord

[1] Kerr, Fraud, 173 (Am. ed.); York Buildings Co. v. Mackenzie, 3 Pat. (Scotch App.) 378; Lowther v. Lowther, 13 Ves. 95, 103; Watt v. Grove, 2 Schoales & L. 492; Woodhouse v. Meredith, 1 Jac. & W. 204; Selsey v. Rhoades, 2 Sim. & S. 41; s. c. 1 Bligh, N. s. 1; Cane v. Allen, 2 Dow, 294; Rothschild v. Brockman, 2 Dow & C. 188; s. c. 5 Bligh, N. s. 165; Barker v. Harrison, 2 Colly. 546; Molony v. Kernan, 2 Dru. & War. 31; Trevelyan v. Charter, 4 Law J. Ch. 209; s. c. 11 Clark & F. 714, 732; Mulhallen v. Marum, 3 Dru. & War. 317; Murphy v. O'Shea, 2 Jones & L. 422, 425; Clarke v. Tipping, 9 Beav. 284; Bloye's Trust, 1 Macn. & G. 488; Lewis v. Hillman, 3 H. L. Cas. 607; Rhodes v. Bate, Law R. 1 Ch. 252; Farnham v. Brooks, 9 Pick. 212; Dobson v. Racey, 8 N. Y. 216; Bank of Orleans v. Torrey, 9 Paige, 649; s. c. 7 Hill, 260; Comstock v. Comstock, 57 Barb. 453; Fisher's Appeal, 34 Penn. 29; Brooke v. Berry, 2 Gill, 83; Moseley v. Buck, 3 Munf. 232; Teakle v. Bailey, 2 Brock. 43; Moore v. Maudelbaum, 8 Mich. 433; Taylor v. Knox, 1 Dana, 391; s. c. 5 Dana, 466; Casey v. Casey, 14 Ill. 112.

The clerk of a vendor's broker, having access to correspondence, is, like the broker himself, disabled from purchasing of the broker's employer without full disclosure. Gardner v. Ogden, 22 N. Y. 327.

[2] Murphy v. O'Shea, 2 Jones & L. 422, 425; Gillett v. Peppercorn, 3 Beav. 78.

Chancellor Sugden observed, of the right to impeach a sale of lands to one's agent, that it was perfectly well settled that it is not necessary to prove under value. A principal selling to his agent was entitled to set aside the sale upon equitable grounds, whatever may have been the price obtained for the property. In the case next cited, the court held a transaction of the agent void on grounds of public policy, without entering into the question of fairness of price. "It is not necessary," said the court, " to show that fraud was intended, or that loss afterwards took place in consequence of these transactions."

Subject to a strict and jealous investigation in equity, an agent may buy from his principal, if the latter, being fully informed who is the proposed purchaser, and laboring under no influence or deception on the part of the agent, be willing to sell to him.[1] But an agent cannot be permitted to act clandestinely, setting up a nominal purchaser, and dealing with his own principal in the name of that person. The principal would be thus thrown off his guard. Instead of a person acting solely with a view to his (the principal's) interest, the agent would be practically contracting with himself, and fixing the price which he is himself to pay. To call such a transaction a contract, it has well been said, would be an abuse of terms. To a contract there must be two parties.[2] Lord Thurlow, indeed, as the writer just referred to has pointed out, seems to have been clearly of opinion that a person employed to sell could not, under any circumstances, be permitted to buy ; and that a purchase by such person could not be supported, though it was made with the knowledge of the party selling.[3]

Except under the restrictions above mentioned, an agent is also prohibited from selling property which he has bought,

---

[1] Morse v. Royal, 12 Ves. 373; Gibson v. Jeyes, 6 Ves. 277.

[2] 1 Hovenden, Fraud, 147.

[3] Crowe v. Bullard, 3 Brown C. C. 120.

under instructions, for his principal. The clearest evidence of consent is necessary to support such a transaction.[1]

Upon these principles, it is considered that, if a person make himself an actual principal in transactions in which he is ostensibly concerned as a broker, he can maintain no suit either at law or in equity in respect of those transactions. A broker is the agent of the buyer or of the seller or of both, and is bound to exercise his skill in favor of those who, for that sole purpose, have confidentially employed him; and, if he were allowed to introduce himself as a principal, his duty and his interest would be set in decided opposition.[2]

And not only where an agent employed to sell property becomes himself the real purchaser, will equity charge him (under the above restrictions) with the value of the estate; but, also, whenever such agent, from corrupt or doubtful motives, has let part of his employer's estate at a rent less than he could have obtained from a responsible tenant, the agent is himself liable in his lifetime, and his estate is liable after his death. As to the latter situation, it is to be observed that, though at common law actions sounding in damages (except trover) generally die with the wrongdoer, the ground of jurisdiction in equity is debt.[3]

Though, in general, mere inadequacy of price will not vitiate a sale, still, if the purchaser be the agent of the vendor, the adequacy of the consideration will be more jealously scrutinized. Such a purchaser must at least show, with indisputable clearness, that he furnished his employer with all the knowledge which he himself possessed,[4] or which he might by due diligence have acquired, as to the value of the subject of sale.[5] For, in order to set aside a purchase at an

[1] Massey v. Davies, 2 Ves. Jr. 321; Attorney-General v. Cochrane, Wightw. 14.
[2] Lowther v. Lowther, 13 Ves. 103; Wren v. Kirton, 8 Ves. 502; Ex parte Dyster, 1 Meriv. 172; s. c. 2 Rose, 355; 1 Hovenden, Fraud, 147.
[3] 4 Ves. 416, 418. [4] Lowther v. Lowther, 13 Ves. 103.
[5] Wren v. Kirton, 8 Ves. 502; Ex parte James, 8 Ves. 347.

15

undervalue by an agent from his employer, it is not necessary that actual fraud should be proved.[1]

An agent who discovers a defect in the title to his principal's land, in the course of his agency relating thereto, cannot avail himself of the discovery to acquire a title against his principal.[2] So, an agent employed to sell a reversionary legacy is not permitted to become the purchaser thereof for himself. And nothing will amount to a confirmation of such a transaction until the vendor is fully apprised that he might be relieved against the transaction, if he should choose to impeach it.[3]

Where an agent for the care of land has fraudulently taken a tax-deed of the property, under which deed he is in possession, the principal may either sue in equity for relief from the fraud, as by asking a conveyance of the title, or he may maintain ejectment, relying on the agent's fraud as ground for estopping him to set up his tax-title.[4]

If a lease be obtained from the steward or other agent of the lessor by means of any misrepresentation, whereby the lessee, even innocently on his part, gains an advantage over the lessor, the lease cannot stand. And, if it be proved that the agent was cognizant of the real facts, he will be answerable to his principal for any loss sustained in consequence of the concealment of that which it was his duty to communicate to his employer.[5]

If a stranger enter into a fraudulent bargain with a servant, acting on behalf of his master; or if a servant by collusion take greater profits than belong to his office, he cannot in either case resist an account of the gains made by such fraud.[6] And when a factor, instead of charging factorage upon pur-

---

[1] Medlicott v. O'Donnell, 1 Ball & B. 165.
[2] Rogers v. Lockett, 28 Ark. 290; Ringo v. Burns, 10 Peters, 279.
[3] Crowe v. Ballard, 2 Cox, 253.
[4] McMahon v. McGraw, 26 Wis. 614.
[5] Abingdon v. Butler, 1 Ves. Jr. 208.
[6] East India Co. v. Henchman, Ib. 289.

chases made for his employers, deals with them as a merchant, and charges mercantile profits, that is a fraud, upon which a court of equity will decree an account. Or if such factor or broker be also a manufacturer, though he might by a rigid, adverse bargain demand what price he thought fit for his goods, yet if, by taking advantage of his character of factor or broker, and of the confidence reposed in him as such, he obtain a price he ought not to have had, that, also, is good ground for an account.[1]

If an agent sell property to his principal as the property of a third person, when in fact it belongs to the agent, the principal will be entitled to rescind the contract.[2] So, too, the concealment by a broker employed to effect a sale of property of the fact that he is himself interested in the property will be fatal to any claim by him for services rendered his employer, in case his own interest in the property, in connection with the terms of sale fixed by the employer, were such as to render a sale by him under such concealment inconsistent with his duty to his principal.[3] But, when the terms of sale as fixed by the principal are such that the concealment of the broker's interest cannot operate adversely to the rights of the former, the rule is otherwise.[4] Thus, where the defendant employed the plaintiff to sell certain land, agreeing to pay him for his services all that he could obtain over thirty-five cents per foot, it was considered that the plaintiff's failure to disclose the fact to the defendant that he was interested in the land as owner or part-owner was immaterial, since it could not operate to the prejudice of the defendant's rights in the matter.[5]

A broker who engages for a commission to find a purchaser

[1] East India Co. v. Keighley, 4 Madd. 35.
[2] Ely v. Hanford, 65 Ill. 267.
[3] Durgin v. Somers, 117 Mass. 55; Smith v. Townsend, 109 Mass. 500. Farnsworth v. Hemmer, 1 Allen, 494; Walker v. Osgood, 98 Mass. 348.
[4] Durgin v. Somers, *supra*.   [5] Ib.

of property at a price to be agreed upon between such purchaser and the vendor, and then becomes himself the purchaser
in part, the vendor accepting him as such, may recover the
commission upon clear proof that such was the agreement;[1]
and the fact that in effecting the sale the broker has acted in
fraud of his co-purchaser, will not affect his right to the commission as between himself and the vendor.[2]

One who conceals from a party who has employed him to
effect a particular transaction the fact that he is the agent of
the other party to the transaction cannot, it is held, recover
from the deceived employer the value of his services.[3]   And
a similar principle applies where the party transacting business for another effects a sale for himself and his employer,
according to the direction of the latter, but conceals from him
the fact that he is acting in the negotiation of the business as
agent of the vendor.   The agent will not be allowed to retain
any advantage gained over his co-vendee.[4]   Thus, in the case
cited, the vendor of land employed the defendant to sell
certain land, agreeing to give him as commission all that he
should get for the property above $6,000.   The defendant
thereupon procured the plaintiff to become a joint purchaser
of the land with himself, concealing from him the fact that he
was acting as the vendor's agent, and inducing the vendor to
demand and the defendant to agree to pay $8,000 for the
property.   A joint purchase was accordingly made, and the
vendor conveyed to the plaintiff a three-fourths interest in
the land, and one-fourth interest to the defendant.   The
plaintiff paid $6,000 for his share; and the defendant pretended
to him that he had paid $2,000 for his.   In fact, he received
that sum back from the vendor, according to the agreement.

[1] Stewart v. Mather, 32 Wis. 344.

[2] Hardy v. Stonebraker, 31 Wis. 540; Grant v. Hardy, 33 Wis. 668.

[3] Meyer v. Hanchett, 39 Wis. 419; Cleveland R. Co. v. Pattison, 15 Ind.
70; Watkins v. Corsall, 1 E. D. Smith, 65; Dunlap v. Richards, 2 E. D.
Smith, 181.

[4] Grant v. Hardy, 33 Wis. 668.

Subsequently, the plaintiff bought the defendant's one-fourth interest, paying $2,100 for the same. Having afterwards discovered the nature of the transaction between the defendant and the former owner of the land, the plaintiff brought suit against the defendant to recover the amount paid to him for his fourth interest; and the action was held maintainable.

An agent cannot purchase from his principal so as to bind the latter, where he conceals the fact that a higher price could have been obtained for the property.[1] Thus, where agents conspiring against their principal represented that certain lands of which they had the management were worth but $20 per acre, and thereby obtained a conveyance of the same from the principal at that price, and then sold the land for $50 per acre, it was held that they were to be treated as trustees for the principal, and that he was entitled to the difference between the two prices.[2] If there be collusion between the agent and the purchaser, the property can be recovered from the latter.[3]

If an agent employed to purchase an estate become the purchaser for himself, equity will treat him as a trustee for his principal.[4] Hence, an agent cannot use for his own benefit, and against his principal, information obtained in investigating a title for his principal.[5]

In considering whether an agent can be allowed the benefit of any voluntary settlement obtained from his employer before the connection between them was absolutely dissolved, it will be necessary to ascertain clearly not only that such settlement was the pure, uninfluenced, and well-understood act of the employer's mind, and that he executed the gift with that full knowledge of all its effects and consequences which it was the agent's duty to communicate; but a further question will

---

[1] Moseley v. Buck, 2 Munf. 232.   [2] Hunter v. Hunter, 50 Mo. 445.

[3] Mann v. Best, 62 Mo. 491; Louguemare v. Busby, 56 Mo. 540.

[4] Lees v. Nuttall, 1 Russ. & M. 53.

[5] Reid v. Stanley, 6 Watts & S. 369.

arise, how that intention was produced, with reference to which the pecuniary circumstances and transactions between the parties must be attended to.[1]

It is no fraud on the principal for the agent to receive to his own use gratuities for incidental benefits derived from services rendered by the agent for his principal, where neither the principal nor the agent had any claim for the amount so received.[2]

It matters not that a party for whom another has been acting in promoting a transaction, in which both are to become partners, obtains a good bargain from the agency of the other in the matter. If the party managing the transaction has secretly obtained an undue advantage, he will not be permitted to retain it. This principle was recently enunciated in an English case. Four out of five persons who had agreed to purchase a mine and to sell it to a company for their joint benefit were deceived by the fifth in the course of effecting the purchase. The latter represented that the owners would not sell the property for less than a certain sum, while at the same time he obtained an agreement from the owners that, on perfecting the sale at such sum, he should be allowed a bonus equal to nearly one-quarter of the purchase price. The purchase was effected accordingly, and two out of the original five joined in forming a company for the purchase of the mine, and in fact bought it, at a considerable advance over the price understood to have been paid to the original owners. The nature of that transaction, however, having been discovered, it was held that the agreement for the bonus was fraudulent and void, not only as against the other four original purchasers, but also as against the company ; and this, too, though it appeared that the mine was cheap at the price paid by the company. It was observed that the company had a right to the best bargain which the two original parties, acting as a committee of man-

[1] Hugenin v. Baseley, 14 Ves. 300; 1 Hovenden, Fraud, 153.
[2] Ætna Ins. Co. v. Church, 21 Ohio St. 492.

agement, would have been in a position, dealing fairly, to give them, had they known the facts.[1]

An agent may, after the termination of his agency, purchase his late principal's property at tax-sale,[2] provided he do not take undue advantage of his knowledge acquired while agent.

The rule of law forbidding the abuse of confidence applies as strongly against those who have gratuitously or officiously undertaken the management of another's property as to those who are retained or appointed for that purpose and paid for it.[3]   Hence, if a person of his own will become a gratuitous agent of another to negotiate a sale of stock, and then receive compensation from a purchaser as a reward for acting in his behalf and procuring a sale for less than the purchaser would have paid, the agent becomes liable to the vendor for the loss sustained by the breach of confidence.[4]

The rule that an agent cannot make himself an adverse party to his principal while the agency continues applies only to such agents as are relied upon for counsel and direction, whose employment is a trust as well as a service.   It does not apply to those who are merely employed as instruments in the performance of some appointed service.[5]   Thus, it does not apply to a person who, claiming an equitable interest in property by an assignment from the father of certain infants, brings a suit in the name of the infants, styling himself their next friend.[6]

[1] Beck v. Kantorowicz, 3 Kay & J. 230.

[2] Moore v. Stone, 40 Iowa, 259.

[3] Rankin v. Porter, 7 Watts, 390; Coggs v. Barnard, 2 Ld. Raym. 900; Doorman v. Jenkins, 2 Ad. & E. 256; Hunsaker v. Sturgis, 29 Cal. 142.

[4] Hunsaker v. Sturgis, *supra*.

[5] Deep River Mining Co. v. Fox, 4 Ired. Eq. 61.

[6] Michael v. Michael, Ib. 349.

§ 4. OF PARTNERS.[1]

It is the duty of partners towards each other to refrain from all concealment in the transaction of the partnership business. If a partner be guilty of any such concealment and derive a benefit therefrom, he will be treated in equity as a trustee for the firm, and compelled to account to his copartners.[2]

This principle will prohibit all clandestine bargains by one partner for his own exclusive benefit, made in contemplation of establishing a partnership with other persons.[3] So each partner is bound to refrain (in the absence of consent by his copartners) from engaging in any other business or speculation which will deprive the partnership of a portion of the skill, industry, diligence, or capital which he is bound to employ therein. In other words, he is not at liberty to deal on his own private account in any matter or business which is obviously at variance with his primary duty to the partnership. The object of this prohibitory rule is to withdraw from each partner the temptation to bestow more attention, and to exercise a sharper sagacity in respect to his own purchases and sales and negotiations than he does in respect to the concerns of the partnership, in the same or in a conflicting line of business.[4] Hence, if one partner should secretly carry on another trade, or the same trade, for his own advantage, especially if actually rather than presumably to the injury of the partnership interests, or should divert the capital or funds of the partnership to such secret or sinister purposes, he will be compelled to account in equity for all the profits made

---

[1] As to frauds on third persons, see *ante*, pp. 146–150.

[2] Story, Partnership, § 172; Russell *v.* Austwick, 1 Sim. 52; Maddeford *v.* Austwick, Ib. 89; Sexton *v.* Sexton, 9 Gratt. 204; Hopkins *v.* Watt, 13 Ill. 298.

[3] Fawcett *v.* Whitehouse, 1 Russ. & M. 132, 148; Hichens *v.* Congreve, 4 Russ. 562; Story, § 174.

[4] Story, § 177; 3 Kent, Com. 51.

thereby.[1] So, if one partner should purchase articles on his own private account in some special trade and business in which the partnership was engaged, the purchase being to the injury of the partnership, he would be held to account in equity for his profits.[2] In cases of this sort, equity will even restrain the partner from carrying on any such trade or business without the consent of his copartners.[3]

Equity will not permit parties bound to each other by express or implied agreement for promoting an undertaking for their common benefit to engage in another enterprise which necessarily gives them an interest directly adverse to their original undertaking. But, if it merely appear that such other enterprise offers a *temptation* to betray the first, this affords no ground for an injunction.[4] One partner cannot treat privately and behind the backs of his copartners for a lease of the premises, where the joint trade is carried on for his own individual benefit. A lease obtained in his own name will be held a trust for the partnership.[5]

A partner cannot make a secret profit out of dealings with the firm. He cannot, for example, supply the firm with goods which he has himself bought for his own use at a lower price, without informing his partners of the facts;[6] unless, indeed, his own purchase was made long before, without any intention of selling at a profit to the firm, the firm having knowledge of his ownership of the property when they bought it.

It is considered no fraud in one member of a partnership,

---

[1] Story, § 178; Long *v.* Majestre, 1 Johns. Ch. 305; Stoughton *v.* Lynch, Ib. 467, 470; Glassington *v.* Thwaites, 1 Sim. & S. 124, 133; Burton *v.* Wookey, 6 Madd. 367; Lock *v.* Leynam, 4 Irish Ch. 188; England *v.* Curling, 8 Beav. 129; Herrick *v.* Ames, 8 Bosw. 115.

[2] Burton *v.* Wookey, *supra.*

[3] Glassington *v.* Thwaites, *supra.*

[4] Glassington *v.* Thwaites, 1 Sim. & S. 133.

[5] Featherstonhaugh *v.* Fenwick, 17 Ves. 311; Wilson *v.* Greenwood, 1 Wils. C. C. 236.

[6] Bently *v.* Craven, 18 Beav. 75; Getty *v.* Devlin, 54 N. Y. 403.

intrusted by the firm with business outside of the operations
of the firm as such, to enter into an arrangement with a
stranger by which the partner shall derive a special benefit
from the outside transaction, not shared by the other partners,
if they, too, have been guilty of fraud.[1] Thus, in the case
cited, a firm engaged in the general produce business held a
mortgage on real estate, which real estate the firm were desirous of purchasing under the mortgage. The business of
so acquiring this property was intrusted to one of the partners ; and he made an arrangement with a third person, without the knowledge of his partners, by which such third person
should buy the property, giving him, the partner, an interest
in it. The mortgage debt having been fully paid into the firm
account, it was determined that the partner thus managing
the matter was not liable to account to the other members
of the firm in respect of the benefit obtained by him in his
private arrangement with the third person ; inasmuch as it
appeared that the other partners had been guilty of fraudulent conduct in relation to the property under mortgage,
having engaged in a scheme to depreciate its value and to
deceive other creditors.

Partners are presumed to have equal access to and knowledge of the books and business of the firm ; and, in the absence of any evidence contrary to this presumption, they stand
upon an equal footing in inter-alienations of their respective
interests. Hence, in the case of such a sale, it will not be
permitted one of the parties to say that the value of his interest was misrepresented by the other. And it has even
been held in such a case that the fact that the purchaser
bought the vendor's interest through a third person, concealing
the real nature of the purchase, was not necessarily a fraud.[3]

---

[1] Wheeler *v.* Sage, 1 Wall. 518.

[2] Geddes's Appeal, 80 Penn. St. 442.

[3] Ib. "That such a concealment," it was said, "was not a fraud *per
se*, as is assumed in this assignment of error, is easily demonstrated. Of

A partner in business, intending to purchase the interest
of his copartner, must, where he (the former) has had the
management of the business or the keeping of the accounts,
make a full disclosure of the extent and situation of the business ; otherwise, the purchase will be liable to impeachment
by the copartner. Thus, it appeared in an English case that
a partner, who had superintended exclusively the accounts of
the business, agreed to purchase his copartner's share therein
for a sum which he knew from accounts in his possession was
inadequate. The transaction was set aside on the ground
that the purchaser had concealed the state of these accounts.[1]

If one party agree to unite with two others in the purchase
of land, each to furnish one-third the purchase-money, and
such party to conduct the negotiations and buy the land for
the least possible price, he assumes a position of trust towards
his associates, and is bound to exercise the utmost good faith

what importance was it to the plaintiff who the purchaser was, provided
he obtained his price or the value of his interest? It is a very common
thing in real estate, and perhaps other transactions for the purchaser to
conceal his name from the vendor, and negotiate through or in the name
of another party. The reasons for this are obvious, and such course
of dealing has never been held to be fraudulent. It is true there might be
a case in which such concealment might be some evidence of fraud. But
it would only be so in its relation to other facts, as to which it formed a
connecting link in a chain of evidence to establish a fraud, where a fraud
in fact had been committed. In this case, we have the fact in proof, that
the relations between the plaintiff and his partners were not of the most
amicable kind. This circumstance may have induced the latter to conceal their real purpose. It is said that, if the plaintiff had known who
the actual purchasers were, it would have put him upon his guard, and
perhaps induced him to demand a higher price for his interest. This, if
true, raises no equity. The argument, to be worth any thing, must go the
extent of supposing that the plaintiff would have used the information for
the purpose of exacting a greater price than his interest was worth. For,
if he got its value, how was he injured? It is possible the defendants
had this in view in withholding the information from him. They had a
right to buy upon as good terms as they could, provided they did no wrong
to the plaintiff."

[1] Maddeford v. Austwick, 1 Sim. 89.

towards them, and share with them all the profits of the bargain. He will not be permitted to conceal the actual price
to be paid, and make a private profit thereon.[1]

§ 5. Of Trustees.

It is the duty of trustees to see that their *cestuis que trust*
are properly advised as to their rights. Where, for instance,
trustees, in order to support a release, rely on the ground that
their *cestuis que trust* were advised by an independent solicitor,
it lies on them to show that the *cestuis que trust* did authorize
an independent solicitor to act for them.[2] The case cited well
illustrates the principle. Two ladies entitled to a trust fund,
which had been improperly lent by the trustees to J. A. (who
stood towards the ladies *in loco parentis*), were induced by
J. A., soon after they came of age, to execute releases to the
trustees, taking from him a security for the money, which
security was known to be worthless. No direct communication took place between the ladies and the trustees, nor did
the trustees render any account to them ; but the ladies were
represented in the transaction by G., a solicitor, who was
known to the trustees to have been for years the confidential
adviser of J. A., and the transaction was conducted by G. and
J. A.'s solicitors. G. was never in fact authorized by the
ladies to act for them, but was nominated by J. A. The
ladies did not at the time consider him to be acting for them.
The Court of Chancery decided that under these circumstances
the trustees could not avail themselves of the releases.

The determination of the question whether necessary information was given to a *cestui que trust* to enable him or his
advisers to form a proper judgment of the condition of the
estate, and decide whether such a release is valid, renders it

---

[1] King *v.* Wise, 43 Cal. 629.
[2] Lloyd *v.* Attwood, 3 DeG. & J. 614.

necessary to examine the circumstances connected with it, such as the conduct and the acts of the parties before its execution, though occurring during the minority of the *cestui que trust*. Thus, where two releases were executed by the *cestui que trust*, one before and one twelve days after he had reached majority, and the necessary information was conveyed at the time of the first release, and a proper examination made by the advisers of the minor as to the condition of the trust fund, such facts were considered as the operating causes for the second release.[1]

A trustee may buy from the *cestui que trust*, provided there is a distinct and clear contract, ascertained to be such after a jealous and scrupulous examination of all the circumstances, that the *cestui que trust* intended that the trustee should buy ; and that there is no fraud or concealment or advantage taken by the trustee in respect of information acquired by him in his fiduciary position.[2]

It is not necessary to show that a trustee who has purchased the trust property has made any profit or obtained any advantage thereby. But it is said that the sale will be supported, if found to be beneficial to the trust estate. This, however, was said of a purchase made under authority of court.[3]

A trustee or agent cannot generally, as intimated, unite in himself the opposite characters of buyer and seller. And, if he do so, the *cestui que trust* or principal, unless, upon the fullest knowledge of all the facts, he elect to confirm the act of the trustee or agent, may repudiate it, or he may charge the profits

[1] Forbes v. Forbes, 5 Gill, 29.

[2] Coles v. Trecothick, 9 Ves. 234, 247. In this case, Lord Eldon said: " I admit it is a difficult case to make out wherever it is contended that the exception prevails." He then explains Fox v. Mackreth, 2 Brown, C. C. 400, as consistent with the exception.

[3] Fawcett v. Fawcett, 1 Bush, 511. Even when the court authorizes, and the *cestui que trust* consents to a purchase by the trustee, it is said that the sale will be looked upon with suspicion. Ib.

When a trustee takes a benefit under his own abuse of the trust, a fraudulent purpose will be presumed. Harrison v. Smith, 2 Heisk. 230.

made by the trustee or agent with an implied trust for his benefit.[1] But the rule that a trustee cannot act in the double capacity of seller and buyer of the trust property does not necessarily apply to all dealings with the person for whom he holds it and towards whom he bears the relation of trustee. He may purchase the property of such person; and if the whole transaction, and the circumstances under which it took place, were fair and open, and no advantage was taken by him over the *cestui que trust*, whether by positive concealment, misrepresentation, or omitting to state any important fact, and no undue influence was exercised, and the *cestui que trust* understood what he was doing, the contract will not be set aside because of the fiduciary relation of the parties.[2]

A trustee may come to an agreement with his *cestui que trust* that, with reference to a proposed contract of purchase, they shall no longer stand in the present trust relation. And if the trustee prove that, through the medium of such an agreement, he had previously to the purchase clearly, distinctly, and honestly removed himself from the position of trustee, his purchase may be sustained.[3] But, though the authorities concede that a man may put off the confidential character of trustee, it may frequently be difficult to determine if he have done so effectually;[4] and this fact will be investigated with jealousy. So, though the connection may have been dissolved, still the trustee cannot use against the interests of the *cestui que trust* any information derived by him while in the trust relation, unless such information has been fully imparted to the *cestui que trust*.[5] But though a

[1] Parker v. Nickerson, 112 Mass. 195; Michoud v. Girod, 4 How. 503; Gillett v. Peppercorne, 3 Beav. 78; York & M. Ry. v. Hudson, 16 Beav. 485; Bentley v. Craven, 18 Beav. 75; Kimber v. Barber, Law R. 8 Ch. 56.

[2] Brown v. Cowell, 116 Mass. 461; Farnam v. Brooks, 9 Pick. 212, 231; Perry, Trusts, § 195.

[3] Sanderson v. Walker, 13 Ves. 601; Downes v. Grazebrook, 3 Meriv. 208.   [4] *Ex parte* Bennett, 10 Ves. 394.

[5] *Ex parte* Lacey, 6 Ves. 626; Coles v. Trecothick, 9 Ves. 248; Oliver v. Court, 8 Price, 161, 164.

trustee may purchase from his *cestui que trust*, where the latter is fully informed, and is not pressed by any undue influence, still the trustee must purchase openly for himself. He cannot set up a nominal purchaser, and deal with his *cestui que trust* in the name of another person.[1]

When trustees depart from that rule of conduct which their duty prescribes, neither they nor those who claim under them with notice can sustain an interest derived from their breach of trust. Nor are the *cestuis que trust* called upon in such cases to prove actual injury, in order to enable them to set aside the transaction.[2] But the *cestuis que trust* may, with full knowledge of the facts, when under no legal disability or undue influence, confirm such acts and debar themselves from future objection, though of course they cannot control the rights of others. If, for instance, the *cestuis que trust* be tenants for life, they cannot by their confirmation conclude the interests of those in remainder.[3]

If a person accept the office of trustee of a marriage settlement by which property is intended to be secured for the separate use of the wife, with remainder to the survivor, but subject to a power of joint appointment reserved to them in the settlement, any private agreement between the husband and the trustee that the property should be held liable to make good the engagements of the husband with the trustee would be fraudulent against the other parties to the settlement. The trustee would be bound to carry the appointment into execution, without himself setting up or allowing any one else to set up any thing to defeat it.[4] And where a creditor of the husband, by suppressing the fact that he is a creditor, procures himself to be appointed one of the wife's trustees, with a view of obtaining payment out of the wife's

---

[1] Woodhouse *v.* Meredith, 1 Jac. & W. 222.

[2] 1 Hovenden, Fraud, 484.

[3] Ib. ; Bowes *v.* East London Waterworks, 3 Madd. 383.

[4] Morris *v.* Clarkson, 1 Jac. & W. 111.

separate property, equity will not permit him to reap the fruits of his imposition by reverting to his character, and setting up the debt which he had suppressed.[1]

If the trustees of a marriage settlement, empowering them to advance to the husband a sum of money upon receiving a written consent of the wife, attested by witnesses, take upon themselves to advance the money without such consent, they cannot justify this breach of trust by alleging a *subsequent* approval of the wife. For the actual advance of the money to the husband, who perhaps may be unable to return it, would create an unfair pressure upon the judgment of the wife, giving to her subsequent assent a very different character from the free consent required by the settlement.[2]

It is a fundamental rule of law that no one can be compelled to answer questions having a tendency to convict himself of a criminal offence. If therefore it be alleged by bill in equity that a trustee has sold a living belonging to his *cestui que trust*, the trustee may demur to any discovery that would tend to fix him with simony, since this is a crime. But if the object of inquiry be to prove payment of money, it is proper, though the effect of the answer may be to prove simony; for no considerations will induce the court to declare that a trustee may so deal with the trust property as to be at liberty to state what he has done only to a limited extent, and compel the *cestui que trust* to rest satisfied with imperfect imformation concerning his property interests.[3]

Leases of charity estates for an unreasonable term, without an adequate consideration, are invalid;[4] *a fortiori*, if they contain a covenant for perpetual renewal.[5] In all such cases, fraud is inferred; and the lessee is held to be a trustee. So, if a corporation, acting as trustee of a charity, demise part of

---

[1] Dalbiac *v.* Dalbiac, 16 Ves. 124.   [2] Bateman *v.* Davies, 3 Madd. 99.

[3] Parkhurst *v.* Lowten, 2 Swanst. 211, 215.

[4] Attorney-General *v.* Moses, 2 Madd. 308.

[5] Attorney-General *v.* Brooke, 18 Ves. 326.

the charity estate to one of their own body at a lower annual rent than might have been obtained from another responsible tenant, it would be impossible for the lessee to support such a lease, if he were aware of the circumstances under which it was executed.[1]

When a sale is made under a trust or devise for payment of debts generally, without a specification of the debts in a schedule, the purchaser is not bound to see to the application of the money. But, if there be a specification of debts, the purchaser must look to the application of the money.[2]

Where trustees join collusively with a remainder-man in putting the tenant for life of the trust estate out of possession, and before the tenant for life is restored to his rights some of the occupiers of the land become insolvent, the trustees will be decreed to make good, not merely what the tenant for life would under the circumstances actually have received, had his possession been uninterrupted, but all he is entitled by his contracts of lease to receive.[3] If, on the other hand, trustees to preserve contingent remainders collude with the tenant for life, and permit him to commit waste in fraud of those in remainder, the trustees will be liable for such misconduct.[4]

It would in ordinary cases be a fraud in mere trustees appointed to preserve contingent remainders to concur in the destruction of the very interests, the protection of which was the object of their appointment;[5] but where they join in the destruction of contingent remainders without any fraudulent motive in fact, after the first tenant in tail has attained the age of twenty-one years, this may be in furtherance of such a fair and reasonable family arrangement as equity, even if it hesitated to direct the act, would not deem a culpable breach

---

[1] *Ex parte* Greenhouse, 1 Madd. 109.   [2] 1 Hovenden, Fraud, 490.

[3] Kaye *v.* Powell, 1 Ves. Jr. 408.

[4] Garth *v.* Cotton, 3 Atk. 753; Stansfield *v.* Habergham, 10 Ves. 278.

[5] Mansell *v.* Mansell, 2 P. Wms. 680; Biscoe *v.* Perkins, 1 Ves. & B. 491.

of trust.[1] *A fortiori*, where the trustee is not merely such, but is also tenant for life of the estate, he will not be deemed guilty of a breach of trust in joining with a remainder-man in tail to bar the entail; for the policy of the law favors the free alienation of property.[2]

Courts of equity look with special jealousy upon the conduct of trustees where infants are the *cestuis que trust*. And where a person has the management of two estates, in one of which he is interested personally and in the other as trustee, he will not be allowed to refer an engagement into which he has entered to one account or the other, as he may think fit, after he has seen the probability of its turning out advantageously or otherwise. If he has once embarked the infant's property, though no part of such trust money has been laid out, the trustee cannot abandon the contract on the part of the infant and take it on his own behalf. For any profits made, he must account: whether he must answer for any loss or not will depend upon his authority so to employ the trust funds, and the diligence and honesty with which he has conducted the transaction.[3]

A general rule obtains in respect of trustees of every description, and of tenants for life, namely, that if, from being in possession, they have and improve an opportunity of renewing a leasehold interest, such renewal will be treated as a graft upon the old lease.[4] They must not obtain a reversionary interest for their own use only;[5] but whatever advantages they obtain by such means they must hold in trust.[6] And purchasers with notice of course stand in the same situation,

---

[1] Moody *v.* Walters, 16 Ves. 307, 310, 311.

[2] Osbrey *v.* Bury, 1 Ball & B. 58.

[3] 1 Hovenden, Fraud, 481; Wilkinson *v.* Stafford, 1 Ves. Jr. 42.

[4] Mulvany *v.* Dillon, 1 Ball & B. 419; James *v.* Dean, 15 Ves. 240.

[5] Pickering *v.* Vowles, 1 Brown, C. C. 198; Randall *v.* Russell, 3 Meriv. 196.

[6] Nesbitt *v.* Tredennick, 1 Ball & B. 46; Rushworth's Case, 2 Freem. 13.

if relief be sought against them without laches.[1] Still, where there has been no contrivance in fraud of those who were interested in the old lease, and where such old lease and all the trusts relating to it are absolutely determined, and there is neither any remnant of the old lease, nor any tenant right of renewal upon which a new lease can be considered a graft, then the party who was trustee is *quoad hoc* no longer in that situation. The fiduciary relation is terminated for want of an object; the trust as to this subject has expired; and there is no ground for excluding the *quondam* trustee from becoming a purchaser of the property for his own benefit.[2] And where a trustee, even during the existence of a trust as to the leasehold interest, purchases the reversion in fee, though it may be objected that by this means he debars the *cestui que trust* of a fair chance of a renewal, yet this fact alone is not of sufficient importance to convert the purchase of the inheritance into a mere graft upon the leasehold interest.[3]

Upon similar principles, though it would be highly improper for an attorney to avail himself of information which he obtained as trustee for tenants for life or years to procure from the right heir a conveyance of the reversion in fee for his own benefit, still, desirous as equity might be to consider him a trustee only, it would not be warranted in doing so in favor of tenants for life who took nothing in the inheritance.[4]

Where a trustee in abuse of his trust has converted the trust property to his own use, the *cestui que trust* has the option to take the original or the substituted property. And, if either has passed into the hands of a *bona fide* purchaser without notice, he may take its value in money. If the trust property come back into the hands of the trustee, that fact does not affect the rights of the *cestui que trust*. The prin-

---

[1] Parker *v.* Brooke, 9 Ves. 587; Senhouse *v.* Earle, Amb. 288; Cordwell *v.* Mackrill, 2 Eden, 347.

[2] Stokes *v.* Clarke, Colles, P. C. 193.

[3] Randall *v.* Russell, 3 Meriv. 197; Hardman *v.* Johnson, Ib. 352.

[4] Norris *v.* Le Neve, 3 Atk. 38.

ciple is, that the wrongdoer shall derive no benefit from his own wrong. The entire profits belong to the *cestui que trust;* and equity will so mould and apply the remedy as to give them to him.[1]

It is an inflexible rule that, when a trustee buys at his own sale, the *cestui que trust* may treat the sale as a nullity, though the trustee paid a fair price, not because there is, but because there is likely to be, fraud,[2] a reason founded of course upon the peculiar relation of the parties. Thus, it has been held that, where shares of stock, standing in the name of a trustee, were assessed by an act of the Legislature and put up at auction for non-payment, and struck off to the trustee, the sale was invalid, and the trustee liable in trover for the value of the shares at the time of the sale and the dividends he had received thereon, with interest, less the amount of the assessments and expenses of sale.[3] And this rule, invalidating purchases by trustees at their own sales, applies as well where the sale is made under a decree of court as where it is made by himself.[4] And a trustee is not only forbidden to purchase for himself, but he cannot buy as agent for another person.[5]

However, if the trustee, in buying, acted without moral turpitude, equity may protect him so far as to give him a lien upon the property for any advances of a reasonable kind which he may have made.[6] And, if the trustee put improvements upon the trust property which he has purchased, he

---

[1] May *v.* Le Claire, 11 Wall. 217, 236. If there be actual fraud in the trustee in the execution of the trust, the *cestui que trust* can recover of him without an offer to reimburse the trustee for moneys which he has expended. McKennan *v.* Pry, 6 Watts, 137.

[2] Brothers *v.* Brothers, 7 Ired. Eq. 150. See Freeman *v.* Harwood, 49 Maine, 195.

[3] Freeman *v.* Harwood, 49 Maine, 195.

[4] Ogden *v.* Larrabee, 57 Ill. 389.

[5] North Baltimore Assoc. *v.* Caldwell, 25 Md. 420; Lewin, Trusts, 377, note.

[6] Mulford *v.* Minch, 3 Stockt. Ch. 16.

will be allowed therefor upon a resale ; provided the premises bring more than the sum agreed to be paid by the trustee.[1]

It is held in Mississippi that the right of a *cestui que trust* to avoid a purchase by the trustee at his own sale does not apply to the same extent as to sales made directly between the trustee and the *cestui que trust*. A trustee may, it is there held, purchase the trust property directly from the *cestui que trust*, or from third persons by his consent. But such transactions are there, as elsewhere, viewed with great suspicion ; and, if attacked, it is incumbent upon the trustee to show that the sale was fair and just in all respects, and consummated on his part with the most abundant good faith ; and that the *cestui que trust* had all the information concerning the property possessed by the trustee.[2]

Where the title to which a trust or mortgage attaches fails absolutely, the trustee or mortgagee, in the absence of fraud or unfair dealing or unfair advantage arising out of the relation sustained to the *cestui que trust* or mortgagor, may purchase and hold for his own benefit an adverse title. The prohibition is not applicable, where there is no title whatever in the party occupying the subordinate position.[3]

If a trustee purchase the trust property at his own sale, and claim to hold the same against the *cestui que trust*, on the ground of acquiescence, it devolves upon him to show notice to the *cestui que trust*, and distinct information to him before the alleged acquiescence began. The sale being *prima facie* fraudulent, the purchaser must be able to prove sufficient to overcome the presumption.[4] Mere notice cannot be enough ; for it does not follow in logic or in any uniform or usual course of events that a *cestui que trust*, having notice of a purchase by his trustee, had sufficient information from the trustee to justify him in making the purchase.

[1] Mason *v.* Martin, 4 Md. 124.　　[2] Jones *v.* Smith, 33 Miss. 215.
[3] Price *v.* Evans, 26 Mo. 30.
[4] Miles *v.* Wheeler, 43 Ill. 124 ; Randall *v.* Irvington, 10 Ves. 427.

The transaction, however, may often be established by long acquiescence in the purchase, in the absence of actual fraud. Thus, an attorney who sells bonds of his client at public sale, and buys them in himself at their full value at the time, cannot, after twelve years' acquiescence by the client, be called to account for them as a trustee.[1]

If the *cestui que trust*, being under no disability, lie by for a considerable time, with full knowledge of the purchase by the trustee, or do not within a reasonable time after his disability is removed seek to set aside the sale, or to treat the trustee as a purchaser for his benefit, it will be considered a case of acquiescence in the sale, and the trustee will not be disturbed.[2]

Though equity will enforce the utmost good faith on the part of a trustee, and vigilantly watch any acquisition by him in his individual character of property which has ever been the subject of his trust, yet, when he has sold the property to another, and the sale has been judicially confirmed after opposition by the *cestui que trust*, the fact that thirteen years afterwards he bought the property from the person to whom he sold it does not of necessity vitiate the transaction. The question in such a case becomes one of actual fraud. Where, therefore, on a bill charging fraud in a sale, the answer denies it in the fullest manner, alleging a purchase *bona fide* and for full value, and that, when the trustee made the sale to the person from whom he has since bought it, the present purchase by himself was not thought of, equity will not pronounce the purchase fraudulent.[3]

The fact even that property was sold by a trustee for a sum less than half its value, and was shortly afterwards sold back to him by the purchaser for the same amount, is not of itself sufficient to fix on the trustee the charge of having committed

---

[1] Marsh *v.* Whitmore, 21 Wall. 178.

[2] Mason *v.* Martin, 4 Md. 124.

[3] Stephen *v.* Beall, 22 Wall. 329.

a fraud. To establish such a fact, there should be proof of an understanding between the trustee and the bidder at or prior to the sale.[1]

To render the ratification of a purchase made by a trustee of trust property for himself effective and binding, the *cestui que trust*, being *sui juris*, must at the time of the ratification be fully aware of every material fact, and his act of ratification must be an independent, substantive act; and he must not only be aware of the facts, but apprised of the law as to how these facts would be dealt with, if brought before a court of equity.[2]

An application by the *cestui que trust* to be allowed to participate in the purchase, which is refused, is not such an acquiescence in the sale to the trustee as to make the sale valid.[3]

As to the taking of accounts between a trustee and his *cestui que trust*, the general rule to be gathered from the cases is, that where there has been great laches on the part of the *cestui que trust* (supposing him to have been *sui juris*), and the trustee has not been guilty of positive fraud, the account will be taken only from the commencement of the suit. But where there has been no laches in seeking the account, or where the parties are not *sui juris*, or where the trustee is

---

[1] Boehlert *v.* McBride, 48 Mo. 505.

[2] Cumberland Coal Co. *v.* Sherman, 20 Md. 134. "The doctrine of a court of chancery," say the court, quoting from Lammott *v.* Bowley, 6 Har. & J. 526, "is not, as has been contended, that equity will not administer relief in cases of mistake of law, upon the principle that every man is bound to know the law. It is not intended to say that the plea of *ignorantia legis* would in all instances be available in civil cases (in criminal it never can be), because some legal propositions are so plain and familiar even to ordinary minds that it would be doing violence to probability to impute ignorance in such cases; but it is only meant to say that where the legal principle is confessedly doubtful, and one about which ignorance may well be supposed to exist, a person acting under a misapprehension of the law in such a case shall not forfeit his legal rights by reason of such mistake."

[3] Ricketts *v.* Montgomery, 15 Md. 46.

chargeable with fraud, the account will be carried back to the time when the fraudulent possession began.[1]

A release obtained by executors and trustees from the *cestuis que trust* for less than the amount due from them is invalid, especially if the beneficiaries reside in another State.[2] So, too, releases from *cestuis que trust* to their trustees, without a settlement of the trust account, are looked upon with jealousy by the courts.[3]

One to whom certain property has been conveyed by his debtor in trust for others is not precluded from purchasing or levying upon other property of the debtor, for his own personal benefit.[4]

Besides those who are trustees *eo nomine*, there are others who occupy that position. The officers and directors of a corporate body, for example, are trustees of the stockholders, and cannot, without being guilty of fraud, secure to themselves advantages not common to the latter.[5] Thus, where a corporation instructed its officers to effect a loan of money, and they, in violation of their duty, proceeded to secure personal claims of their own against the company, they were held guilty of a fraudulent breach of trust, and the transaction was declared void as against the stockholders.[6]

---

[1] Miles v. Wheeler, 43 Ill. 123; Bowes v. East London Waterworks, 3 Madd. 375; Drummond v. St. Albans, 5 Ves. 432; Pettinard v. Prescott, 7 Ves. 541; Dormer v. Fortescue, 3 Atk. 130.

[2] Bixler v. Kunkle, 17 Serg. & R. 298.

[3] Shartel's Appeal, 64 Penn. St. 25.

[4] Eldridge v. Smith, 34 Vt. 484.

[5] Jackson v. Ludeling, 20 Wall. 616; Simmons v. Vulcan Oil Co., 61 Penn. St. 202; Koehler v. Black River Iron Co., 2 Black, 715; Charitable Corp. v. Sutton, 2 Atk. 404; Robinson v. Smith, 3 Paige, 222; Hodges v. New England Screw Co., 1 R. I. 321; York & N. M. Ry. Co. v. Hudson, 19 Eng. L. & E. 361.

[6] Koehler v. Black River Iron Co., *supra.* " In executing this mortgage," said the court, " and thereby securing to themselves advantages which were not common to all the stockholders, they were guilty of an unauthorized act, and violated a plain principle of equity applicable to trustees. The directors are the trustees or managing partners, and the

While, however, the officers of a corporation cannot make a personal profit out of the business of the company, still, as in other cases of fiduciary relations, transactions for the individual benefit of the directors are supported where the fiduciary relation has ceased before the particular transaction, or where it was entered into with the consent of the stockholders, or where by acquiescence they have precluded themselves from objecting.[1]

A director of a company is not in the position of a trustee of his shares for the general body of shareholders, and under ordinary circumstances he may deal with them as freely as any other shareholder, provided he does not part with his qualification. But he is a trustee of his power of making calls for the general body of shareholders, and must not use it for his own benefit, without regard to their interests.[2]

It has been held in Indiana that the relation existing between the president of a railroad corporation and a non-official stockholder is not such as to require a disclosure of facts in transactions in the corporation stock between such persons.[3] In the case cited, the president of a railroad company, who was also one of its directors, having knowledge by reason of his official position that the true value of the stock of the company was very largely in excess of its nominal market value, purchased at much less than its real worth the stock of a non-official stockholder, who was ignorant of the company's financial condition, and of facts giving an extraordinary value to the stock, without disclosing to the seller the facts and circumstances within his knowledge as to

stockholders are the *cestuis que trust*, and have a joint interest in all the property and effects of the corporation; and no injury that the stockholders may sustain by a fraudulent breach of trust can, upon the general principles of equity, be suffered to pass without a remedy." Angell & Ames, Corporations, § 312.

[1] Ashhurst's Appeal, 60 Penn. St. 290.
[2] Gilbert's Case, Law R. 5 Ch. 559.
[3] Tippecanoe Co. v. Reynolds, 44 Ind. 509.

its true value. It was held that in the absence of actual fraud
the sale was valid. It was considered that such a case did
not disclose a relation of trustee and *cestui que trust*. But the
decision was not unanimous, and the subject is worthy of
further consideration. The court were possibly correct in
holding that the president of the company was not, in strictness, a trustee towards the vendor;[1] but it is quite another
thing to say that no relation of confidence and trust existed
between the parties. And that is all that is necessary to
require disclosure.[2] But this decision is not to be understood
as in any way impugning the well-established doctrine, that
the duties of corporate officers require them to forego all
personal interests except in so far as their personal interests
are the same as the interests of the corporation. The authorities upon this point were commented upon and conceded to
be correct.[3]

§ 6. OF GUARDIAN AND WARD.

Property transactions between guardian and ward, with
the exception of gifts or bequests by a guardian to his ward,
are *prima facie* fraudulent as against the guardian; but the
guardian is entitled to show, if he can by the clearest proof,
that he dealt with the ward exactly as with a stranger, taking
no advantage of his influence over him, or of his superior

[1] See Spering's Appeal, 71 Penn. St. 11, 20 ; Bliss *v.* Matteson, 45
N. Y. 22 ; Bedford R. Co. *v.* Bowser, 48 Penn. St. 29 ; Koehler *v.* Black
River Co., 2 Black, 715.

[2] To the same effect as Tippecanoe Co. *v.* Reynolds, *supra*, see Carpenter *v.* Danforth, 52 Barb. 581.

[3] Robinson *v.* Smith, 3 Paige, 222 ; Verplank *v.* Mercantile Ins. Co.,
1 Edw. Ch. 84 ; Cumberland Coal Co. *v.* Sherman, 30 Barb. 553 ; Butts
v. Woods, 38 Barb. 181 ; Hodges *v.* New England Screw Co., 1 R. I.
312 ; European Ry. Co. *v.* Poor, 59 Maine, 277 ; York Ry. Co. *v.* Hudson, 19 Eng. L. & E. 361 ; Great Luxembourg Ry. Co. *v.* Maguay, 25
Beav. 586 ; *Ex parte* Bennett, 18 Beav. 339.

knowledge in relation to the subject-matter of the transaction, and that the ward's act was the result of his own volition and upon full deliberation [1] and legal advice.

A guardian has the power to sell his ward's personal estate, but he has no right to use his power for his individual benefit. If he appropriate his ward's property, or the proceeds of a sale of it, to pay his own debt, he commits a fraud on the ward.[2] But the fraud of the guardian will not of itself invalidate the transaction. If a guardian dispose of his ward's property as his own (the guardian's) to an innocent purchaser without notice, actual or constructive, such purchaser is not affected by the fraud.[3]

A guardian who has fraudulently converted stock of his ward will be held to account at the highest price reached by the stock after the conversion.[4] And, on the other hand, improvements put by a guardian upon land fraudulently purchased from his ward need not be paid for by the ward.[5] In the absence of actual fraud, however, the case would probably be otherwise.

The principle of law which protects wards in transactions with their guardians extends to the execution of a will by a ward in favor of his guardian; and hence a testament made by a ward in favor of his guardian will be held void, unless the legal presumption of undue influence is rebutted by proof.[6] The same principles apply to cases of acknowledgment of debts. Thus, in an English case it appeared that the plaintiff had married while a minor, and had thereby placed himself in a position of great embarrassment. The defendant, an attorney, made him considerable advances of money, but did not appear to have acted for him in any professional capac-

---

[1] Meek v. Perry, 36 Miss. 190.
[2] Hunter v. Lawrence, 11 Gratt. 111. [3] Ib.
[4] Lamb's Appeal, 58 Penn. St. 142.
[5] Eberts v. Eberts, 55 Penn. St. 110.
[6] Meek v. Perry, 36 Miss. 190.

ity. Two months after coming of age, the plaintiff signed an
acknowledgment, stating, as the defendant alleged (but this
was disputed) that he was indebted to the defendant above
£1,300. The court treated the case as one of guardian and
ward, and held that he could not be permitted to conclude
the plaintiff by an acknowledgment, signed by him within a
short time after coming of age, and without the intervention
of any friend or adviser.[1]

The jurisdiction of equity will be exercised to restrain
an action at law upon a negotiable security obtained by a
guardian from his ward while under the influence, though
absolved from the connection, of the confidential relation.
In an English case, it appeared that a lady, two years and
a half after she came of age, had at the request of her
late guardian, with whom she was still living, indorsed a
promissory note, made in his favor. The paper came into
the defendant's hands for value, but with notice of the
circumstances. Upon a bill filed by the young lady, the
defendants were restrained from suing her at law upon her
indorsement.[2]

When a man acts as guardian, or trustee in the nature of
guardian, for an infant, the courts are extremely watchful to
prevent such person taking any advantage, immediately upon
the attaining majority by his ward or *cestui que trust*,[3] and
also at the time of settling accounts or delivering up the trust,
because an undue advantage may then be easily taken. The
occasion would give an opportunity, either by flattery or by
force, to take such an advantage; and therefore the rule of

---

[1] Revett *v.* Harvey, 1 Sim. & S. 502. Of course, a mere acknowledgment of debt would not be conclusive in any case, unless under seal; but
in this case the defendant alleged that the instrument was signed after a
regular settlement of accounts and delivery of vouchers, and there was
no suggestion of mistake.

[2] Maitland *v.* Backhouse, 16 Sim. 58. See Maitland *v.* Irving, 15
Sim. 437.

[3] Tuck *v.* Buckley, 43 Iowa, 415.

the courts is to treat the situation as one coming under the head of public utility, like the case of bonds obtained from young heirs, and rewards given an attorney pending a cause. Gifts under such circumstances are not in general permitted to stand, though perhaps in the particular case there may not have been any actual unfairness. Still such bounties by wards just come of age are not universally invalid. A ward in such a situation may bind himself by a gift to his guardian ; as where, being actually in possession of an estate, and fully *sui juris*, he makes a gift by way of reward for care and trouble, with his eyes open.[1]

A person entering upon the estate of an infant, whether the infant had been in possession or not, will be fixed with a fiduciary relation as to the infant : first, whenever he is the natural guardian of the infant ; secondly, when he is so connected by relationship or otherwise with the infant as to impose upon him a duty to protect, or at least not to prejudice, the infant's rights ; or, thirdly, where he takes possession with knowledge or express notice of the infant's rights.[2] One who occupies such a position towards an infant comes, it should seem, within the general prohibition against treating by way of contract or purchase with reference to the infant's estate.

Deeds of release and acquittance as well as of gift, made by a ward to his guardian, or to a person who has borne the part of a guardian, shortly after the ward's arrival at majority, but before the delivery of the ward's estate and without a settlement of accounts, are considered void, without proof of actual fraud.[3] So, too, if a guardian buy property from his ward at a greatly inadequate price, shortly after the ward arrives at majority, the sale will be set aside at the suit of the ward.[4] But undue influence will not be presumed to exist on-

[1] Hylton *v.* Hylton, 2 Ves. 548.

[2] Quinton *v.* Frith, Law R. 2 Irish Eq. 396.   See also Revett *v.* Harvey, 1 Sim. & S. 502.   [3] Waller *v.* Armistead, 2 Leigh, 11.

[4] Eberts *v.* Eberts, 55 Penn. St. 110.

the part of a guardian over his former ward in a settlement between them made more than three years after the ward has attained his majority.[1]

The settlements and allowances of a guardian in a Probate Court, in the matter of his guardianship, have the force, it has been said, of judgments, and can be set aside only upon proof that they were procured by fraud.[2]   And it is not a fraud for the guardian to give his individual note for the maintenance of the ward, and then to obtain an allowance therefor in the settlement.[3]

§ 7. OF EXECUTORS AND ADMINISTRATORS.

Executors and administrators also come under the general designation of parties holding confidential relations to others, and the general principles already stated apply to them.   In a recent case,[4] a widow had yielded the right of administration upon her husband's estate to the husbands of children by a former marriage of the deceased.   Between the widow and these children and their husbands the most affectionate relations existed.   The husbands had in their hands or within their control personal property of the deceased amounting to sixty thousand dollars or more, to one-third of which the widow was entitled absolutely by law.   She had, in fact, great confidence in the men, as she evinced by renouncing her right to the administration of her husband's estate in their favor.   Soon after the qualification of the administrators, a deed was executed between all the parties above-named, whereby they agreed to abide by the terms of a defective will made by the deceased in the disposition of his estate.   The effect of this

[1] Kittredge v. Betton, 14 N. H. 401.
[2] Brent v. Grace, 30 Mo. 253; Mitchell v. Williams, 27 Mo. 399.
[3] Brent v. Grace, *supra.*
[4] Statham v. Ferguson, 25 Gratt. 28.

arrangement was the giving up, on the part of the widow, of some $25,000. Upon the evidence in the case, it was considered that, in the situation of the parties, undue influence had been exerted on the widow, and that she was not sufficiently informed of the value of the estate or of her rights; and therefore, though no actual fraud had been practised, the deed was set aside.

As we have elsewhere seen, in considering the duties of agents, a person cannot legally purchase, on his own account, that which his duty requires him to sell on account of another; nor can he purchase, on account of another, that which he sells on his own account. He cannot unite the opposite characters of buyer and seller. And this rule applies to purchases by executors at open sale, though they were empowered by the will to sell the estate of their testator for the benefit of heirs and legatees, of whom they themselves were part.[1] And an administrator can no more buy the estate of the deceased through a third person acting on his behalf than he can do so directly.[2] Thus, where property sold at an administrator's sale is purchased by his attorney and his brother, and he (the administrator) afterwards negotiates sales of the same, deriving profits thereby, equity will set aside the original purchase, unless the property has since passed into the hands of innocent third persons.[3]

The rule which restrains executors and administrators, and persons in situations of trust generally, from buying the property under their charge, does not go so far as to prevent them from buying the property from one who has purchased the same for value and in good faith. Provided there be no connivance or collusion between such parties, the executor or trustee may treat for the purchase, and acquire the title to the property immediately after it is sold from the estate in

---

[1] Michoud v. Girod, 4 How. 503.

[2] Scott v. Umbarger, 41 Cal. 410.

[3] Read v. Howe, 39 Iowa, 553.

trust.[1] But the fact that a purchaser at an administrator's sale was a man of no pecuniary means, that on the same day on which the administrator conveyed the property to him he reconveyed it to the administrator, is sufficient proof, in the absence of an adequate explanation, that the first purchase was made for the benefit of the administrator; and the transaction may be avoided by the parties in interest.[2]

If an executor, ignorant of the rules of the Court of Chancery, openly purchase assets of his testator with the full approbation of the parties interested, he will not be held answerable, after a considerable lapse of time, for the profit he has made, provided he has purchased honestly. But, if it appear that the purchase was made with a fraudulent intention, the rule will be enforced. The purchase will be set aside, and the executor required to account for the accumulations.[3]

A purchase by an administrator of one of the distributees, shortly after the distributee became of age, of all his interest in his father's estate, the administrator having rendered no inventory of the estate or stated an account, and the purchase being made at a grossly inadequate price, will be considered fraudulent and voidable at the election of the distributee, if application is made for that purpose within a reasonable time afterwards, or within reasonable time after obtaining knowledge of the fraud.[4] Fraud, however, in an administrator's sale, will not be presumed from the mere fact that the purchaser afterwards conveyed the property to the administrator. Actual fraud should be proved in such a case.[5]

A purchase of bonds from an executor at a discount of eighteen per cent., with knowledge that the condition of the

[1] Wortman v. Skinner, 1 Beasl. 358.
[2] Obert v. Obert, 2 Stockt. 98.   See Scott v. Gamble, 1 Stockt. 235; Mulford v. Bowen, Ib. 797; Michoud v. Harris, 4 How. 563.
[3] Whatton v. Toone, 5 Madd. 54.   [4] Johnson v. Johnson, 5 Ala. 90.
[5] Vasquez v. Richardson, 19 Mo. 96.

estate does not require the sale, is a fraud on the part of the purchaser, though he may not know that the bonds do not amount to more than the executor's interest (as one of the legatees) in the estate. And in such a case, where the executor has not paid to the other legatees their portion of the estate, such purchaser may be compelled to repay the money to them.[1] So, too, if the sureties of the executor have been compelled to pay the amount to the legatees, they may recover over from the purchaser.[2]

If an administrator charge himself in settlement with the appraised value of the estate, while the sale-bill returned by him shows that the amount for which the property sold exceeded its appraised value; or if he apply the money of the estate to the purchase of property in his own name and right, equity will open the settlement for fraud.[3] And the same is true where such a party, in his trust capacity, collects notes due and drawing interest, without charging himself with such interest, though there be no evidence of positive fraud.[4]

A party who voluntarily interferes with and manages an estate in behalf of heirs as their representative, and as such

---

[1] Pinckard v. Woods, 8 Gratt. 140. "It is the duty of an executor," said the court, "not to sell, but to collect the debts due to the estate of his testator, including those arising out of sales of goods made by the executor in the course of his administration; and, if he sells such debts at a price below their value, he thereby commits a *devastavit*, unless he makes it appear that such sale was manifestly required by the interests of the estate. And this he can never do without showing in the first place that the proceeds thereof have been applied to the purposes of the estate. The appropriation by the executor of the proceeds of such a sale to his own individual uses presents the case of a fraudulent breach of trust on his part, for which, of course, he is personally liable to creditors legatees, and others injuriously affected by such improper diversion of the assets. And the purchaser himself, so acquiring such debt at a profit, if he has reason to believe at the time that the same belongs to the estate, and is so disposed of by the executor for his individual uses, thereby concurs in such fraudulent breach of trust by the executor, and therefore incurs the like liability."

[2] Ib.

[3] Osborne v. Graham, 30 Ark. 66.　　[4] Ringgold v. Stone, 20 Ark. 526.

acquires information to which a stranger would not have access, stands in the situation of an administrator or executor duly appointed. And, in treating with the heirs for the purchase of the estate, he is bound to disclose every matter which it is important they should know, or the sale will be invalid, unless such disclosure is distinctly waived.[1]

It has been doubted whether a gift will be looked upon with such suspicion as to cast the burden of proving fairness upon the donee, where the situation of the donee was merely that of a person transacting the business of the donor as administratrix of the estate of the donor's husband, and of attending to her out-of-doors affairs generally. If, however, the situation were to be deemed that of an agency, subject to the severest scrutiny of the law, there was nothing in the evidence to cast the slightest suspicion upon the transaction; and it was accordingly upheld.[2]

When an executor's purchase at his own sale is set aside, the executor will not be held to take the property at what it was worth upon the estimate of witnesses. The property will be put up for sale again; but, if more cannot be obtained for it than the executor was to pay, his purchase will be confirmed.[3]

A court of equity will not assist in carrying into effect compositions of claims by executors or administrators, unless

---

[1] Casey v. Casey, 14 Ill. 112.

[2] Millican v. Millican, 24 Tex. 426, 451. See Hunter v. Atkins, 3 Mylne & K. 113. In Millican v. Millican, the court say: " The agency which existed in this case was such as every widowed mother, who is under the necessity of administering upon her deceased husband's estate, would be likely to intrust to a son, if she have one competent to transact the business; and it will scarcely be contended that in every such case the performance of so reasonable a service and duty on his part will disqualify the son from receiving a gratuity from his mother, or from becoming the object of her bounty equally with others who have not rendered such services. Undue influence is not to be inferred as the legal consequence of such an agency."

[3] Bailey v. Robinsons, 1 Gratt. 4.

the party praying it will first disclose all the circumstances of
the case, that the court may see that there has been no fraud,
and that every thing was fair.[1]

§ 8. OF MORTGAGOR AND MORTGAGEE.

The law upon the subject of the right to redeem mortgaged
property, where the mortgagor has conveyed to the mortgagee
the equity of redemption, is well settled. It is characterized
by a jealous and salutary policy. Principles are applied almost
as stern as those which govern where a sale by a *cestui que
trust* to his trustee is drawn in question. To give validity to
such a sale by a mortgagor, it must be shown that the conduct
of the mortgagee was in all things fair and frank, and that
he paid for the property what it was worth. He must hold
out no delusive hopes; he must exercise no undue influence;
he must take no advantage of the fears or poverty of the other
party. Any indirection or obliquity of conduct is fatal to his
title. Every doubt will be resolved against him. The fact
that the mortgagor may have knowingly surrendered and
never intended to reclaim is of no consequence. If there be
vice in the transaction, the law, while it will secure to the
mortgagee his debt with interest, will compel him to give back
that which he has taken with unclean hands.[2]

A sale under a power in a mortgage will be set aside upon
proof of the slightest fraud or unfair conduct.[3] This, however, does not mean that countervailing evidence is not to

---

[1] Clay *v.* Williams, 2 Munf. 105.

[2] Villa *v.* Rodriguez, 12 Wall. 323, 339, *per* Swayne, J.; Morris *v.*
Nixon, 1 How. 118; Russell *v.* Southard, 12 How. 139; Wakeman *v.*
Hazleton, 3 Barb. Ch. 148; Holmes *v.* Grant, 8 Paige, 245; 4 Kent, Com.
143.

[3] Burr *v.* Borden, 61 Ill. 389; not, however, as was inaccurately stated
in Longwith *v.* Butler, 3 Gilm. 42, upon the *slightest proof* of fraud or
unfair conduct. Ib.

be taken into account.   The whole evidence must be fairly weighed.   The sale will not be set aside upon slight proof of unfairness, if met by preponderating evidence on the other side.[1]

A mortgagee under a power of sale is a trustee in law; he is also a *cestui que trust*, and his interest as such may absorb the whole estate.   It is pledged to him for his protection; and his security might be greatly impaired or even sacrificed at such sale, if he were not permitted under any circumstances to become a purchaser.   It has been accordingly held that where the mortgagor was privy to the sale, assented to it, and to the acquisition of title by the mortgagee, and concurred in that result after it was reached, and there was no suspicion of fraudulent practice, the sale to the mortgagee would stand.[2]   It has been held in Texas that a mortgagee with a power of sale may purchase at his own sale through a third party, and that such sale is not subject to impeachment in the absence of proof of unfairness, attempt to stifle competition, or other fraudulent acts.[3]   So, too, it has been held in New York that a mortgagee, holding a power of attorney from the mortgagor, may sell and convey through a third party to himself, provided he act therein with the knowledge and concurrence of the mortgagor.[4]   A mortgagee selling under a power of attorney, and a mortgagee acting under a power of sale incorporated in the mortgage, stand upon the same footing.   In the latter case, the mortgage deed itself is treated, for this purpose, as a power of attorney.[5]

In deciding upon transactions between mortgagor and mortgagee, equity will jealously examine whether the latter has taken advantage of the necessities of the former.   When the loan has been coupled with or followed by any other transaction beneficial to the lender, the inequality of the situations

---

[1] Burr *v.* Borden, 61 Ill. 389.

[2] Medsker *v.* Swaney, 45 Mo. 273.   [3] Howards *v.* Davis, 6 Tex. 174.

[4] Dobson *v.* Racy, 4 Seld. 216.   See Ives *v.* Ashley, 97 Mass. 198.

[5] Medsker *v.* Swaney, 45 Mo. 273, 277.

of the parties will be evidence that the dealing was produced by the influence derived from the mortgage. And on this ground it will be set aside as fraudulent.[1] Thus, sales of equities of redemption may be set aside whenever, by the influence which the incumbrance gives him, a mortgagee has purchased for less than others would have given, and there has been any evidence of misconduct on his part in obtaining the purchase.[2] However, when mortgaged premises are to be sold under orders in bankruptcy against the mortgagor, the mortgagee may, by application to the court, obtain permission to become purchaser, if he prove to be the highest bidder at the sale.[3]

If the mortgagee of leasehold premises obtain a renewal, either by being in possession or by clandestine conduct towards the mortgagor, the renewal lease will be treated as a graft upon the old one ; and the mortgagee will not be allowed to retain it for his own benefit, but will hold it in trust.[4]

§ 9. OF PARENT AND CHILD.

In respect of bounties by children in favor of their parents, Lord Eldon has said that the Court of Chancery will not look on such transactions in the light of reversionary bargains, but will regard them as family arrangements, with a reasonable degree of jealousy, and will not look into all the motives and feelings which might actuate the parties in entering into such arrangements.[5] This principle has been reasserted in later cases. Lord St. Leonards, after quoting the above

[1] Webb v. Rorke, 2 Schoales & L. 673; Spurgeon v. Collier, 1 Eden, 59; Vernon v. Bethell, 2 Eden, 113; Tooms v. Conset, 3 Atk. 261; 2 Hovenden, Fraud, 180.

[2] Gubbins v. Creed, 2 Schoales & L. 221.

[3] *Ex parte* Duncane, Buck, 18; *Ex parte* Hammond, Ib. 465.

[4] Nesbitt v. Tredennick, 1 Ball & B. 46.

[5] Tweddell v. Tweddell, 1 T. R. 1.

language, has said that if it could be shown on the whole
that the son understood what he was doing, and that the
case was one of family arrangement, he would be most unwilling to look narrowly into the consideration.[1] And both
of these statements have been cited with approval in a recent
case.[2] This was the case of a bounty by a son, entitled in remainder to real estate expectant on the lives of his mother
and father, by whom he had been educated and maintained.
A few days after he attained majority, the son, in order to relieve his parents (who had mortgaged their life interest as a
security for moneys borrowed and partly expended in improv-
ing the property) from keeping on foot certain life insurance
policies, executed a deed, charging the inheritance with the
mortgage debt. He subsequently filed a bill to have the
deed set aside on the ground of fraud, which was disproved,
and of undue influence ; but the bill was dismissed with costs.
It was considered that the benefit conferred upon the inheritance would support the deed.[3] Whether it would have been

---

[1] Wallace v. Wallace, 2 Dru. & War. 470.   See also Rhodes v. Cook,
2 Sim. & S. 489.

[2] Baker v. Bradley, 2 Smale & G. 531, 559.

[3] "It was argued, indeed," said the court, "that a judicious friend
would have advised the plaintiff that it was useless to attempt to relieve
his father by joining in the security, and that his better course was to
preserve unincumbered his reversionary estate. But, to justify the propriety and wisdom of any such advice, it will be necessary to show some
other scheme of life and of intermediate subsistence for the plaintiff during
the life of the father and mother. But no such scheme has been shown.
Upon a fair view of the whole transaction, there seems nothing unfair,
nothing unreasonable in it as a family arrangement, even if the money
expended by the father on the estate was not a sufficient consideration.
That the plaintiff perfectly understood the transaction is proved by various circumstances. . . . Looking at this case with that reasonable degree of jealousy required in the investigation of all such transactions, it
would seem that the previous expenditure by the father for the improvement of the estate, and the advantages which were likely to accrue to the
plaintiff in point of position and future prospects in his profession [sur-
veying] by his concurring to preserve the family establishment, are considerations enough to support the securities given in September, 1848, as

supported in the absence of such a consideration does not appear.

In cases of gifts to a parent by a child shortly after the child attains majority, the courts look with jealousy upon the transaction; and the more especially when the parent has, during the minority of the child, been guardian of his property, and in receipt of the rents of a considerable estate. The burden of proof rests upon the parent to show (and he should show plainly) that the gift was made, not in consequence of representations on his part, but by the spontaneous act of the child, and that the child had full knowledge of the nature of the deed by which the gift was effected, and of his own position and rights in reference to the property.[1]

A gift by a child just come of age to his father or mother is not, however, *per se* voidable; nor, it is held in this country, is it *prima facie* voidable. The true interpretation of the cases on this subject is said to be to the effect that there must be some ingredient of undue influence exercised by the parent, operating upon the fears or hopes of the child; thus showing reasonable ground to presume that the act was not perfectly free and voluntary on the part of the child.[2] But the natural and just influence which a parent has over a child renders it peculiarly important for courts of justice to watch over and protect the interests of the latter. And therefore all contracts and conveyances whereby benefits are secured by children to their parents are objects of jealousy; and if they be not entered into with scrupulous good faith, and are not

a reasonable family arrangement. It has, indeed, been said on behalf of the plaintiff that this is the case of a father urged, by the threat of a creditor, to exercise his parental influence to induce his son to do what was wholly to his detriment. But it is impossible, on a fair view of the facts, to consider that some advantage did not accrue to the son, and that the expenditure of the father on the estate was not a valuable consideration."

[1] Wright *v.* Vanderplank, 2 Kay & J. 1; s. c. 8 DeG., M. & G. 133.
[2] Taylor *v.* Taylor, 8 How. 183, 201; Jenkins *v.* Pye, 12 Peters, 241.

reasonable under the circumstances, they will be set aside, unless third persons have acquired an interest under them.[1] Hence, where a deed of gift was made by a female child just of age, and living with her parents, to a trustee for the benefit of one of those parents, and was executed under the influence of misrepresentations by the parents, and contained false recitals, the instrument was ordered to be set aside and the property to be reconveyed to the grantor.[2]

The influence which a child may exert over a parent by acts of filial duty and obedience is not undue influence. That influence is proper which one person gains over another by acts of pure kindness and attention, and by correct conduct. In the case of a gift from a child to a parent, undue influence may be inferred from the relation itself, but never where the gift is from the parent to the child. In the former case, it may be inferred that the donation proceeded from the exercise of parental authority. It is natural that the known wishes of a parent should be strongly felt by a child accustomed from infancy to implicit confidence and obedience, even after the child has attained majority; to the extent of affecting the child's freedom of will, especially if he continue to reside with the parent and to look to him or her for protection and support. But, where the gift is from the parent to the child, there is no such inference. A parent does not yield obedience to the child further than affection or duty prompts; and it is in accordance with the promptings of nature that parents should make gifts to their children.[3]

Notwithstanding the favor with which family settlements are regarded, they seem to stand upon no peculiar footing, when effected under the influence of one in whom a special confidence, from his familiarity and connection with the estate, is placed. Thus, it has been laid down that where a father

---

[1] 1 Story, Equity, § 309.   [2] Taylor v. Taylor, 8 How. 183.

[3] Millican v. Millican, 24 Tex. 426, 446; Saufley v. Jackson, 16 Tex. 579.

devises an estate to a son and daughters, the son, knowing
its value, and the daughters not knowing it, should be scrupu-
iously careful to apprise them, when entering upon a treaty
with them for a different settlement of the estate, of its value,
of their rights, and of every circumstance necessary to enable
them to treat upon terms of perfect equality with him. Any
positive concealment or misrepresentation on his part, calculated to put them at a disadvantage, will, it is clear, be sufficient ground for annulling the settlement.[1]

There is no such relation of confidence between a grantor
and his son, or grandson, or son-in-law, as to raise a presumption of fraud in the case of deed granting to such persons a
bounty, though the instrument were executed without the
aid of legal counsel but eight days before the grantor's death,
and while he was confined to his bed by sickness.[2]

The principles applicable to gifts by children to their parents
apply where the natural position of the parties has become
reversed, and the child has become the guardian of his aged
or infirm parent.[3] Thus, it has been held that a son, the
principal legatee of an infirm mother, who was generally
under his influence, must produce the most satisfactory evidence of the good faith of his conduct.[4]

If no undue or improper means be used by a son to procure
a voluntary deed from his father, the mere fact that the
father regarded him with more favor than another child, and
that the deeds were executed when the father was in some

---

[1] Hewitt v. Crane, 2 Halst. Ch. 159; Van Meter v. Jones, 2 Green's
Ch. 520.

[2] Beanland v. Bradley, 2 Smale & G. 339. " There is no rule of this
court," said Stuart, V. C., " which prohibits a man by a voluntary deed
from bestowing a benefit upon his son, or his grandson, or his son-in-law,
even though only a few days before his death. To provide for his children
or grandchildren is, or may be, a necessary duty; and, where a father dis
charges that duty, this court will not presume fraud. If fraud is alleged,
it must be proved in the ordinary way."

[3] Highberger v. Stiffler, 21 Md. 352.

[4] Simpler v. Lord, 28 Ga. 52. As to evidence to rebut the presumption against the legatee, see Glover v. Hayden, 4 Cush. 580.

degree intoxicated, but not enough to be insensible of what he was doing, will not be sufficient to set aside the gift.[1]

A son employed by his father to procure a deed making a certain disposition of his property thereby assumes a fiduciary relation towards his father. Hence where a son so employed procured a deed to himself and a brother, in exclusion of the other heirs, the father being at the time aged, infirm, and in a distressed state of mind, though capable of making a deed, and there being indications that the father had been imposed upon, the sons were held to strict proof of the fairness of the transaction.[2]

There is no such relation of trust and confidence existing between a son-in-law and his mother-in-law, by force of the mere relationship, that in dealings between them the latter should be supposed to act upon the presumption that there would be no concealment of facts from her.[3]

§ 10. Of Physician and Patient.

On the principle of correcting abuse of confidence, equity will also look with favor on the claim of a patient against his medical attendant in respect of relief from gifts made to him. Relief has been granted against the liability of the maker of a promissory note, taken by his medical attendant (who had rendered no account) from a poor patient on the occasion of an accession of fortune for an amount beyond what was due for his services on the most extravagant scale of charges.[4] So, too, an agreement obtained by a physician or surgeon from a deceased patient will be set aside, if the court be satisfied

---

[1] Belcher v. Belcher, 10 Yerg. 121.

[2] Martin v. Martin, 1 Heisk. 644.

[3] Fish v. Cleland, 33 Ill. 238; Cleland v. Fish, 43 Ill. 282.

[4] Bellage v. Southee, 9 Hare, 534. " Why," said the court, " was the amount of the debt which was due from the poor man to be altered, because his position in life was about to be changed? And why was the alteration to be made without any account being rendered or any explanation being offered? It is said that he intended to be liberal, and that this

that the patient never did agree to, or intend to direct, what in the agreement he was represented as agreeing to and directing ; and if his signature must have been obtained by fraud, or under such circumstances as render it the duty of the court to protect the patient and his estate from prejudice. And the relief stands upon the general principle applicable to all the variety of relations in which dominion may be exercised by one person over another.[1]

The mere fact, however, that a vendor was afflicted with a chronic disease, and that the purchaser was his family physician, will not be sufficient to raise a presumption of fraud in the sale against the purchaser.[2]

§ 11. OF DRAFTSMAN OF WILL TAKING BENEFIT.

Besides the foregoing cases, there are others in which (from the peculiar circumstances under which an instrument, especially a will, is executed) a presumption of fraud arises, or at least a suspicion of unfairness or imposition sufficiently strong as matter of law to require the party claiming the bounty to prove the perfect fairness of the transaction and the freedom of action of the giver. Such a case occurs where a will is written or procured to be written by a person benefited by its provisions, or by one standing in the relation of attorney or counsel, who is benefited by its provisions. Such a circumstance is sufficient to excite close scrutiny, and to require strict proof of volition and capacity.[3] There is,

court would not prevent him from being so; and no doubt it would not, if such were his intention. But intention imports knowledge, and liberality imports the absence of influence; and I see no evidence in this case either of knowledge or of the absence of influence. And, where a gift is set up between parties standing in a confidential relation, the *onus* of establishing it by proof rests upon the party who has received the gift.''

[1] Dent *v.* Bennett, 4 Mylne & C. 269.

[2] Doggett *v.* Lane, 12 Mo. 215.

[3] Breed *v.* Pratt, 18 Pick. 115; Coffin *v.* Coffin, 23 N. Y. 9; Clark *v.* Fisher, 1 Paige, 171; Duffield *v.* Robeson, 2 Harr. (Del.) 384; Tompkins *v.* Tompkins, 1 Bailey, 92; Patton *v.* Allison, 7 Humph. 320; Crispell *v.*

however, no necessary incompatibility between the positions of acting as a draftsman of a will and of receiving a benefit under its provisions. The only effect of occupying both positions is to require the party to show the volition and capacity of the testator.[1] The presumption against the validity of the bequest will, however, be still stronger if the disposition be different from the previously expressed intention of the testator.[2]

It follows from the statement of this proposition (to wit, that the writing a will or the procuring it to be written by a beneficiary under it raises a suspicion against his right to the bounty) that the rule is independent of any allegation as to the capacity and volition of the testator by the party contesting the testament. In fact, however, most of the cases upon this subject are cases in which there was asserted to be more or less weakness of mind in the testator. But this cannot affect the correctness of the proposition. Parties do not generally contest the validity of a will without some allegation of the incapacity of the testator or of fraud practised upon him, and some attempt to support the allegation by proof. If, however, it were insisted, even without such allegation, that a beneficiary who had written the will should make clear proof of the capacity and volition of the testator, the court, it is apprehended, would require it.

On the other hand, it is not conclusive against the validity

Dubois, 4 Barb. 393; Beall *v.* Mann, 5 Ga. 456; Adair *v.* Adair, 30 Ga. 102; Newhouse *v.* Godwin, 17 Barb. 236; Durling *v.* Loveland, 2 Curteis, 225; Greville *v.* Tylee, 7 Moore, P. C. 320; Baker *v.* Batt, 2 Moore, P. C. 317; Dodge *v.* Meech, 1 Hagg. 612; Shelford, Lunacy, 317–334; 1 Jarman, Wills, 42 (4th Am. ed.). But see Wright *v.* Howe, 7 Jones, Eq. 412.

[1] Shelford, Lunacy, 319; Davis *v.* Rogers, 1 Houst. 44.

[2] Lee *v.* Dill, 11 Abb. Pr. 214. A will written for a testator *in extremis* by one who takes under it is not *ipso facto* invalid. Downey *v.* Murphey, 1 Dev. & B. 82. If the draftsman of a will be one of the nearest relations of the testator, the fact that he is made executor will not in ordinary cases raise a presumption of fraud; nor will the case be different, if a small legacy and a contingent remainder be given him and several other relations in the same degree. Coffin *v.* Coffin, 23 N. Y. 9.

of the bounty to the draftsman of the will that the testator
was at the time of executing the testament a person of weak
mind.[1] Thus, in the case first cited, it appeared that the
testator was a person of slender capacity, of retiring disposition, indolent habits, addicted to drinking, singular in his
appearance, frivolous, and even childish at times in his amuse-
ments and occupations. However, there was no evidence to
show that he was insane, or that he lacked the capacity to
make a will. Indeed, it was not disputed on the one side that
he was of testamentary capacity, or on the other that he was
of weak mind. The court accordingly declared that, even
admitting that the weakness went to the extent claimed by
the party contesting the will, the only consequence was to
add to the suspicion against the draftsman and beneficiary (a
solicitor), who was to take no less than a fourth of the estate,
the legatees taking the rest to the exclusion of the testator's
family, and to call upon the court to watch the proof of the
will itself with increased jealousy and suspicion.[2] Hence, it
is laid down that the increased strictness of scrutiny and
proof required in cases where the person by whom, or by
whose procurement or direction, a will is drawn, receives a
benefit from it, and in cases of doubtful capacity (and *increased*
scrutiny states the whole difference between such and other
cases, since the party propounding a will must in all cases
establish it, and some scrutiny is always necessary), is only
such as to give full and entire satisfaction to the court or jury
that the testator was not imposed upon, and that he knew
what he was doing, and the dispositions he was making, when
he executed the will.[3]

[1] Barry *v.* Butlin, 1 Curteis, 637; Harvey *v.* Anderson, 12 Ga. 69;
Boyd *v.* Boyd, 3 Hill (S. Car.), 341.

[2] See also Chambers *v.* Wood, 1 Jarman, Wills, 45 (4th Am. ed.);
Wrench *v.* Murray, 3 Curteis, 623; Crispell *v.* Dubois, 4 Barb. 393; Hill
v. Barge, 12 Ala. 687.

[3] Duffield *v.* Robeson, 2 Harr. (Del.) 384, 385; Davis *v.* Rogers, 1
Houst. 44; Barry *v.* Butlin, 1 Curteis, 637; Durnell *v.* Corfield, 1 Robt.
Ecc. 51, 63.

The doctrine, as declared by a distinguished judge,[1] is that proof of the knowledge of the contents of the will may be given in any form; that the degree of proof required depends upon the circumstances of each case; that, in the case of perfect capacity, knowledge of contents may be presumed, but when the capacity is weakened, and the benefit to the drawer of the will is large, the presumption is weaker and the suspicion stronger. The proof in such case must be more stringent, and the court must be satisfied of the knowledge of the contents beyond the proof of execution by the testator. And then the nature of the instrument is to be considered, — its simplicity or complexity. In cases of suspicion, therefore, the proof is to be in proportion to the degree of suspicion; and the greater the loss of capacity, the more stringent will be the court to require adequate proof of knowledge of the contents of the testament.

It is not necessary in ordinary cases, then, in order to establish the will, that the person claiming under it should prove that it was read over to the testator in the presence of the attesting or other witnesses.[2] The law presumes in general that the will was read over by or to the testator. But if evidence be given that the testator was blind, or from any cause unable to read, or if a reasonable ground is laid for believing that it was not read to him, or that fraud or imposition of any kind was practised upon the testator, it is incumbent upon those who would support the will to meet such proof by evidence, and to satisfy the jury either that the will was read or that the contents were known to the testator.[3]

---

[1] Dr. Lushington in Durnell v. Corfield, 1 Robt. Ecc. 51, 63.

[2] Harrison v. Rowan, 3 Wash. C. C. 580, 584.

[3] Day v. Day, 2 Green, Ch. 549. See Gerrish v. Nason, 22 Maine, 438; Harding v. Harding, 18 Penn. St. 340; Clifton v. Murray, 7 Ga. 564; Vernon v. Kirk, 30 Penn. St. 218.

§ 12. Of Engagement to Marry.

Undue influence may be exercised under the intimate relation created by an engagement to marry. Thus, if a woman
give a man land upon a promise of marriage, and he then
refuse to marry her and continue to hold the land, this is a
fraud for which the law will give the woman proper relief.[1]
So, on the other hand, if a man should, after much solicitation
and hesitancy, convey land without adequate pecuniary consideration to a woman who had promised to marry him, and
who had thereby gained great influence over him, her refusal
to marry him would afford him ground for rescinding the
conveyance.[2]

§ 13. Of Illegal Marriages or Relations.

In England, the marriage of a widower with the sister of
his deceased wife is not lawful; and a conveyance obtained
without full consideration by a widower so marrying, without
advice to the sister-in-law as to the character of the act and
of her legal *status*, is voidable at the suit of the latter. And
the burden of proof is upon the widower to show that, at the
time of entering into the transaction, she was fully, fairly,
and truly thus informed.[3] This principle is probably applicable to such transactions in all cases of illegal marriage.

The existence of an unlawful relation between the testator
and the object of his bounty at the time of the execution of
the will is considered sufficient to raise a presumption of undue influence against the beneficiary, at least where there are
natural objects of his bounty who are thus pushed aside.[4]

---

[1] 3 Black. Com. 174.   [2] Rockafellow *v.* Newcomb, 57 Ill. 186.

[3] Coulson *v.* Allison, 2 DeG., J. & F. 521.

Dean *v.* Negley, 41 Penn. St. 312.

§ 14. OF SPIRITUAL ADVISERS.

The relation of spiritual adviser, where the person holding it procures a will to be drawn and superintends its execution, by which a church in which he is interested is benefited, raises sufficient for a presumption of undue influence.[1] It is also to be observed that one who prevails over another through spiritualistic means to obtain a gift of property may be compelled to restore or make good the property so obtained.[2] In the case cited, a widow of advanced years was induced by the defendant, acting as a spiritual medium, to adopt him as her son, to transfer to him a large amount of property, to make her will in his favor, and to settle upon him a large reversionary interest. Having afterwards instituted a suit to set aside these gifts, it was held that the relation existing between the parties implied the exercise of dominion by the defendant over her mind; and the latter having failed to show that the gifts were the pure, voluntary, and well-understood acts of the plaintiff, she was entitled to judgment. The burden of proof rests upon the defendant in such cases, just as in those of attorney and client, guardian and ward, and the like.[3]

§ 15. OF VOLUNTEERS.

A person cannot take advantage of circumstances arising from a project communicated to him by another, to secure a benefit from the action of the person making the communication, to the exclusion of such person; especially if he advised the latter to take the course pursued.[4] Thus, in the case cited, a creditor having knowledge that part of the real estate

[1] *In re* Welsh, 1 Redf. 238.
[2] Lyon *v.* Home, Law R. 6 Eq. 655.
[3] Ib.
[4] Buswell *v.* Davis, 10 N. H. 413.

of his debtor was mortgaged, apparently to its full value, was informed by another creditor that he proposed to effect an arrangement by which that mortgage should be removed, and one taken to himself. The former advised the latter to effect the arrangement; and after the arrangement had been made and the first mortgage discharged, but before the new one was executed, levied an attachment upon the land to secure himself. It was held on a bill filed by the injured creditor that the attachment was fraudulent. A levy under such circumstances, it was well observed, was not a fair exercise of superior diligence.[1]

If a party voluntarily undertake to aid another in obtaining possession of his property in the hands of third persons, he thereby assumes a relation of confidence towards the party whom he proposes to assist; and if he take advantage of this relation, and by deception or improper influence induce him to part with his property without an adequate consideration, equity will afford redress.[2] And it would seem on principle that the presumption of law would be against the volunteer and in favor of the other party, so as to cast the burden upon the former of establishing the fairness of the transaction; but the case cited does not support this position. This point, however, was not considered by the court.

§ 16. OF COTENANTS. TENANTS FOR LIFE.

Tenants in common of property, not jointly engaged in making purchases and sales, do not stand in a relation of trust and confidence towards each other with reference to the common property; and they may deal with each other for the purchase of the entire ownership thereof, as if they

[1] Beckett v. Cordley, 1 Brown, C. C. 357; Temple v. Hooker, 6 Vt. 240; Jackson v. Burgott, 10 Johns. 461; Chickering v. Lovejoy, 13 Mass. 51.

[2] Harkness v. Fraser, 12 Fla. 336.

were owners of separate property.[1] Thus, a tenant in common of a vessel, in contracting with his cotenant for the purchase of his share at a certain price, is under no legal obligation to disclose that a third person had previously agreed with him to purchase the whole of the vessel at a higher rate.[2] So, too, the purchase of an estate in remainder or reversion by a tenant for life, though open to objection, is not to be impeached on general principles.[3]

§ 17. OF JOINT PURCHASERS.

Joint purchasers of property stand in such a relation to each other that one of them will not be permitted to acquire a secret advantage over the others in the purchase.[4] And the same is true of joint owners of property.[5] Hence, if a person procure another to enter into a contract for the purchase of property at a price which the former says he can obtain it for, when in fact he has the refusal of it at a considerably less price, it is a fraud upon the latter, and such wrongdoer cannot compel him to carry out the agreement.[6]

§ 18. OF EXPECTANT HEIRS.

Generally speaking, a contract cannot be avoided on the ground that advantage has been taken of distress, when the advantage, if any, depended upon subsequent contingencies, the result of which must have been equally uncertain to each party at the time of the contract.[7] The case of an expectant heir, dealing for his expectancy during his father's life, is an

---

[1] Matthews v. Bliss, 22 Pick. 48.   [2] Ib.
[3] Lloyd v. Johnes, 9 Ves. 37.
[4] Willink v. Vanderveer, 1 Barb. 599.   [5] Ib.
[6] Barry v. Bennett, 45 Cal. 80.   See King v. Wise, 43 Cal. 629.
[7] Ramsbottom v. Parker, 6 Madd. 6; Paine v. Meller, 6 Ves. 352; Pritchard v. Ovey, 1 Jac. & W. 403; Revell v. Hussey, 2 Ball & B. 287; Gowland v. DeFaria, 17 Ves. 25; 1 Hovenden, Fraud, 497.

exception. To that class of persons equity has extended a
degree of protection approaching nearly to fixing an incapacity to bind themselves by any contract.[1] And though the
sale of a reversion by an expectant heir may be supported,
still, if it appear that the vendor is a young man, desirous of
raising money on *post obit* obligations, payable at his father's
death, and the sale is to take place at auction without proper
safeguards for the protection of the young man's interests, he
will be considered as in the power of those who deal with
him. A sale by auction, under such circumstances, would
not afford fair evidence of the market price of the property.[2]
And where the dealing is substantially for the expectation of
an heir, a colorable disguise of the character of the bargain,
such as including a small present possession, will not avail
the purchaser.[3] Relief in these cases will be given on grounds
of inadequacy.

In an English case, it appeared that a reversionary interest,
worth at least £1,900, was bought for £1,700. The rever-
sioner was a man under twenty-three years of age, somewhat
straightened in circumstances, and very desirous of obtaining
money; but there was no evidence of fraud. The sale was,
however, set aside.

It has been said by an eminent English judge that it is
incumbent upon those who have dealt with an expectant heir
relative to his reversionary interest to make good the bargain
by showing that a full and adequate consideration was paid.[4]
And, though some doubt was once suggested as to the correctness of this principle,[5] it appears to express the established

[1] Chesterfield v. Janssen, 2 Ves. 125, 157. See Peacock v. Evans,
16 Ves. 514; Marsack v. Reeves, 6 Madd. 109; Gwynne v. Heaton,
1 Brown, C. C. 9.
[2] Fox v. Wright, 6 Madd. 112.
[3] Davis v. Marlborough, 2 Swanst. 154.
[4] Sir William Grant, in Gowland v. De Faria, 17 Ves. 24.
[5] Sir Knight Bruce in the course of the argument in Edwards v.
Browne, 2 Coll. C. C. 100, 104; Sir John Leach in Hinksman v. Smith,
3 Russ. 433, 435.

rule of equity.[1] But by this rule is meant, not the valuation
which may be set upon the interest by actuaries on the tables
of mortality, but the fair market price at the time of dealing.[2]
The rule itself has recently been changed by statute in England; and it is now provided in that country that no purchase
made *bona fide*, and without fraud or unfair dealing, of any
reversionary interest in real or personal property, shall be
opened or set aside merely on the ground of undervalue.[3]
The common-law rule still prevails, generally, in America.[4]

The application of this rule is not prevented either by the
fact that the transaction was a charge and not a sale, or that
the expectant heir was a person of mature age, or that he
perfectly understood the nature and extent of the transaction.
Nor is it necessary for the heir to show that he was in pecuniary distress at the time. That fact is assumed from the
circumstance of his having dealt with another upon such a
footing; and the assumption that the person advancing the
money has possibly taken advantage of that distress is the
reason why the courts throw upon him the burden of proving
that the bargain was reasonable.[5] When, however, the transaction is set aside for mere inadequacy, the proof failing
to disclose actual fraud, the conveyance will be decreed to
stand as a security for the money paid, and interest. The
suit in such case is considered as in the nature of a bill of
redemption; and the vendor is charged with the costs of the
suit.[6]

---

[1] Aldoborough v. Trye, 7 Clark & F. 436, and notes, Am. ed.

[2] Ib. To this extent Gowland v. De Faria was overruled.

[3] 31 Vict. ch. 4.

[4] 1 Story, Equity, §§ 336 *et seq.*; 1 Lead. Cas. in Equity, 580 (3d
Am. ed.). It is, however, held in Virginia that where there is no actual
fraud, and no fiduciary relation between the purchaser of a reversionary
interest and his vendor, mere inadequacy of consideration is not sufficient
to avoid a sale; unless, indeed, it be so great as to shock the moral
sense. Mayo v. Carrington, 19 Gratt. 74; Cribbins v. Markwood,
13 Gratt. 495.

[5] Bromley v. Smith, 26 Beav. 644.

[6] Bawtree v. Watson, 3 Mylne & K. 339. See 1 Story, Equity, § 344.

It is held in England that the doctrines of equity, as to the relief of expectant heirs from unconscionable bargains, have not been affected by the repeal of the usury laws, or by the alteration of the law as to sales of reversionary interests. The changes of the law in these particulars have not altered the *onus probandi* in those cases, which, according to Lord Hardwicke, raise a presumption of fraud " from the circumstances or conditions of the parties contracting, — weakness on one side, usury on the other, or extortion, or advantage taken of that weakness." [1]

Fraud in such cases does not mean deceit or circumvention : it means an unconscientious use of the power arising out of such circumstances and conditions. And, when the relative position of the parties is such as *prima facie* to raise this presumption, the transaction cannot stand, unless the person claiming the benefit of it is able to repel the presumption by contrary evidence, proving it to have been in point of fact fair, just, and reasonable.[2]

Where an expectant heir, under pecuniary pressure, mortgages his reversionary estate to obtain an advance of money or credit for a purchase of goods, and the party in present possession of the property so mortgaged stands *in loco parentis* to such heir, and approves of the transaction, the heir cannot afterwards obtain a rescission of the mortgage.[3]

The sale of a legacy which has become absolute and fixed, the amount and time of payment of which have become certain, is not the sale of an expectancy or reversionary interest within the rule which protects young heirs or reversioners from the consequences of " catching bargains." And this is equally true, though the vendor of the legacy be shown to be a reckless, dissipated, and weak-minded man, provided no actual fraud or undue influence be practised upon him.[4]

---

[1] Aylesford v. Morris, Law R. 8 Ch. 484, citing Chesterfield v. Janssen, 2 Ves. Sr. 125.   [2] Aylesford v. Morris, *supra*, Lord Selborne.

[3] King v. Hamlet, 2 Mylne & K. 456 ; affirmed, 3 Clark & F. 218.

[4] Parmelee v. Cameron, 41 N. Y. 392.

§ 19. OF SAILORS.

The courts treat with great indulgence the rights and interests of common sailors in the mercantile and naval service, considering them as standing upon the same footing with young heirs and expectants.[1] The contracts of seamen are watched with great jealousy, and will generally be set aside whenever any inequality appears in the bargain or any undue advantage has been taken.[2]

§ 20. OF AGED PERSONS.

In an English case, a deed of gift was set aside where one of the donees had married the niece of the donor, it appearing that the donor had entire trust and confidence in the donees, that she was eighty-four years old, and nearly blind, and that she was dependent upon their kindness and assistance. It was considered that they stood in a relation to her which so much exposed her to their influence that they could not maintain the transaction without showing that the act was the result of her own free will, and had been effected by the intervention of some indifferent person.[3] Old age alone, however, in the donor of a gift, is not a ground for presuming imposition or undue influence. It is merely a circumstance which may be taken into consideration in deciding upon the fairness of a transaction, where there is other evidence tending to show imposition.[4]

[1] How *v.* Weldon, 2 Ves. 516, 518; Taylor *v.* Rochford, 2 Ib. 281. See Chesterfield *v.* Janssen, Ib. 137.

[2] 1 Story, Equity, § 332.

[3] Griffiths *v.* Robins, 3 Madd. 191.

[4] Millican *v.* Millican, 24 Tex. 426, 449; Lewis *v.* Pead, 1 Ves. Jr. 19, note. See also Ellis *v.* Mathews, 19 Tex. 390; *post*, pp. 279–287.

§ 21. Of Illiterate, Weak-minded, and Drunken Persons.[1]

Though evidence of mere undervalue, except where the undervalue is very gross, will not afford ground for interference with a completed purchase, still, where the seller is an illiterate person, unable to judge of the precautions to be taken in selling, or of the mode of sale, or of the mode of securing the price when not paid down, and acts without professional advice, these circumstances, added to inadequacy of price, will afford such person ground in equity for relief.[2] Thus, in a recent case,[3] certain real estate

---

[1] As to *actual* fraud on such persons, see *ante*, pp. 74, 75, 155, 156.

[2] Clark *v.* Malpas, 4 DeG., F. & J. 401. "The seller," said Lord Justice Bruce, "was a man in humble life, imperfectly educated, and unable of himself to judge of the precautions to be taken in selling, or of the mode of sale, or of the mode of securing the price which was not at once paid down. He was helpless in the matter, without advice, without protection. Now, in the transactions only one solicitor was employed, and, though the evidence may be conflicting, I am perfectly satisfied, without meaning any reflections on Mr. Cooper, that if Mr. Cooper was not the solicitor of the purchaser alone in the matter, he was more the solicitor of the purchaser than of the seller. The bargain was not an ordinary one; it was to sell these cottages, forming the whole of the seller's property, in consideration of a weekly annuity for his life, and a dwelling to be provided for him, and a sum of £100 to be paid after his death, with power to him to require £10 of it to be paid in his lifetime. The seller was made to convey absolutely at once, without taking any security for the annuity, for the dwelling-house, or for the £100. A title was not shown, perhaps a marketable title could not be shown, nor any title without expense, but that did not justify making the seller enter into absolute covenants for title which on eviction would render him liable to repay the whole purchase money. For the annuity he had only the personal liability of the purchaser, probably a substantial person, but who might die at any moment or fall into adverse circumstances. He might sell the property, and then fail or die, and from what source was then the annuity to come? The same observations apply to the £10 and £100. So that not only was there completion at an undervalue, which alone might be nothing, but there was completion under circumstances of gross imprudence, on terms on which the seller ought not to have

---

[3] Baker *v.* Monk, 4 DeG., J. & S. 388.

had been sold by an elderly, uneducated woman in humble life to a person far above her in station. The agreement was made without the intervention of any one acting on her behalf; and, it appearing that the consideration paid was inadequate, the sale was set aside, though there was no evidence of fraud on the part of the purchaser. It was said that the purchaser and vendor were in such relative positions as that, according to established principles of equity, it lay on the purchaser to show affirmatively that the price given represented the true value of the estate.[1]

But slight circumstances will be sufficient, such perhaps as the refusal of the complainant to employ counsel may suffice, to overturn the presumption of fraud.[2] So, too, it is held that proof that the grantor in a deed was a very ignorant and illiterate man, and could not read writing, and that the deed was not read to him, is not, it is said, sufficient to avoid the deed, unless he requested that it be read to him.[3]

However, it is held that a person dealing with an illiterate person, unable to read or write, and taking from him a prom-

---

been allowed to complete. It does not appear that Cooper called attention to any of these considerations. No counterpart or copy of the conveyance was kept for the seller: he was left helpless. If he had been bred to the law, if he had had the advantages of education, the case might have stood differently.''

[1] "Here is a transaction," said Turner, L. J., "between an old woman (and I will say no more than that), said to be a very shrewd old woman, but still an old woman dealing with a person far superior to her in position, there being no advice given to her and no assistance rendered to her in the course of the treaty for the purchase and agreement for the sale of the fee-simple of the property for an annuity of 9s. a week, to last during the life of this old lady, who could know no more about what the pecuniary value of that annuity was than any person whom you might meet walking along the streets at the time. I think there was that distinction between the parties which rendered it incumbent on the appellant to throw further protection around this lady before he made the bargain with her.''

[2] See Harrison v. Guest, 6 DeG., M. & G. 424.

[3] Hallenbeck v. Dewitt, 2 Johns. 404. See Jackson v. Croy, 12 Johns. 427.

issory note for the payment of money, and also a deed for property in trust to secure the payment, is bound to show, when he seeks to enforce his securities, that they or the material parts of them were read and fully explained to the party before they were executed, and that he fully understood their meaning and effect.[1]   But, if this be shown, evidence is not admissible to prove that the contract agreed upon was different from that which was reduced to writing.   To make such evidence admissible, it must be proved that the party was deceived and misled as to the contents of the written instrument.[2]

If a weak-minded person is, notwithstanding his weakness, *compos mentis*, he can make a valid sale of his property, so far as his own capacity is concerned.[3]   That is implied in being *compos*.   And, if he can make a valid sale of his property, he can make a valid gift of it; for there is no authority of law for requiring greater strength of mind for the latter act than for the former.   Mental capacity admitted for the exercise of one class of acts, *ex contractu* in character, and the capacity for all classes of such acts follows.   But evidence that the injured party is a person of weak understanding puts him in a position more favorable than the position of one of perfectly sound understanding, in that such a person is more easily circumvented.   If, then, it appear that the weak-minded person has parted with property at an inadequate price, it is natural to suppose that he has been cheated; and the law accordingly raises a presumption of fraud against the party who has obtained the advantage.[4]   But this presumption cannot be a conclusive one, since the injured party has the capacity to make a sale or a gift; and there may be a good and substantial reason for the sale at the inadequate price, a reason perfectly consistent with the highest honor and good

[1] Selden *v.* Myers, 20 How. 506.   [2] Ib.

[3] Smith *v.* Beatty, 2 Ired. Eq. 456; Sprague *v.* Duel, Clarke, 90.

[4] Wiest *v.* Garman, 4 Houst. 119, 140.

faith on the part of the purchaser. It is the purchaser's duty, however, to show that such a reason existed, and to completely remove the suspicion resting upon him. So of a gift, except that, instead of receiving an inadequate consideration, the grantor receives none at all. But the presumption can hardly be stronger in his favor than in the case of a sale ; at all events, it cannot be conclusive. The fact may be that the recipient was a most worthy object of the grantor's bounty, and that he may not only not have used any improper means to obtain it, but he may not have used any means at all, and may not even have known that the grantor had any intention of making it until after the act was done. In such cases, the gift should be allowed to stand. There would be no more propriety in setting aside such transactions as the above (either the sale or the gift) than there would be if the party were perfectly sound of mind. Having the capacity, and his weakness not having been imposed upon, he indeed stands in precisely the situation of other men.[1]

It is, however, distinctly laid down that one who deals in property matters with an aged and feeble person is bound to prove the fairness of the transactions.[2] Hence it is declared that though a contract made by a man of sound mind and fair understanding may not be set aside merely because it is a rash, improvident, or hard bargain, still, if the same contract be made with a person of weak understanding, there arises an inference that it was obtained by fraud or undue influence.[3] *A fortiori* is this true if the defendant occupied an actual confidential relation to the complainant.[4]

---

[1] See Russell *v.* Russell, 4 Dana, 40, 43, which implies that such transactions may be binding; Harris *v.* Wamsley, 41 Iowa, 671; Galpin *v.* Wilson, 40 Iowa, 90, which implies that a weak-minded person, if not imposed upon, may bind himself as surety for another; Darnell *v.* Rowland, 35 Ind. 342; Wallace *v.* McVey, 6 Ind. 300; Rogers *v.* Higgins, 56 Ill. 244 ; Lindsey *v.* Lindsey, 50 Ill. 79 ; Miller *v.* Craig, 36 Ill. 109.

[2] Wartemberg *v.* Spiegel, 31 Mich. 400.

[3] Ellis *v.* Mathews, 19 Tex. 390.   [4] Seeby *v.* Price, 14 Mich. 541.

Equity will set aside a contract for the sale of real estate and a conveyance thereunder, where it appears that the capacity for business on the part of the grantor has been greatly weakened by trouble and distress of mind, and the price was grossly inadequate. In such a case, the grantee will be liable for timber taken by him from the premises, and for the rental value thereof during possession. But the rental value may be diminished by circumstances arising after the sale and not under the control of the purchaser, such as the prevalence of a freshet which destroyed the fences of the land.[1]

A confession of judgment and release of equity will be supported, though made by a man of weak understanding, in the habit of making improvident bargains, and addicted to intoxication, and embarrassed in circumstances, and though such confession was induced by the plaintiff's giving him time to pay the money; provided no other influence was exerted, and no fraud committed in obtaining the confession, and the confession was deliberately made, whether by the defendant personally or by virtue of a power of attorney deliberately and voluntarily executed by him.[2]

It may therefore be laid down in general that the acts and contracts of weak-minded persons will be held invalid in equity, if the nature of the act or contract justify the conclusion either that the party through undue influence has not exercised a deliberate judgment, or that he has been imposed upon, circumvented, or overreached by cunning or artifice. Where inadequacy of consideration or undue influence is joined to imbecility or weakness of mind arising from old age, sickness, intemperance, or other cause, equity will set aside the transaction at the suit of the injured party.[3]

What is that degree of mental imbecility which may be

[1] Perkins *v.* Scott, 23 Iowa, 237.
[2] Mason *v.* Williams, 3 Munf. 126.
[3] Tracey *v.* Sackett, 1 Ohio St. 54.

taken into account as one of the elements necessary for relief
is often a difficult matter to decide.   No definite rule of law
can be laid down.   A set of examples has been given by the
Court of Chancery of Maryland,[1] of which the following may
be mentioned : It has been laid down in general terms that it
is fraudulent to obtain a deed by the exercise of undue influence over a man whose mind had ceased to be a safe guide
of his actions,[2] or from a man who was of small understanding, and not able to manage the lands which had descended to
him.[3]   A woman who could read and write, and had taught
a child to read, was still held to be a person of weak understanding.[4]   So, too, it was in another case considered no proof
of sanity that a person could repeat scraps of Latin and read
classic authors, because what a person learns in youth leaves
a very lasting impression ; and such a person may still be
weak-minded.[5]   In another case, a person is spoken of as
being seventy-two years of age, and a weak man, easily imposed upon.[6]   Again, a grantor is said to be eighty-four years
of age, blind, or nearly so, and altogether dependent upon the
kindness and assistance of others.[7]   From these examples, it
is suggested that by weakness of mind is meant a sort of
mental imbecility approaching to the condition of one who is
actually *non compos mentis,* and analogous to childishness and
dotage.[8]

[1] Owing's Case, 1 Bland, 370, 391.
[2] Harding *v.* Handy, 11 Wheat. 125; Chesterfield *v.* Janssen, 2 Ves.
156.
[3] Twyne's Case, 3 Coke, 83.   [4] White *v.* Small, 2 Ch. Cas. 103.
[5] Bennet *v.* Vade, 2 Atk. 325.
[6] Clarkson *v.* Hanway, 2 P. Wms. 204.
[7] Griffith *v.* Robins, 3 Madd. 191.
[8] Owing's Case, 1 Bland, 370, 392; Henderson *v.* McGregor, 30 Wis.
78 ; Johnson *v.* Chadwell, 8 Humph. 145.
Where a person, though not positively *non compos* or insane, is yet of
such great weakness of mind as to be unable to guard himself against
imposition, or to resist importunity or undue influence, he will be protected in a court of equity when an unfair advantage has been taken of
his weakness.   And it is immaterial from what cause such weakness arose,

The circumstances which, taken in connection with this weakness of mind, constitute grounds of fraud whereby to annul pecuniary transactions are various. Among them the following may be mentioned : Where an ignorant old man was induced to execute a deed, surrendering to his children a large fund to which he was entitled, by being informed by them of the opinion of a lawyer whom they had employed, and in whom he had great confidence, that he had no right to the property, and also by the false representations of one of the children as to what they had agreed to give him, and as to the purpose for which the deed was to be used, it was held that equity would grant relief.[1] So, too, an agreement with a weak old man, whereby he makes an assignment of his whole estate upon the consideration of the assignee's personal covenant to maintain him for life out of the profits of the estate, imports undue advantage ; and this without reference to any confidential relation between the parties, or to any state of anxiety or alarm on the part of the assignor.[2] The fact that a deed has never been left for the grantor's perusal ; or that it has not been read by him ; or that it was prepared by the grantee and obtruded upon the grantor ; or that the gift was excessively large ; or that the other party had not the means to pay ; or that the grantee had acquired a commanding influence over the grantor, and had exercised it in the transaction ; or that the consideration was greatly inadequate ;[3] or that a relation of trust and confidence existed between the

whether from illness, hereditary misfortune, the infirmity of old age, or from depressions resulting from sudden fear or overwhelming calamity. Tally v. Smith, 1 Cold. 290, 298 ; 1 Story, Equity, § 234. And a degree of weakness of intellect far below that which would justify a commission of lunacy, coupled with other circumstances showing that advantage had been taken of the weakness, will be sufficient to set aside the conveyances of such a person. Walker v. McCoy, 3 Head, 103.

[1] Powell v. Cobb, 3 Jones, Eq. 456.

[2] Buffalow v. Buffalow, 2 Dev. & B. Eq. 241.

[3] Cadwallader v. West, 48 Mo. 483 ; Freeland v. Eldridge, 19 Mo. 325.

parties;[1] or that the grantor had conveyed all of his property, leaving himself to be fed and clothed at the pleasure of the grantee, — in all of these and similar cases, the weakness of mind of the party, though it does not render him *non compos*, will be sufficient, in connection with the other facts, to establish a presumption of fraud, and entitle the party wronged to relief.[2]

Contracts made by persons under the influence of liquor, even when not completely intoxicated, are governed by the same principles which apply to other cases, where one party is in a position to expose him to the exercise of an improper influence by the other. If carried so far that the reasoning powers are destroyed, the contract is void; but, when it falls short of this, the contract will not be avoided, unless undue advantage (which, however, the law seems to presume) has been taken of the condition of the drunken party. Thus, if a party while excited by liquor has been led into a hard and disadvantageous bargain, the contract will be set aside in equity. And the same is true of transactions with persons whose minds are enfeebled by habitual intoxication, though not intoxicated when the contract was made.[3]

Gifts also of property, made by a person in a state of mental imbecility owing to habitual intoxication, will often be treated as void upon the presumption of imposition. Thus, a person in such a condition made a voluntary and irrevocable deed of

---

[1] Cadwallader *v.* West, 48 Mo. 483 ; Freeland *v.* Eldridge, 19 Mo. 325; Morisso *v.* Philliber, 30 Mo. 145.

[2] See Hervey *v.* Hervey, 1 Atk. 564; Mountain *v.* Bennet, 1 Cox, 353; Nantes *v.* Corrock, 9 Ves. 183; White *v.* Small, 2 Ch. Cas. 103; Portengton *v.* Eglington, 2 Vern. 189 ; Donegal's Case, 2 Ves. 408; Bridgman *v.* Green, Ib. 627; Norton *v.* Rilly, 2 Eden, 286; Wright *v.* Proud, 13 Ves. 136 ; Huguenin *v.* Basely, 14 Ves. 273; Harvey *v.* Pecks, 1 Munf. 518; Rutherford *v.* Ruff, 4 Dessaus. 350; Rowland *v.* Sullivan, Ib. 518; Brogden *v.* Walker, 2 Har. & J. 285; Gibson *v.* Jeyes, 6 Ves. 275.

[3] Birdsong *v.* Birdsong, 2 Head, 289.

gift of his whole estate to a cousin german, to the disherison of his half-sister, reserving however the use to the donor during his life. No reasonable motive was assigned for the act; and it was held that fraud and imposition might be inferred from the very nature of the transaction.[1]

---

[1] Samuel *v.* Marshall, 3 Leigh, 567; Adams *v.* Ryerson, 2 Halst. Ch. 328; Hale *v.* Brown, 11 Ala. 87. As to *actual* fraud upon drunken persons, see *ante*, pp. 155, 156.

CHAPTER VI.

NOTICE.

§ 1. OF PUTTING ONE ON INQUIRY.

A PURCHASER of property with knowledge or notice that the title of the vendor is to be disputed for fraud is entitled to no consideration at law or in equity, if the fraud be established. He stands in the precise situation of his vendor.[1] Of actual knowledge or notice we need not stop to speak; it needs no explanation. But there is another kind of notice that deserves attention, to wit, constructive notice, or notice by construction of law, the consequences of which are equally fatal with those attending actual knowledge.

The general proposition of law concerning constructive notice is, that, if facts are brought to the knowledge of a party which would put him, as a man of common sagacity, upon inquiry, he is bound to inquire; and, if he neglect to do so, he will be chargeable with notice of what he might have learned upon examination.[2] Where, for example, a party has had actual notice that property in dispute was in fact charged, incumbered, or in some way affected with the claims

---

[1] Peter v. Wright, 6 Ind. 183; Adams v. Stevens, 49 Maine, 362, and cases cited *infra, passim.*

[2] Warren v. Swett, 31 N. H. 332; Cambridge Bank v. Delano, 48 N. Y. 326; Acer v. Wescott, 46 N. Y. 384; Willis v. Vallette, 4 Met. (Ky.) 186; Woodworth v. Paige, 5 Ohio St. 70; James v. Drake, 3 Sneed, 540; Colquitt v. Thomas, 8 Ga. 258; Martel v. Somers, 26 Tex. 551; Jones v. Smith, 1 Hare, 43; Kennedy v. Green, 3 Mylne & K. 718.

of others, he is considered as under constructive notice of all facts and instruments to a knowledge of which he would have been led by an inquiry after the charge, incumbrance, or other fact affecting the property.[1] Hence, a person is chargeable with notice of an unrecorded lien, though he have no knowledge of its existence, if he have notice of the contents of the instrument giving the lien.[2] The omission of indorsements of interest paid on a note or bill is not alone, however, sufficient to fix a purchaser with notice of equities existing between prior parties.[3]

In accordance with the above rule, that that which is sufficient to put a party upon inquiry is notice of whatever the inquiry, reasonably prosecuted, would disclose,[4] it has been held that if the purchaser of corn from a tenant know of the existence of the tenancy, and that his vendor, as tenant, has raised the corn on the demised premises, this will be notice to him of any *statutory* lien the landlord may have upon the premises for unpaid rent.[5]

If, however, there be no fraudulent turning away from knowledge of the facts which the *res gestæ* would suggest to a prudent mind ; if mere want of caution, as distinguished from fraudulent and wilful blindness, is all that can be imputed to a purchaser of property, the doctrine of constructive notice will not apply to him.[6] Hence, a party cannot be charged with notice of an advertisement in a newspaper, in the absence of statutory provision, merely because he is a subscriber to the paper.[7]

[1] Willis *v.* Vallette, 4 Met. (Ky.) 186.

[2] Ib.; Tiernan *v.* Thurman, 14 B. Mon. 279.

[3] National Bank *v.* Kirby, 108 Mass. 497. But see Hart *v.* Stickney, 41 Wis. 630; Newell *v.* Gregg, 51 Barb. 263.

[4] Russell *v.* Ranson, 76 Ill. 167; Watt *v.* Scofield, Ib. 261; Kennedy *v.* Green, 3 Mylne & K. 699; Dickey *v.* Lyon, 19 Iowa, 544.

[5] Watt *v.* Scofield, *supra.*

[6] Jones *v.* Smith, 1 Hare, 43 ; Woodworth *v.* Paige, 5 Ohio St. 70.

[7] Watkins *v.* Peck, 13 N. H. 360; Clark *v.* Ricker, 14 N. H. 44; Lincoln *v.* Wright, 23 Penn. St. 76. But see King *v.* Paterson R. Co., 5 Dutch. 82.

Notice must be definite and certain. Mere rumor is not notice. To hear, for example, floating reports about an incumbrance upon land about to be bought does not affect the party with notice.[1] But it is said to be otherwise of general reputation and belief.[2] With regard to the question, what constitutes notice of fraud in a conveyance, while it is settled that vague and general assertions, resting on mere hearsay and made by strangers, may be disregarded, still a direct statement to a purchaser of the existence and nature of an adverse claim or title will operate as notice, whether it was made by or on behalf of the holder of the adverse title, or by a mere stranger.[3]

The general doctrine is that notice cannot be binding, unless it proceed from a person interested in the property, and in the course of a treaty for its purchase; but this rule applies only to notice in its limited sense, as distinguished from knowledge or such information as is substantially equivalent to knowledge. If it be shown that the purchaser knew or was informed of the existence of fraud, it is immaterial whether his knowledge was obtained from parties in interest or from third persons. From whatever quarter it may proceed, it will be sufficient if it be so definite as to enable the purchaser to ascertain whether it is authentic or not, and sufficiently clear and definite to put the purchaser on inquiry, and enable him to conduct that inquiry to an ascertainment of the fact.[4] The statements of third persons may be sufficient for this purpose; and it has been suggested that the existence of a fact may acquire such a notoriety as to have the same effect.[5] But this is venturing upon doubtful ground.

One who, prior to the issuing of a patent from the State to his grantor, knew that the State authorities claimed that the lands covered by it were reserved from sale, and knew of ineffectual attempts to purchase them from the State, has

---

[1] Colquitt v. Thomas, 8 Ga. 258; James v. Drake, 3 Sneed, 540.
[2] James v. Drake, supra.   [3] Martel v. Somers, 26 Tex. 551.
[4] Martel v. Somers, supra.   [5] Ib.

sufficient to put him upon inquiry, and to subject him to any
equities growing out of any mistake or fraud under which
the patent may have been issued. He is not a *bona fide*
purchaser.[1] So, too, one who purchases land with notice
that another has a contract for the purchase of the same property is bound to inquire into the nature of such contract, and
takes subject to it, if valid, though he may not have notice
that it is in writing.[2]

If a person purchase an instrument with constructive
notice that it is void, he can neither recover thereon against
the maker, nor (in the absence of fraud on the part of the
vendor) can he recover from the latter the purchase price
paid.[3] For example, a person is chargeable with notice of all
the facts appearing upon the face of a county warrant purchased by him; and, if they are invalid in law, he must suffer
the loss of the purchase-money, unless the vendor was guilty
of fraud or warranted the instrument good.[4]

But while fraud does not render a contract void, so as
ipso facto to cut off the claims of subsequent purchasers for
value, it must be observed that little is sometimes required
to impose upon such purchasers the duty of inquiry; failing in the performance of which, their claims must yield to
those of the original party defrauded. Where a purchaser
in such cases is fixed with notice of a fact which would
have put him on an inquiry which he neglects to make, it
is his own negligence in not pursuing the inquiry that oc-
casions the loss. Thus, where the defendants, who claimed
as subsequent purchasers of a mortgage interest, were aware
at the time of their purchase that the plaintiff had been
a mortgagee of the same property, they were considered as
fixed with knowledge of the particulars of his security from

---

[1] Attorney-Gen. *v.* Smith, 31 Mich 359.

[2] Connihan *v.* Thompson, 111 Mass. 270.

[3] Christy *v.* Sullivan, 50 Cal. 337. See Lamert *r.* Heath, 15 Mees.
& W. 487 ; Lawes *v.* Purser, 6 El & B. 930.

[4] Christy *v.* Sullivan, *supra.*

which the title offered to them was derived, and with the
evidences of fraud which there appeared.[1] But though a
party have notice of facts putting him upon inquiry, still, if
with due diligence he make inquiry and become satisfied by
evidence upon which a reasonable man may rely that a particular fact does not exist, he is to be regarded as not affected
with notice.[2]

This doctrine of constructive notice, by which a party is
considered as so fixed with knowledge in law of an illegality
as not to be able to complain of it, is applicable only between
the party alleged to be affected with it and third persons, not
parties to the illegality.   If, indeed, a party have actual
notice of a fraud, and allow the party committing it to go on,
giving assent to his conduct, he cannot afterwards repudiate
his acts, and claim to have the matter made good. *Injuria
non fit volenti.*   But constructive notice has no such effect.
It would be very absurd to say that a client should not have
a remedy against his attorney for the attorney's fraud, on the
ground that the client knew what his attorney knew, and
therefore had constructively assented to his fraud.   And
scarcely less absurd would it be to consider the client barred
of relief, where others besides the attorney were involved in the
misconduct complained of, on the ground that the client was
affected with his attorney's knowledge of the facts.[3] The
doctrine of constructive notice rests upon the ground of
protecting innocent persons, not of shielding wrongdoers.

[1] Ogilvie *v.* Jeaffreson, 2 Giff. 353; Kennedy *v.* Green, 3 Mylne & K.
699, 718.

[2] Hoyt *v.* Shelden, 3 Bosw. 267.

[3] See Sankey *v.* Alexander, Law R. 9 Irish Eq 259, 298. "There are
some defences," said Lawson, C. S., "which a party is estopped from
relying on by the rules of law and common sense ; and in this case, where
all the defendants are charged with a common fraud, and where it was
essential to the success of their design that facts should be suppressed,
and where the facts were suppressed by the person who was their agent,
it is impossible for them to call in aid the doctrine that, under another
state of facts and between different parties, the agent would be deemed
to have communicated them." See *post*, p. 316.

And this is none the less true where the client finds it
necessary to his case to impute to himself part of the knowledge of the attorney, and repudiate the rest.[1]

Again, when, even in a case otherwise appropriate for the
application of this doctrine, it appears that it was understood
that the person through whose knowledge the constructive
notice was alleged to arise was to suppress the facts from his
principal or employer, the doctrine of constructive notice will
not be applied. Thus, where it appeared that the defendants had communicated the existence of a settlement to the
plaintiff's solicitor, and he told them that he should not
inform his client lest it might make him feel nervous, it was
considered that the client was not affected with constructive
notice of the existence of the settlement.[2] Such, too, is the
rule where there is a moral certainty that there will be no
disclosure to the principal.[3]

If a man take a conveyance of land from one, while another
is in the open and visible possession of the estate, he will
be affected with notice of every thing in relation to the title
which could be known upon the most diligent inquiry. And,
if in such case the person in possession have an equitable title
to the land, the taking of the conveyance will be deemed a
fraud; and nothing will pass to the grantee which can avail
him against such equitable title.[4] Hence, actual possession
by a *cestui que trust* is constructive notice to a purchaser that
there is some claim, title, or possession of the property,
adverse to the vendor.[5]

---

[1] Sankey v. Alexander, Law R. 9 Irish Eq. 259, 318.

[2] Sharpe v. Foy, Law R. 4 Ch. 35.

[3] Kennedy v. Green, 3 Mylne & K. 699, 718; Atlantic Bank v. Harris,
118 Mass. 147; Thompson v. Cartwright, 33 Beav. 178. See also Atter-
bury v. Wallis, Law R. 4 Ch. 35; Sankey v. Anderson, Law R. 9 Irish
Eq. 298, 319; *post*, p. 316.

[4] Hadduck v. Wilmarth, 5 N. H. 181; Hathaway v. Noble, 56 N. H.
508; Eli v. Gridley, 27 Iowa, 376; Van Orman v. Merrill, Ib. 476, and
cases cited in the following notes.

[5] Johns v. Norris, 12 C. E. Green, 485; Daniels v. Davison, 16 Ves.
249; McDavit v. Pierrepont, 8 C. E. Green, 42.

It has been thought in England that notice of a tenancy is not notice of the title of the lessor.[1] But, by the weight of authority, the rule of law in this country is different.[2] The ground of the American rule is that a purchaser from the assumed owner is put upon notice that his grantor's ownership is not complete; and, having notice of such fact, due diligence requires him to ascertain how far short of a perfect ownership the grantor comes. That is, he must ascertain all that can be ascertained by reasonable diligence from the existence of the tenancy and the record of the lease, if there be a written lease.

The possession of land which will afford notice of the party's rights must be as open, notorious, and exclusive as is required to constitute adverse possession under the limitation laws.[3] If land upon which there are no buildings be used for pasture by the grantee and others, this is not such visible, notorious, and exclusive possession by the grantee as amounts to constructive notice of ownership. The possession for such purpose must be actual and distinct, and be manifested by such acts of ownership as will naturally be observed and recognized by others.[4] So, where real estate is ostensibly as much in the possession of the husband as of the wife, there is no such actual possession by the wife as will import notice of an equitable interest possessed by her in the land to a

[1] Barnhart v. Greenshields, 9 Moore, P. C. 18. But see Daniels v. Davidson, 16 Ves. 254; s. c. 17 Ves. 433.

[2] Dickey v. Lyon, 19 Iowa, 544; Smith v. Jackson, 76 Ill. 254; Pittman v. Gaty, 5 Gilm. 186; Sailor v. Hertzog, 4 Whart. 259; Hood v. Fahnestock, 1 Penn. St. 470; Kerr v. Day, 14 Penn. St. 112; Wright v. Wood, 23 Penn. St. 120, 130; Morrison v. March, 4 Minn. 422; Bank of Orleans v. Flagg, 3 Barb. Ch. 317; Buck v. Holloway, 2 J. J. Marsh. 180. Contra, Flagg v. Mann, 2 Sum. 486; Beattie v. Butler, 21 Mo. 313.

[3] Smith v. Jackson, 76 Ill. 254; Brown v. Volkening, 64 N. Y. 76.

[4] Coleman v. Barklew, 3 Dutch. 357; Holmes v. Stout, 3 Green, Ch. 492; s. c. 2 Stockt. 419; McMechan v. Griffing, 3 Pick. 149; Butler v. Stevens, 26 Maine, 484; Powell v. Thompson, 9 Ala. 409.

purchaser at execution sale, under a judgment against the husband, in whom the legal title apparently was at the time of the rendition of the judgment.[1]

In cases of fraudulent sales or mortgages, the rights of a subsequent purchaser are materially affected by the question of possession on the part of the intermediate vendor. Want of possession in him will generally operate as notice to his vendee. A learned English judge has quoted with approval the following proposition of law on this point: If B obtains a conveyance of land from A by fraud, and A *quits the possession* to B, and B sells the land for a valuable consideration to C, *bona fide* and without notice, A can never obtain the land against C, because the fraudulent conveyance, with the quitting of possession, transfers an interest. And then, when C has obtained an interest at law for his money, *bona fide*, a court of equity ought not to take it from him.[2]

The rule of notice by possession does not apply in favor of a vendor remaining in possession, so as to require a purchaser from his grantee to inquire whether he has reserved any interest in the land conveyed. So far as the purchaser is concerned, the vendor's deed is conclusive. Having declared by his deed that he makes no reservation, he cannot afterwards set up any secret arrangement by which his grant is

---

[1] Thomas v. Kennedy, 24 Iowa, 397.

[2] Sir John Stuart, V. C., in Ogilvie v. Jeaffreson, 2 Giff. 353, 379, quoting Gilbert, Frauds, 287. "It is impossible, I apprehend," said Stuart, V. C., as cited, "to question the soundness of this statement of the principle, which sustains the defence of purchase for valuable consideration without notice. In the case of Jones v. Powles, 3 Mylne & K. 581, the mortagor, who obtained his title by fraud and forgery of a bill, was in actual possession of the estate; and the mortgagor, who claimed by derivative title from him, was also in possession. Therefore, the defence of purchaser for valuable consideration by the mortgagee was sustained, not only on the ground that there was no reasonable cause to suspect that the bill was forged, but expressly because a long possession had followed the alleged devise; and no reasonable diligence could have led to a discovery of the forgery."

impaired.[1] Nor has the doctrine of constructive notice of defects in the title to land, arising out of the neglect of the purchaser to investigate, any application to cases of adverse possession and outstanding claim.[2] Indeed, it is not fraudulent to purchase and take possession of land with actual notice of an outstanding claim.[3] The question in such a case is, simply, who has the better title? The doctrine of fraud operates against the purchaser with notice, only when the opposing claimant had an equity in the land superior to the right of the purchaser's vendor.

This doctrine as to possession does not always require the subsequent purchaser to have taken actual possession. It was indeed considered by Lord Rosslyn that the defence of a purchase for value without notice was a shield to protect the possession of property, and was not available in any case except to protect the actual possession.[4] But Lord Eldon overruled that doctrine, and decided that possession by the purchaser was not necessary, provided he purchased from an apparent owner, who was actually in possession.[5] And this doctrine has recently been reaffirmed.[6]

A person who holds stock as trustee for another has no right, *prima facie*, to pledge it to secure a debt of his own growing out of a transaction independent of his trust.[7] It is the duty of a trustee to use all reasonable diligence to pre-

---

[1] Van Keuren *v.* Central R. Co., 9 Vroom, 165.

[2] Sands *v.* Hughes, 53 N. Y. 287 ; Clapp *v.* Brumagham, 9 Cowen, 558.

[3] Sands *v.* Hughes, *supra.*   [4] Strode *v.* Blackburne, 3 Ves. 222.

[5] Wallwyn *v.* Lee, 9 Ves. 24.

[6] Ogilvie *v.* Jeaffreson, 2 Giff. 353, 379. "According to the doctrine now fully established," said the court, "unless Catharine Jones had taken possession, and, being in possession as apparent owner, had sold and conveyed to the defendant for valuable consideration paid to her, they are not such purchasers as can defend themselves against the plaintiff's right to relief against the fraudulent conveyance [from him] to Catharine Jones, and all those who claim by derivative title from her."

[7] Shaw *v.* Spencer, 100 Mass. 382.

serve the trust property; and no one can acquire an interest therein as against the *cestui que trust*, who purchases the property with notice of the failure of the trustee to use proper diligence in preserving it to the beneficiary.[1]

To convict a purchaser of fraudulent participation in a breach of trust by an executor having authority to sell, the evidence of notice of the fraudulent intent on the part of the executor ought to be very strong. The purchaser has a right to presume, in the absence of direct and plain proof to the contrary, that the executor is exercising his power fairly and faithfully.[2]

One who purchases property from an executor below its value, under circumstances which should put him upon inquiry as to the right of the executor to make the sale, becomes thereby, in case the sale is fraudulent, a party to the fraud. As to what should put a purchaser upon inquiry, it is held that the purchase from an executor of bonds payable to the testator is sufficient to indicate that *prima facie* they belong to the testator's estate; and the purchaser, buying at an inadequate price, acts at his peril.[3] Hence, if a certificate of stock expressed to be in the name of A, trustee, be by A pledged to secure his own debt, the pledgee is, by the language of the certificate, put on inquiry as to the character and limitations of the trust.[4] So, too, a note payable upon its face to a guardian or agent affords notice that the obligation belongs to the ward or principal, and a holder can acquire no rights adverse to those of the parties in whose interest the restriction is made.[5]

[1] Joor v. Williams, 38 Miss. 546.   [2] Davis v. Christian, 15 Gratt. 11.

[3] Pinckard v. Woods, 8 Gratt. 140.

[4] Shaw v. Spencer, 100 Mass. 382 ; Sturtevant v. Jaques, 14 Allen, 523; Duncan v. Judson, 15 Wall. 165.

[5] McMasters v. Dunbar, 2 La. An. 577 ; Nicholson v. Jacobs, Ib. 666 ; Louisiana Bank v. Orleans Nav. Co., 3 La. An. 294; Holmes v. Carman, 1 Freem. Ch. 408 ; Miller v. Helm, 2 Smedes & M. 687 ; Davis v. Henderson, 25 Miss. 549 ; Livermore v. Johnson, 27 Miss. 284.

Where the property or the paper of a firm is taken in payment of the private debt of one of the partners, the law charges the creditor with notice of an abuse of trust, and imposes upon him the burden of repelling the presumption. The rule is founded upon the principle that the employment of the partnership funds by one of the partners for his private benefit is *prima facie* a fraud upon the partnership, and the creditor participating in the transaction is a party to the fraud.[1]

It will not take a case out of this principle that a negotiable note of the firm, made payable to a third person and by him indorsed, is found before maturity in the hands of one of the partners, and is by him indorsed to the plaintiff. The presumption in such case is that the note is accommodation paper, the property of the firm, and not of the individual member; and, if such note be transferred to a creditor for the private debt of the partner in whose possession it is, the creditor takes it charged with knowledge that it is firm property. The presumption, however, that the note belongs to the firm may be rebutted by the creditor, by showing that it has been regularly negotiated in due course, and has become the property of the individual partner.[2]

Purchasers of scrip dividends, though for value and without actual notice of fraud, may be affected with notice by the issuance of certificates of indebtedness in connection with the scrip. Thus, while negotiations between two gas companies for consolidation upon a certain basis of indebtedness were pending, one of the companies passed a resolution without the knowledge of the other, declaring a scrip dividend of ten per cent. upon the amount of their capital stock, thus increasing their indebtedness by so much. Certificates of indebtedness were issued in accordance with the resolution. Consolidation was effected without knowledge on the part of the other company of this transaction. Upon a bill being

[1] Mecutchen *v.* Kennady, 3 Dutch. 230 ; Halstead *v.* Shepard, 23 Ala. 538.   See *ante*, pp. 146, 147.   [2] Mecutchen *v.* Kennady, *supra*.

filed for such purpose, the scrip was declared void, and the company issuing it were restrained from recognizing it as a valid obligation and from permitting its transfer. It was considered that the certificates of indebtedness should have put the purchasers of the scrip upon inquiry, though in fact purchased without notice and for value. The rule as to negotiable instruments is not applicable to such certificates.[1]

A purchaser of property for a valuable consideration is bound, when charged with notice of fraud, to answer all the allegations which *tend* to show that he had notice of the fraud.[2] Thus, in the case cited, the plaintiff, seeking to impeach a deed as obtained by fraud on the part of the defendant vendors, alleged that certain suspicious circumstances appeared on the back of the deed, which tended to show such fraud. The court accordingly required the deed to be produced for inspection, though the defendants had no actual notice of the fraud; and, on further hearing, the defendant's purchase was set aside.

In a proceeding charging a purchaser from a trustee with notice that the sale was in fraud of the rights of the beneficiary, it is not enough for the purchaser to say in his answer (though the answer be not replied to) that the trustee informed him that he needed the money obtained to meet debts contracted for his *cestui que trust*, and that from all the information he had he was led to believe that the trustee wanted the funds for proper purposes. Nor, in such a case, is it enough for the trustee himself to say that the necessities of the beneficiary required a sale of the trust fund, and that he had properly applied the proceeds to his use. He should state how they were applied.[3]

A person who purchases land from one who has only a bond for title is affected with constructive notice of any lien

---

[1] Bailey *v.* Gaslight Co., 12 C. E. Green, 196. No account of interest was ordered.

[2] Kennedy *v.* Green, 6 Sim. 6.   [3] Cocke *v.* Minor, 25 Gratt. 246.

upon the property for unpaid purchase-money due by the holder of the title bond to the obligor.[1]

§ 2. Of Lis Pendens.

There are other classes of cases of constructive notice to which the above principle of the duty of inquiry has no application; as to which, indeed, no amount of inquiry, or no want of suggestions to inquiry, would afford any excuse.[2] The first of these classes of cases to be considered is known as *lis pendens*.

A person purchasing property *pendente lite* is treated as a purchaser with notice, and is subject to all the equities of the person under whom he claims, and is bound by the decree that may be made against the person from whom he derives title;[3] and this, too, even though the vendor fraudulently conceal the pending trial.[4] But the rule applies only to cases in which the purchaser derives title from one of the litigating parties. If he claim adversely to both, by title paramount, the proceedings will not bind him. The judgment or decree settles the rights of the parties to the suit only, and those claiming under or deriving title from them.[5] Nor does the rule apply to purchasers at tax-sales. The authority of the State to make a tax-sale is paramount to the rights of

---

[1] McLaurie *v.* Thomas, 39 Ill. 292.

[2] It will indeed often happen that we shall meet with the case of facts suggesting inquiry in connection with the present subject; but, upon examination, it will generally be found that such facts are merely incidental, and not necessary to establish the main feature of the notice.

[3] Allen *v.* Morris, 5 Vroom, 159 ; Bishop of Winchester *v.* Paine, 11 Ves. 194; McPherson *v.* Housel, 2 Beasl. 301; Murray *v.* Ballou, 1 Johns. Ch. 574 ; Griswold *v.* Jackson, 2 Edw. Ch. 466 ; Metcalfe *v.* Pulvertoft, 2 Ves. & B. 205; Sorrell *v.* Carpenter, 2 P. Wms. 482 ; Moore *v.* McNamara, 2 Ball & B. 187.

[4] Blanchard *v.* Ware, 43 Iowa, 530.   [5] Allen *v.* Morris, *supra.*

the owner and of all others; and, when made in accordance with law, the sale is conclusive against all persons.[1]

The reason of the doctrine of *lis pendens* is that, if a transfer of interest pending a suit were to be allowed to affect the proceedings, there would be no end to litigation; for, as soon as a new party was brought in, he might transfer to another, and render it necessary to bring that other into court; and hence the suit might be interminable. This reason, however, has no application to a third person whose interest existed before the suit was commenced, and who might have been made an original party.[2]

A purchaser who has constructive or actual notice of a pending suit can only be held chargeable with knowledge of facts of which the record in the cause, as it existed at the time of the purchase, would have informed him. If these facts inform him that the vendor is committing a fraud in making the sale, he becomes, by purchasing, a party to the fraud. But he cannot be charged with a knowledge of facts afterwards brought into the case.[3] The burden of proving such a case as this, however, would doubtless rest upon the party claiming the property. It seems pretty clear at all events that, if a party's claim to property in litigation arose before the litigation began, he must show the fact.[4]

Mere service of a *subpœna* is not a sufficient *lis pendens*, unless a bill or declaration be afterwards filed. But, when the bill or declaration is filed, the doctrine of *lis pendens* relates to the service of the *subpœna*.[5] And the question must relate to the estate, and not merely to money securities upon it.[6] So, if the suit fail for a defect of process, there is no *lis pendens*. Thus, where there is a defect in an attachment, the

---

[1] Wright *v.* Walker, 30 Ark. 44.

[2] Murray *v.* Lylburn, 2 Johns. Ch. 441.

[3] Davis *v.* Christian, 15 Gratt. 11.   [4] Hall *v.* Jack, 32 Md. 253.

[5] Sugden, Vendors, 534, Perkins's ed.

[6] Ib.; Worsley *v.* Scarborough, 3 Atk. 392.

debtor can convey a good title to a purchaser for value without notice of the attachment proceedings.[1]

§ 3. Of Registration of Instruments.

The second class of cases above referred to [2] is that of the registration of instruments under recording acts.

The doctrine of constructive notice in relation to registered deeds has in England been divided into two classes of cases: First, cases in which the party charged has had actual notice that the property in dispute was in fact charged, encumbered, or in some way affected; and the courts have thereupon bound him with constructive notice of facts and instruments, to a knowledge of which he would have been led by an inquiry after the charge, encumbrance, or other circumstance affecting the property of which he had actual notice. Secondly, cases in which the courts have been satisfied from the evidence before them that the party charged had designedly abstained from inquiry.

The proposition of law upon which the former class of cases proceeds is, not that the party charged had notice of a fact or instrument which in truth related to the subject in dispute without his knowing that such was the case, but that he had actual notice that it did so relate. The proposition of law upon which the second class of cases proceeds is, not that the party charged had incautiously neglected to make inquiries, but that he had designedly abstained from such inquiries for the purpose of avoiding knowledge; a purpose which, if proved, would clearly show that he had a suspicion of the truth and a fraudulent determination not to learn it. In short, if there be not actual notice that the property is in some way affected, and no fraudulent turning away from a knowledge of facts

---

[1] Burchard v. Fairhaven, 48 Vt. 327.

[2] *Ante*, p. 300.

which the *res gestæ* would suggest to a prudent mind, — if mere want of caution as distinguished from wilful blindness is all that can be imputed, — the doctrine of constructive notice will not apply.[1] In accordance with these principles, it is held that, in order to affect the priority of a registered deed over an unregistered security by reason of fraud in the grantor, actual notice of the fraud must be fixed upon the grantee of such deed.[2]

A purchaser is constructively affected by the registration of a deed required to be put on record with such knowledge as the index entries afford ; and, if they are such as to necessarily put a cautious and prudent man upon inquiry, such inquiry will be considered to have been made, and notice given accordingly.[3]

The extent to which constructive notice is sometimes carried takes the subject entirely beyond the proper limits of constructive fraud. It is quite proper to declare that a purchaser who will not examine the registry to ascertain the condition of the title of a party about to convey to him shall be held to be postponed to the rights of a prior encumbrancer, lessee, or grantee whose deed has been recorded ; and this on the ground of constructive fraud, even apart from the express language of the statute making the registration notice. Knowledge of the place of deposit of muniments of title-deeds would alone require a purchaser to examine the estate of his grantor's title. But this is not the extent of the rule concerning notice by registration, at least as held by some courts. The doctrine has been carried so far as to require a purchaser to take notice of that of which he can in fact have no knowledge from the books of registration, except by examining every

---

[1] Jones *v.* Smith, 1 Hare, 55; Ratcliffe *v.* Barnard, Law R. 6 Ch. 654; Chadwick *v.* Turner, Law R. 1 Ch. 319 ; Whitbread *v.* Jordan, 1 Younge & C. 32; Agra Bank *v.* Barry, Law R. 6 Irish Eq. 128, 144.

[2] Agra Bank *v.* Barry, *supra*, criticising Wormald *v.* Maitland, 35 Law J. Ch. 69, and *In re* Allen, Law R. 1 Eq. 455.

[3] Bostwick *v.* Powers, 12 Iowa, 456; Doyle *v.* Teas, 4 Scam. 202.

recorded instrument therein. Thus, it has been decided that
the registration of a deed required to be recorded constitutes
notice to subsequent purchasers, though the record of the
instrument be not indexed.[1] This, however, is upon the
ground that under the statute as to registration the index is
no part of the record: it could not well be sustained on the
ground of constructive fraud. A man cannot be guilty of
constructive fraud of this kind, except by shutting his eyes to
facts to which he has a plain and adequate clew. The case
simply turns upon a question of statutory interpretation; and,
as to this, it is proper to remark that there is strong authority to the contrary of the cases above referred to.[2]

By the law of California, a grantee of land must ascertain
whether any of the preceding grantors of the property had
made an earlier conveyance of the same, which, remaining unrecorded until after the registration of the second grant under
which the present claimant holds, was then put upon record.
If such were the facts, the present claimant, though a purchaser for value without actual notice, is considered to have
constructive notice of such prior (and for a time) unrecorded
grant.[3] It may well be doubted, however, in the absence of a
clear intent to this effect on the part of the Legislature,
if this is not transcending the purpose of the registry acts.[4]
But authorities in support of that rule are not wanting.[5]

[1] Mutual Life Ins. Co. v. Dake, 4 Cent. L. J. 340; Curtis v. Lyman,
24 Vt. 338; Bishop v. Schneider, 46 Mo. 472. See also Schell v. Stein,
76 Penn. St. 398; Chatham v. Bradford, 50 Ga. 327, and other cases cited
in the Central Law Journal, ut supra.

[2] Barney v. McCarty, 15 Iowa, 510; Miller v. Bradford, 12 Iowa, 14;
Whalley v. Small, 25 Iowa, 184; Noyes v. Horr, 13 Iowa, 570; Breed v.
Conley, 14 Iowa, 269. See Barney v. Little, 15 Iowa, 527; 4 Cent. L. J.
387, and cases cited.

[3] Clark v. Sawyer, 48 Cal. 133; Mahoney v. Middleton, 41 Cal. 41.

[4] See Rawle, Covenants, 428 (4th ed.); Bates v. Norcross, 14 Pick.
224.

[5] Jarvis v. Aikens, 25 Vt. 635; Doe d. Potts v. Dowdall, 3 Houst.
369; Tifft v. Munson, 57 N. Y. 97; McCusker v. McEvey, 9 R. I. 525.
See Bigelow, Estoppel, 326 (2d ed.).

A mortgage duly recorded certainly operates as notice until discharged; and hence where a mortgagor has regained possession by fraudulent practice, and has then conveyed to a purchaser for value, who has no knowledge of the mortgage, the mortgagee may foreclose against him.[1] But this is a very different case from the above.

Though land be bid off at an administrator's sale for the administrator by a nominal purchaser, who after confirmation of the sale received a conveyance from the administrator, and subsequently conveyed to the latter, still subsequent purchasers for value are not, it is said, chargeable with notice of the fraud by the mere record of the conveyances between the administrator and nominal purchaser.[2] But this proposition deserves further consideration.

The registration of a deed defectively acknowledged is not constructive notice to a subsequent *bona fide* purchaser for value.[3] And the registration of any deed is notice of only such fraud as appears on the face of the instrument: it is not notice of fraud perpetrated in its execution.[4] And, again, the registration of a deed is notice only to those who claim through or under the grantor.[5] The purchaser of land is not bound to take notice of a registered lien or incumbrance upon the estate, created by any person other than those parties through whom he is compelled to make title.[6]

The doctrine of constructive notice to a purchaser by registration does not apply where there is a false representation that the vendor has an unincumbered title. In such a case, the purchaser can, without an eviction,[7] enjoin the collection

---

[1] Grimes v. Kimball, 8 Allen, 153; s. c. 3 Allen, 518.

[2] Wells v. Polk, 36 Tex. 120.   [3] Cockey v. Milne, 16 Md. 200.

[4] Godbold v. Lambert, 8 Rich. Eq. 155; Hoffman v. Strohecker, 7 Watts, 86.

[5] Corbin v. Sullivan, 47 Ind. 356; Ely v. Wilcox, 20 Wis. 523, 530; Maul v. Rider, 59 Penn. St. 167.

[6] Harper v. Bibb, 34 Miss. 472.   [7] See *ante*, p. 68.

of the price agreed upon, though the conveyance contain covenants of warranty.[1]

The prior registration of a conveyance obtained in fraud of a grantee registering later will be of no avail against the rights of the latter. Thus, if after knowledge of a sale to another, a person should procure another conveyance to himself from the vendor, and have the deed recorded before the registration of the deed to the first grantee, he would be compellable in equity to surrender his fraudulent claim to the latter.[2] But it is said to be necessary for a party relying upon an unregistered deed against a subsequent purchaser or attaching creditor to prove that the latter had actual notice of the deed.[3]

It is, however, clear that the kind and degree of notice sufficient to stand as a substitute for an actual record of a deed must be such as to charge a party with fraud in taking the second conveyance. He must know of the prior conveyance, and intend to defeat it. A floating rumor or a vague suspicion is insufficient. Possession may or may not be notice of an unrecorded deed. Notice is not to be inferred from a possession which commenced before and has continued after a conveyance, without any change in the manner of the possession or use indicating an altered estate.[4] It has well been said that it would materially impair the security which men generally feel in a public registry, and greatly infringe upon the beneficent policy of the registry laws, to charge the public with notice of any estate that a party in possession might acquire. Possession has in fact no tendency in such cases to put men upon inquiry.[5] Thus, if a tenant in possession were to receive a conveyance of the reversion, and fail to record it before the registration of another conveyance of the lessor to a purchaser for value without notice, the latter would not be

[1] Napier v. Elam, 6 Yerg. 108. See ante, p. 68.
[2] Mercier v. Hemme, 50 Cal. 606.
[3] Spofford v. Weston, 29 Maine, 140. Sed quære.
[4] Emmons v. Murray, 16 N. H. 385.
[5] Bell v. Twilight, 18 N. H. 159, 164.

affected with notice of his grantor's fraud by the mere possession of the tenant. So, too, if a grantor of land should take
from the grantee a lease of the property and remain in possession, and the grantee, having recorded the conveyance to
himself, should afterwards mortgage the premises for value
to one having no notice of the lease, the mortgagee's rights
would prevail over the lessee's, notwithstanding the possession of the latter.[1]

A purchaser for value without notice of a prior unregistered conveyance may make a valid conveyance to one who
has such notice.[2] And the same is true of the case of a mistake in a conveyance.[3] And it would seem by analogy
that the same rule would hold where the grantee had notice
that the estate had been obtained from a remote grantor by
fraud. If he derive title from a *bona fide* purchaser without
notice, his claim to the estate should stand. The doctrine is
explained on the ground that, but for the rule, the *bona fide*
purchaser would not be able to enjoy the full benefit of his
own unexceptionable title.[4]

§ 4. Of Purchasers without Value.

The third of the above-mentioned[5] classes of cases is that of
purchasers without consideration. We have under this head
to consider, then, who are, and who are not, purchasers for
value. It will, however, be convenient and sufficient to point

[1] Bell *v.* Twilight, 18 N. H. 159.

[2] Bell *v.* Twilight, *supra;* Harrison *v.* Forth, Prec. in Ch. 51 ; Lowther *v.* Carlton, 2 Atk. 139; Sweet *v.* Southcote, 2 Brown, C. C. 66;
Trull *v.* Bigelow, 16 Mass. 406; Boynton *v.* Reese, 8 Pick. 329; Fenno
v. Sayre, 3 Ala. 458 ; Price *v.* Martin, 46 Miss. 489; Ledyard *v.* Butler,
9 Paige, 132.

[3] Prescott *v.* Hawkins, 16 N. H. 122, 127; Bumpus *v.* Platner, 1 Johns.
Ch. 213; Varick *v.* Briggs, 6 Paige, 323.

[4] 1 Story, Equity, § 409.

[5] *Ante,* p. 300.

out the meaning of the term purchasers for value ; and it will be understood that all purchasers not coming under the definitions are affected with notice.

A *bona fide* purchaser for value obtains a good title, notwithstanding his vendor's title was obtained by fraud.[1] Hence, where a man already married went through the ceremony of marriage again with another person, and then joined with her as his wife in assigning her property to a purchaser, the assignment was supported, though the woman had been deceived.[2] So, if a trustee be in actual possession of the

---

[1] Thompson *v.* Lee, 3 Watts & S. 479 ; Ball *v.* Shell, 21 Wend. 222; Moody *v.* Blake, 117 Mass. 23 ; Hoffman *v.* Noble, 6 Met. 68; Rowley *v.* Bigelow, 12 Pick. 307 ; Spindler *v.* Atkinson, 3 Md. 409 ; Toole *v.* Darden, 6 Ired. Eq. 394; Thorpe *v.* Beavans, 73 N. Car. 241; Bradley *v.* Obear, 10 N. H. 477; Gage *v.* Gage, 29 N. H. 533; Shufelt *v.* Pease, 16 Wis. 659.

But such vendor must have acquired a *title* in order to this result, unless the conduct of the real owner was fraudulent. A person buying goods without authority, for another, who refuses to receive them, cannot himself acquire title to them by taking possession upon such refusal ; nor is the case different when the party falsely represents himself to be a member of a firm for whom the goods are without authority purchased. He cannot take possession and convey a title even to a *bona fide* purchaser for value. Moody *v.* Blake, 117 Mass. 23.

So, if a person sell goods to another, or has been led to believe that he has sold them to such person, and deliver them, as he supposes, to such person, and the person who has led him into that belief receive and carry off the goods and dispose of them to another, there has not been a sale to the person who has thus fraudulently represented himself to be a servant or agent of the supposed purchaser; and he cannot confer a good title on any one else, the property never having vested in him. Hardman *v.* Booth, 1 Hurl. & C. 803; Lindsay *v.* Cundy, Law R. 2 Q. B. Div. 96, Court of Appeal, reversing Law R. 1 Q. B. Div. 348.

A purchaser at an execution sale cannot be held liable for any device of the defendant in the execution of which he was ignorant. Thorpe *v.* Beavans, 73 N. Car. 241. But the public policy in favor of sustaining judicial sales does not go so far as to protect a purchaser who has himself been guilty of trick or artifice in obtaining the property at an under-value. Stewart *v.* Nelson, 25 Mo. 309; Schweitzer *v.* Tracy, 76 Ill. 345 ; Young *v.* Bradley, 68 Ill. 553; Michigan Cent. R. Co. *v.* Phillips, 60 Ill. 190; Jennings *v.* Gage, 13 Ill. 610.

[2] Sturge *v.* Starr, 2 Mylne & K. 195.

trust estate, and convey it to an innocent purchaser for value, the remedy of the *cestui que trust* is against the trustee alone. The purchaser gets a good title.[1] A person, however, receiving money raised on trust property in fraud of the *cestui que trust*, is said to be liable for the amount to the latter, though the money was obtained for value and without notice of the trust.[2] Thus, in the case cited, the defendant had received money fraudulently raised on real property which had been settled on the plaintiff and her children; and, though the defendant was trustee of this marriage settlement, he had no notice or knowledge that the money referred to had been raised on the trust property. But the plaintiff, her husband having deceased, was held entitled to follow the fund into the defendant's hands, and recover the same for herself and (as next friend) for her children. And it was thought immaterial that the defendant had been discharged in insolvency since the money was put into his hands.[3]

Proof of fraud in a sale casts the burden upon a subsequent purchaser of showing that he bought for value and without notice.[4] But the purchaser of a fraudulent title must be able to show clearly that he is a *bona fide* purchaser without notice, and has paid the purchase-money, of which the receipt of the vendor will not be sufficient evidence.[5]

A purchaser for value is one who, at the time of his purchase, advances a new consideration, surrenders some security, or does some other act which, if his purchase were set aside,

[1] Grove *v.* Robards, 36 Mo. 523.

The ownership of a trust fund is unaffected by a change of the custodian, or where it is taken by a volunteer or one who has notice of the trust. Kepler *v.* Davis, 80 Penn. St. 153.

[2] Buckeridge *v.* Glasse, Craig & P. 126.

[3] The debt was not shown to have been in the defendant's schedule; but the court thought the result would have been the same, even if it had been proved to be there.

[4] Easter *v.* Allen, 8 Allen, 7.

[5] Hoffman *v.* Strohecker, 9 Watts, 183. See s. c. 7 Watts, 86.

would leave him in a worse than his original situation,[1] or (according to most of the authorities) which would leave him in a worse situation than he *might* have been but for the purchase.[2] Thus, a person who takes a negotiable bill of exchange in payment, absolute or conditional, of a pre-existing debt; or as security for a debt simultaneously created with the giving of the bill or note, where such instrument is part of the inducement to the credit; or, according to the strong tendency and weight of authority, where the bill or note is taken as security for a pre-existing debt, whether there be an agreement to extend the time of the original credit or an agreement *not* to extend the time, — in all of these cases, the holder of the paper is a holder for value; and, if he have no notice of fraud or other defence available in an action between the original parties, his right to recover is perfect.[3]

In New York and in some other States, it is held that one to whom property, purchased through fraud, has been delivered by the defrauding buyer, in payment of a preceding debt, or in performance of an executory contract of sale made prior to acquiring possession of the property in question, though a consideration was paid at the time of the contract, is not a holder for value, and cannot hold the property as against the party who originally owned and was defrauded of his posses-

[1] Boon v. Barnes, 23 Miss. 136. Hence, a purchaser of property who has not paid any thing for it, though he may have agreed to pay full value, is not protected. Hicks v. Stone, 13 Minn. 434. But the case would be otherwise, where he had given security for payment. Starr v. Strong, 2 Sandf. Ch. 139.

[2] Blanchard v. Stevens, 3 Cush. 162 ; Bank of Republic v. Carrington, 5 R. I. 515; Redf. & B. Lead. Cas. 208, 209.

[3] The cases at variance with the last of these propositions, mainly in New York, are considered in the note to Swift v. Tyson, Redf. & B. Lead. Cas. 186, 195. The whole subject of holders for value under the circumstances stated in the text is there presented, and the authorities, American and English, examined. See, further, the late reaffirmance of the rule in New York (requiring the actual parting with some value, or otherwise positively changing the party's position), in Moore v. Ryder, 65 N. Y. 438.

sion of the property.[1] But payment, even in New York, is
not necessary to make one a purchaser for value. The giving
of securities is equally good.[2]

In accordance with the above rule of law in New York,
one who has innocently received from a husband, to secure
the purchase price of goods then presently sold and delivered
to him, and also to secure a prior indebtedness, a mortgage
executed by the wife of the debtor upon her own property,
which as to the prior indebtedness was a fraud upon the wife,
cannot claim to have equities superior to hers, so long as the
avoiding of the mortgage to the extent of such prior debt
will not place him in any worse position than he originally
occupied.[3] To make the claim of the mortgage superior to
that of the wife, it must appear that, in relation to the prior
debt, he has done something, or parted with something, in
reliance upon the mortgage, which will make the effect of
defeating the mortgage as a security to that extent operate to
his injury.[4]

It is further held in New York that an execution creditor
does not become a *bona fide* purchaser by buying goods at a
sale thereof without making an advance upon them, when the
goods were fraudulently purchased by the defendant in the
execution. Such a proceeding, it is said, gives the creditor
no better title than a mere delivery would from the fraudulent
defendant. The creditor advances nothing, and loses nothing
by the proceeding. That is, the creditor had no right, under
the circumstances, to levy on the goods in question ; and the
mere sale had therefore conferred no title to him.[5]

A mere attaching creditor cannot be regarded as a *bona fide*

---

[1] Barnard *v.* Campbell, 58 N. Y. 73.

[2] Starr *v.* Strong, 2 Sandf. Ch. 139.

[3] Smith *v.* Osborn, 33 Mich. 410.

[4] Ib.; McWilliams *v.* Mason, 31 N. Y. 294.

[5] Devoe *v.* Brandt, 53 N. Y. 462. This was quite clear for the
further reason that there was evidence that the creditor had notice of
his debtor's fraud.

purchaser for value. The claim of an attaching creditor is considered as not of equal strength with that of such a purchaser. He parts with nothing in exchange for the property, nor does he take it in satisfaction of any debt. The property is merely seized for the purpose of having it afterward so appropriated. The attaching creditor, by his attachment, obtains but a lien. It is a well-settled rule, at least in equity, that the general assignees of a bankrupt take his estate subject to every equitable claim existing against it in favor of third persons; and so it is with judgment creditors in regard to the lien of their judgment.[1] But if the property attached be afterwards sold under the levy, and the creditor become purchaser, paying cash or giving a valid security for payment, he will be a purchaser for value, even under the New York rule.

One who claims against a prior donee or creditor as a purchaser for value must prove a fair consideration, not necessarily equal to the full value of the property, but a price paid which does not cause surprise or warrant a suspicion of fraud or contrivance on the part of the purchaser.[2] Indeed, if the price paid be grossly below the value of the property, he will not be regarded as a purchaser for value as against a creditor, though in fact his purchase was made without knowledge of any fraudulent intent on the part of the vendor.[3]

If any interest *ad rem* remain in the intermediate fraudulent vendor of property, it seems that the original vendor can follow the property into the hands of a *bona fide* purchaser for value to the extent of such interest. That is, he can sue upon the rights of the purchaser's vendor, and recover to the extent of such rights.[4] But, in the absence of trust or agency, this

---

[1] Schweizer v. Tracy, 76 Ill. 345, 351; *Ex parte* Howe, 1 Paige, 125; Gibson v. Warden, 14 Wall. 249; Tousley v. Tousley, 5 Ohio St. 78; Nathan v. Giles, 5 Taunt. 558. See McLaughlin v. Shepherd, 32 Maine, 143.

[2] Worthy v. Caddell, 76 N. Car. 82; Fullenwider v. Roberts, 4 Dev. & B. 278.   [3] Ib.   [4] See Justh v. National Bank, 56 N. Y. 478.

right of the intermediate vendor must, it should seem, be in the nature of a lien upon the property,[1] and not a mere right of action for the breach of a contract; since the original, defrauded owner would not be a party to the contract.

If the fraud practised on the owner of the property be of such a character as to prevent the passing of a title to the supposed vendee, the latter of course can convey no title to a subsequent purchaser, though the purchase be made without notice and for value. Thus, where under the pretence that an instrument was a deed of covenant to procure title-deeds, a solicitor obtained from his client a mortgage of property to secure the payment of an alleged debt not shown to exist, the deed thus procured was held to be void, not merely against the solicitor, but also against an assignee for value from him without notice of the fraud.[2]

No title passes to a *bona fide* purchaser for value of land, who claims under a deed which was surreptitiously and fraudulently taken from the grantor's house, before signature and delivery.[3]   And it is held in Ohio that if the fraudulent purchaser of goods does not obtain a delivery of them under the contract, but subsequently acquires possession of them through fraud and misrepresentation, he cannot convey a good title to them as against the owner, even to a *bona fide* purchaser for value.[4]

The distinction between the two classes of cases is found in the fact that in the latter there is no valid execution of the instrument. If the solemnities of signing, sealing, and delivering are tainted with imposture or deceit, these solemnities have no binding effect; and the instrument to which they

---

[1] Justh *v.* National Bank, 56 N. Y. 483, 484.   See also Pennell *v.* Deffell, 4 DeG., M. & G. 372.

[2] Vorley *v.* Cooke, 1 Giff. 230.   See also *ante*, pp. 130, 157.

[3] Van Armringe *v.* Morton, 4 Whart. 382.

[4] Dean *v.* Yates, 22 Ohio St. 388.

have been fraudulently applied cannot be the act and deed of him who had no intention to execute such an instrument. By the common-law rules of pleading, evidence of imposture, falsehood, or fraud can be given in evidence under the plea of *non est factum*. The instrument is no more a genuine deed than it would be, had the signature been forged.[1] But where the imposition consists merely in false representations of the condition or value of the property, or of the state of the title, or of claims upon it, or the like matters, the conveyance, though obtained by fraud, is good until set aside, even as between the parties, and is unimpeachable as to subsequent purchasers for value and without notice. In cases of this kind, there is an intention to convey the property, and that intention will be upheld, subject to the right of the injured party to relief from the consequences of the fraud of the other party, or of others who claim under him with notice or as volunteers. In the one case, the original party intends to alienate the particular property; in the other, he does not.

One who buys property from another who acquired the title by fraud must, in order to protect himself in his purchase, have been ignorant of any of the facts constituting the fraud, not only at the time of his purchase, but also at the time of paying the purchase price.[2] To constitute one a purchaser without notice, he should have paid the purchase-money in whole or in part[3] before notice.[4] Hence, a person receiving notice after having contracted for the purchase of land, but before the delivery of the deed or adjustment of

---

[1] Vorley *v.* Cooke, *supra.*

[2] Scott *v.* Umbarger, 41 Cal. 410; Blanchard *v.* Ely, 12 Mich. 339; Warner *v.* Whittaker, 6 Mich. 133.

[3] Hardin *v.* Harrington, 11 Bush, 367. See Pickett *v.* Baum, 29 Barb. 505; 2 Story, Equity, § 1502.

[4] Paul *v.* Fulton, 25 Mo. 156; Vattier *v.* Hude, 7 Peters, 252; Doswell *v.* Buchanan, 3 Leigh, 365; Dellard *v.* Crocker, 1 Speer, Eq. 20; Bash *v.* Bash, 3 Strobh. Eq. 131; Kyle *v.* Tait, 6 Gratt. 44; Cole *v.* Scott, 2 Wash. 141.

the consideration, is not a purchaser without notice.[1] But notice to a purchaser after his purchase does not affect him.[2]

To be a purchaser of land without notice, it is held that the party must have acquired the legal title : a purchaser of an equitable title is not within the protection.[3] Nor is one who holds title under a quit-claim deed regarded as a *bona fide* purchaser without notice.[4]

§ 5. OF PRINCIPAL AND AGENT, CLIENT AND ATTORNEY, &c.[5]

The fourth and last of the classes of cases of notice above referred to [6] is that arising between principal and agent.

The doctrine of constructive notice of fraud depends upon two considerations: first, that certain things existing in the relation or the conduct of parties, or in the case between them, beget a presumption of actual knowledge so strong that the law holds the knowledge to exist, because it is highly improbable it should not ; and, next, that policy and the safety of the public forbid a person to deny knowledge, while he is so dealing as to keep himself ignorant, or so as that he may keep himself ignorant, and yet all the while let his agent know, and himself perhaps profit by that knowledge. And under one or both of these heads comes the other principle, that whatever is notice enough to excite attention, and put the party on his guard and cause him to make inquiry, is also notice of every thing to which it is afterwards found that such

---

[1] Prescott *v.* Hawkins, 16 N. H. 122; Blair *v.* Owles, 1 Munf. 38; Hoover *v.* Donally, 3 Hen. & M. 316; Jewett *v.* Palmer, 7 Johns. Ch. 65; Simms *v.* Richardson, 2 Litt. 274.

[2] Low *v.* Blinco, 10 Bush, 331.   [3] Wailes *v.* Cooper, 24 Miss. 208.

[4] Watson *v.* Phelps, 40 Iowa, 482; May *v.* Le Clare, 11 Wall. 217; Oliver *v.* Pratt, 3 How. 333 ; Bragg *v.* Paulk, 42 Maine, 502 ; Smith *v.* Bank of Mobile, 21 Ala. 125 ; Boon *v.* Chiles, 10 Peters, 177; Vattier *v.* Hinde, 7 Peters, 252.

[5] See also *post*, Chap. IX. § 4.   [6] *Ante*, p. 300.

inquiry might have led, though (for the want of the investigation) all was unknown.[1]

Upon the first of these principles, while it is a general rule of law that a principal or client is affected with notice to his agent or attorney, received in the performance of the matter of the agency, the rule is to be limited to those cases in which the presumption of knowledge by the principal is a reasonable one. It does not apply to cases in which the contrary presumption arises. Thus, where an agent or attorney himself commits the fraud upon his principal or client, he would of course conceal it. To fix the principal with constructive notice of the fraud in such case would be absurd and unjust. There must be something more than this to effect that result.[2]

The rule that a purchaser is in equity chargeable with constructive notice of facts and circumstances which came to the knowledge of his attorney or agent for the purchase, and the rule that notice of a deed is constructive notice of its contents, do not apply to controversies between the vendor and purchaser in relation to their own rights. These rules as to constructive notice are adopted only for the protection of the prior equitable rights of third persons against subsequent purchasers who claim in hostility to such rights.[3]

The notice to the counsel, attorney, or agent must be in the same transaction in which he is employed, according to the more general rule.[4] In Vermont, however, it is settled that it is not necessary that the notice should reach the attorney or agent in the same transaction. If the attorney or

[1] Kennedy v. Green, 3 Mylne & K. 693, 719. See *ante*, pp. 288, 289.

[2] Kennedy v. Green, *supra;* Sharpe v. Foy, Law R. 4 Ch. 35; Atlantic Bank v. Harris, 118 Mass. 147; National Ins. Co. v. Minch, 53 N. Y. 144.

[3] Champlin v. Laytin, 6 Paige, 189; s. c. 18 Wend. 407.

[4] 2 Sugden, Vendors, 532, Perkins; Bracken v. Miller, 4 Watts & S. 102; Bank of United States v. Davis, 2 Hill, 451; Howard Ins. Co. v. Halsey, 4 Seld. 271; McCormick v. Wheeler, 36 Ill. 114; Willis v. Vallette, 4 Met. (Ky.) 186; Jones v. Bamford, 21 Iowa, 217; Wilde v. Gibson, 1 H. L. Cas. 614, 624.

agent has the notice, though acquired while acting in another and different transaction, the client or principal will be affected by it, the law presuming that the notice was communicated.[1] And such seems to be now substantially the rule of law in England,[2] and in the Supreme Court of the United States, except where the situation and fact are such that the notice would not be likely to be communicated.[3] And it would probably be conceded by all the courts that where one transaction is closely followed by and connected with another, or where it is clear that a previous transaction was present to the mind of the agent when engaged in another transaction, the notice to him will bind his principal.[4]

If the agent of one principal, in the course of his employment, collude with the agent of another to defraud either principal, and succeed, it is held that the defrauded principal cannot maintain an action therefor against the other principal.[5] The ground of this decision was said to be that, if the fraud were committed in the course of the principal's business, the principal would be affected by the agent's knowledge; but knowledge of an agent's fraud upon his *principal* cannot be imputable to the principal. If it could be, the principal would be barred from proceeding *ex delicto* against his own or the colluding agent, and might even be liable criminally, where the act was a crime. The true ground for such a rule of law must lie in the fact that collusion against an agent's principal cannot be within the scope of any legitimate business, and can only render the opposite principal liable, when it was expressly authorized or ratified by him.

If a party, with an understanding between himself and another that they shall be jointly interested, purchase prop-

---

[1] Hart v. Farmers' & M. Bank, 33 Vt. 252; Abell v. Howe, 43 N. H. 403.

[2] Dresser v. Norwood, 17 Com. B. N. s. 466, Ex. Ch., reversing s. c. 14 Com. B. N. s. 574.

[3] Distilled Spirits, 11 Wall. 356, 366.

[4] 2 Sugden, Vendors, 532, Perkins.

[5] Scofield Co. v. State, 54 Ga. 635.

erty from a third person in his own name, committing a fraud upon the vendor in the transaction, and then let into the purchase the party so to be jointly interested, the latter is bound by the fraud of the purchaser; and this, too, though he had no actual notice of the fraud, and paid value for his interest in the property. Though in a sense such party may be a *bona fide* purchaser for value, still the first purchaser is in law his agent, and he is bound by his fraud. The sale may therefore be rescinded as against both parties.[1]

The directors of a corporation cannot be charged with notice of all of the acts of the managing officers, so as to be personally liable for their fr..uds.[2] And, as to false representations made by the latter, the directors are not liable in the absence of proof that (knowing the representations to have been made) they (the directors) believed, or had reason to believe, at the time the managers made them, that the representations were false, and that they were for that reason fraudulently made; or that the directors assumed, or intended to convey the impression, that they had actual knowledge of their truth, though conscious that they had no such knowledge.[3]

Notice to a husband is not notice to his wife, unless he is her agent, and, it is held, is engaged upon the business of the agency when he receives the notice.[4] And the same would doubtless be true of notice to the wife to affect the interests of the husband.

The rule that the presence of facts sufficient to put a man of fair intelligence upon inquiry is notice of such facts does not apply to the case of a party residing in a distant State, who has an agent at the place of the sale or other transaction, by whom the fraud is perpetrated.[5]

[1] McLean *v.* Clark, 47 Ga 24.

[2] Wakeman *v.* Dalley, 5ι N. Y. 27.

[3] Ib.; Meyer *v.* Amidon, 45 N. Y. 169; Oberlander *v.* Spiess, Ib. 175, explaining Bennett *v.* Jordan, 21 N. Y. 238.

[4] Snyder *v.* Sponable, 1 Hill, 567; s. c. 7 Hill, 427.

[5] Livermore *v.* Johnson, 27 Miss. 284.

PART II.

ADJECTIVE LAW OF FRAUD.

PROCEDURE AND INCIDENTS THEREOF.

PART II.

ADJECTIVE LAW OF FRAUD.

PROCEDURE AND INCIDENTS THEREOF.

CHAPTER VII.

JURISDICTION.

SUBJECT to a few exceptions, courts of equity exercise a general jurisdiction in cases of fraud, sometimes concurrent with, and sometimes exclusive of, other courts.[1] There are, however, many cases, such, for example, as those involving fraud in the sale of land, where the injured party may apply to either a court of law or a court of equity for redress. There are other cases, such, for example, as those involving fraud in trusts, where the injured party must apply to a court of equity in order to obtain an adequate remedy. There are other cases, such, for example, as those involving fraud in the probate of a will of real estate, where the injured parties must find their remedy in a court of common law.[2] There are still other cases, such, for example, as those involving fraud in the probate of a will of personalty, where the parties injured must in most cases resort to another court altogether, —

---

[1] 1 Story, Equity, § 184.

[2] Ib.; Webb v. Claverden, 2 Atk. 424 ; Kerrich v. Bransby, 7 Brown, Parl. Cas. 437 (Tomlins); Pemberton v. Pemberton, 13 Ves. 297.

the Court of Probate in this country, or the Ecclesiastical Court in England.[1]

A court of equity can grant relief from the consequences of fraud in a manner and upon terms which a court of law cannot do. There are cases, for example, where equity will give relief against the operation of instruments which are not void at law. A court of law will not pronounce a deed void on the ground of misrepresentation of matters *dehors* the instrument, where it appears that the exercise of ordinary capacity, with ordinary care, might have guarded against it.[2] And yet equity will often refuse to order a specific performance in such cases. In the case cited, it appeared that, upon the execution of a lease, the lessor misrepresented his title to demise the premises, by stating that he had the consent of parties interested therein, and that they would not interfere or disturb the possession of the lessee. In covenant by the lessor upon the lease, the lessee pleaded that the deed was obtained from the defendant by fraud and covin on the part of the plaintiff in making this false representation. But the court held that a court of law could not grant relief in such a case.[3]

---

[1] Kerrich v. Bransby, *supra;* Allen v. McPherson, 1 Phill. 133; s. c. 1 H. L. Cas. 191; Broderick's Will, 21 Wall. 503. As to this point, see *post,* pp. 333, 334.

[2] Hovenden v. Tilly, 5 Irish L. R. 462.

[3] " The defendant," said the court, " appears from the beginning to have been apprised of the existence and nature of the claims by which he has been since disturbed in his possession ; that he knew of these claims at the time he took the lease and executed the counterpart ; that he knew the terms, and understood the import of the terms of the lease ; and what he was told by the plaintiff himself was sufficient to make him aware that it was necessary, to his having a good title under the lease, that the persons having those claims should be consenting parties to it. This was surely of itself sufficient to lead his mind to the consideration of the manner in which he was to be protected from the consequences of those claims. . . . That in the exercise of his judgment he was or might be affected by the untrue representations made to him of their willingness to concur in or confirm the lease may be reasonably presumed ; but the ques-

It is an established doctrine that, when the legal estate in property has been acquired by fraud, the taker is regarded in equity as trustee of the party defrauded; and such party may recover the estate or its avails, when distinctly identified, from the party or parties charged with the fraud.[1] And the injured party is entitled not only to enforce his equitable title to the property, but also to compel payment of all damages he may have suffered. This whole purpose he could not accomplish at law, and hence he may resort to equity for the entire relief.[2] In ejectment, the grantor of a deed, regularly executed and registered, cannot set up fraud in the procurement of the instrument. His remedy is to be found in a court of equity.[3]

A deed of gift executed and acknowledged by one having legal capacity to convey cannot be avoided at law by proof that it was obtained by undue influence. The remedy is in equity.[4] So, too, a person who has executed a deed to a trustee cannot at law impeach for fraud in the purchaser a deed regularly executed by the trustee of the trust property. He should go into equity.[5] So, also, conveyances in fraud of the marital rights of the husband are good at law. The remedy therefor is in equity.[6] The remedy for fraud upon a partner

tion is, whether such representations, made under such circumstances, can at law have the effect of avoiding the deed *ab initio*. I conceive that they cannot have that effect. . . . They would amount at most only to a promise that the claimants would join in the lease; but that would only be a promise by parol. And to hold that the legal existence of the deed as a deed should depend upon the truth of that representation, or the performance of that promise, would be to put such a representation or promise upon the same footing as an express covenant in the deed."

[1] Cheney v. Gleason, 117 Mass. 557; Small v. Attwood, Younge, 507; Adams, Equity, 144.

[2] Cheney v. Gleason, *supra;* Dodd v. Cook, 11 Gray, 495; Whittemore v. Cowell, 7 Allen, 446.   [3] Ferguson v. Coleman, 5 Heisk. 378.

[4] Truman v. Lore, 14 Ohio St. 144; Clary v. Clary, 2 Ired. 85.

[5] Taylor v. King, 6 Munf. 358.

[6] Logan v. Simmons, 1 Dev. & B. 13.

in the settlement of partnership accounts is also by bill in equity. Assumpsit, for example, cannot be maintained.[1] But this rule does not apply to the case of money obtained by such copartner from his fellow for the partnership, when the formation of the partnership and the obtaining the money were a fraud by the former upon the latter, practised for the sake of obtaining money for individual purposes. In such a case, the defrauded party may recover his money at law.[2]

Equity has jurisdiction of a bill alleging a conspiracy between the defendants to defraud the plaintiff of his land, and setting forth the acts done in pursuance of the objects of the conspiracy.[3]

A bill in equity is maintainable against a defendant who, claiming title under a deed alleged to be fraudulent, has taken possession of, and converted to his own use, sundry articles of personal property ; the plaintiff praying the court to set aside the fraudulent deed, and to compel the defendant to render a just account of the property so wrongfully taken, and pay the value thereof to the plaintiff. This is not a mere action of trover.[4]

In a suit brought for partition by a purchaser of the interests of devisees, it is not regular to impeach for fraud or mistake the conveyance made to him. An application to a court of equity for partition does not seem to be an application to the sound discretion of the court, to be granted or refused according to the circumstances of the case, as in cases of specific performance and other cases. It is a remedy substituted for the difficult and perplexed remedy by writ of partition. The only indispensable requisite to entitle the plaintiff to relief is that he shall show a clear legal title. If his title be disputed or doubtful, the decree for partition will be suspended until

---

[1] Holyoke v. Mayo, 50 Maine, 385; Chase v. Garvin, 19 Maine, 211.

[2] Hale v. Wilson, 112 Mass. 444.

[3] Dwinal v. Smith, 25 Maine, 379.

[4] Cocke v. Bromley, 6 Munf. 184.

he establishes his title at law by ejectment or other remedy.[1]

Notwithstanding the fact that courts of equity generally have concurrent jurisdiction over fraud with courts of law, a determination at law of a question of fraud will conclude a re-examination of the same matter in equity, except perhaps where the complaining party was under some disability which prevented him from bringing his case fully and fairly before the court of law.[2]

Though courts of equity and courts of law have in most cases a concurrent jurisdiction in cases of fraud, still if a suit be first brought in a court of law, in which, upon the issues, the question of fraud should be tried and determined, the party injured by the fraud must make his defence there ; and, if he neglect to do so, equity has no jurisdiction to relieve him.[3] But this rule is probably to be understood of cases in which the defrauded party was bound to set up the fraud in the action at law. It can hardly be true of cases in which such party is entitled to bring a cross suit for the fraud.[4]

Equity will entertain a bill to set aside an order of court obtained for a fraudulent purpose, and a sale made thereunder, notwithstanding the fact that the plaintiff might have accomplished the same object by mere motion in the court which granted the order, if it be not clear that the rights of the parties could be so well protected and disposed under a motion. But where a full, adequate, and perfect remedy is attainable by motion, as in respect of orders fraudulently obtained for foreclosure sales, an independent proceeding is not allowed.[5]

[1] Wiseley v. Findlay, 3 Rand. 361 ; Wilkin v. Wilkin, 1 Johns. Ch. 111; Philips v. Green, 3 Johns. Ch. 302.

[2] Smith v. McIver, 9 Wheat. 532.

[3] Haden v. Garden, 7 Leigh, 157.

[4] See Bigelow, Estoppel, 107, 138 (2d ed.).

[5] Hackley v. Draper, 60 N. Y. 88, overruling a *dictum* in Libby v. Rosekrans, 55 Barb. 202, 219; Brown v. Frost, 10 Paige, 243 ; American Ins. Co. v. Oakley, 9 Paige, 259 ; McCotter v. Jay, 30 N. Y. 80; Gould v. Mortimer, 26 How. Pr. 167.

In any case of fraud, if the injured party is entitled to go into equity for relief as to any matter arising out of the contract or transaction in which he has been defrauded, he may there obtain full relief without resorting to a court of law. Equity having entertained jurisdiction as to part of the case will entertain jurisdiction as to the whole, and give final relief to the injured party.[1]

While a court of equity will not interfere in cases of fraud where a court of law has first taken jurisdiction and can furnish a full and adequate remedy, a court of equity will in a proper case intervene and order a fraudulent instrument, sought to be enforced in a law court, to be delivered up and cancelled. But the exercise of this power is to be regulated by sound discretion, as the circumstances of the particular case may require ; and, to be sustained, the resort to equity must be expedient, either because the instrument is liable to abuse, or because he defence not arising upon the face may be difficult or uncertain at law, or because of other special circumstances peculiar to the case which render a resort to chancery proper, and clear of all suspicion of design to promote expense and litigation.[2]

At common law, it has generally been held incompetent to a defendant sued at law on a specialty to plead that the instrument was obtained by false representations. Such defence must be made in equity. But it is otherwise of the *execution* of the instrument, as where the bond is misread to the obligor, or where his signature is obtained to an instrument which he did not intend to sign. In such cases, fraud may be alleged at law.[3]

[1] Bradley v. Bosley, 1 Barb. Ch. 125.

[2] Glastenbury v. McDonald, 44 Vt. 450; Bank of Bellows Falls v. Rutland & B. R. Co., 28 Vt. 470 ; Hamilton v. Cumings, 1 Johns. Ch. 517.

[3] Taylor v. King, 6 Munf. 358; Wyche v. Macklin, 2 Rand. 426; Dorr v. Munsel, 13 Johns. 430 ; Vrooman v. Phelps, 2 Johns. 177 ; Franchot v. Leach, 5 Cowan, 506 ; Champion v. White, Ib. 509 ; Dale v. Roosevelt, 9 Cowen, 307 ; Belden v. Davies, 2 Hall, 433 ; Stryker v. Vanderbilt, 1 Dutch. 482 ; Holley v. Younge, 27 Ala. 203 ; Wood v. Goodrich, 9 Yerg. 266.

The ground of this rule seems to be, that to admit evidence of fraud not relating to the execution of the deed would be to allow the obligor to disprove the presumption of consideration; which presumption in the case of a specialty is an absolute one, not to be rebutted. Some courts, however, admit the plea of fraud as to the consideration, as well as to the execution of the instrument ; and in other courts it is allowed by statute.[1] And in any case, if the plaintiff traverse the plea, he waives the estoppel, and the evidence of fraud becomes admissible.[2]

The doctrine that fraud not in the execution of a deed cannot be availed of at law applies not only to actions upon contracts under seal, but also to conveyances.[3] Thus, in the case cited, a party proposed to convey a tract of land in trust, and his brother undertook to have the deed drawn, and thereupon, without the knowledge of the grantor, inserted a conveyance also of another tract of land in trust for himself. Upon presenting the deed for execution, in reply to a question from the grantor, the brother said it was " all right," whereupon it was executed without reading. It was held, in an action of trespass *quare clausum fregit*, that the deed was binding. The remedy of the grantor was to be sought in equity. The fraud was deemed not to have been perpetrated in the *factum* of the grant.

As to what is considered fraud in the *factum* or execution of a deed, as distinguished from fraud relating to the con-

---

[1] Phillips v. Potter, 7 R. I. 289; Hoitt v. Holcomb, 23 N. H. 535, 552. See 3 Phillips, Evidence, 1448, note 969, Cowen's ed. In Hoitt v. Holcomb, *supra*, the court hold that fraud not relating to the execution of a specialty is not necessarily fraud relating to the consideration; and it was considered that the cases which refuse to admit evidence not relating to the execution have fallen into confusion in overlooking this distinction. It was conceded that no inquiry into the consideration of a deed could be made at law.

[2] Wormley v. Moffet, 6 Munf. 120; Wyche v. Macklin, 2 Rand. 426.

[3] McArthur v. Johnson, Phill. (N. Car.) 317.

sideration, the authorities afford various examples. One
instance of fraud in the *factum* is where the grantor of a
conveyance intends to execute a certain deed, and another
deed is surreptitiously substituted in its place.[1] Another is
afforded by the case of a deed executed by a blind or illiterate
person, when, upon request to read the deed, it has been
falsely read to him.[2]

The principle upon which such cases as the above proceed is that the party was fraudulently caused to sign, seal,
and deliver a different instrument from that intended. It
could not therefore be properly called his deed. But, where
the party knowingly executes the very instrument which he
intended, but is induced to do so by some fraud in the treaty,
the fraud relates to the consideration, and cannot be set up
at law. Of this species of fraud is that practised upon a
man who can read the instrument which he signs, seals, and
delivers, but refuses to do so. "If the party," says the
Touchstone, "that is to seal the deed can read himself, and
doth not, or, being an illiterate or a blind man, doth not
require to hear the deed read, or the contents thereof declared; in these cases, albeit the deed be contrary to his
mind, yet it is good and unavoidable at law; but equity may
correct mistakes, frauds, &c."[3] Nothing, therefore, which
would be discoverable upon the reading of the instrument can
make the deed invalid at law, unless the duty of reading devolve upon the opposite party, and that duty is abused.[4]

If in an action at law upon a sealed instrument there be
fraud (not relating to the consideration) on the part of the

---

[1] Canoy v. Troutman, 7 Ired. 155; Gant v. Hunsucker, 12 Ired. 254;
Nichols v. Holmes, 1 Jones, 360; McArthur v. Johnson, Phill. (N. Car.)
317.

[2] 2 Black. Com. 304; Manser's Case, 2 Coke, 3; McArthur v. Johnson, *supra.*   [3] Shep. Touch. 561.

[4] McArthur v. Johnson, *supra*, overruling McKerall v. Cheek, 2
Hawkes, 343, which was said to be decided without argument or proper
consideration.

plaintiff, the court will hear evidence in resistance of the action. But a court of law will not allow evidence on the part of the *plaintiff* of fraud in the defendant; as, for example, in the date of the deed. He should go into equity for relief.[1] And, in a suit in equity for the correction of an alleged mistake in a bond, the defendant can allege that the bond was obtained by fraud, though no attempt is made to enforce it in such suit. It is not necessary for the defendant to wait until he is sued at law upon the bond, even in those States in which such fact would be available at law.[2]

There is no equity to restrain the overseers of a railroad made over the plaintiff's land from using the road after its completion, or from interrupting the plaintiff's workmen in attempting to remove it and to restore the land to its original state, though the possession of the land for the purpose of constructing the railroad may have been obtained from a tenant of the plaintiff by means of circumvention and fraud.[3] The question in such a case relates merely to the right of way; and, if the railroad company have not acquired the right, they are trespassers, and liable accordingly. The remedy is not by injunction.[4]

An action cannot be maintained at law by stockholders of a corporation, in behalf of themselves and other stockholders, against the directors, for the benefit of the corporation, to recover profits supposed to have been gained, to its prejudice and damages, for losses suffered by it through the misconduct of the directors. And, ordinarily, the same rule will apply in equity. It is only from the necessity of the case, and to prevent a failure of justice, that suits in equity for such purpose are allowed. To justify a bill in equity, it must be shown that suitable redress is not attainable through the action of the corporation. To this extent, all of the author-

---

[1] Wood *v.* Goodrich, 9 Yerg. 266.

[2] Hogencamp *v.* Ackerman, 2 Stockt. 267.

[3] Deere *v.* Guest, 1 Mylne & C. 516.   [4] Ib.

ities agree. There is some diversity, however, as to what will satisfy the requirement. Whether there must be an effort to move the corporate body to the redress of its own injuries, and to that end an attempt to procure a meeting and vote of the stockholders, or whether an application to the present board of officers by whom the corporate affairs are managed, and a refusal by them to allow proceedings in its name and behalf, would be sufficient, does not seem to have been determined by any clear concurrence of decision.

The question may depend somewhat upon the nature of the corporate organization, and the extent of powers confided to its officers for the time being. Where the stockholders retain no control of the corporate business except by means of an annual election of officers, those officers, during their term of service, represent the corporation for all purposes; and a refusal by them to take proper action for the protection of its interests, or to allow the use of the corporate name for that purpose, ought to be sufficient to justify a proceeding in behalf of the individual stockholders, making the corporation a party defendant. A formal application and refusal need not be alleged, if enough appear to show that such an application would be unavailing. Where the directors themselves are the parties charged with the wrong, or by whose fraud or collusion the wrong has been accomplished, and the suit is to be brought against them, they are by the very nature of the case incapacitated for the service of representing the corporation in any action for the restoration of its rights, whether by suit or by proceedings *in pais*. If the corporate action is under the control of such parties, it is sufficient reason to warrant proceedings by suit in the name and behalf of the individual stockholders.[1]

In accordance with these principles, laid down by Mr. Justice Wells in the case cited, it was there held that a bill for the

[1] Mr. Justice Wells, in Brewer *v.* Boston Theatre, 104 Mass. 378. See *post*, pp. 351, 352.

purpose above indicated, which did not allege that any effort
had been made to set the corporation in motion for the purpose of securing its own redress, or that any application had
been made to the directors to take action in the matter, could
not be maintained, if the bill did not clearly show that such
effort or application would be unavailing.

A creditor cannot maintain an action at common law against
his debtor, or against persons conspiring with him, for fraudulently disposing of his property in order to avoid the payment of his debts.[1] The debtor in such a case has, indeed,
committed a fraud upon others, to their damage; but the
law has provided a more suitable mode of procedure to meet
such cases. If such an action were to be allowed, the result
would generally be to prevent the possibility of a ratable
division of the debtor's property among his creditors; for it
often happens that the estate of the debtor is insufficient to
meet all the claims of the creditors, and, if an action for
damages were to be allowed, the plaintiff would be entitled
to recover the amount of his debt. This would be more than
he would be entitled to under a distribution of the effects in
bankruptcy. It is true a debtor may prefer one creditor
over another in many cases, or one creditor may by diligence
secure an advantage over other creditors; but the proceedings
in such cases must be according to established methods, of
which an action for damages is not one.

This principle will not be affected by the circumstance that
the debtor has made false and fraudulent representations to
his creditors as to his financial condition, by which they were
deceived, and led to refrain from making attachments upon
his property until it was too late.[2] The same objection to

[1] Austin v. Barrows, 41 Conn. 287; Cowles v. Day, 30 Conn. 410;
Smith v. Blake, 1 Day, 258; Adler v. Fenton, 24 How. 407; Lamb v.
Stone, 11 Pick. 527; Wellington v. Small, 3 Cush. 145; Moody v. Burton, 27 Maine, 427.
[2] Austin v. Barrows, 41 Conn. 287; Moody v. Burton, 27 Maine, 427.

the action will arise which exists in the case above stated.
A further reason was also suggested in the case first cited,
that the loss of an attachment which had not been undertaken in the least was not a reasonably certain effect of the
fraud. But if it had appeared that the plaintiffs had actually
levied an attachment upon the defendant's property, and
were prevented from retaining their lien by the defendant's
fraudulent representations, we apprehend that the case would
have been considered different, and the action held maintainable.[1]

Where an agreement against which a complainant in equity
asks for relief is perpetual in its nature, and the keeping it
on foot is a fraud on the party complaining, so that the only
effectual relief against it is to have it annulled, the case is
one for equity, not for law.[2]

There is some conflict of authority upon the question
whether a party can resort to equity for redress by reason of
fraud in cases in which an adequate redress is obtainable at
law. Thus, in cases of breach of warranty, misrepresentation, and the like, in respect of personal or real property,
where the sole object of the party making complaint is to
obtain damages for the wrong, and not rescission, injunction,
or other peculiar remedy of equity, it is held by many of the
authorities that resort must be had to the courts of common
law.[3] Upon this view, it has been held that a court of equity
will not enjoin a proceeding at law on a policy of life insurance,
on the ground that the same was obtained by fraud, where it

---

[1] Bradley v. Fuller, 118 Mass. 239; *ante*, p. 86.

[2] Jones v. Bolles, 9 Wall. 364.

[3] Life Assoc. of Scotland v. McBlain, Law R. 9 Irish Ch. 176; Hoare v.
Bremridge, Law R. 14 Eq. 522 ; s. c. Law R. 8 Ch. 22 ; Teft v. Stewart,
31 Mich. 367 ; Russell v. Clark, 7 Cranch, 89; Hardwick v. Forbes, 1
Bibb, 212; Boardman v. Jackson, 119 Mass. 161; Suter v. Matthews,
115 Mass. 253; Williams v. Mitchell, 30 Ala. 299; Russell v. Little, 28
Ala. 160 ; Denny v. Gilman, 26 Maine, 149 ; Woodman v. Freeman, 25
Maine, 531 ; Learned v. Holmes, 49 Miss. 290.

appears that the fraud consists merely in false representations of the habits of the assured. Such facts are properly cognizable by a jury.[1] But a contrary view has been expressed by Lord Eldon and by Chancellor Kent.[2] And it is held in Indiana that where a vendor of real estate fraudulently represents that he has a perfect title to the land sold, and the purchaser is thereby induced to purchase, he can enjoin the collection of the purchase-money until the title shall be made good.[3] It seems clear, however, that if in such cases some further relief than that of damages be sought, and that relief is of an equitable nature, the party must apply to equity for his redress.[4]

It seems equally true that a court of equity may grant relief in certain cases relating to the probate of wills.[5] Indeed, some of the early cases entertained a wide jurisdiction in this respect.[6] But it has since been settled that equity will not set aside a will for fraud. However, though equity will not set aside a will, nor indeed restrain the probate of it in the proper court (for this is equally true), still, if the fraud be proved, it will not assist the party practising it, but will leave him to make such advantage of it otherwise as he can.[7] But, further, equity may, according to the real intention of the testator, declare a trust upon a will, though it be not contained in the will itself, in at least three cases: first, in the case of a notorious fraud upon a legatee, as if the draftsman of the will should insert his own name instead of that of the legatee; secondly, where the words imply a trust for the re-

---

[1] Life Assoc. of Scotland v. McBlain, *supra;* Hoare v. Bremridge, *supra.*

[2] Evans v. Bicknell, 6 Ves. 182 ; Bacon v. Bronson, 7 Johns. 201.

[3] Hinkle v. Margerum, 50 Ind. 240 ; Warren v. Carey, 5 Ind. 319; Wiley v. Howard, 15 Ind. 169 ; Strong v. Downing, 34 Ind. 300.

[4] Denny v. Gilman, 26 Maine, 149.

[5] See Maundy v. Maundy, 1 Ch. Rep. 66; Well v. Thornagh, Prec. Ch. 123; Goss v. Tracy, 1 P. Wms. 287.

[6] Fonblanque, Equity, Bk. 1, c. 2, § 3, note *u.*

[7] Fonblanque, *ut supra.*

lations, as in the case of a specific devise to the executors
without a disposition of the residue ; thirdly, in the case of
a legatee promising the testator to stand as a trustee for
another.[1] So, too, Lord Hardwicke has said that fraud in
making or obtaining a will must be inquired into and determined by the Ecclesiastical Court, but that fraud in procuring
a will to be established in that court, fraud not upon the
testator, but upon the person disinherited thereby, might be
the subject of inquiry in equity.[2] And the same distinction
has been recognized by other judges.[3] So, where the fraud
does not go to the validity of the whole will, but only to that
of some particular clause, or where the fraud consists in un-
duly obtaining the consent of the next of kin to the probate,
courts of equity will interpose to declare the executor a
trustee for the next of kin.[4] And it has been held that a will
which has been fraudulently destroyed or suppressed may be
set up in equity.[5] But beyond cases of this kind, as to which
the Court of Probate itself could afford no suitable relief, the
jurisdiction of that court is as to proper cases exclusive, and
its decision beyond review.

The result of the authorities relating to jurisdiction in
matters of fraud may be thus stated : The Ecclesiastical or
Probate Court has exclusive jurisdiction, when the question
pertains to a will of personal property, and the decision of
such court as to the validity of the will is binding upon all
other courts, except in respect of matters concerning which
such courts cannot give an adequate relief. The courts of
common law have jurisdiction of matters of fraud relating to

[1] Marriot *v.* Marriot, Gilb. 203, 209 ; Allen *v.* McPherson, 5 Beav.
469 ; s. c. 1 Phill. 133; 1 H. L. Cas. 191.

[2] Barnesley *v.* Powell, 1 Ves. Sr. 284.

[3] Meadows *v.* Duchess of Kingston, Amb. 762; Kennell *v.* Abbott,
4 Ves. 802. See Allen *v.* McPherson, *ut supra.*

[4] 1 Story, Equity, § 440.

[5] Buchanan *v.* Matlock, 8 Humph. 390; *ante*, p. 128.

wills of real property, concurrent with that of the Court of Chancery; they have also jurisdiction of matters of fraud for which damages alone are sought. The Court of Chancery has jurisdiction of matters of fraud in wills of personalty, in cases over which the Ecclesiastical or Probate Court can exercise no adequate authority; it has jurisdiction concurrent with courts of law of matters of fraud arising in respect of wills of real estate; it has also concurrent jurisdiction with the same courts in actions for damages, where a further and equitable relief is sought; and finally, subject to the exception arising upon the first case above mentioned, it has jurisdiction in all cases proper for relief of some kind, as to which no adequate relief can be elsewhere obtained.[1]

An action for deceit in the sale of a patent is maintainable in a State court, though the case involves collaterally the construction and validity of the letters-patent.[2]

[1] See also 1 Story, Equity, § 184.
[2] David v. Park, 103 Mass. 501.